Forbidden Dance

ALSO AVAILABLE FROM TOKYOPOP

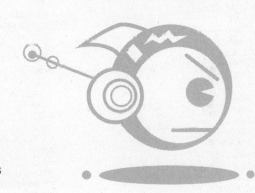

For more
information visit
www.TOKYOPOP.com

01.09.04T

ALSO AVAILABLE FROM TOKYOPOP®

MANGA

.HACK//LEGEND OF THE TWILIGHT
@LARGE
ABENOBASHI
A.I. LOVE YOU
AI YORI AOSHI
ANGELIC LAYER
ARM OF KANNON
BABY BIRTH
BATTLE ROYALE
BATTLE VIXENS
BRAIN POWERED
BRIGADOON
B'TX
CANDIDATE FOR GODDESS, THE
CARDCAPTOR SAKURA
CARDCAPTOR SAKURA - MASTER OF THE CLOW
CHOBITS
CHRONICLES OF THE CURSED SWORD
CLAMP SCHOOL DETECTIVES
CLOVER
COMIC PARTY
CONFIDENTIAL CONFESSIONS
CORRECTOR YUI
COWBOY BEBOP
COWBOY BEBOP: SHOOTING STAR
CRESCENT MOON
CULDCEPT
CYBORG 009
D.N. ANGEL
DEMON DIARY
DEMON ORORON, THE
DEUS VITAE
DIGIMON
DIGIMON ZERO TWO
DIGIMON TAMERS
DOLL
DRAGON HUNTER
DRAGON KNIGHTS
DREAM SAGA
DUKLYON: CLAMP SCHOOL DEFENDERS
ERICA SAKURAZAWA COLLECTED WORKS
EERIE QUEERIE!
ET CETERA
ETERNITY
EVIL'S RETURN
FAERIES' LANDING
FAKE
FLCL
FORBIDDEN DANCE
FRUITS BASKET
G GUNDAM
GATE KEEPERS

GETBACKERS
GIRL GOT GAME
GRAVITATION
GTO
GUNDAM SEED ASTRAY
GUNDAM WING
GUNDAM WING: BATTLEFIELD OF PACIFISTS
GUNDAM WING: ENDLESS WALTZ
GUNDAM WING: THE LAST OUTPOST (G-UNIT)
HAPPY MANIA
HARLEM BEAT
I.N.V.U.
IMMORTAL RAIN
INITIAL D
ISLAND
JING: KING OF BANDITS
JULINE
KARE KANO
KILL ME, KISS ME
KINDAICHI CASE FILES, THE
KING OF HELL
KODOCHA: SANA'S STAGE
LAMENT OF THE LAMB
LES BIJOUX
LEGEND OF CHUN HYANG, THE
LOVE HINA
LUPIN III
MAGIC KNIGHT RAYEARTH I
MAGIC KNIGHT RAYEARTH II
MAHOROMATIC: AUTOMATIC MAIDEN
MAN OF MANY FACES
MARMALADE BOY
MARS
MINK
MIRACLE GIRLS
MIYUKI-CHAN IN WONDERLAND
MODEL
ONE
PARADISE KISS
PARASYTE
PEACH GIRL
PEACH GIRL: CHANGE OF HEART
PET SHOP OF HORRORS
PITA-TEN
PLANET LADDER
PLANETES
PRIEST
PRINCESS AI
PSYCHIC ACADEMY
RAGNAROK
RAVE MASTER
REALITY CHECK
REBIRTH
REBOUND

01.09.04T

Forbidden Dance 4

created by **Hinako Ashihara**

TENSHI NO KISS

Translator - Takae Brewer
English Adaptation - Tisha Ford
Editor - Jodi Bryson
Retouch and Lettering - Rubina Chabra
Cover Layout - Matt Alford

Sr. Editor - Julie Taylor
VP of Production - Ron Klamert
President & C.O.O. - John Parker
Publisher & C.E.O. - Stuart Levy

A TOKYOPOP® Manga

TOKYOPOP Inc.
5900 Wilshire Blvd. Suite 2000
Los Angeles, CA 90036

Email: editor@TOKYOPOP.com
Come visit us online at www.TOKYOPOP.com

"TENSHI NO KISS" 4

ISBN: 1-59182-348-X

First TOKYOPOP printing: March 2004

10 9 8 7 6 5 4 3 2 1

Printed in the USA

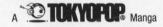

Forbidden Dance

Volume 4

Written and Illustrated by Hinako Ashihara

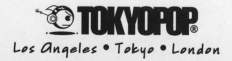

Los Angeles • Tokyo • London

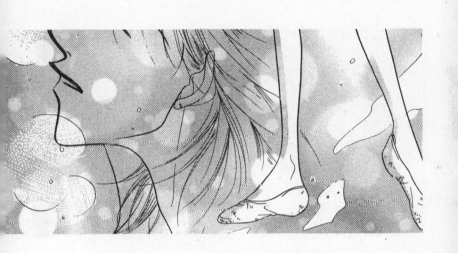

Forbidden Dance

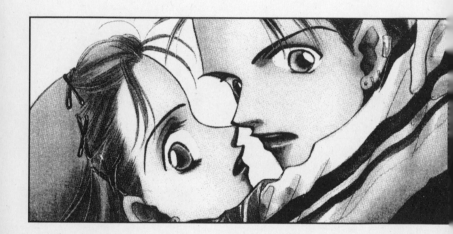

FORBIDDEN DANCE 4

CONTENTS

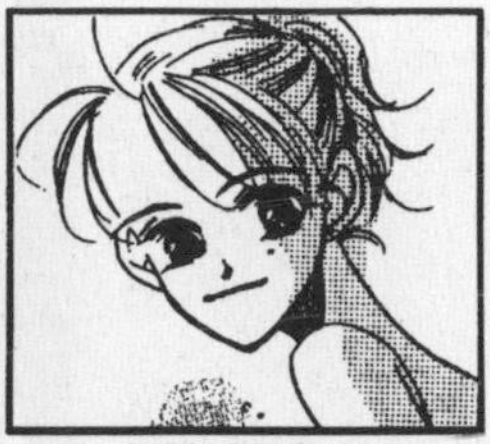

AYA FUJII
HIGH SCHOOL STUDENT. SHE HAS BEEN TRAINING IN CLASSICAL BALLET SINCE SHE WAS VERY YOUNG.

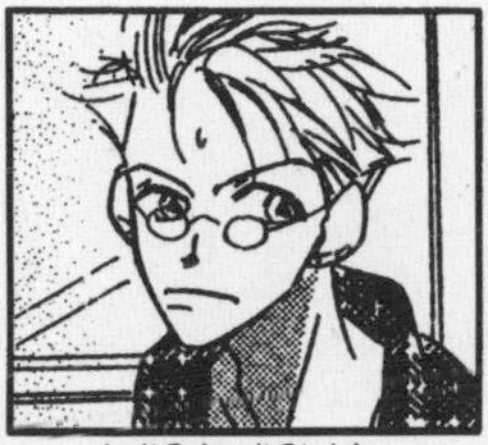

AKIRA HIBIYA
LEADER OF THE ALL-MALE DANCE TROUPE "COOL."

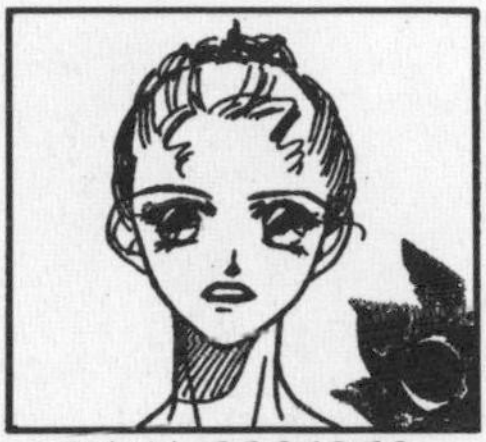

DIANA ROBERTS
A WORLD FAMOUS BALLERINA.

STORY

AYA IS A HIGH SCHOOL STUDENT WHO LOVES BALLET. ONE DAY, AYA GOES TO A BALLET PERFORMANCE BY "COOL" AND BECOMES DEEPLY MOVED BY AKIRA'S STYLE OF DANCE. AYA WISHES TO JOIN "COOL," THE ALL-MALE DANCE TROUPE. DESPITE THE STRICT REQUIREMENT SET FORTH BY AKIRA, AYA SUCCESSFULLY JOINS "COOL."
DIANA ROBERTS, A WIDELY RECOGNIZED BRITISH DANCER, COMES TO SEE AKIRA. SHE CAME FOR A BIG PERFORMANCE IN JAPAN, HIDING THE FACT SHE HAS A SEVERE ANKLE INJURY, WHICH PUTS HER CAREER AS A PROFESSIONAL DANCER AT RISK.
AFTER FINDING OUT SHE CAN NO LONGER DANCE ON THE LEVEL SHE WAS ACCUSTOMED TO, DIANA BEGINS TO SUFFER FROM A MAJOR NERVOUS BREAKDOWN. ONLY A FEW WEEKS AWAY FROM "COOL'S" ANNIVERSARY PERFORMANCE, AKIRA DECIDES TO TAKE DIANA BACK TO ENGLAND. AKIRA LEAVES JAPAN, TELLING AYA THAT HE WILL TRY TO GET BACK AS SOON AS POSSIBLE. AKIRA HASN'T RETURNED TO JAPAN EVEN ON THE DAY BEFORE "COOL'S" BIG PERFORMANCE, MAKING EVERYONE ANXIOUS...

* BETSU COMI FLOWER COMICS*

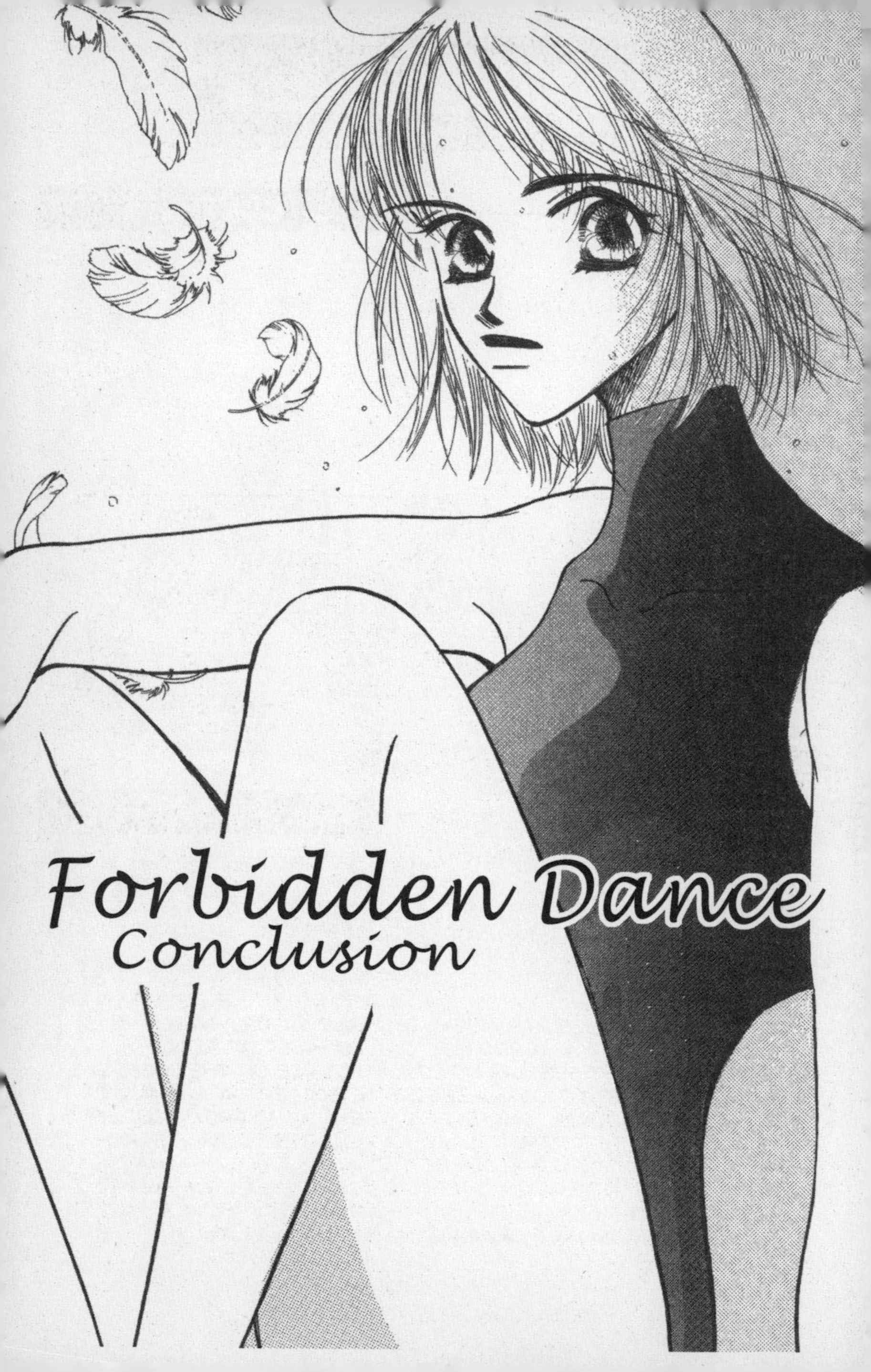
Forbidden Dance
Conclusion

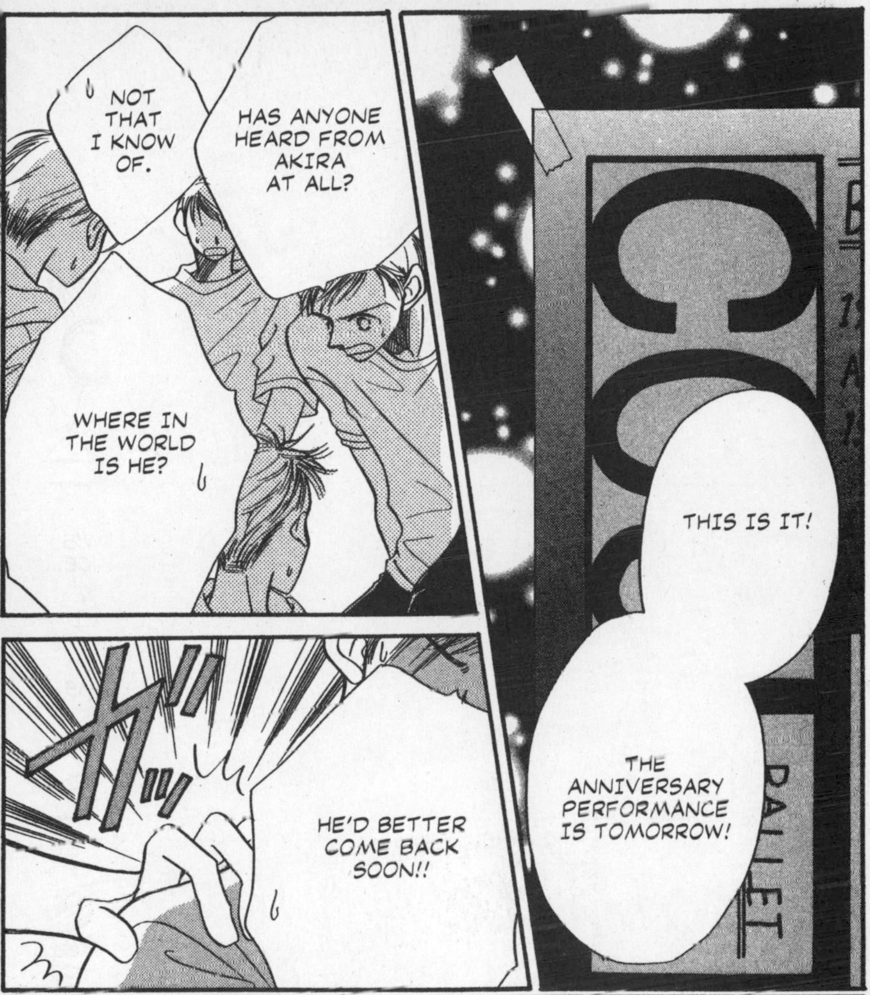
THIS IS IT!
THE ANNIVERSARY PERFORMANCE IS TOMORROW!
BALLET
HAS ANYONE HEARD FROM AKIRA AT ALL?
NOT THAT I KNOW OF.
WHERE IN THE WORLD IS HE?
HE'D BETTER COME BACK SOON!!

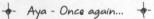

-✦- Aya - Once again... -✦-

She is a cheerful and active character who was easy to draw. While drawing Aya, I was wishing I could be as honest as her. She is a woman of action, and very candid. She doesn't hesitate to express her emotions--her delight, anger, sorrow, and pleasure. It's not always easy to be like that, you know?

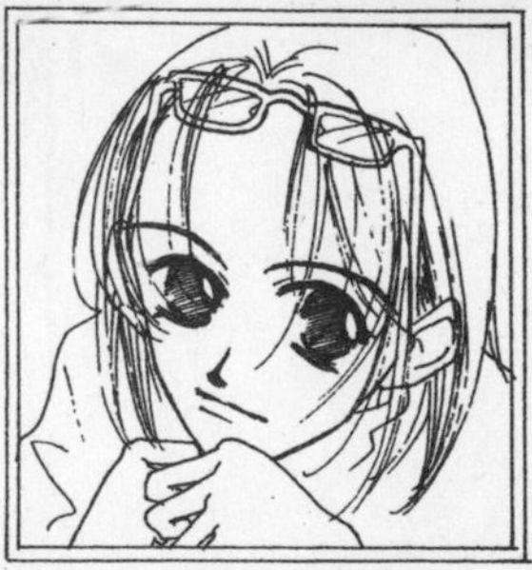

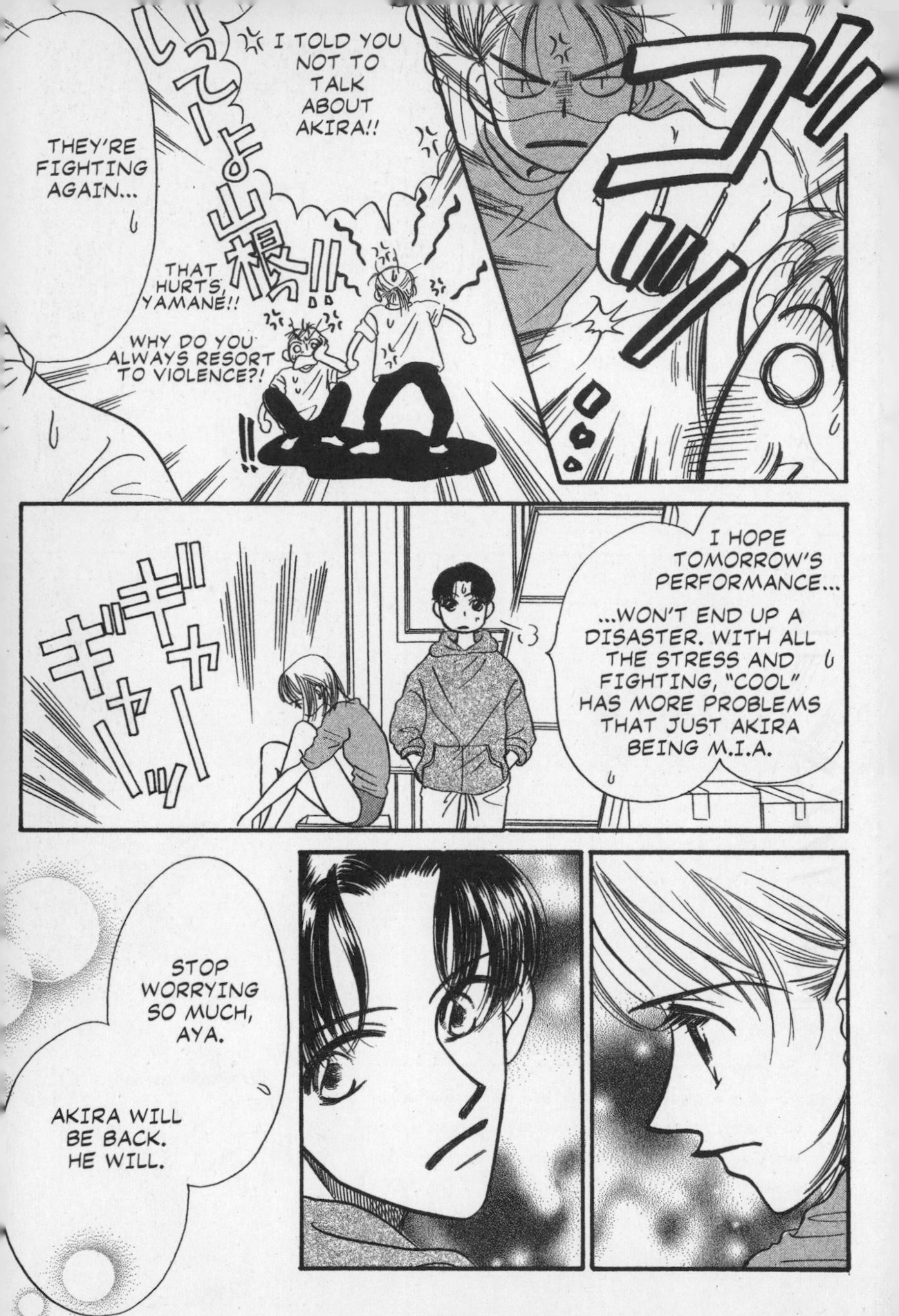

I TOLD YOU NOT TO TALK ABOUT AKIRA!!
いってーよ山根!!
THAT HURTS, YAMANE!!
WHY DO YOU ALWAYS RESORT TO VIOLENCE?!
THEY'RE FIGHTING AGAIN...
I HOPE TOMORROW'S PERFORMANCE...
...WON'T END UP A DISASTER. WITH ALL THE STRESS AND FIGHTING, "COOL" HAS MORE PROBLEMS THAT JUST AKIRA BEING M.I.A.
STOP WORRYING SO MUCH, AYA.
AKIRA WILL BE BACK. HE WILL.

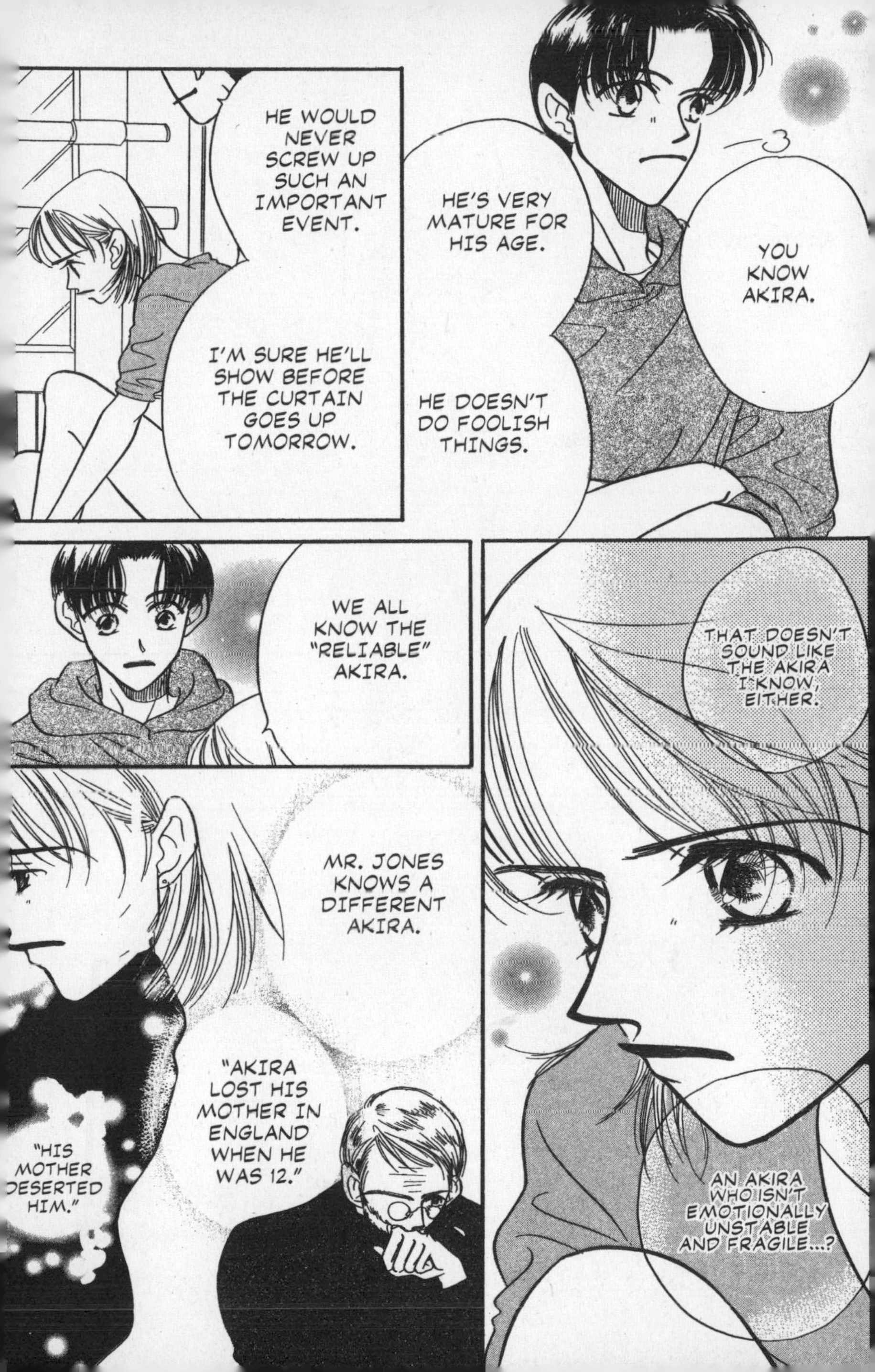
YOU KNOW AKIRA.
HE'S VERY MATURE FOR HIS AGE.
HE DOESN'T DO FOOLISH THINGS.
HE WOULD NEVER SCREW UP SUCH AN IMPORTANT EVENT.
I'M SURE HE'LL SHOW BEFORE THE CURTAIN GOES UP TOMORROW.
THAT DOESN'T SOUND LIKE THE AKIRA I KNOW, EITHER.
AN AKIRA WHO ISN'T EMOTIONALLY UNSTABLE AND FRAGILE...?
WE ALL KNOW THE "RELIABLE" AKIRA.
MR. JONES KNOWS A DIFFERENT AKIRA.
"AKIRA LOST HIS MOTHER IN ENGLAND WHEN HE WAS 12."
"HIS MOTHER DESERTED HIM."

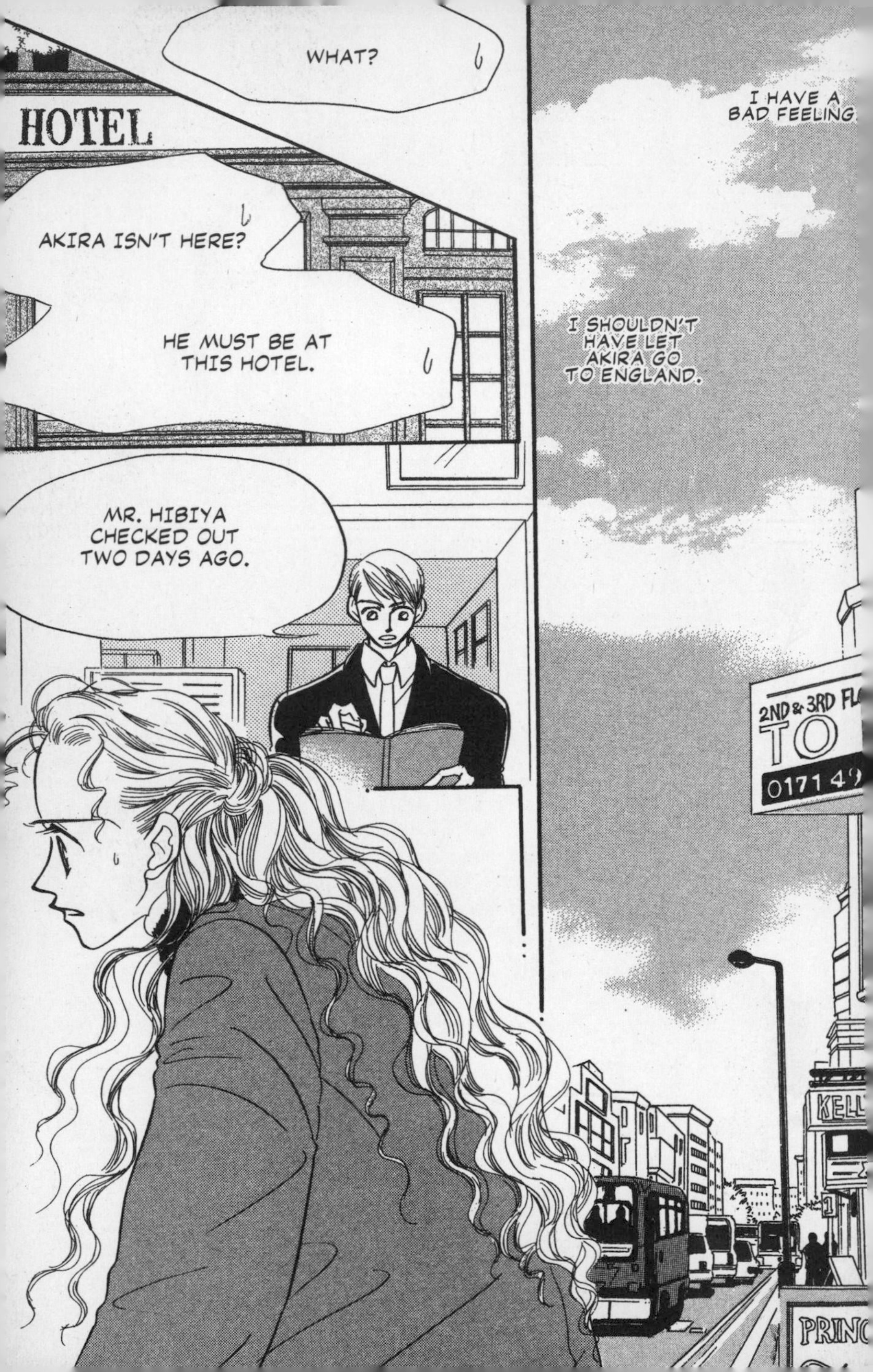
I HAVE A BAD FEELING.
I SHOULDN'T HAVE LET AKIRA GO TO ENGLAND.
WHAT?
HOTEL
AKIRA ISN'T HERE?
HE MUST BE AT THIS HOTEL.
MR. HIBIYA CHECKED OUT TWO DAYS AGO.

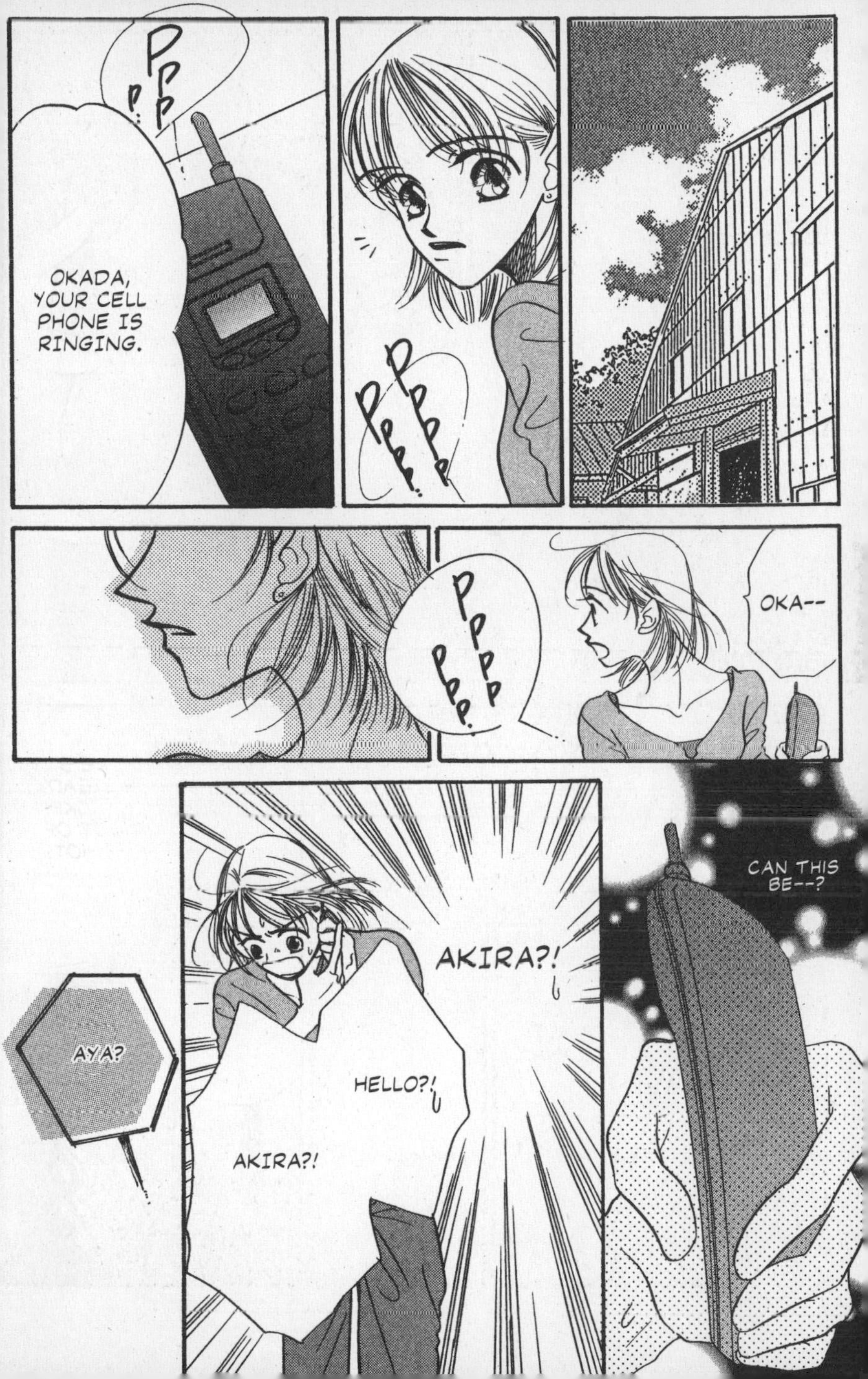
OKADA, YOUR CELL PHONE IS RINGING.
OKA--
CAN THIS BE--?
AKIRA?!
HELLO?!
AKIRA?!
AYA?

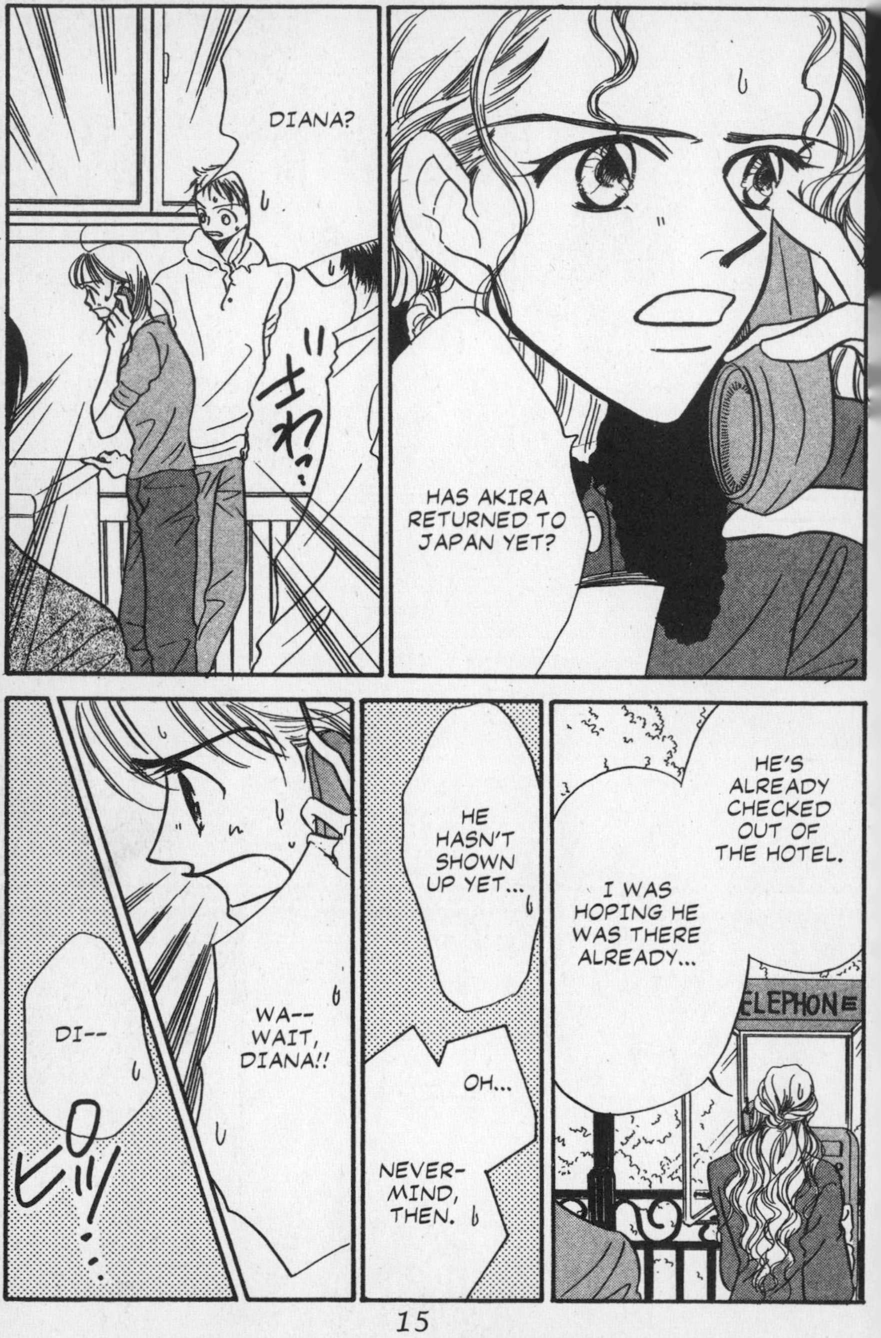
HAS AKIRA RETURNED TO JAPAN YET?
DIANA?
ざわっ
HE'S ALREADY CHECKED OUT OF THE HOTEL.
I WAS HOPING HE WAS THERE ALREADY...
ELEPHONE
HE HASN'T SHOWN UP YET...
OH...
NEVER-MIND, THEN.
WA-- WAIT, DIANA!!
DI--
ピッ

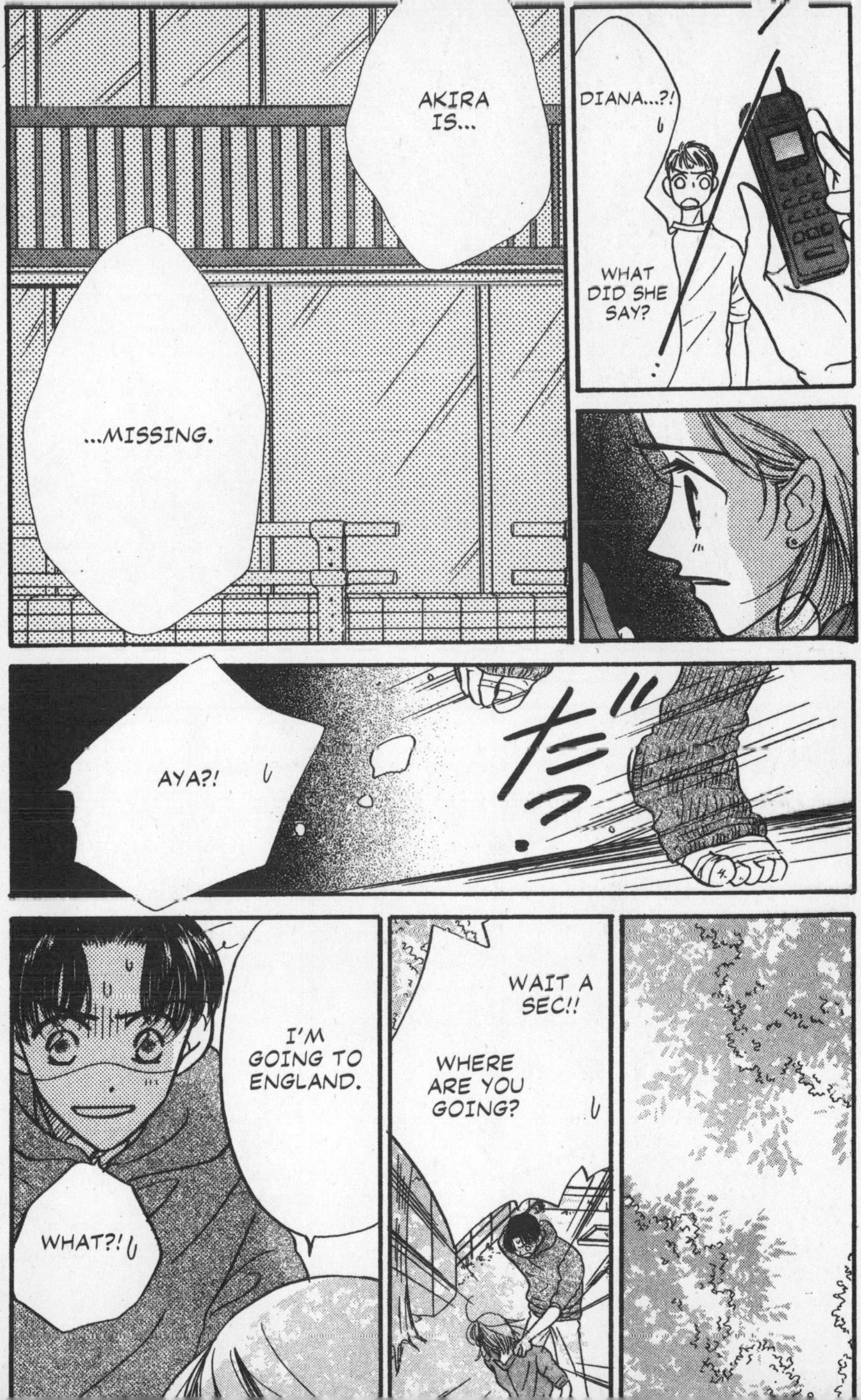
DIANA...?!
WHAT DID SHE SAY?
AKIRA IS...
...MISSING.
だっ
AYA?!
WAIT A SEC!!
WHERE ARE YOU GOING?
I'M GOING TO ENGLAND.
WHAT?!

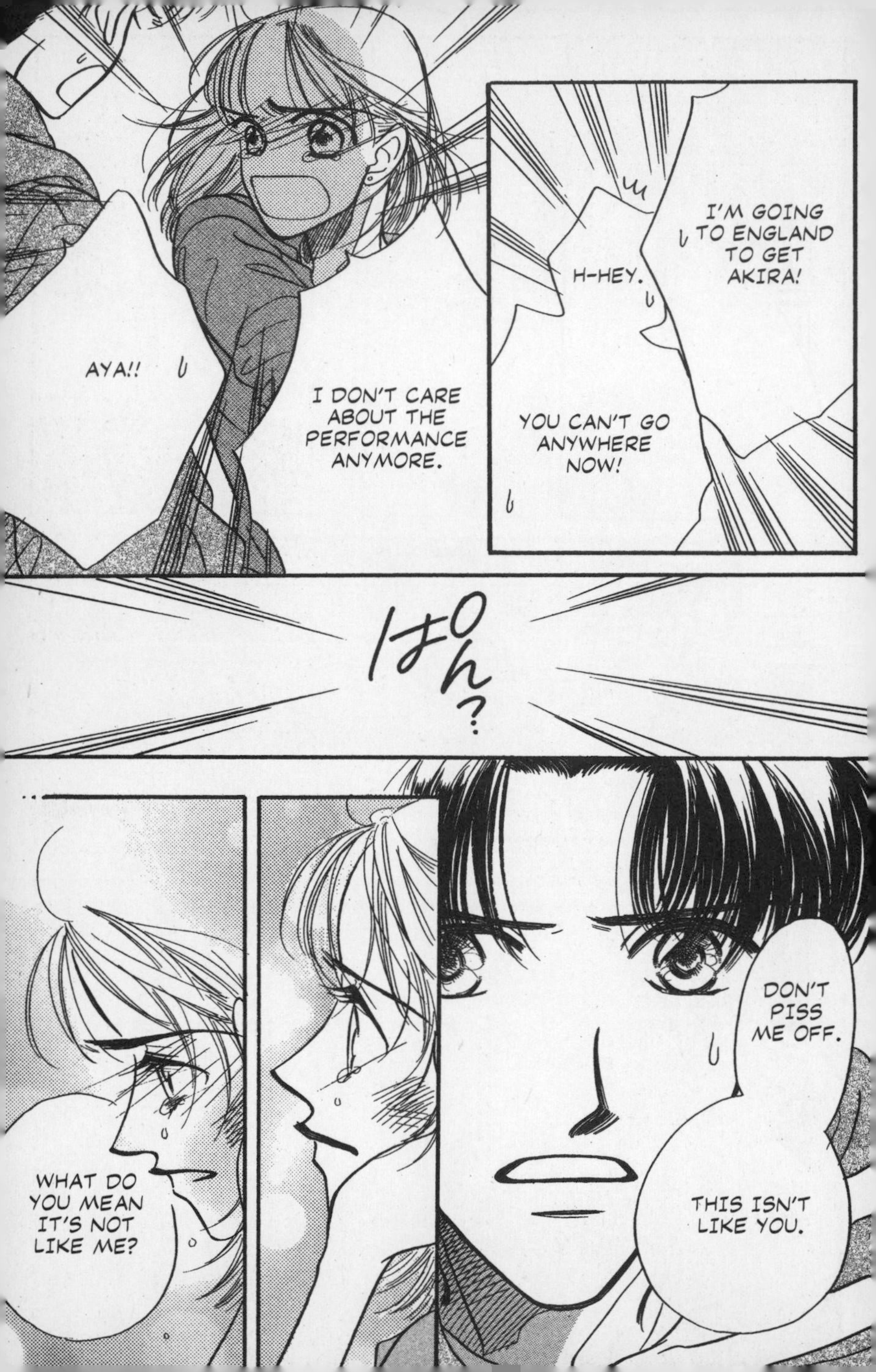
I'M GOING TO ENGLAND TO GET AKIRA!
H-HEY.
YOU CAN'T GO ANYWHERE NOW!
I DON'T CARE ABOUT THE PERFORMANCE ANYMORE.
AYA!!
ぱん?
DON'T PISS ME OFF.
THIS ISN'T LIKE YOU.
WHAT DO YOU MEAN IT'S NOT LIKE ME?

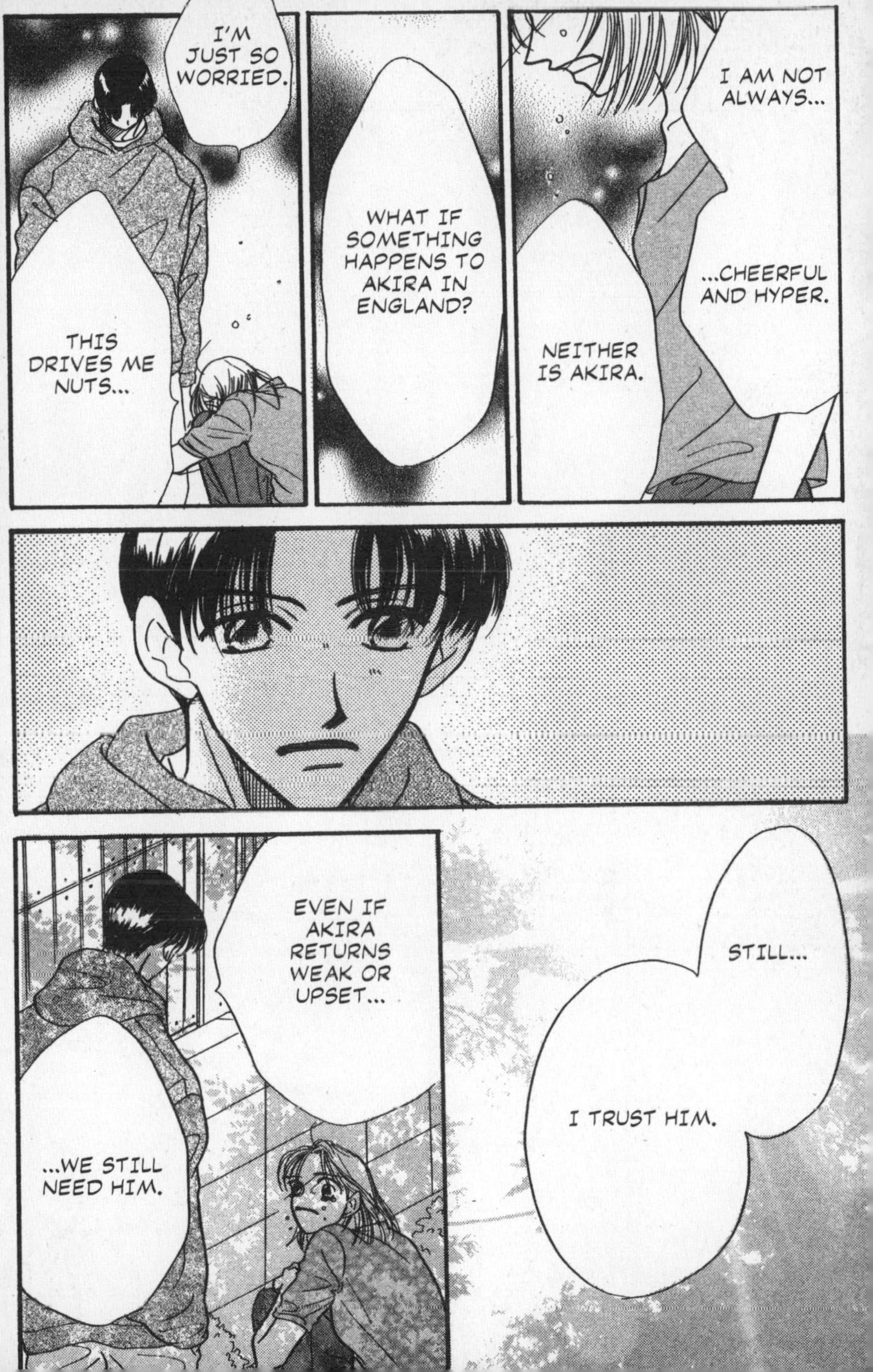
I AM NOT ALWAYS...
...CHEERFUL AND HYPER.
NEITHER IS AKIRA.
WHAT IF SOMETHING HAPPENS TO AKIRA IN ENGLAND?
I'M JUST SO WORRIED.
THIS DRIVES ME NUTS...
STILL...
I TRUST HIM.
EVEN IF AKIRA RETURNS WEAK OR UPSET...
...WE STILL NEED HIM.

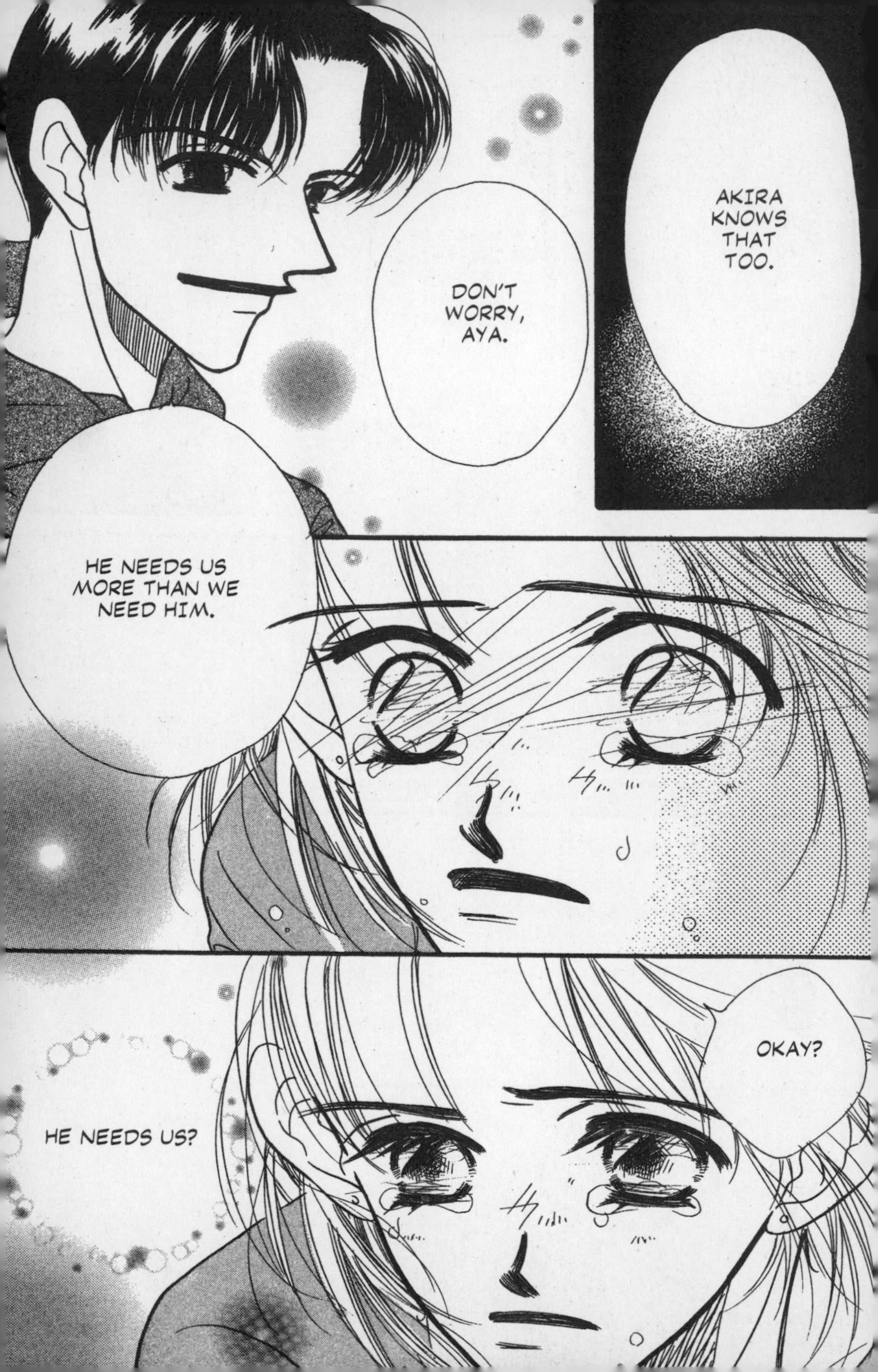
AKIRA KNOWS THAT TOO.
DON'T WORRY, AYA.
HE NEEDS US MORE THAN WE NEED HIM.
OKAY?
HE NEEDS US?

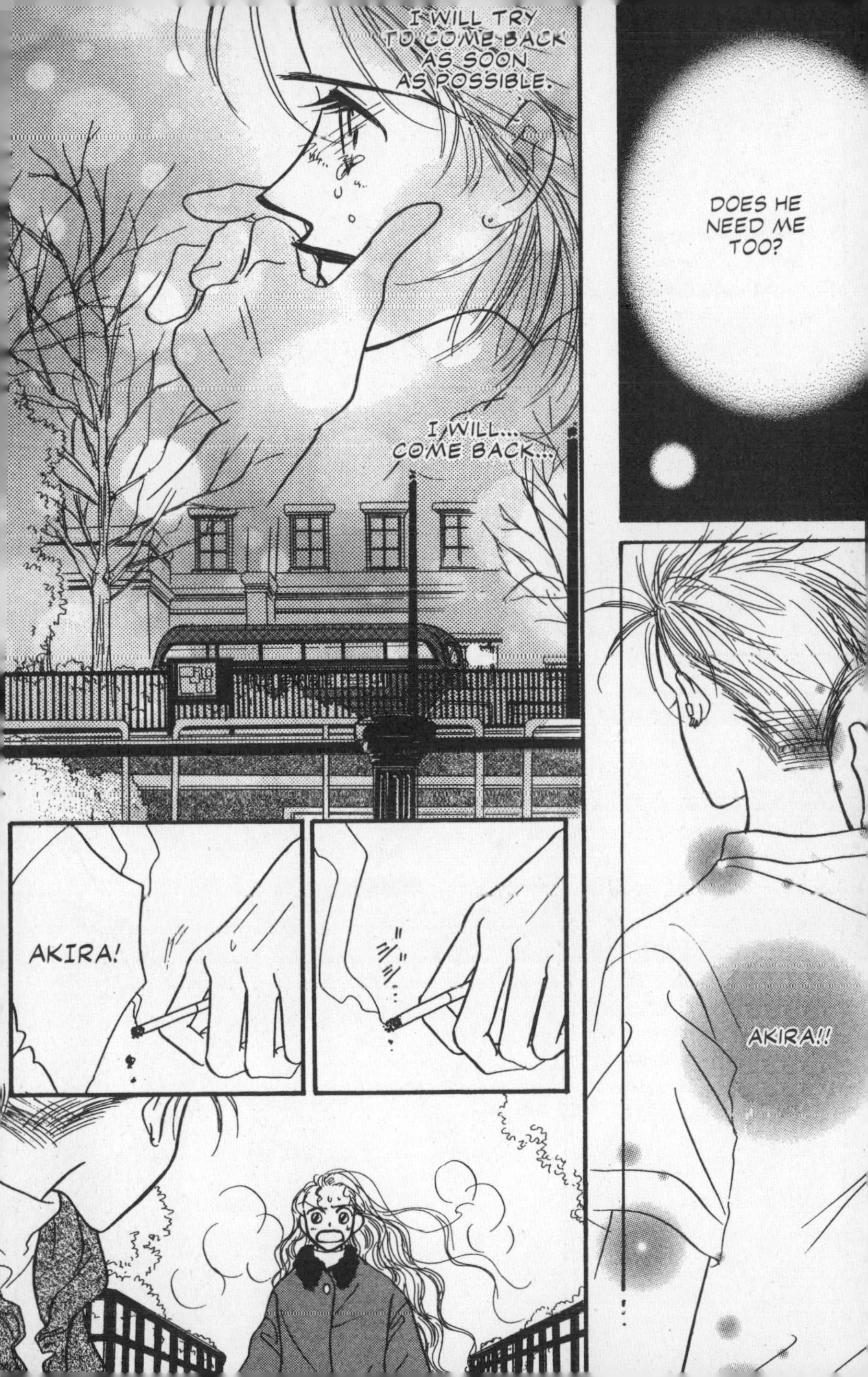
DOES HE NEED ME TOO?
I WILL TRY TO COME BACK AS SOON AS POSSIBLE.
I WILL... COME BACK...
AKIRA!!
AKIRA!

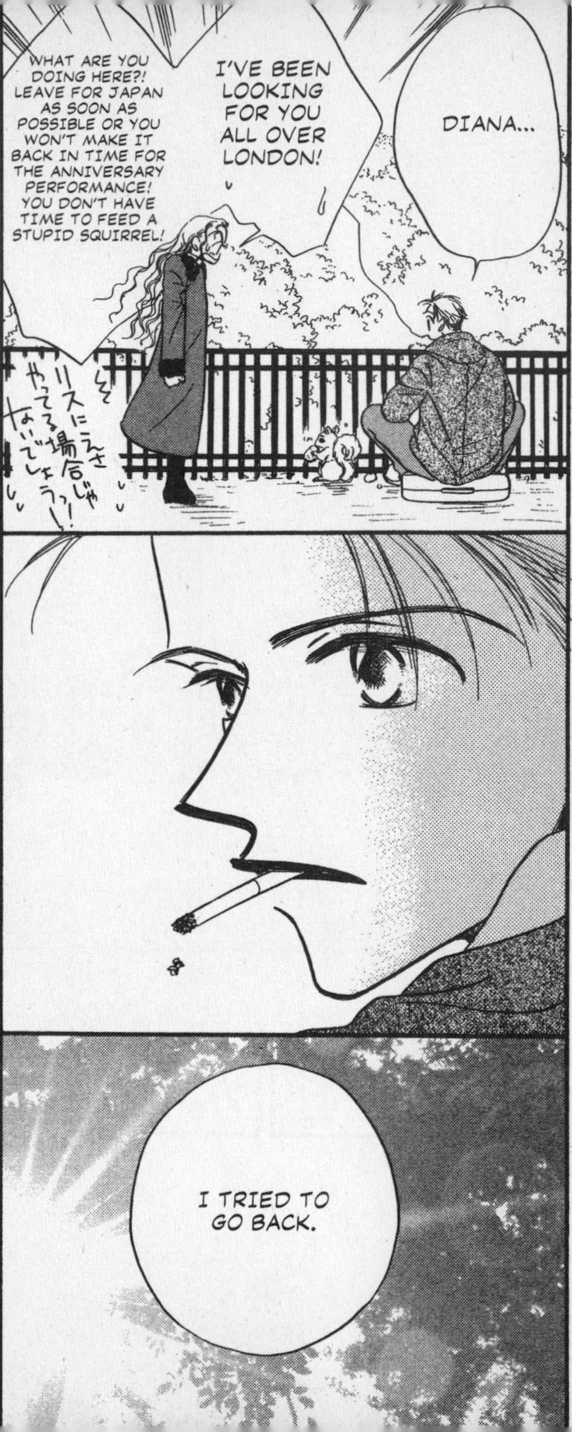
DIANA...
I'VE BEEN LOOKING FOR YOU ALL OVER LONDON!
WHAT ARE YOU DOING HERE?! LEAVE FOR JAPAN AS SOON AS POSSIBLE OR YOU WON'T MAKE IT BACK IN TIME FOR THE ANNIVERSARY PERFORMANCE! YOU DON'T HAVE TIME TO FEED A STUPID SQUIRREL!
リスにえさやってる場合じゃないでしょうっ!!
I TRIED TO GO BACK.

Ashihara's Diary

No. 1

This is the very last volume of Forbidden Dance. Thanks for reading the story until the end.

When I started to write the series, I didn't know much about how to work on a serial story. Fortunately it turned out to be an enjoyable experience for me. I learned a lot in the process, and hope to use the valuable experience to create a better series in the future. I would like to express my appreciation to all who supported me.

*I received a lot of letters from fans who said, "I love Aya, a character who sticks it out to achieve her goals." I like people who do their best, too. It's very pleasant to see a character like her pursuing her dreams. Having goals is great no matter how small they are-academic success, romantic success, or whatever.

To be continued

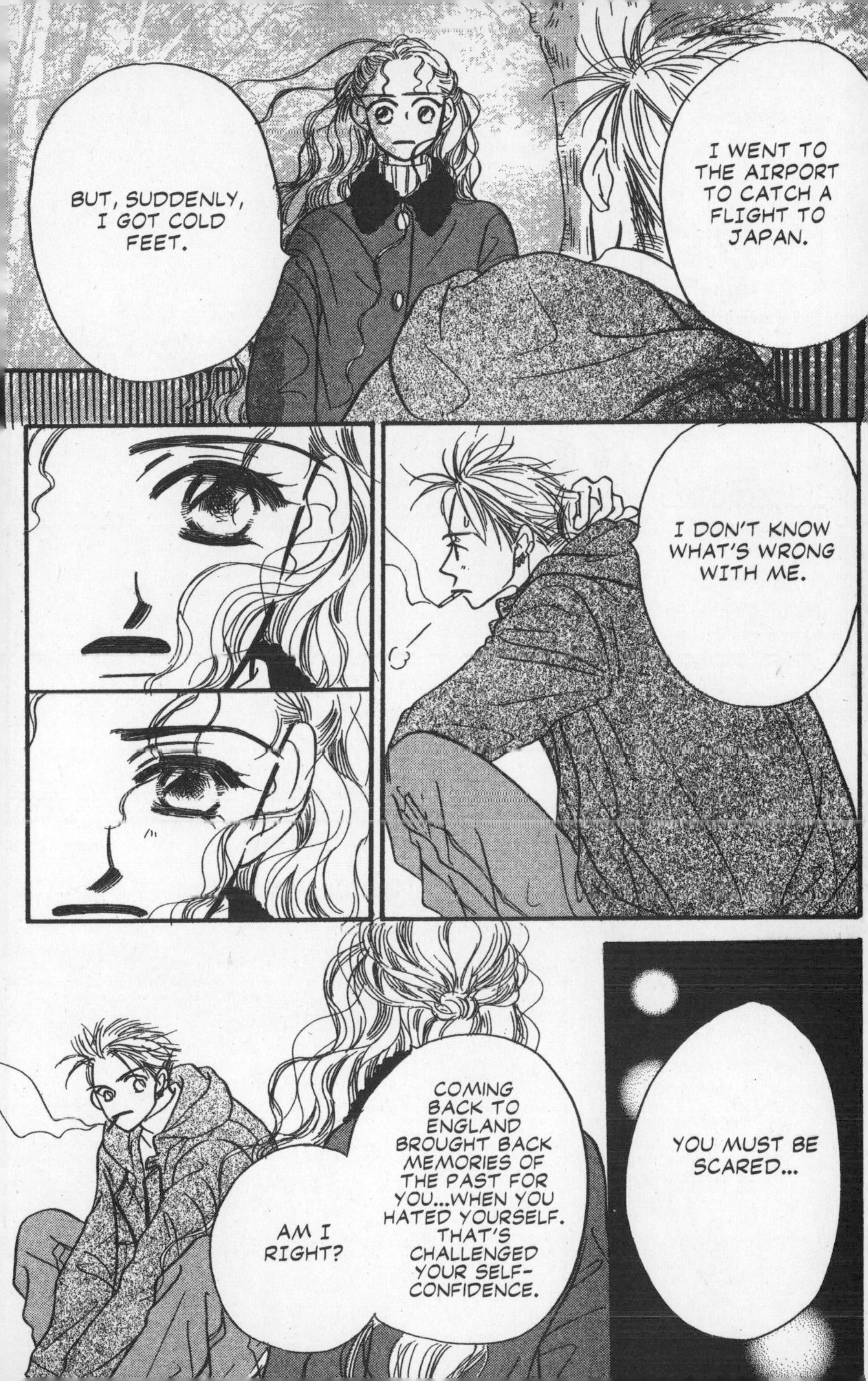
I WENT TO THE AIRPORT TO CATCH A FLIGHT TO JAPAN.
BUT, SUDDENLY, I GOT COLD FEET.
I DON'T KNOW WHAT'S WRONG WITH ME.
YOU MUST BE SCARED...
COMING BACK TO ENGLAND BROUGHT BACK MEMORIES OF THE PAST FOR YOU...WHEN YOU HATED YOURSELF. THAT'S CHALLENGED YOUR SELF-CONFIDENCE.
AM I RIGHT?

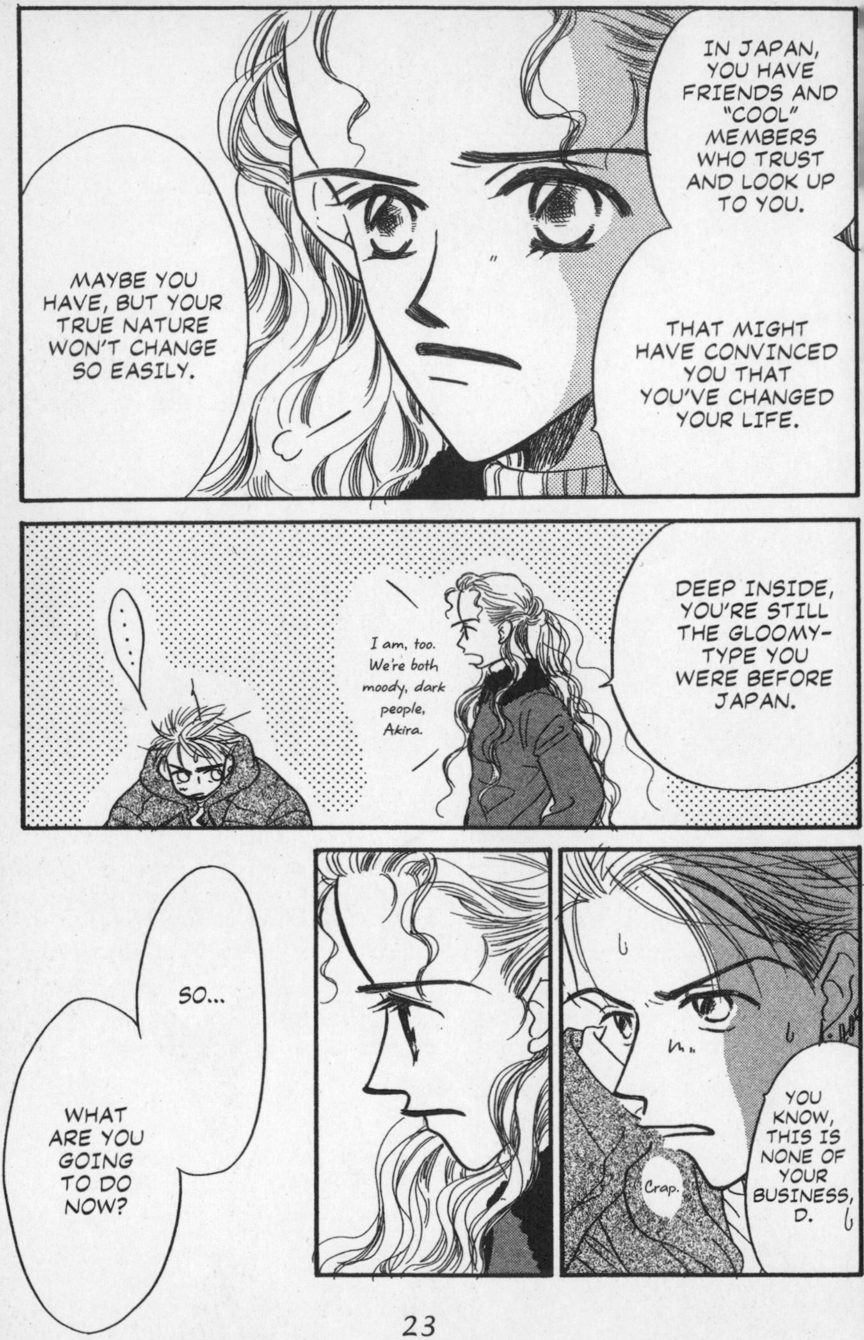
IN JAPAN, YOU HAVE FRIENDS AND "COOL" MEMBERS WHO TRUST AND LOOK UP TO YOU.
THAT MIGHT HAVE CONVINCED YOU THAT YOU'VE CHANGED YOUR LIFE.
MAYBE YOU HAVE, BUT YOUR TRUE NATURE WON'T CHANGE SO EASILY.
DEEP INSIDE, YOU'RE STILL THE GLOOMY-TYPE YOU WERE BEFORE JAPAN.
I am, too. We're both moody, dark people, Akira.
.....
YOU KNOW, THIS IS NONE OF YOUR BUSINESS, D.
Crap.
SO...
WHAT ARE YOU GOING TO DO NOW?

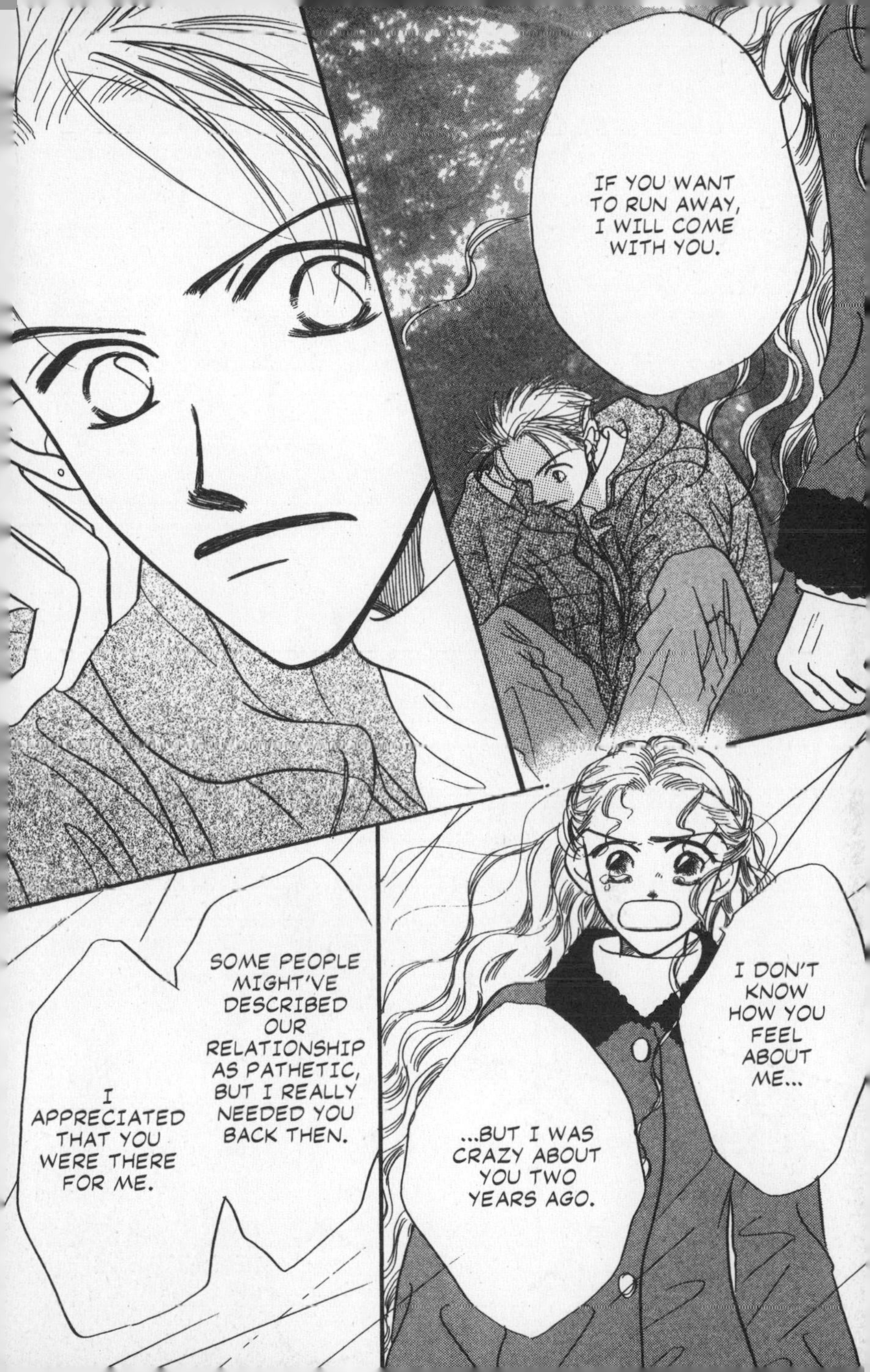
IF YOU WANT TO RUN AWAY, I WILL COME WITH YOU.
I DON'T KNOW HOW YOU FEEL ABOUT ME...
...BUT I WAS CRAZY ABOUT YOU TWO YEARS AGO.
SOME PEOPLE MIGHT'VE DESCRIBED OUR RELATIONSHIP AS PATHETIC, BUT I REALLY NEEDED YOU BACK THEN.
I APPRECIATED THAT YOU WERE THERE FOR ME.

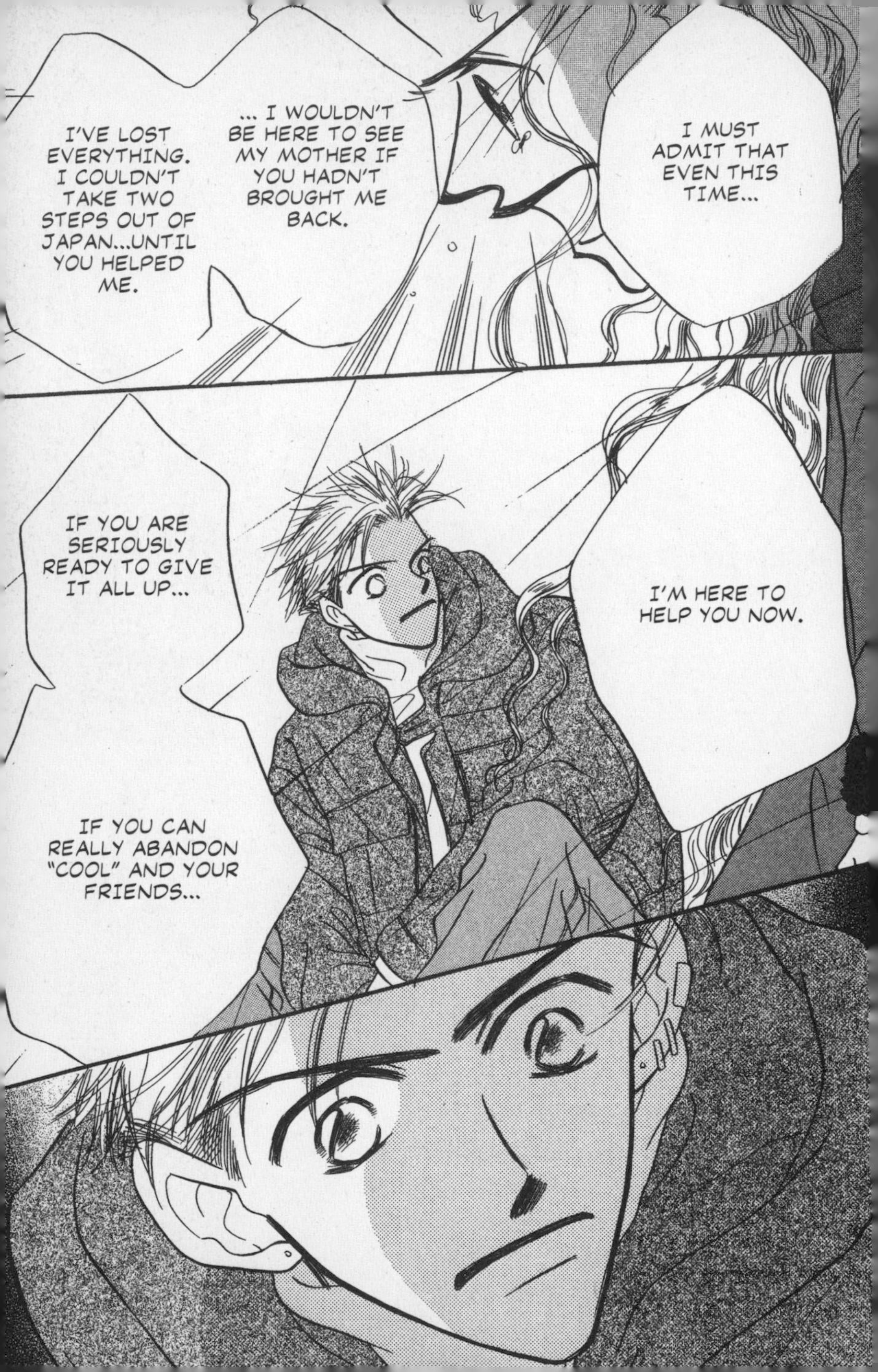
I MUST ADMIT THAT EVEN THIS TIME...
... I WOULDN'T BE HERE TO SEE MY MOTHER IF YOU HADN'T BROUGHT ME BACK.
I'VE LOST EVERYTHING. I COULDN'T TAKE TWO STEPS OUT OF JAPAN...UNTIL YOU HELPED ME.
I'M HERE TO HELP YOU NOW.
IF YOU ARE SERIOUSLY READY TO GIVE IT ALL UP...
IF YOU CAN REALLY ABANDON "COOL" AND YOUR FRIENDS...

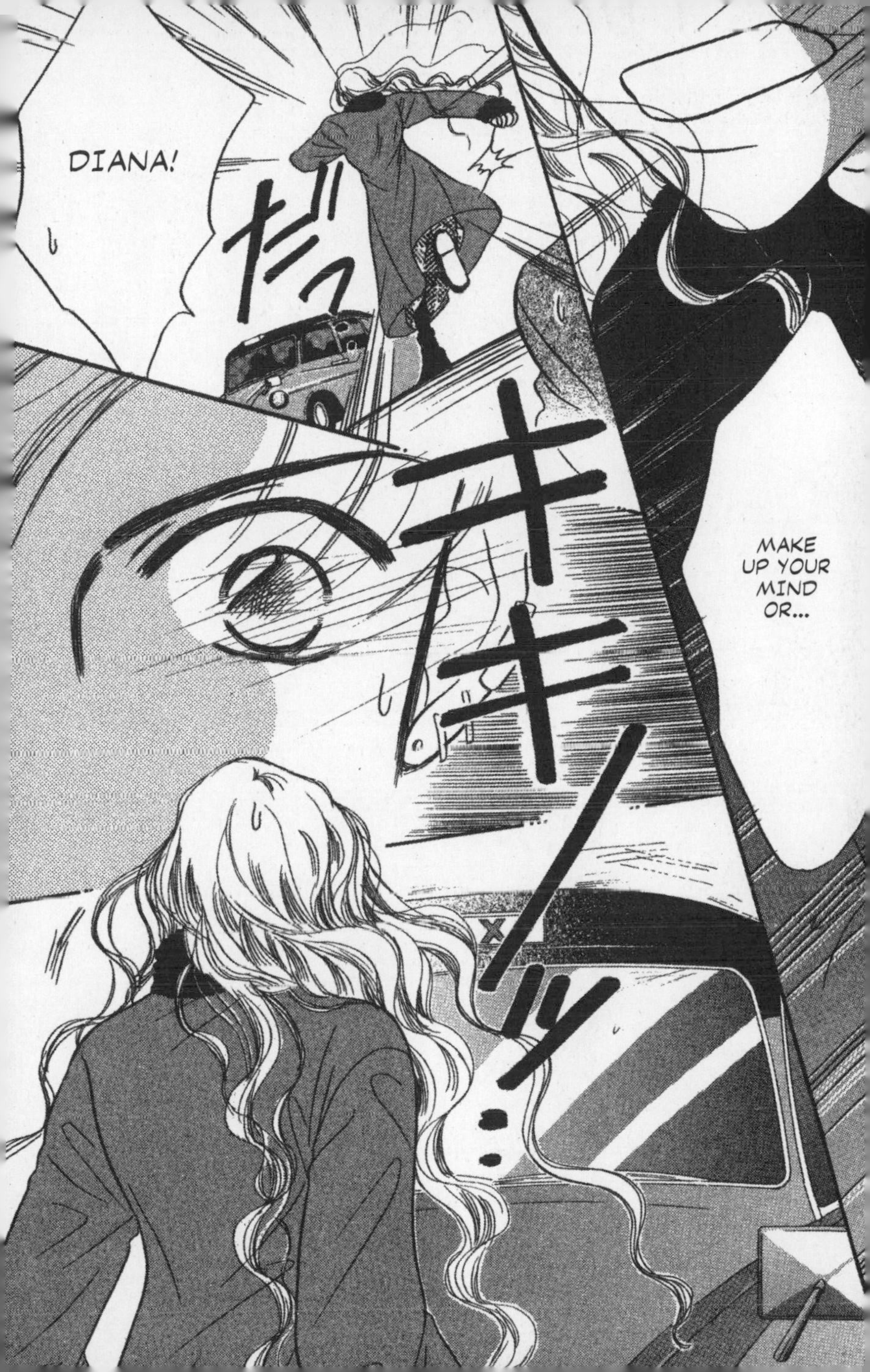
MAKE UP YOUR MIND OR...
DIANA!
ダッ
キキーッ…

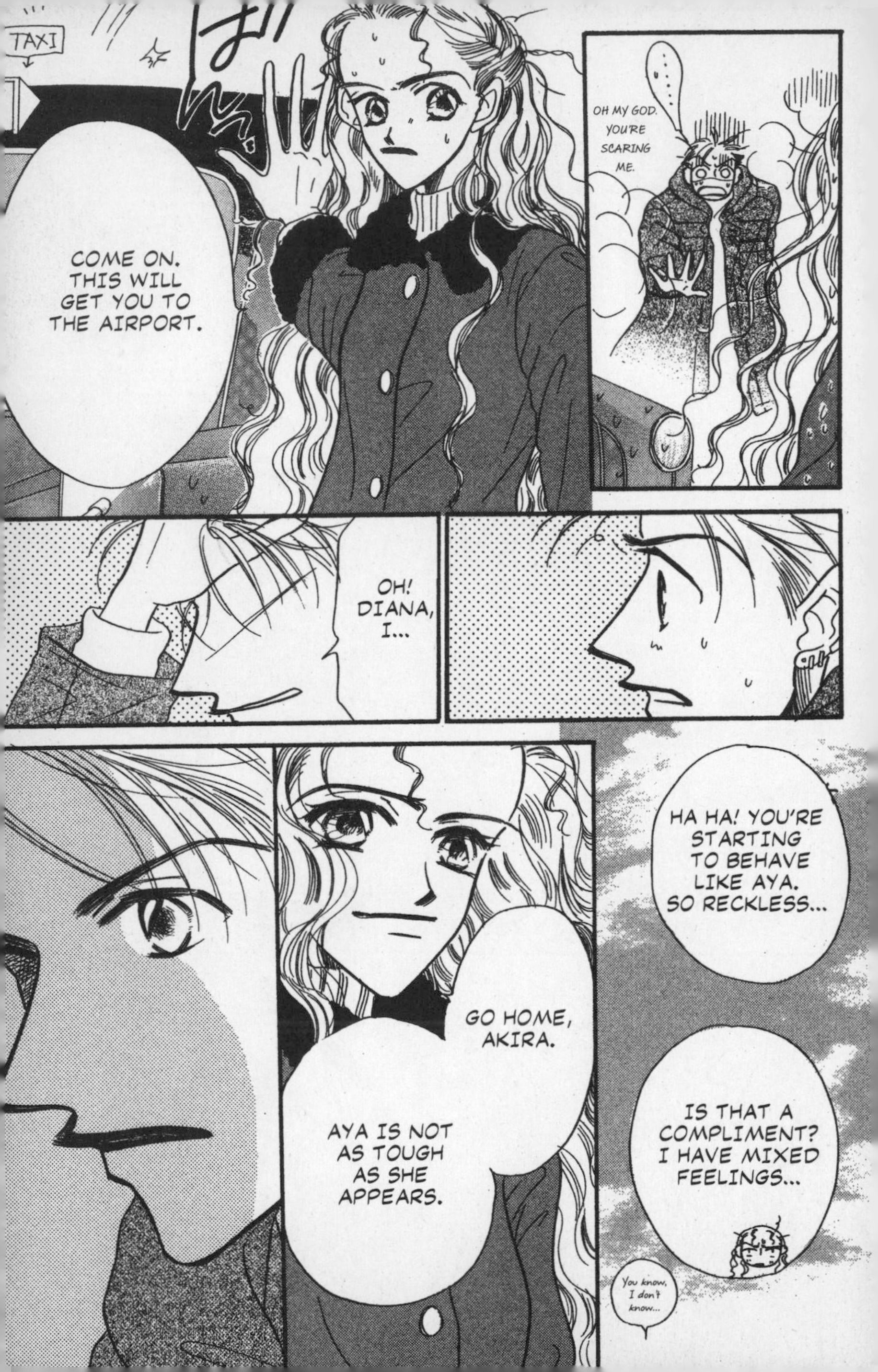
OH MY GOD. YOU'RE SCARING ME.
TAXI
ばん
COME ON. THIS WILL GET YOU TO THE AIRPORT.
OH! DIANA, I...
HA HA! YOU'RE STARTING TO BEHAVE LIKE AYA. SO RECKLESS...
IS THAT A COMPLIMENT? I HAVE MIXED FEELINGS...
You know, I don't know...
GO HOME, AKIRA.
AYA IS NOT AS TOUGH AS SHE APPEARS.

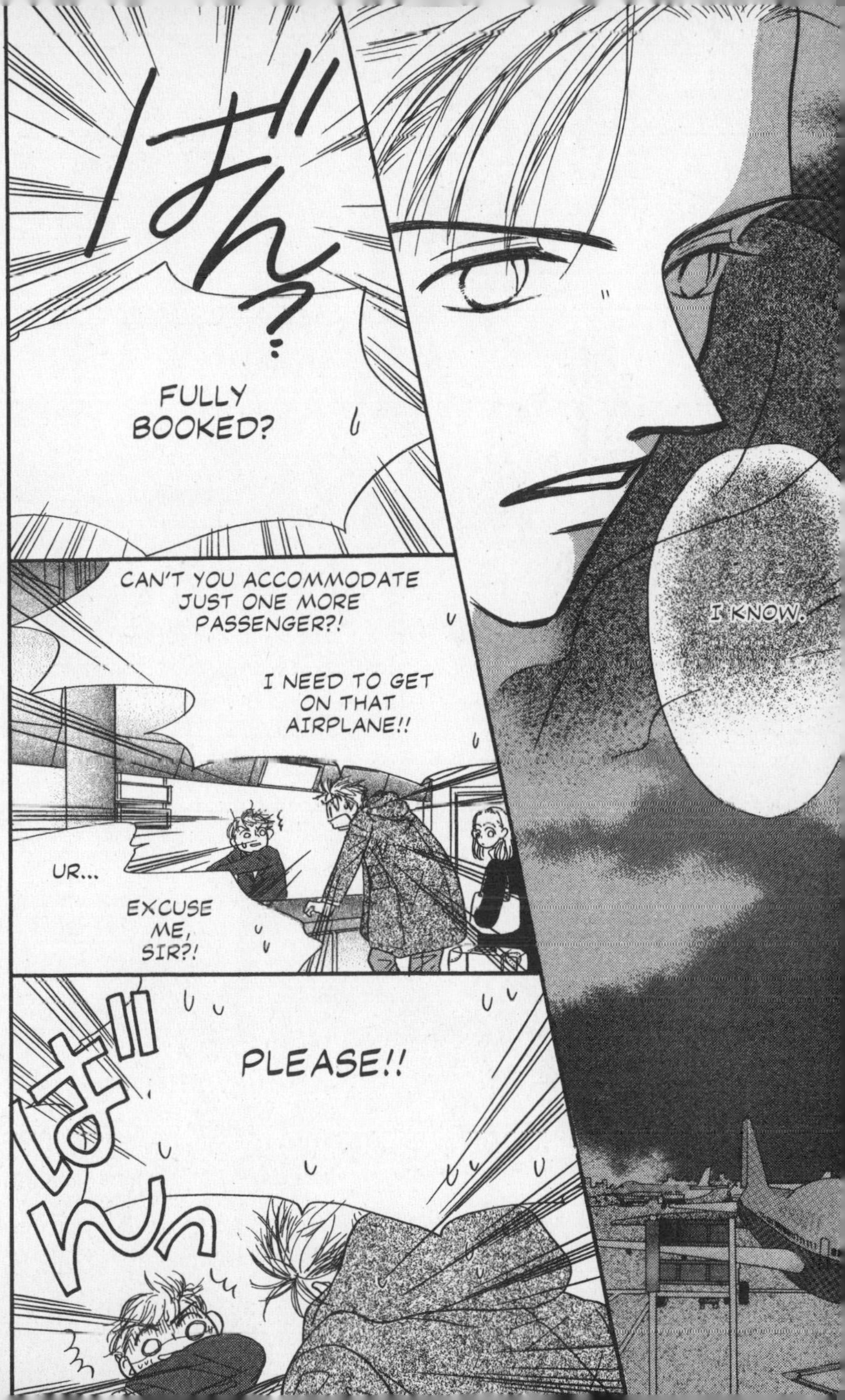
I KNOW.
ばん
FULLY BOOKED?
CAN'T YOU ACCOMMODATE JUST ONE MORE PASSENGER?!
I NEED TO GET ON THAT AIRPLANE!!
UR...
EXCUSE ME, SIR?!
ばん
PLEASE!!

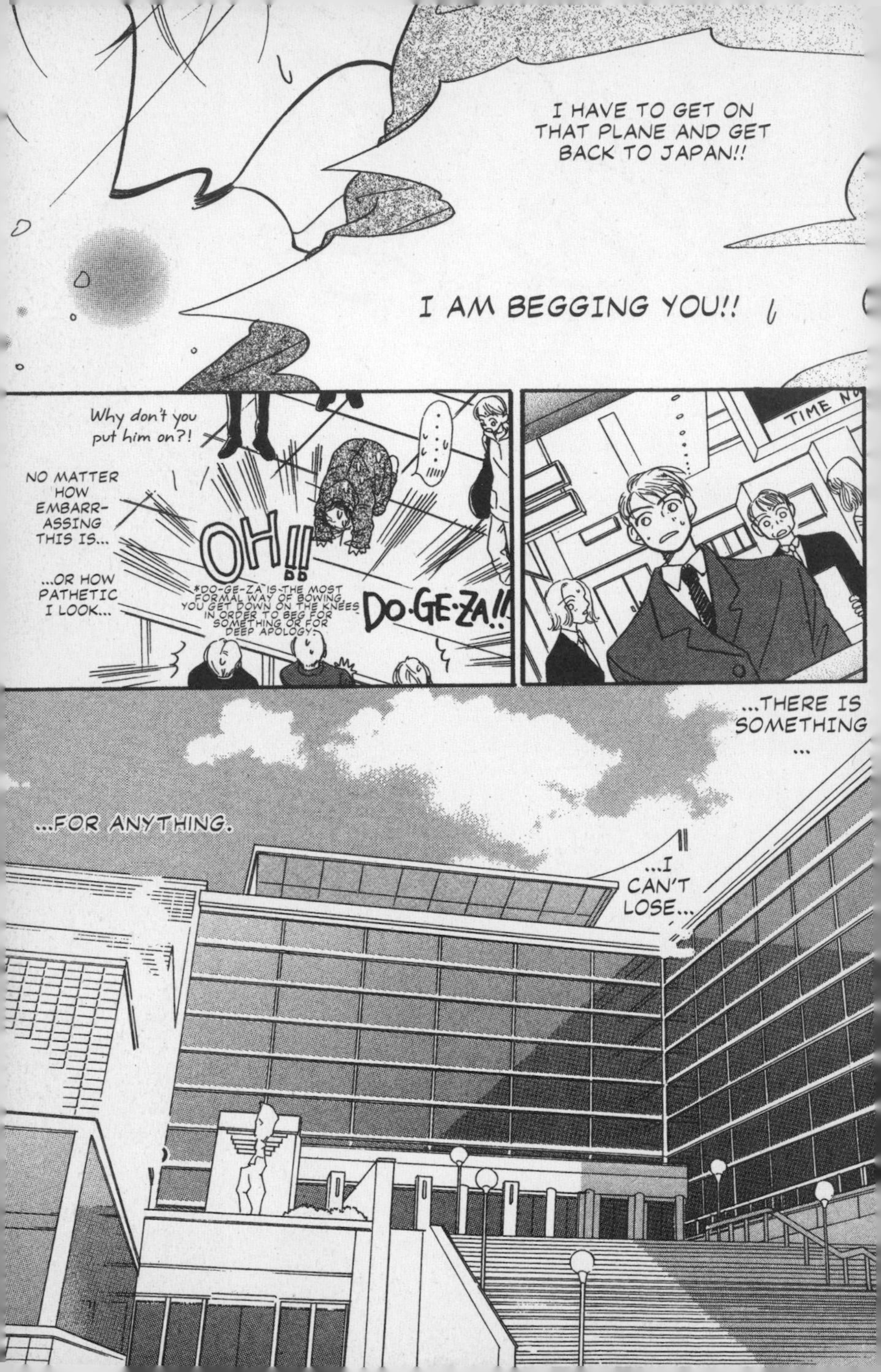
I HAVE TO GET ON THAT PLANE AND GET BACK TO JAPAN!!
I AM BEGGING YOU!!
TIME N
DO·GE·ZA!!
*DO-GE-ZA IS THE MOST FORMAL WAY OF BOWING. YOU GET DOWN ON THE KNEES IN ORDER TO BEG FOR SOMETHING OR FOR DEEP APOLOGY.
OH!!
Why don't you put him on?!
NO MATTER HOW EMBARR-ASSING THIS IS...
...OR HOW PATHETIC I LOOK...
...THERE IS SOMETHING ...
...I CAN'T LOSE...
...FOR ANYTHING.

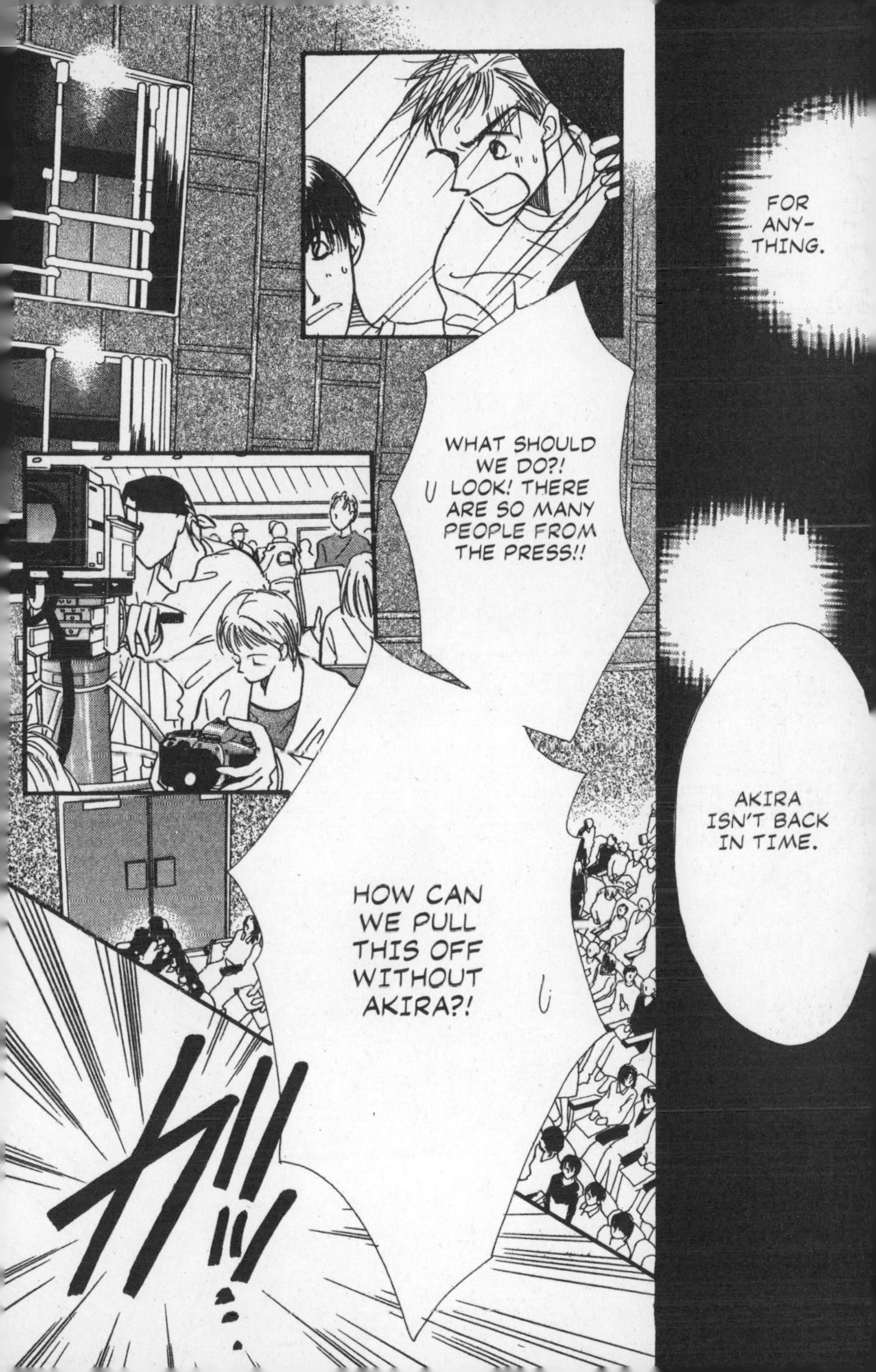
FOR ANY-THING.
AKIRA ISN'T BACK IN TIME.
WHAT SHOULD WE DO?! LOOK! THERE ARE SO MANY PEOPLE FROM THE PRESS!!
HOW CAN WE PULL THIS OFF WITHOUT AKIRA?!

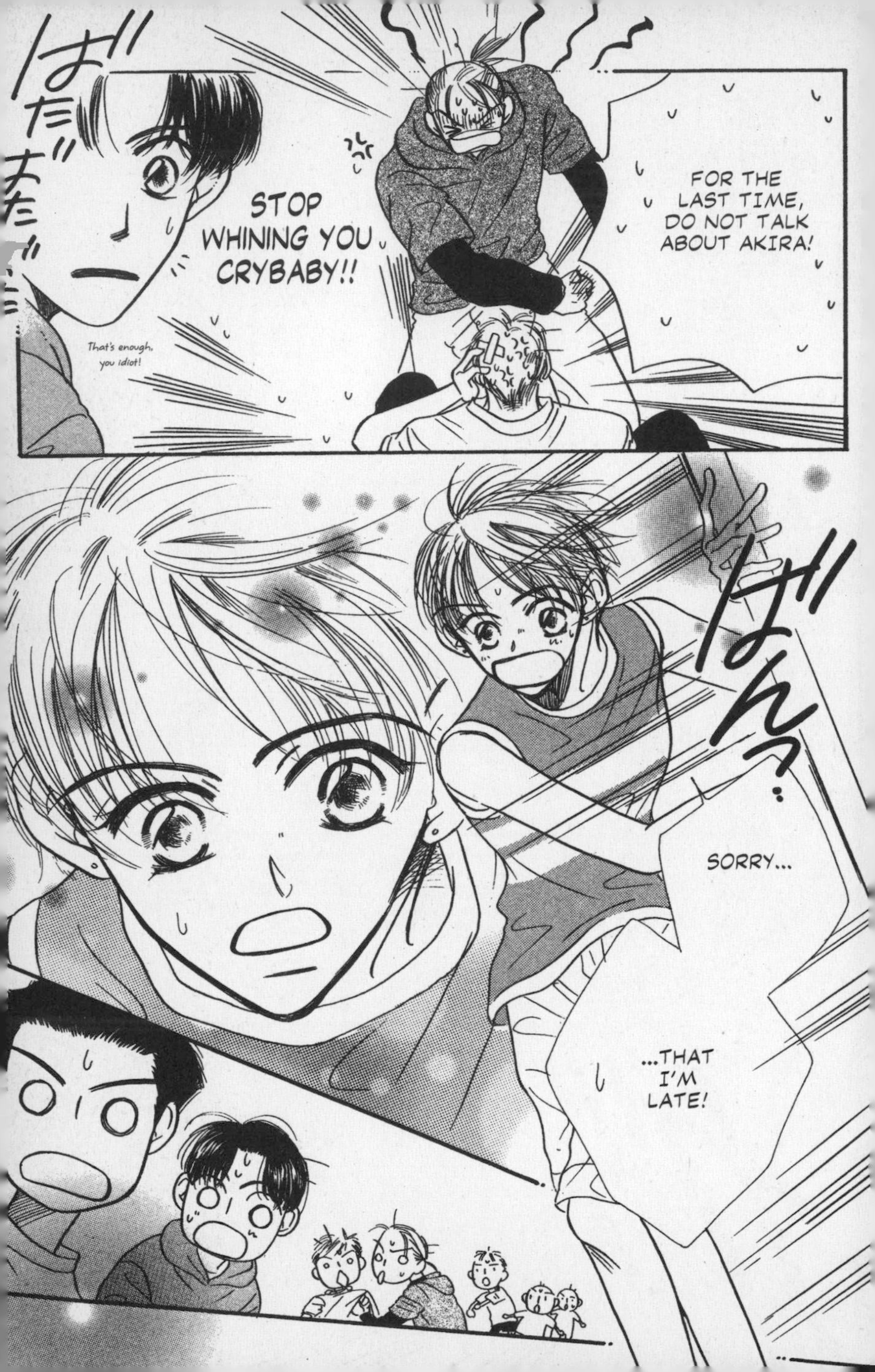
FOR THE LAST TIME, DO NOT TALK ABOUT AKIRA!
STOP WHINING YOU CRYBABY!!
That's enough, you idiot!
ばん
SORRY...
...THAT I'M LATE!

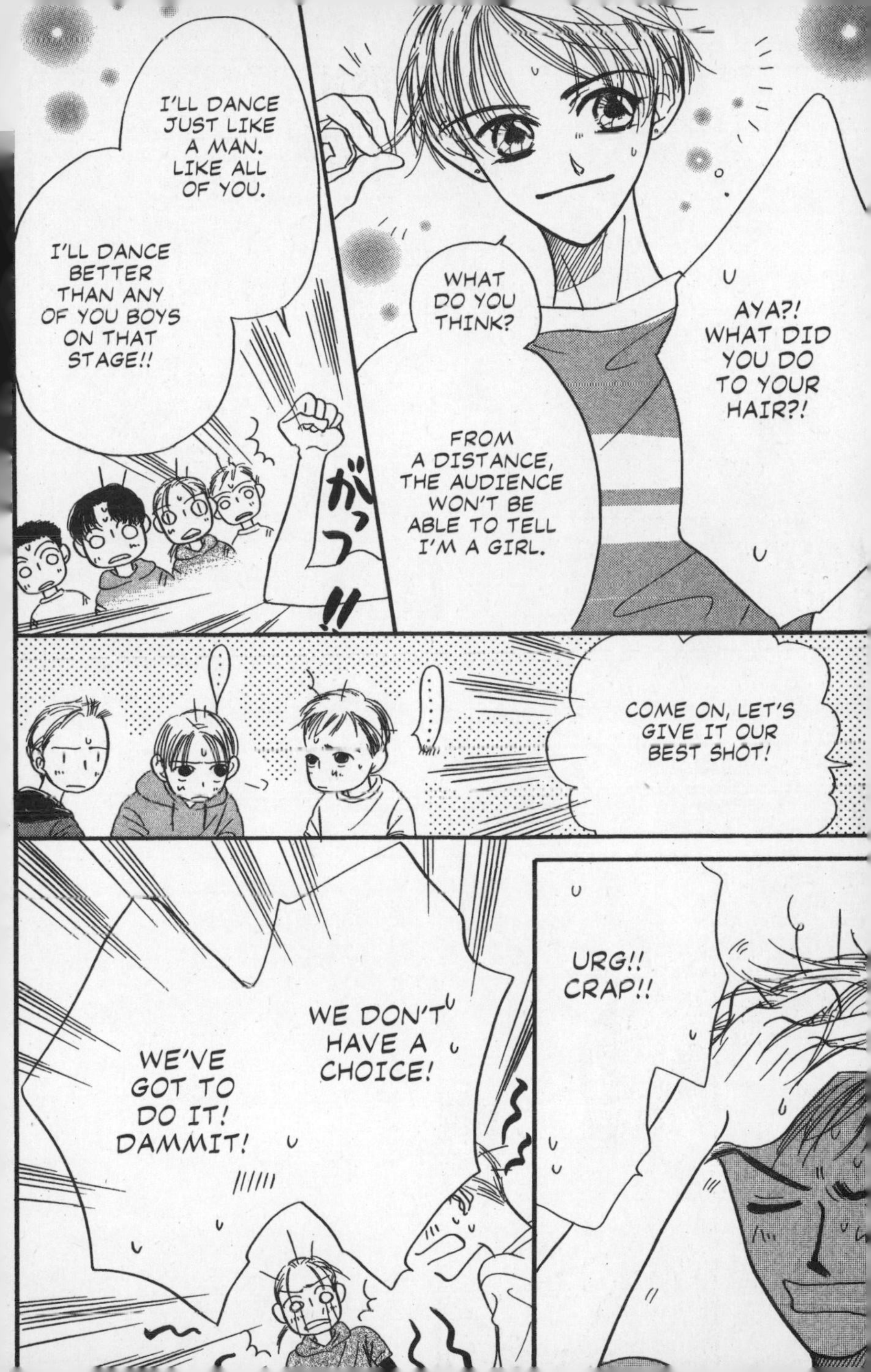
AYA?! WHAT DID YOU DO TO YOUR HAIR?!
WHAT DO YOU THINK?
FROM A DISTANCE, THE AUDIENCE WON'T BE ABLE TO TELL I'M A GIRL.
I'LL DANCE JUST LIKE A MAN. LIKE ALL OF YOU.
I'LL DANCE BETTER THAN ANY OF YOU BOYS ON THAT STAGE!!
がっつ!!
COME ON, LET'S GIVE IT OUR BEST SHOT!
......
!
URG!! CRAP!!
WE DON'T HAVE A CHOICE!
WE'VE GOT TO DO IT! DAMMIT!

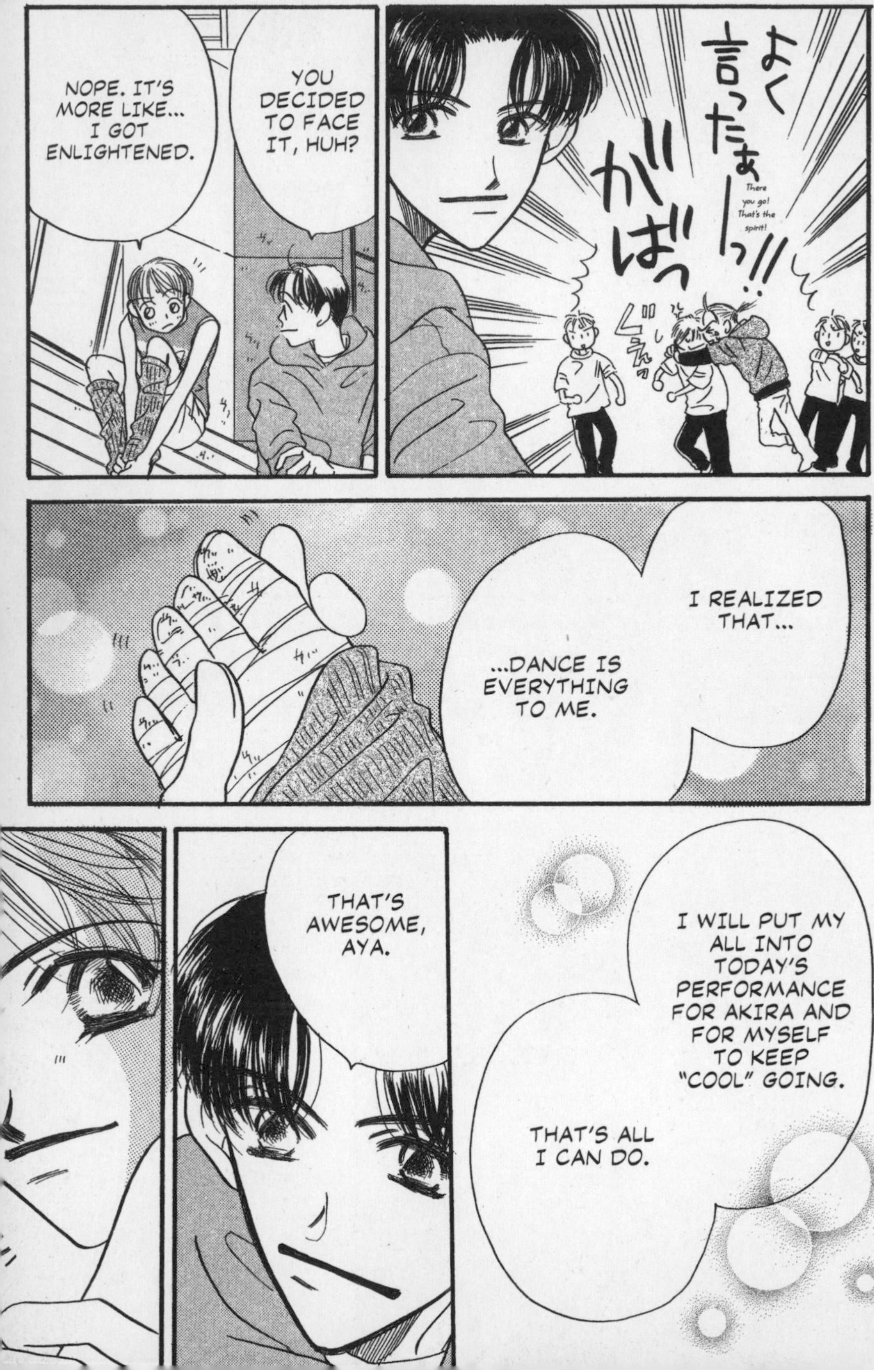
よく言ったぁーっ!!
がばっ
There you go! That's the spirit!
YOU DECIDED TO FACE IT, HUH?
NOPE. IT'S MORE LIKE... I GOT ENLIGHTENED.
I REALIZED THAT...
...DANCE IS EVERYTHING TO ME.
I WILL PUT MY ALL INTO TODAY'S PERFORMANCE FOR AKIRA AND FOR MYSELF TO KEEP "COOL" GOING.
THAT'S ALL I CAN DO.
THAT'S AWESOME, AYA.

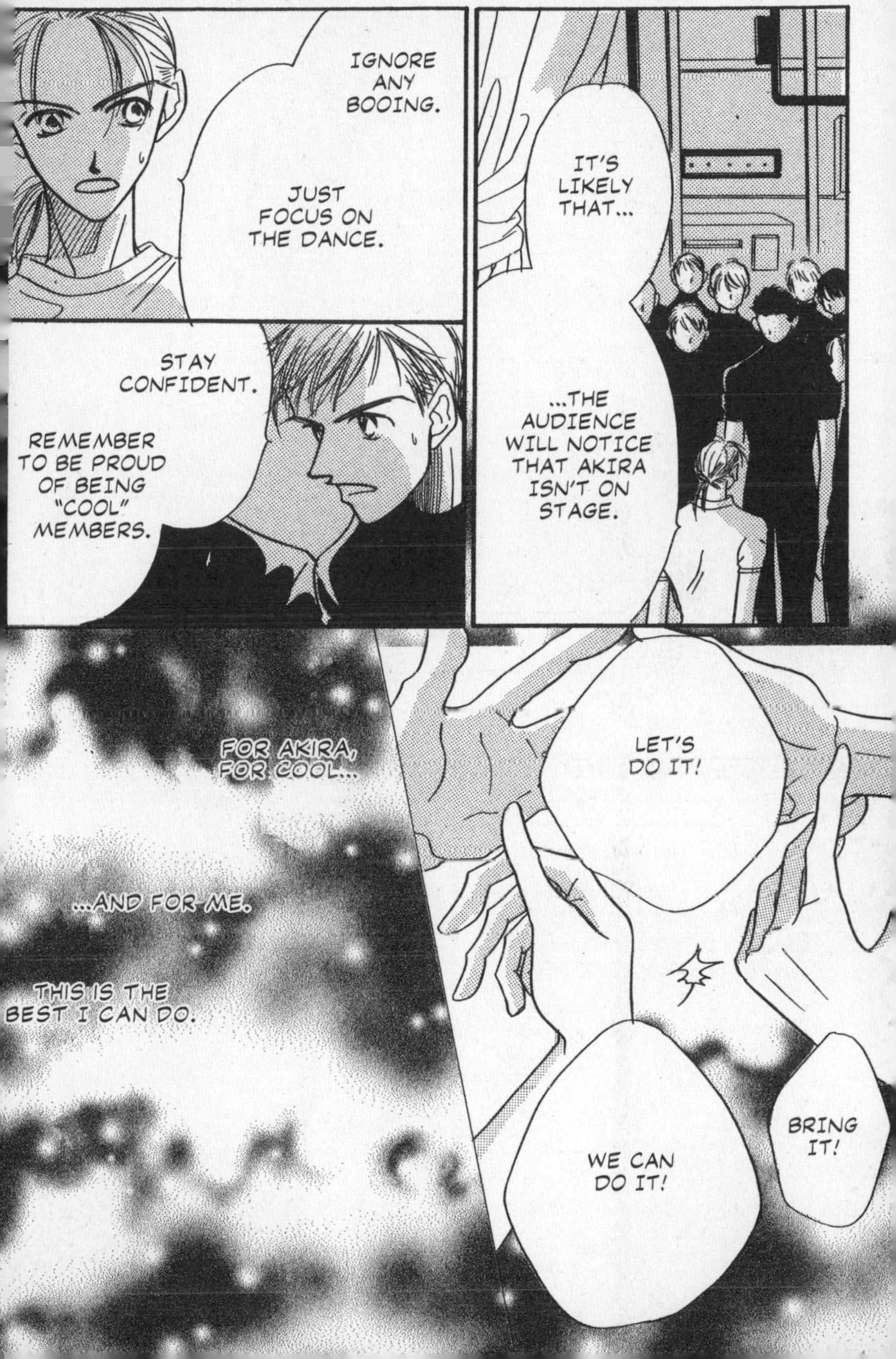
IT'S LIKELY THAT...
...THE AUDIENCE WILL NOTICE THAT AKIRA ISN'T ON STAGE.
IGNORE ANY BOOING.
JUST FOCUS ON THE DANCE.
STAY CONFIDENT.
REMEMBER TO BE PROUD OF BEING "COOL" MEMBERS.
LET'S DO IT!
BRING IT!
WE CAN DO IT!
FOR AKIRA, FOR COOL...
...AND FOR ME.
THIS IS THE BEST I CAN DO.

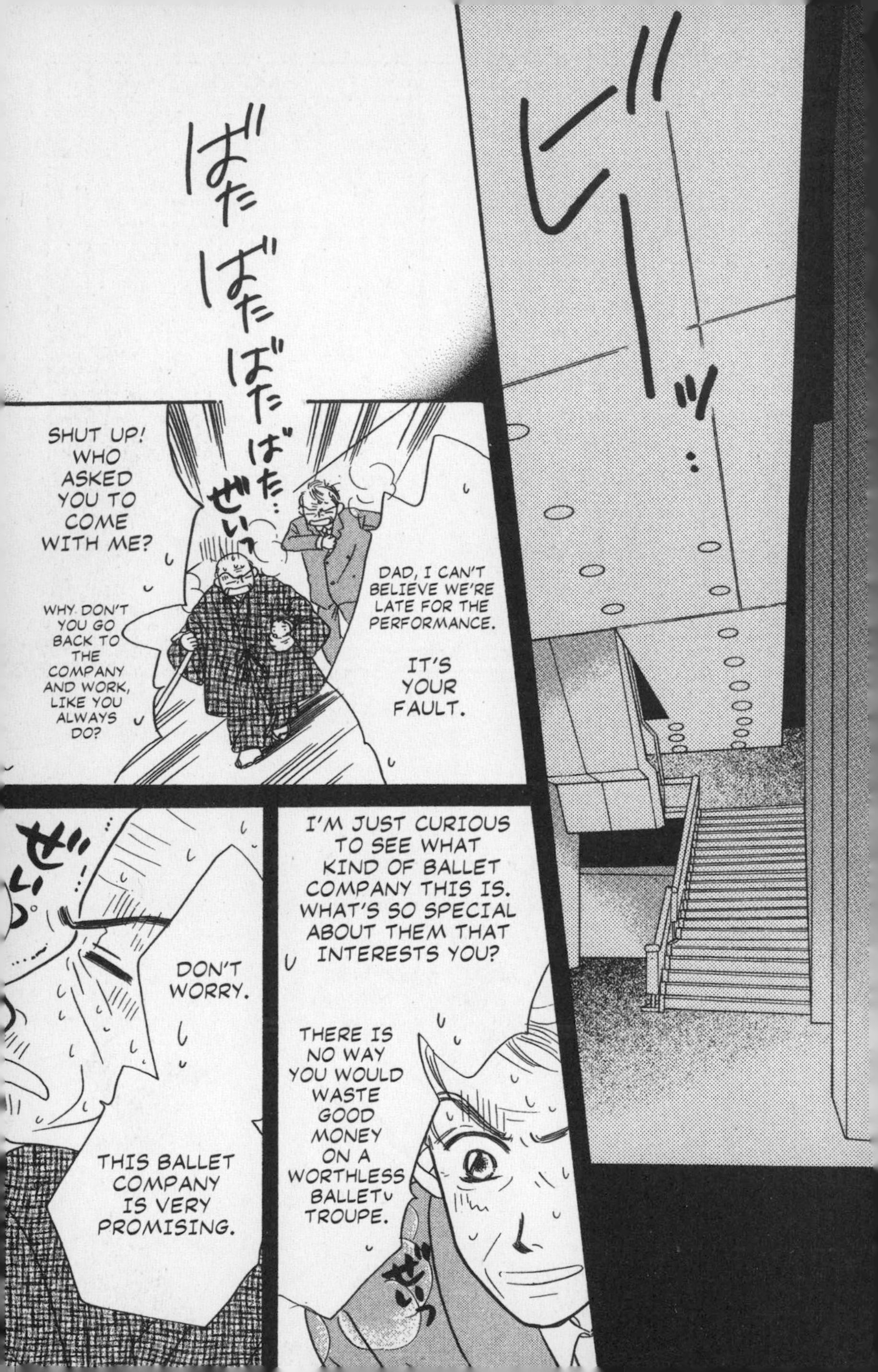
ビーーッ
ばたばたばたばた
DAD, I CAN'T BELIEVE WE'RE LATE FOR THE PERFORMANCE.
IT'S YOUR FAULT.
ぜいっ
SHUT UP! WHO ASKED YOU TO COME WITH ME?
WHY DON'T YOU GO BACK TO THE COMPANY AND WORK, LIKE YOU ALWAYS DO?
I'M JUST CURIOUS TO SEE WHAT KIND OF BALLET COMPANY THIS IS. WHAT'S SO SPECIAL ABOUT THEM THAT INTERESTS YOU?
THERE IS NO WAY YOU WOULD WASTE GOOD MONEY ON A WORTHLESS BALLET TROUPE.
ぜいっ
ぜいっ
DON'T WORRY.
THIS BALLET COMPANY IS VERY PROMISING.

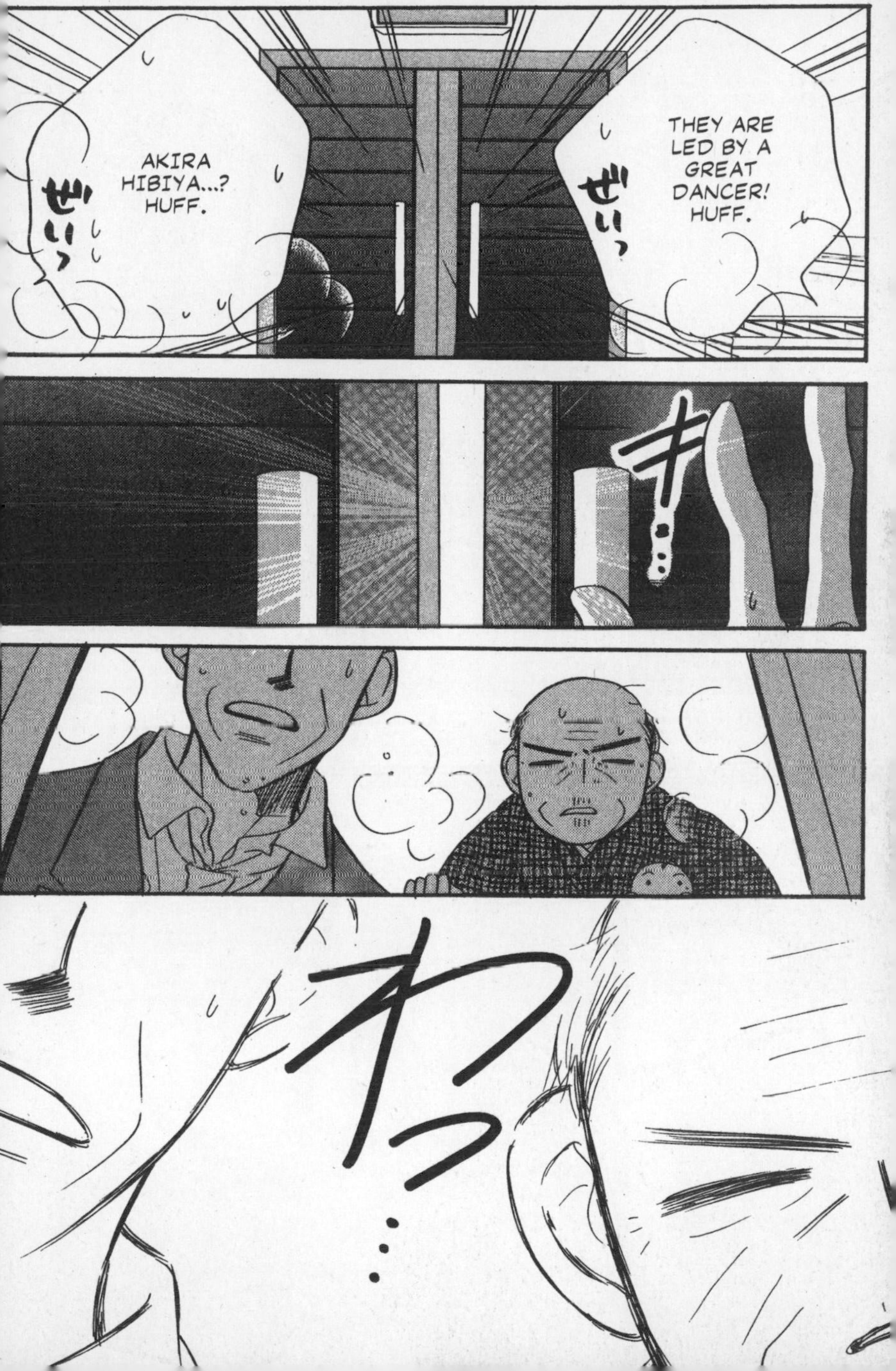
THEY ARE LED BY A GREAT DANCER! HUFF.
ぜいっ
AKIRA HIBIYA...? HUFF.
ぜいっ
わっ…

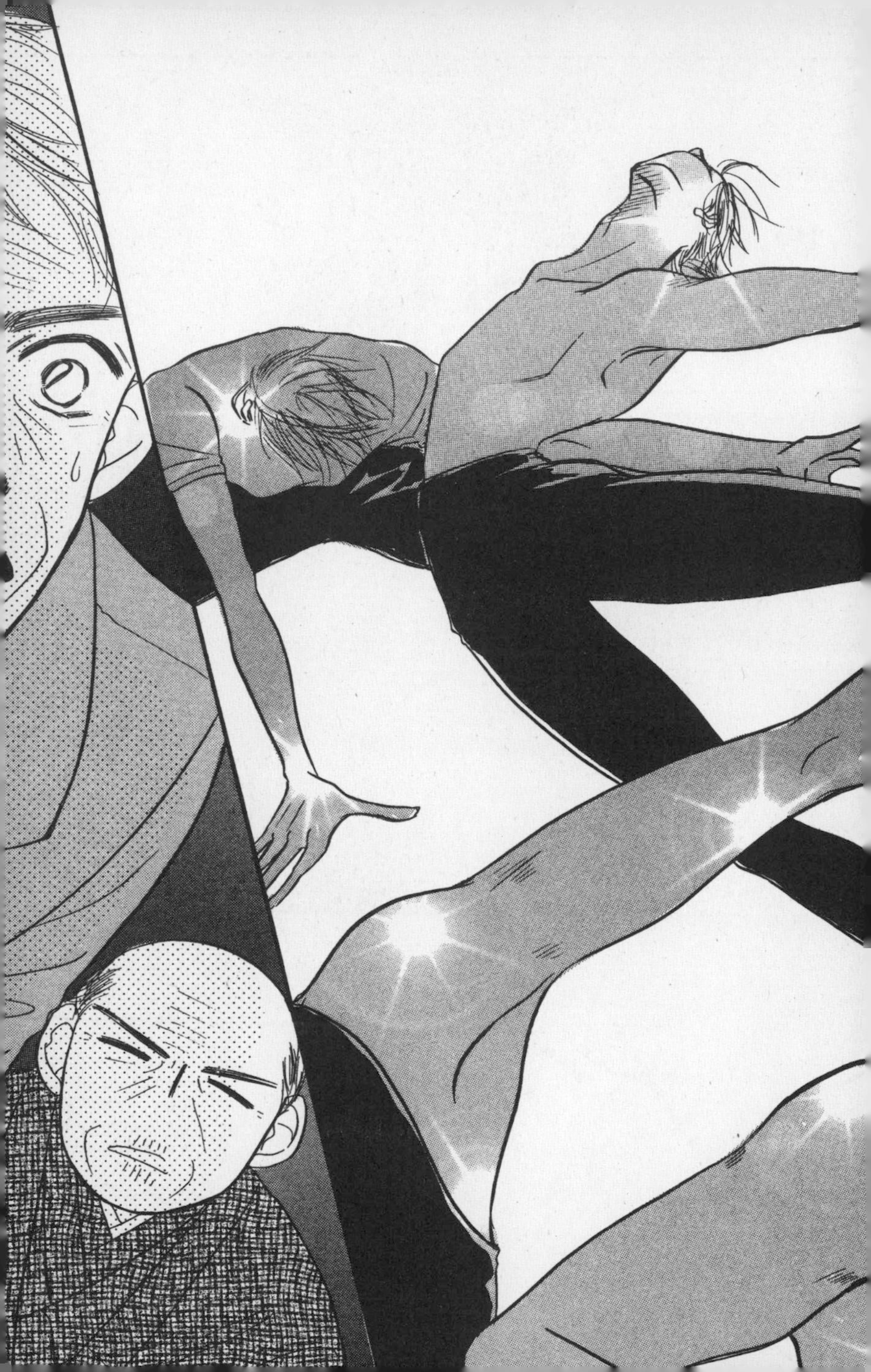

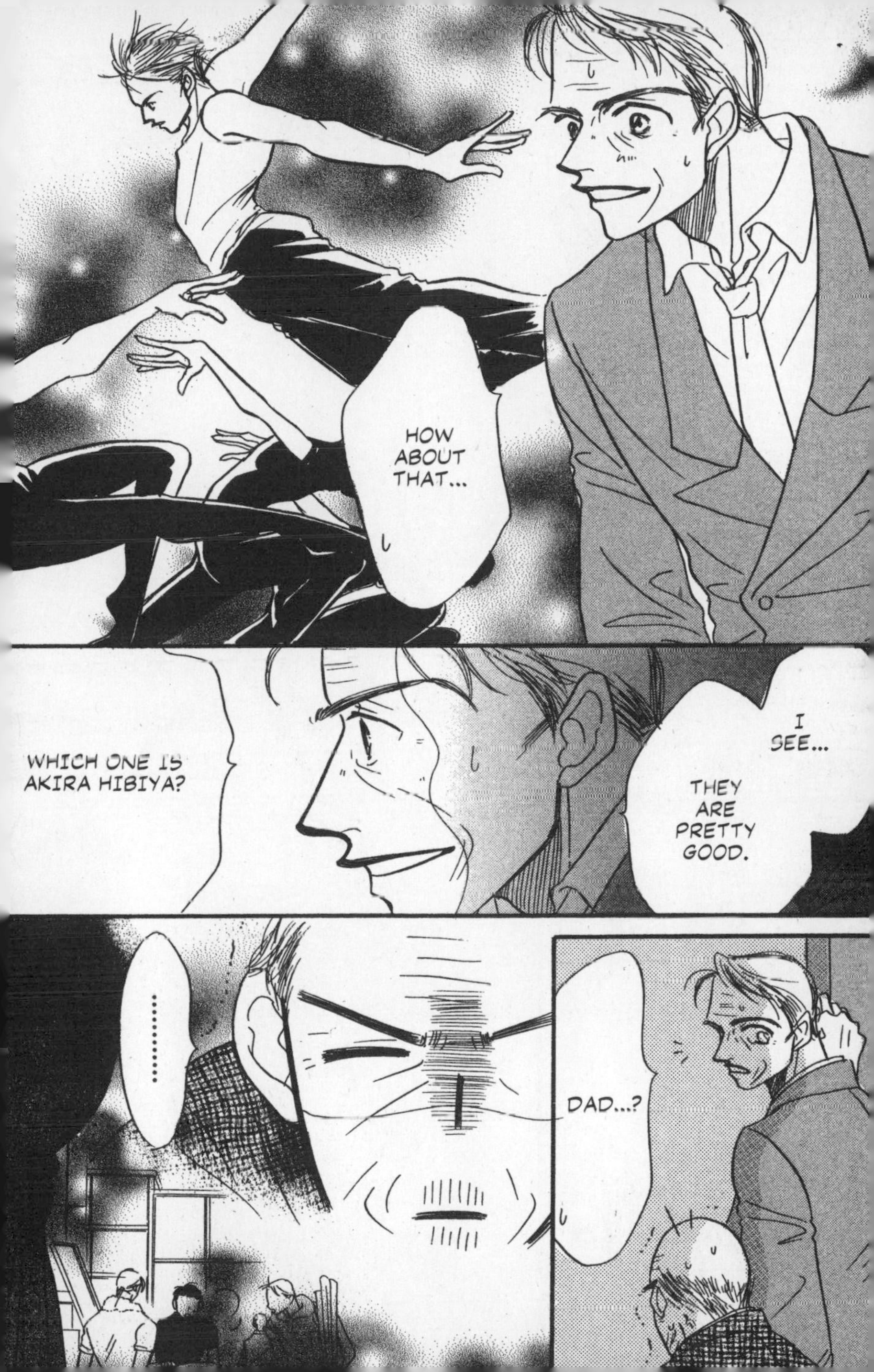
HOW ABOUT THAT...
I SEE...
THEY ARE PRETTY GOOD.
WHICH ONE IS AKIRA HIBIYA?
DAD...?
....

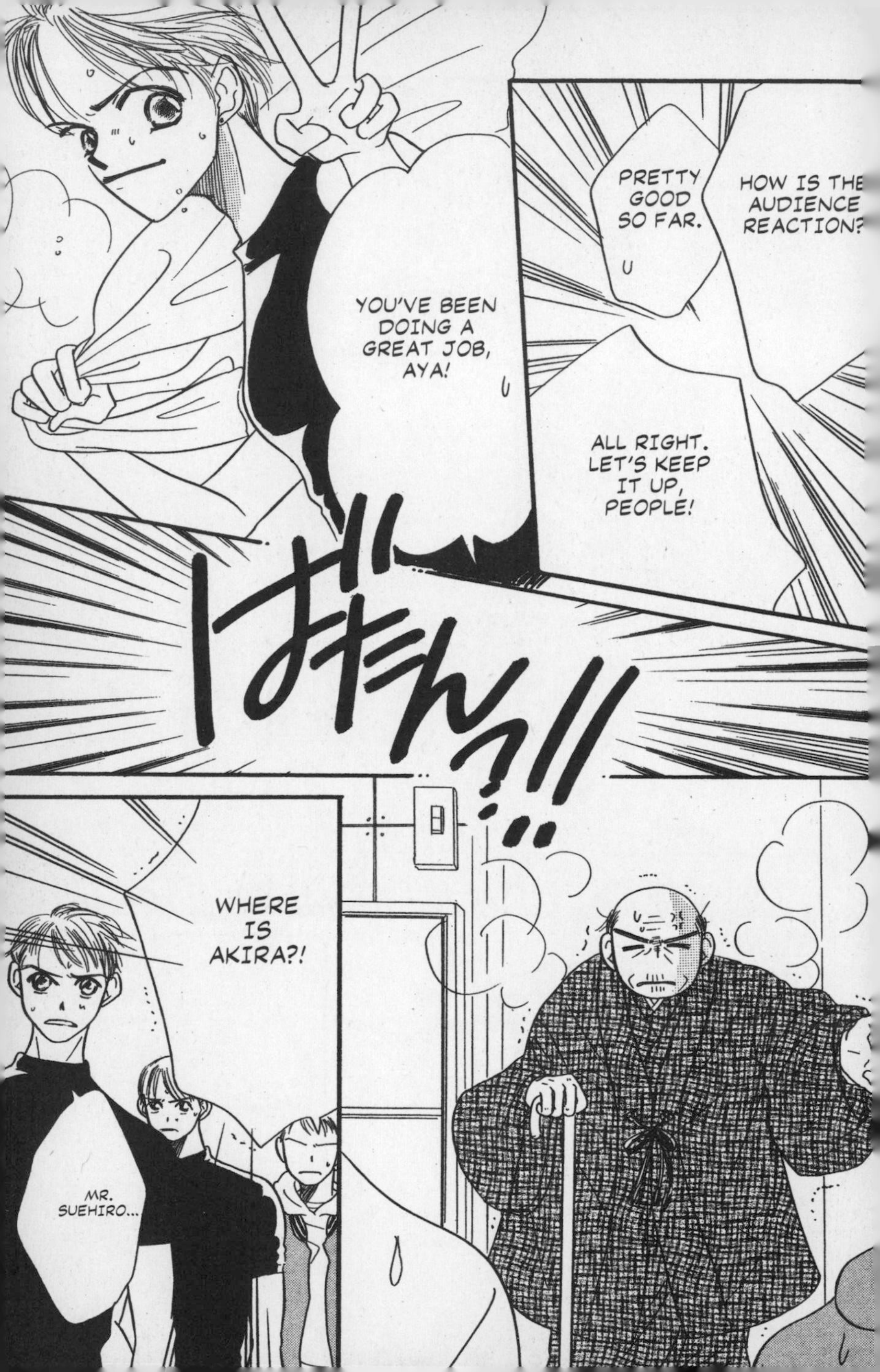
HOW IS THE AUDIENCE REACTION?
PRETTY GOOD SO FAR.
ALL RIGHT. LET'S KEEP IT UP, PEOPLE!
YOU'VE BEEN DOING A GREAT JOB, AYA!
ばたん?!!
WHERE IS AKIRA?!
MR. SUEHIRO...

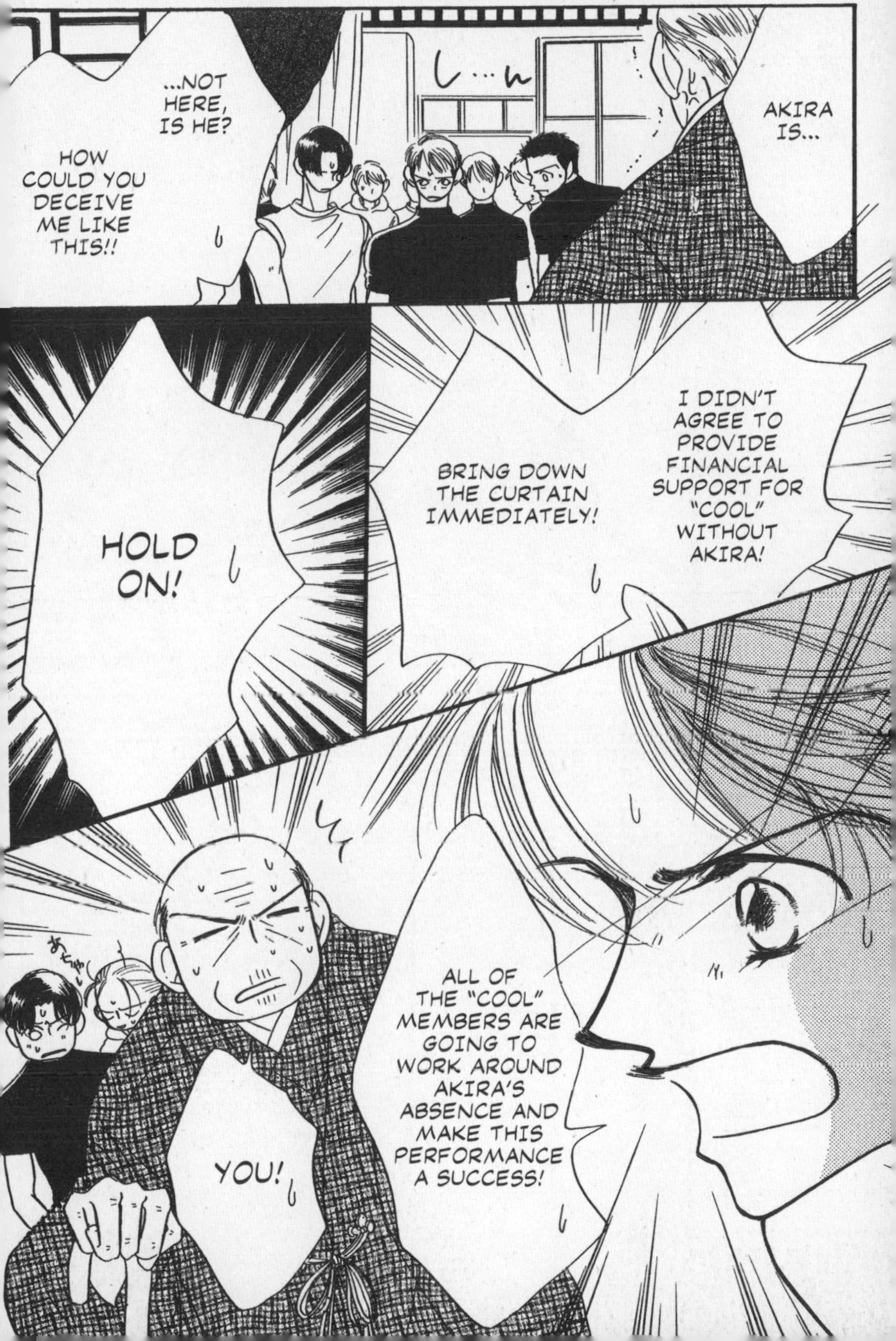
AKIRA IS...
し…ん
...NOT HERE, IS HE?
HOW COULD YOU DECEIVE ME LIKE THIS!!
I DIDN'T AGREE TO PROVIDE FINANCIAL SUPPORT FOR "COOL" WITHOUT AKIRA!
BRING DOWN THE CURTAIN IMMEDIATELY!
HOLD ON!
ALL OF THE "COOL" MEMBERS ARE GOING TO WORK AROUND AKIRA'S ABSENCE AND MAKE THIS PERFORMANCE A SUCCESS!
YOU!

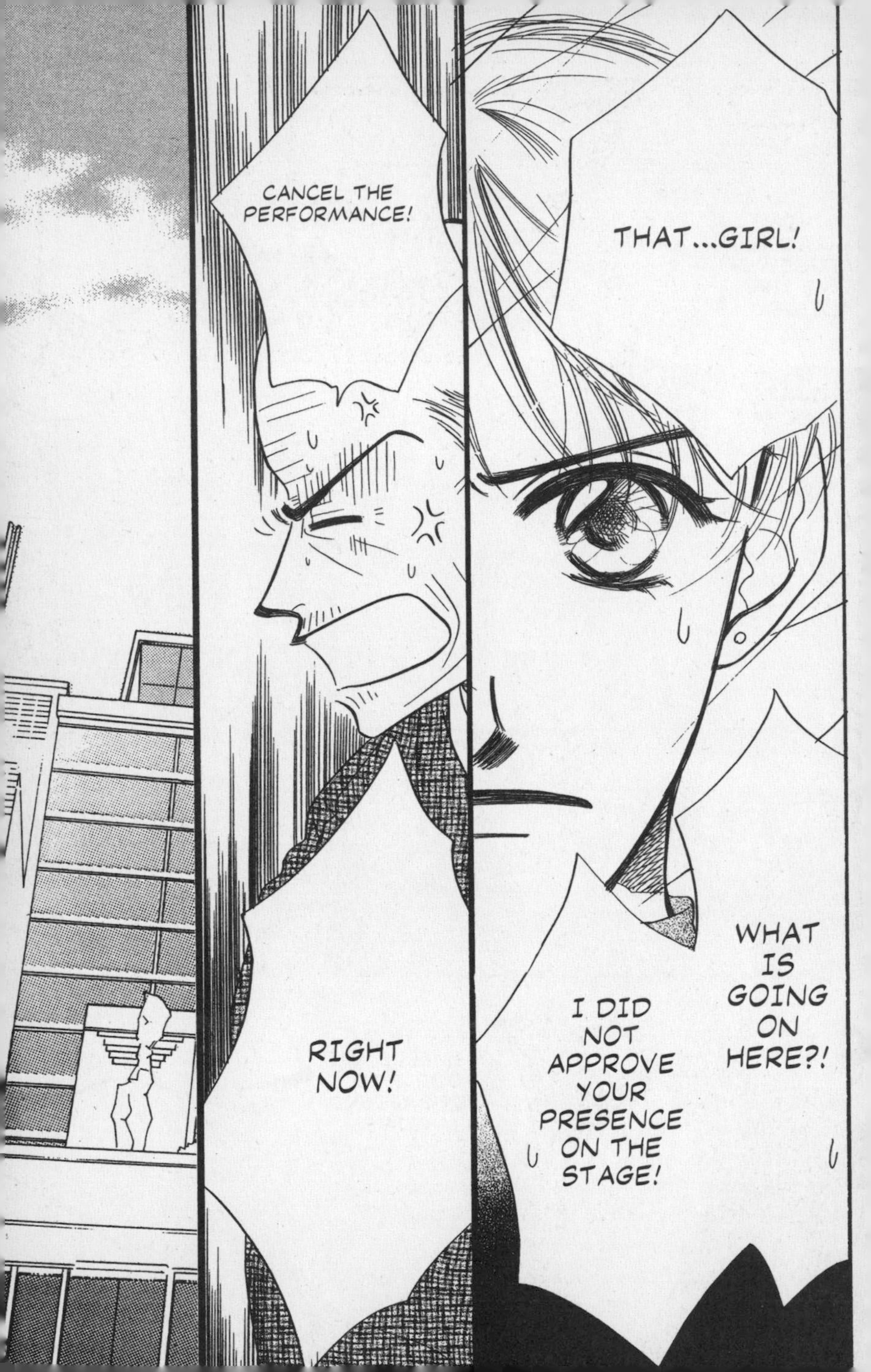
THAT...GIRL!
WHAT IS GOING ON HERE?!
I DID NOT APPROVE YOUR PRESENCE ON THE STAGE!
CANCEL THE PERFORMANCE!
RIGHT NOW!

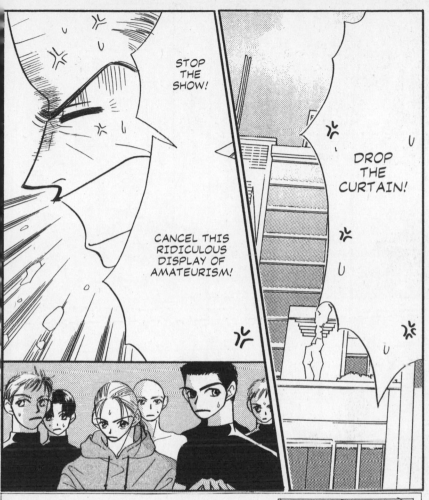

DROP THE CURTAIN!
STOP THE SHOW!
CANCEL THIS RIDICULOUS DISPLAY OF AMATEURISM!

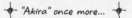

"Akira" once more...

His hair style was hardest to draw. Still, many fans wrote, saying that they would like to see more Aya and Akira romantic scenes. Sorry! I didn't manage to include such scenes. Was it due to bad page allocation? Akira and Aya are not good at expressing their feelings toward one another. But I greatly enjoyed writing their silly conversations.

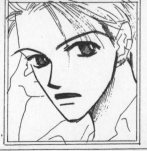

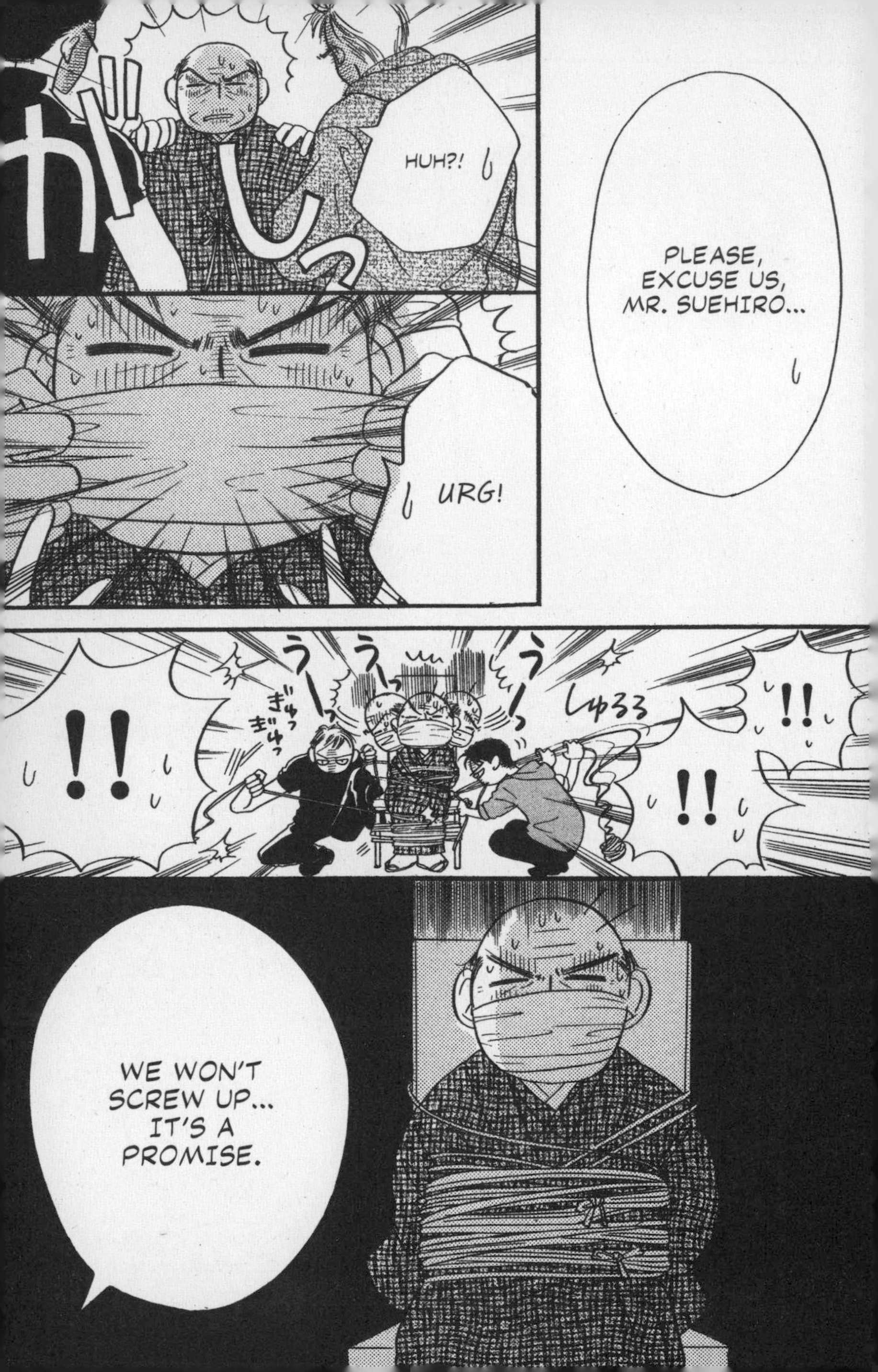
PLEASE, EXCUSE US, MR. SUEHIRO...
わしっ
HUH?!
URG!
う
!!
!!
しゅるるる
う
う
ぎゅっ ぎゅっ
!!
WE WON'T SCREW UP... IT'S A PROMISE.

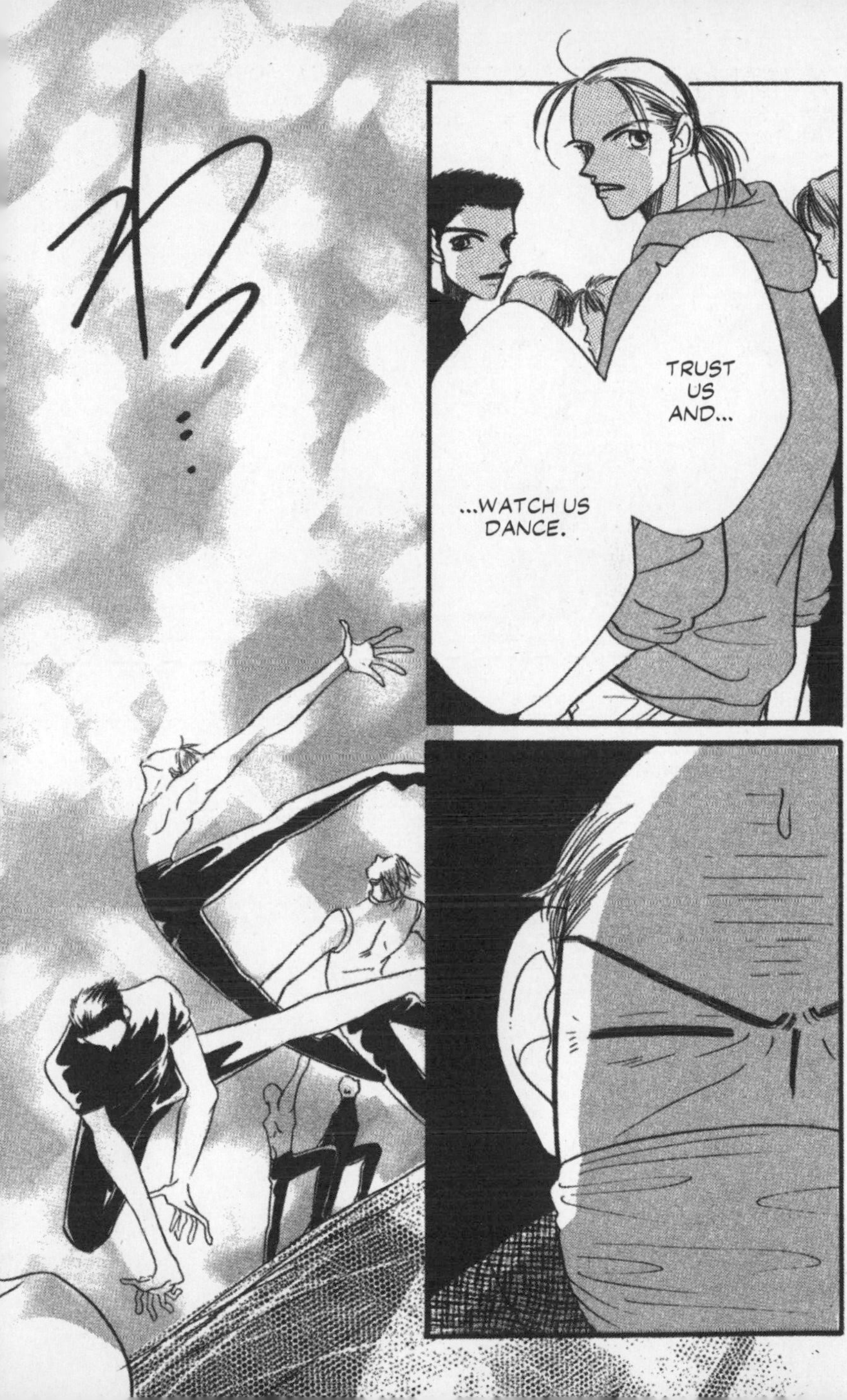
TRUST US AND...
...WATCH US DANCE.

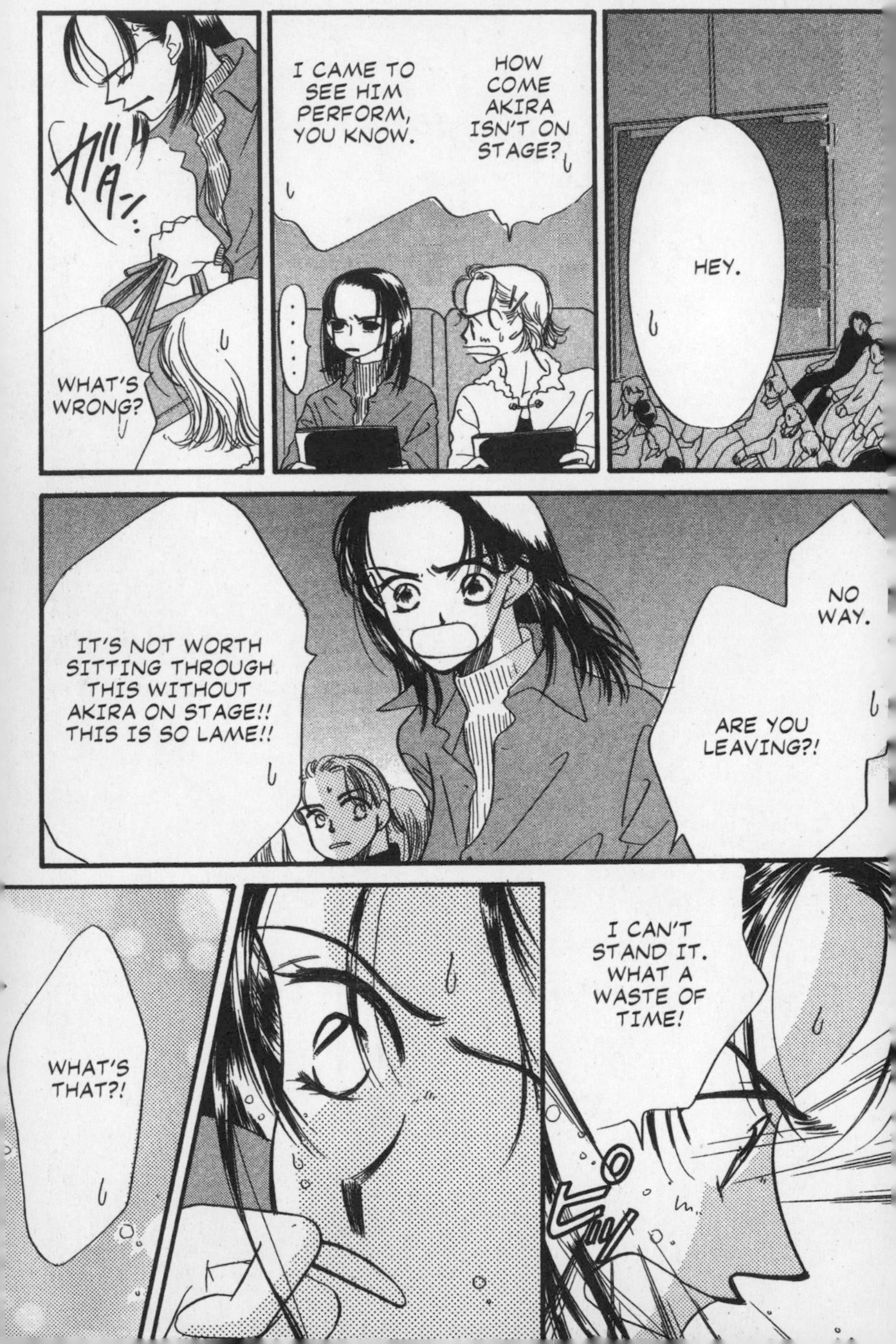
HEY.
HOW COME AKIRA ISN'T ON STAGE?
I CAME TO SEE HIM PERFORM, YOU KNOW.
...
WHAT'S WRONG?
NO WAY.
ARE YOU LEAVING?!
IT'S NOT WORTH SITTING THROUGH THIS WITHOUT AKIRA ON STAGE!! THIS IS SO LAME!!
I CAN'T STAND IT. WHAT A WASTE OF TIME!
WHAT'S THAT?!

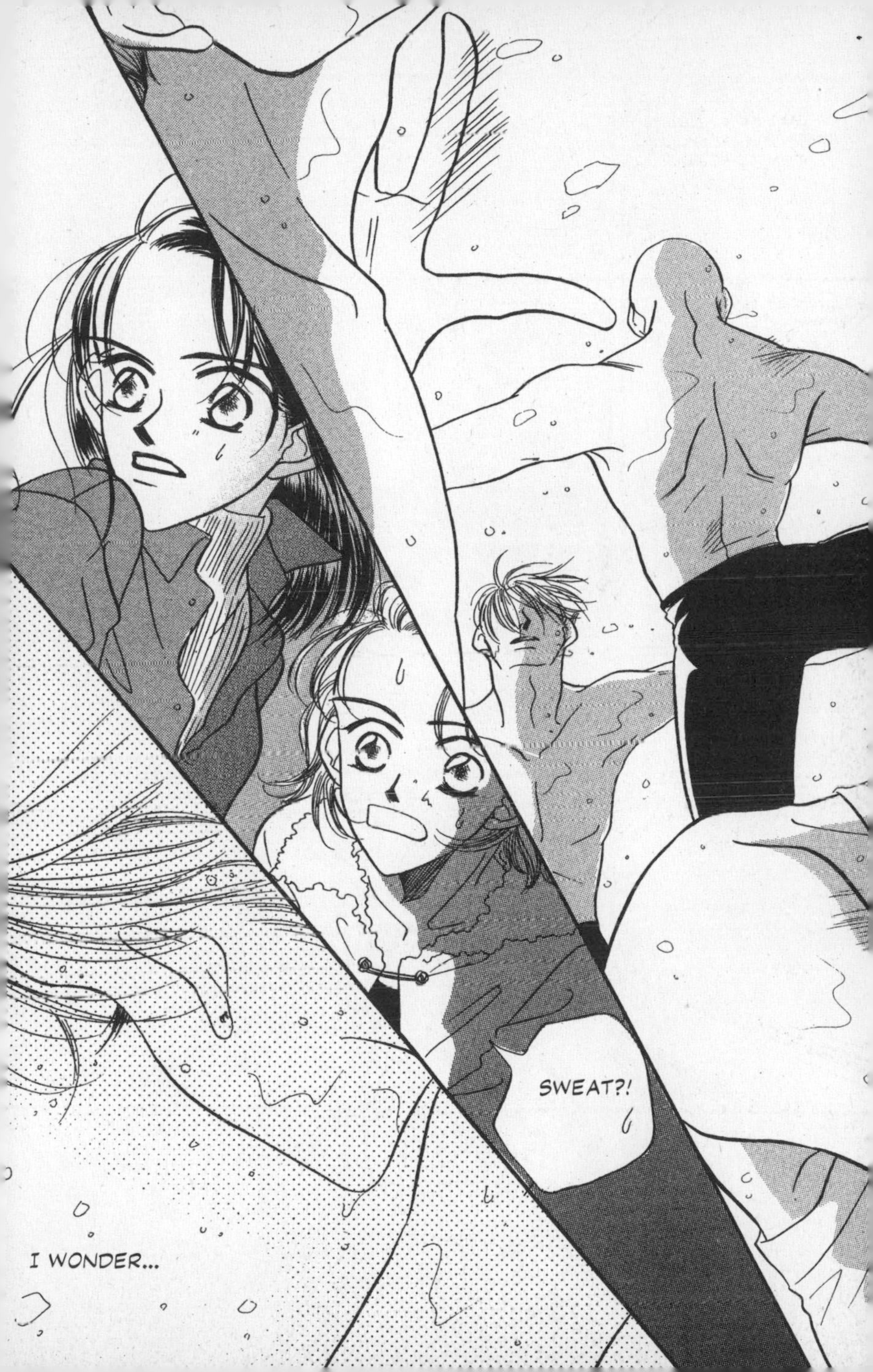
SWEAT?!
I WONDER...

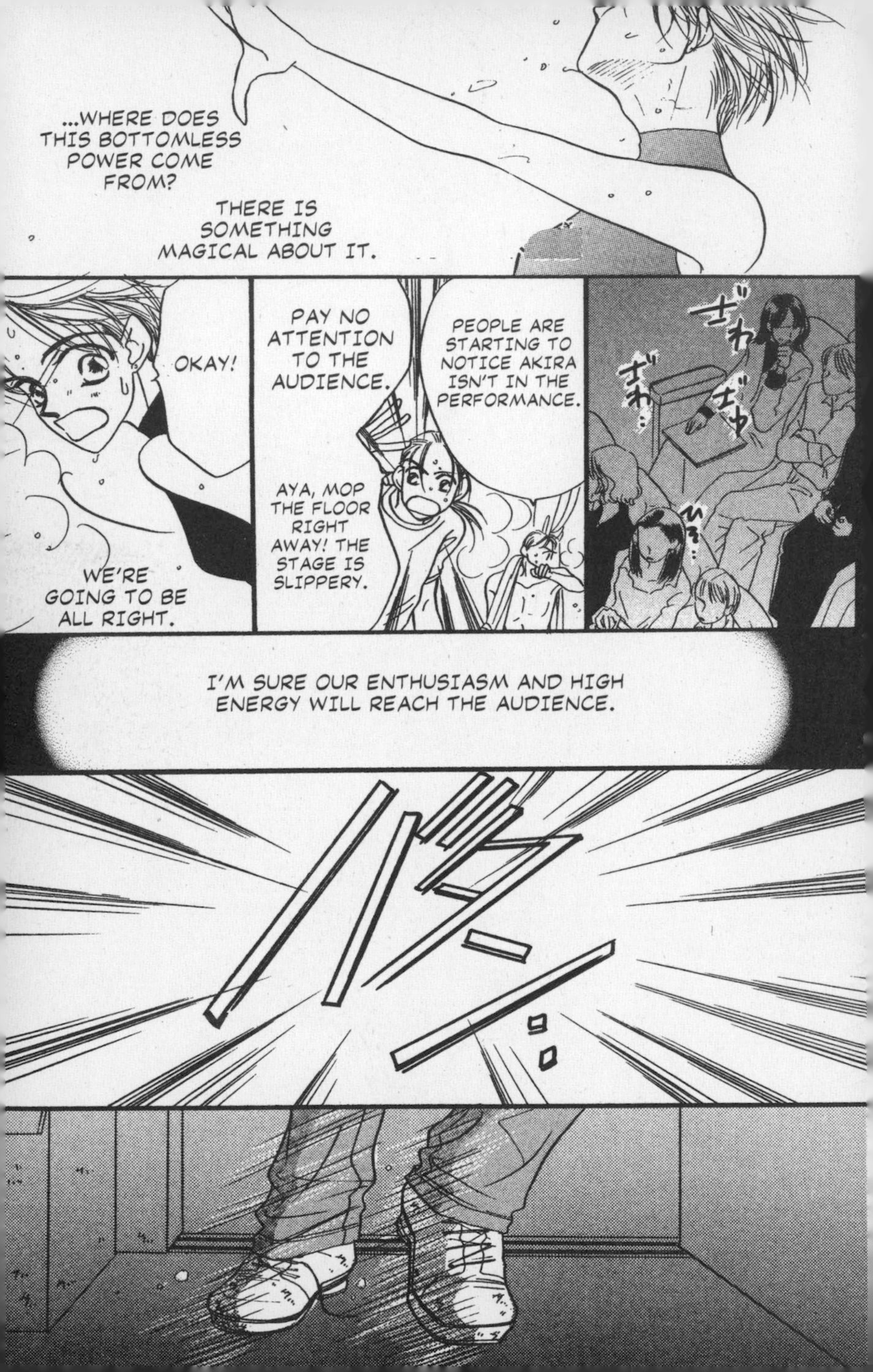
...WHERE DOES THIS BOTTOMLESS POWER COME FROM?
THERE IS SOMETHING MAGICAL ABOUT IT.
ざわ
ざわ
ひそ...
PEOPLE ARE STARTING TO NOTICE AKIRA ISN'T IN THE PERFORMANCE.
PAY NO ATTENTION TO THE AUDIENCE.
AYA, MOP THE FLOOR RIGHT AWAY! THE STAGE IS SLIPPERY.
OKAY!
WE'RE GOING TO BE ALL RIGHT.
I'M SURE OUR ENTHUSIASM AND HIGH ENERGY WILL REACH THE AUDIENCE.

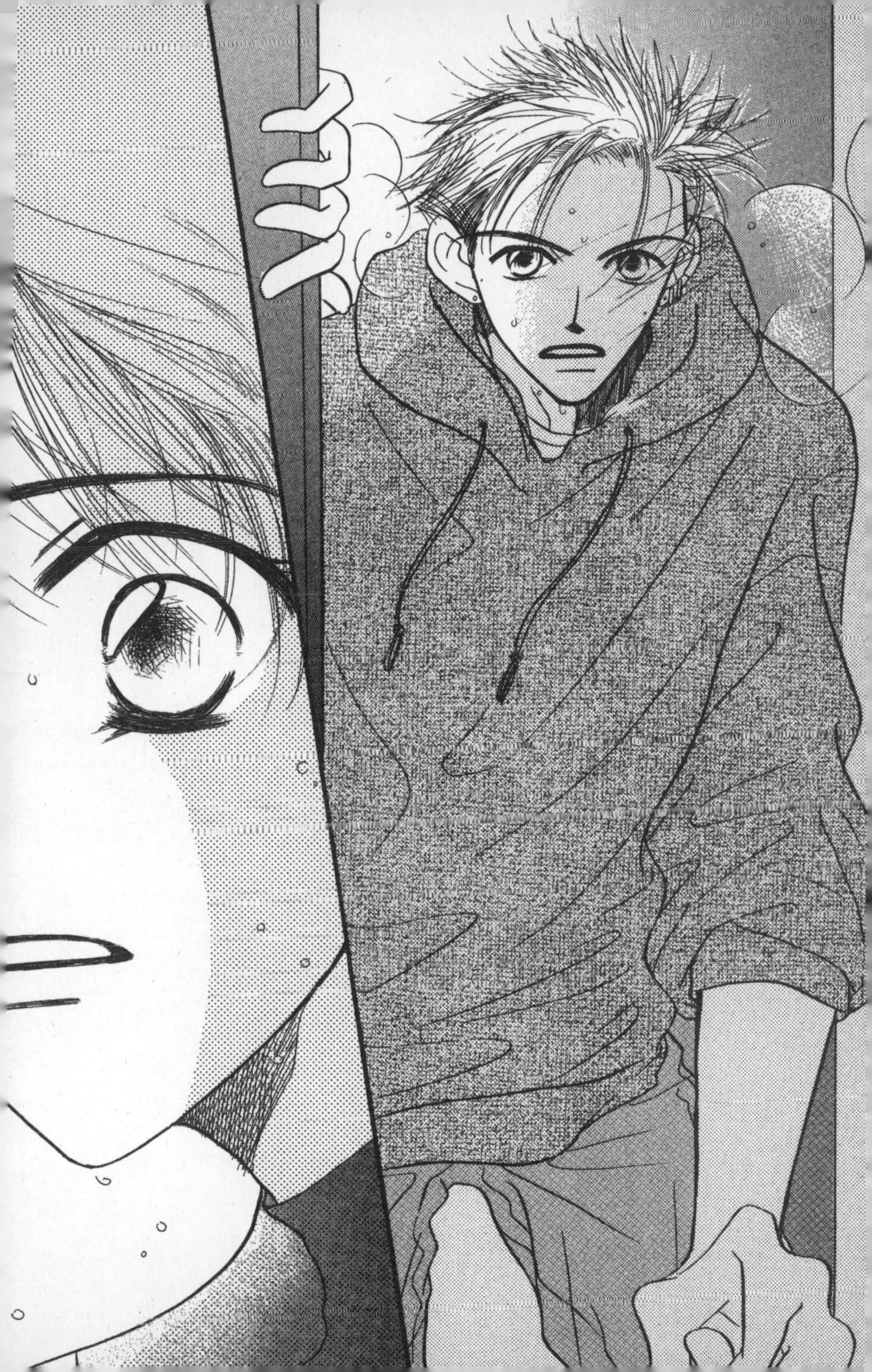

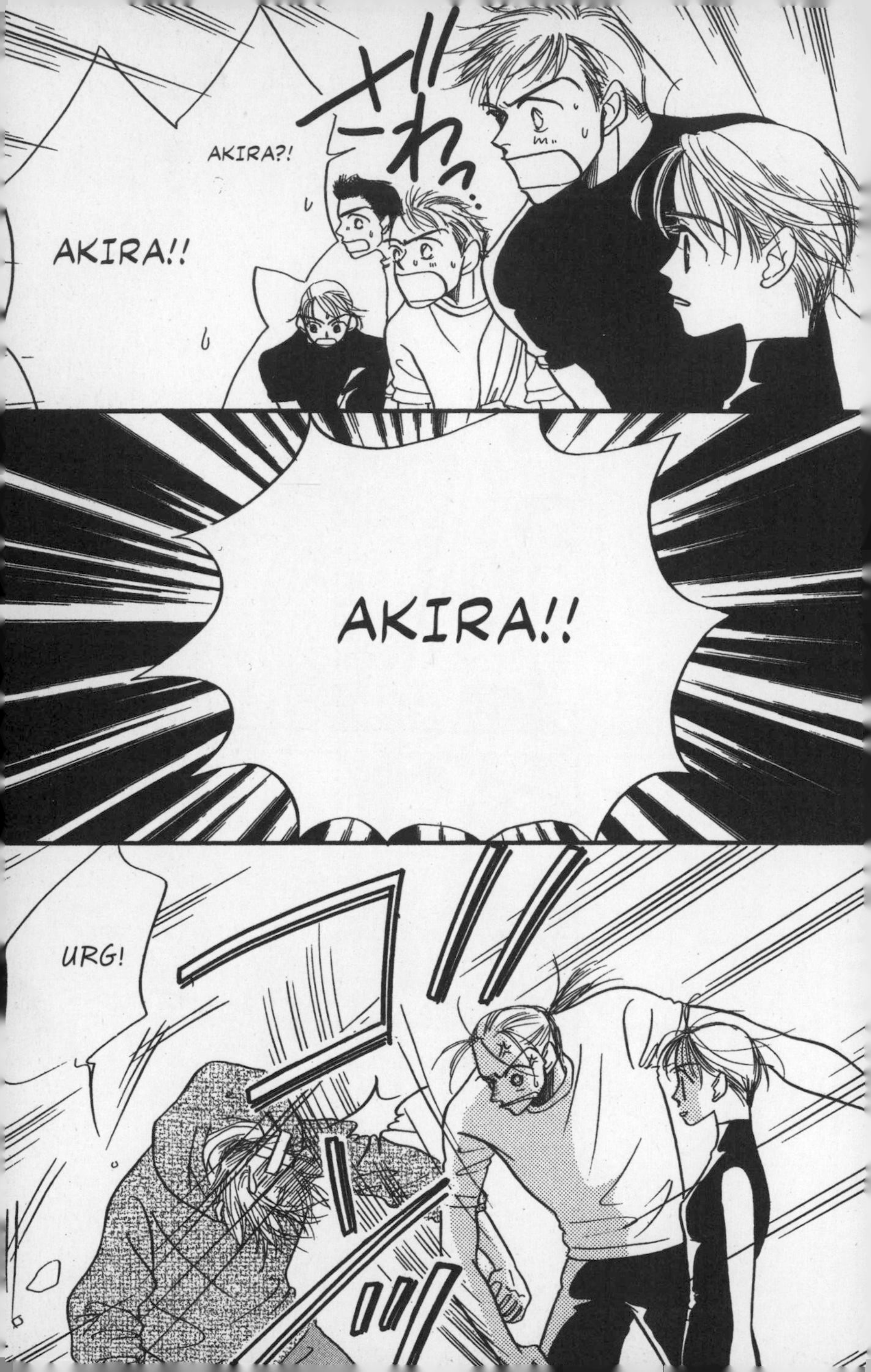
ざわっ
AKIRA?!
AKIRA!!
AKIRA!!
URG!

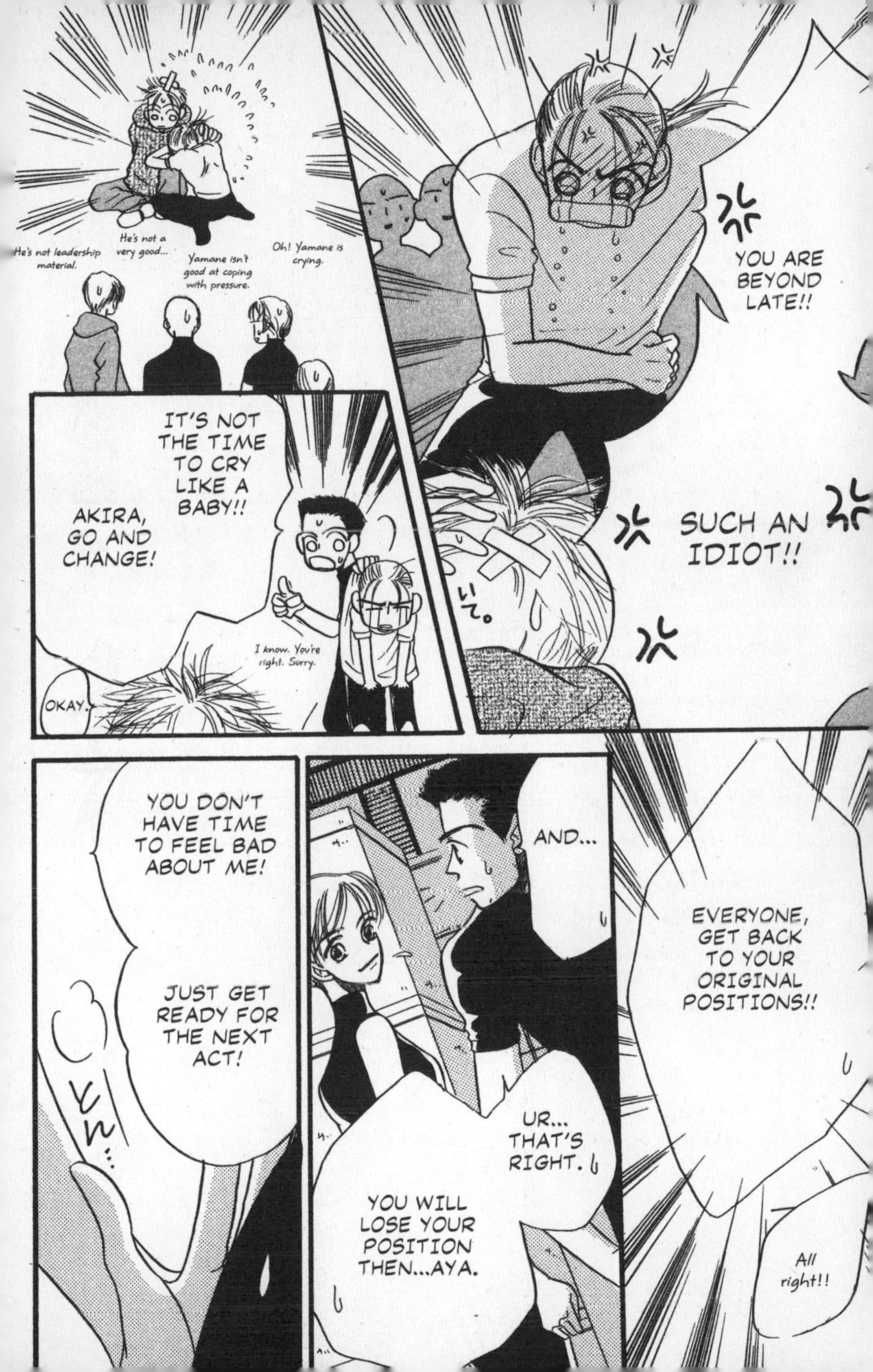
YOU ARE BEYOND LATE!!
SUCH AN IDIOT!!
いて。
Oh! Yamane is crying.
Yamane isn't good at coping with pressure.
He's not a very good...
He's not leadership material.
IT'S NOT THE TIME TO CRY LIKE A BABY!!
AKIRA, GO AND CHANGE!
I know. You're right. Sorry.
OKAY.
EVERYONE, GET BACK TO YOUR ORIGINAL POSITIONS!!
All right!!
AND...
UR... THAT'S RIGHT.
YOU WILL LOSE YOUR POSITION THEN...AYA.
YOU DON'T HAVE TIME TO FEEL BAD ABOUT ME!
JUST GET READY FOR THE NEXT ACT!
うん…

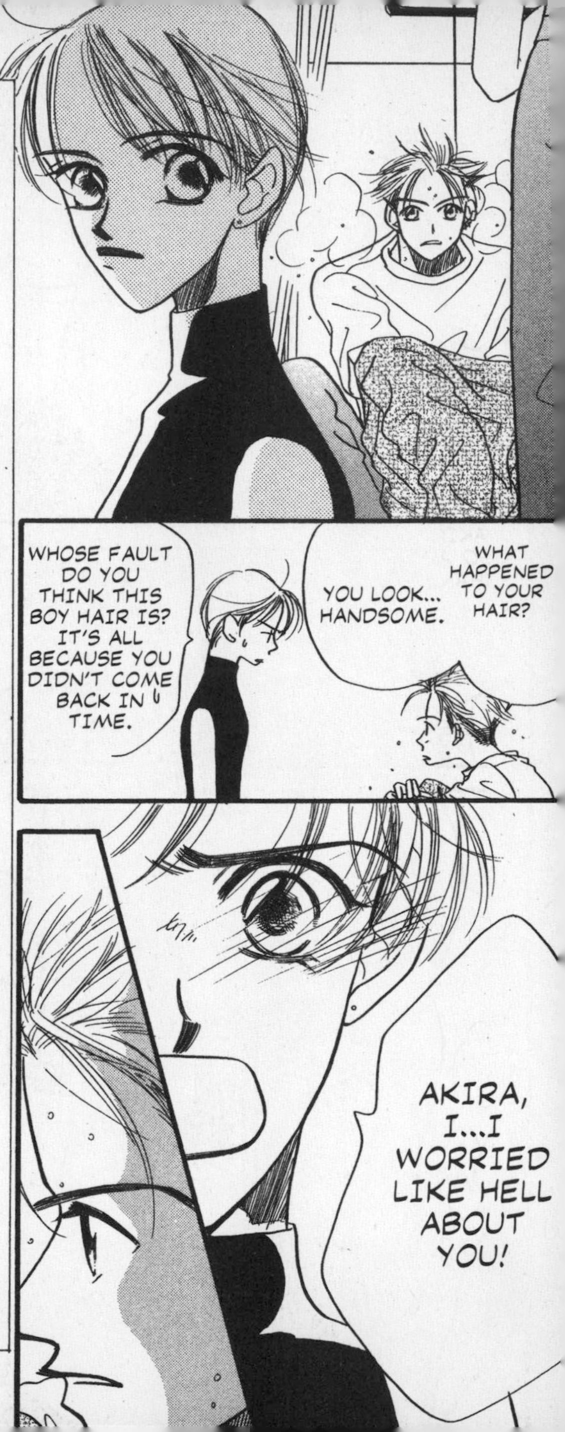
WHAT HAPPENED TO YOUR HAIR?
YOU LOOK... HANDSOME.
WHOSE FAULT DO YOU THINK THIS BOY HAIR IS? IT'S ALL BECAUSE YOU DIDN'T COME BACK IN TIME.
AKIRA, I...I WORRIED LIKE HELL ABOUT YOU!

Ashihara's Diary

No. 2

In Forbidden Dance, I wanted to write a story about a girl who strives hard for her goal. When I was younger, I was not as focused as Aya. I wish I had positive goals to strive for back then. Writing the story was a kind of compensation for what I had missed. I used to envy friends who had specific goals and dreams. I probably feel this way more strongly now because I can't go back to the past.

*In this volume, Forbidden Dance comes to a close and is followed by a side story called "Kiss + alpha". It's written from the perspective of Tetsuya, who is a shy supporting character in the series.

When you have a chance, please read other stories of mine. Once again, deep appreciation to all the fans.

October, 1998
Hinako Ashihara

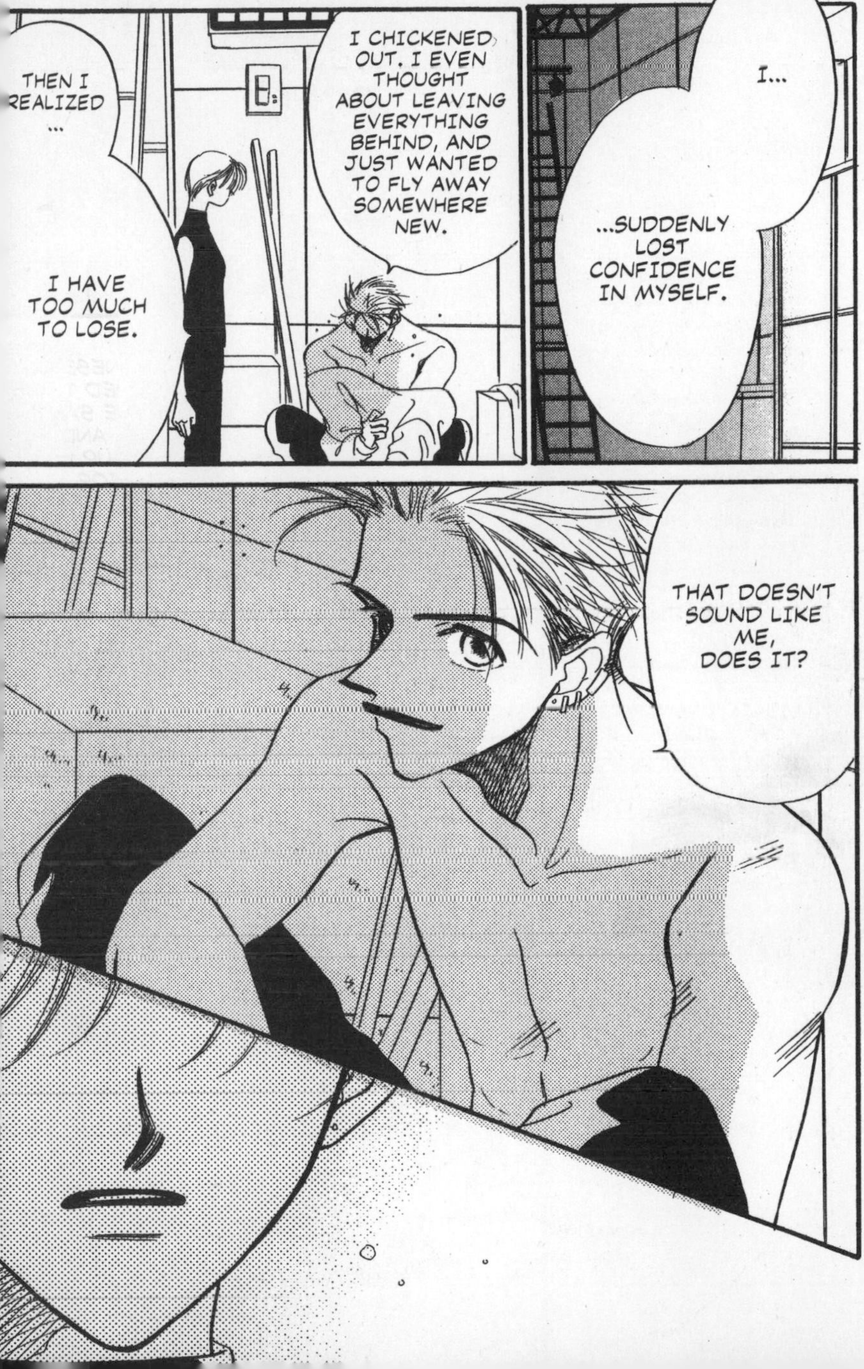
I...
...SUDDENLY LOST CONFIDENCE IN MYSELF.
I CHICKENED OUT. I EVEN THOUGHT ABOUT LEAVING EVERYTHING BEHIND, AND JUST WANTED TO FLY AWAY SOMEWHERE NEW.
THEN I REALIZED ...
I HAVE TOO MUCH TO LOSE.
THAT DOESN'T SOUND LIKE ME, DOES IT?

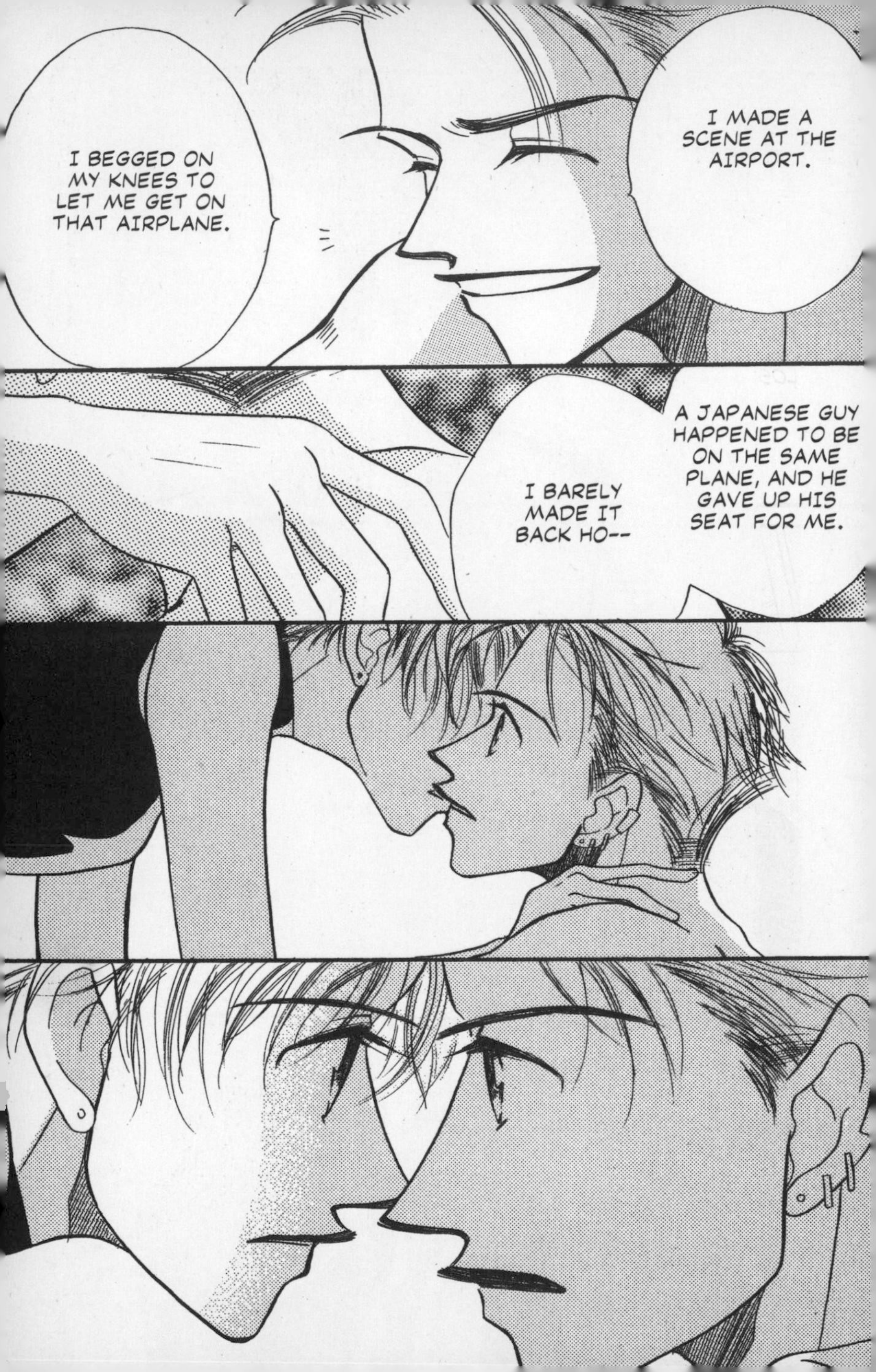
I MADE A SCENE AT THE AIRPORT.
I BEGGED ON MY KNEES TO LET ME GET ON THAT AIRPLANE.
A JAPANESE GUY HAPPENED TO BE ON THE SAME PLANE, AND HE GAVE UP HIS SEAT FOR ME.
I BARELY MADE IT BACK HO--

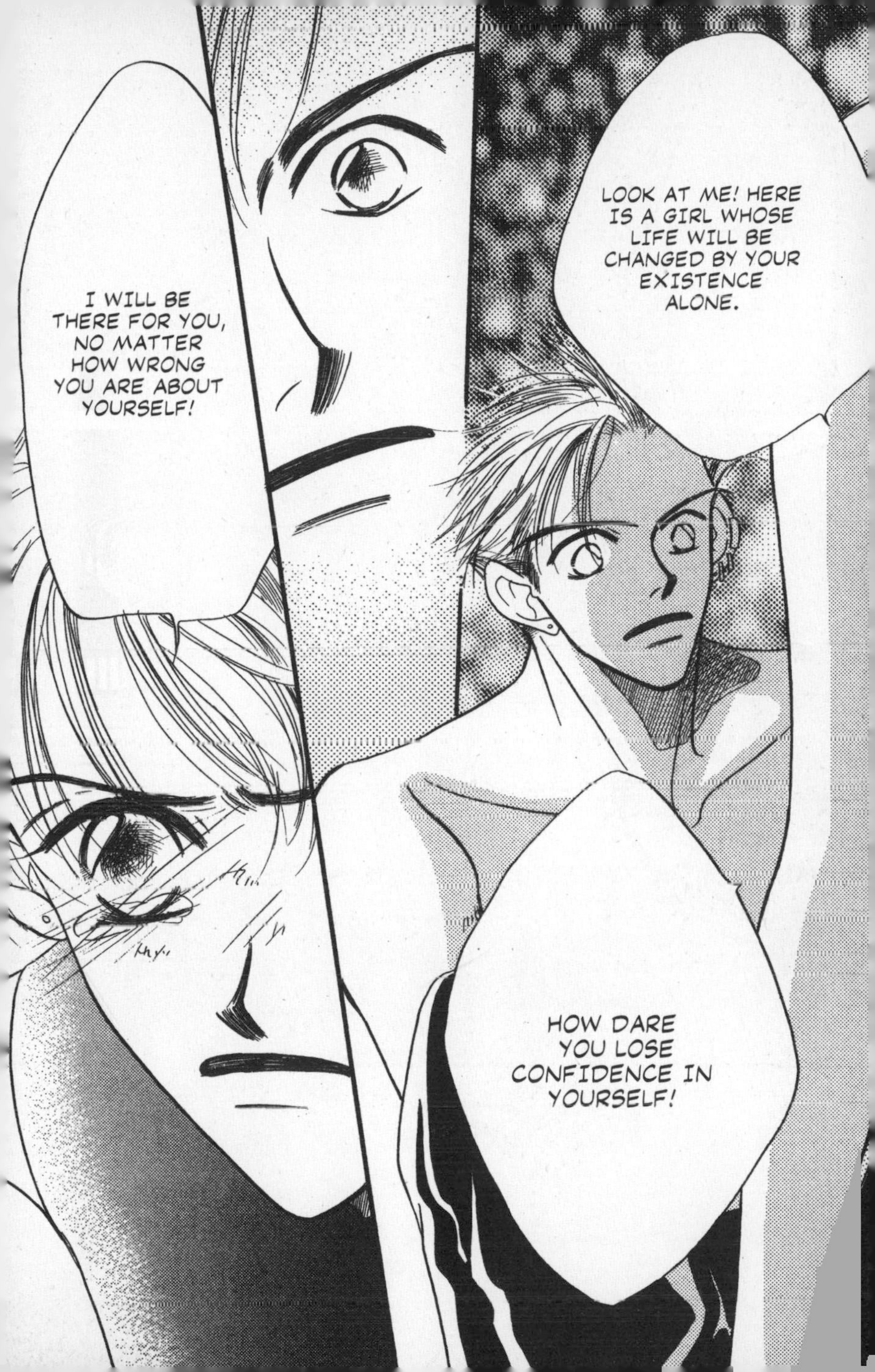
LOOK AT ME! HERE IS A GIRL WHOSE LIFE WILL BE CHANGED BY YOUR EXISTENCE ALONE.
I WILL BE THERE FOR YOU, NO MATTER HOW WRONG YOU ARE ABOUT YOURSELF!
HOW DARE YOU LOSE CONFIDENCE IN YOURSELF!

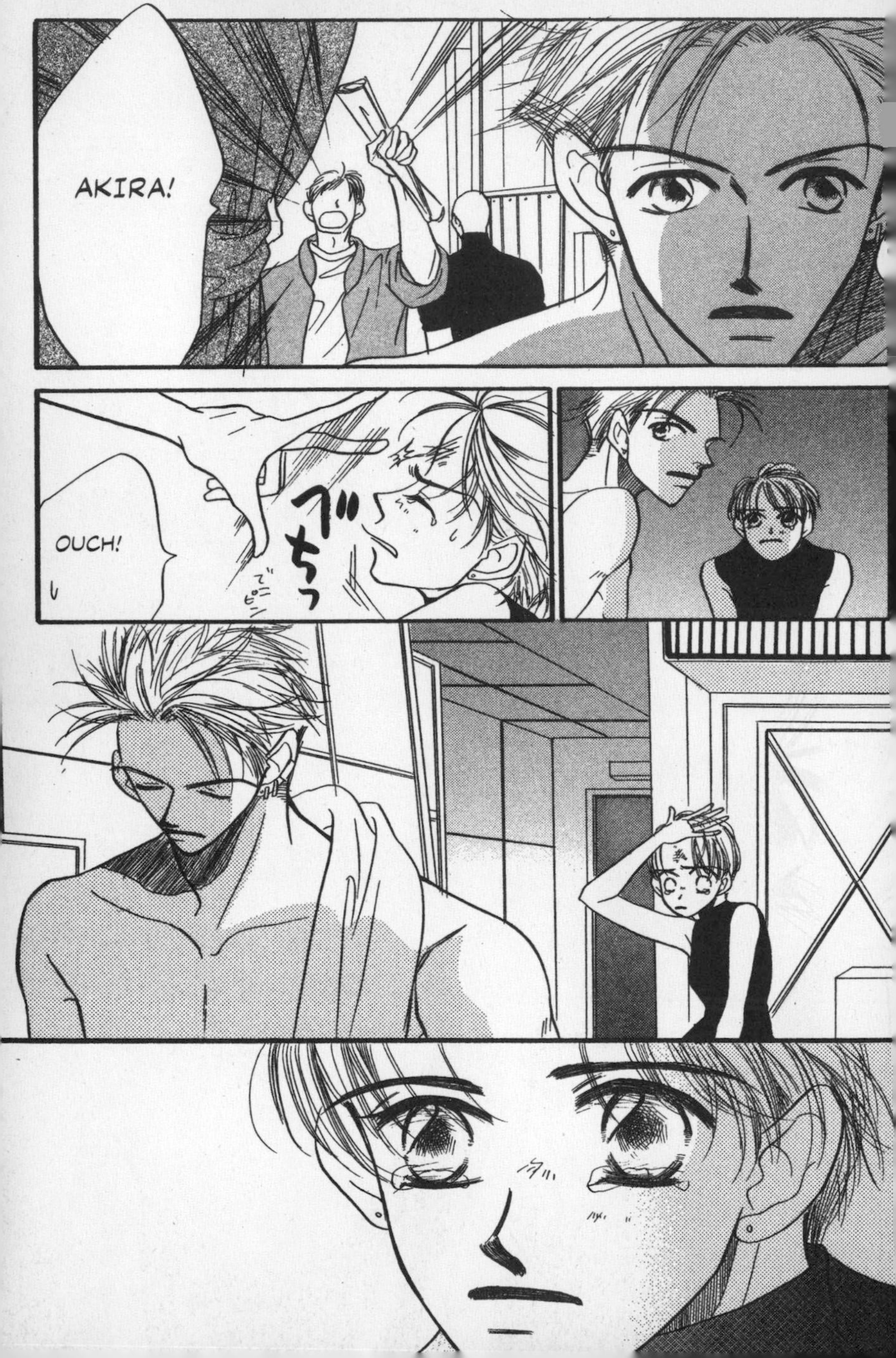
AKIRA!
ブちっ
でピーン
OUCH!

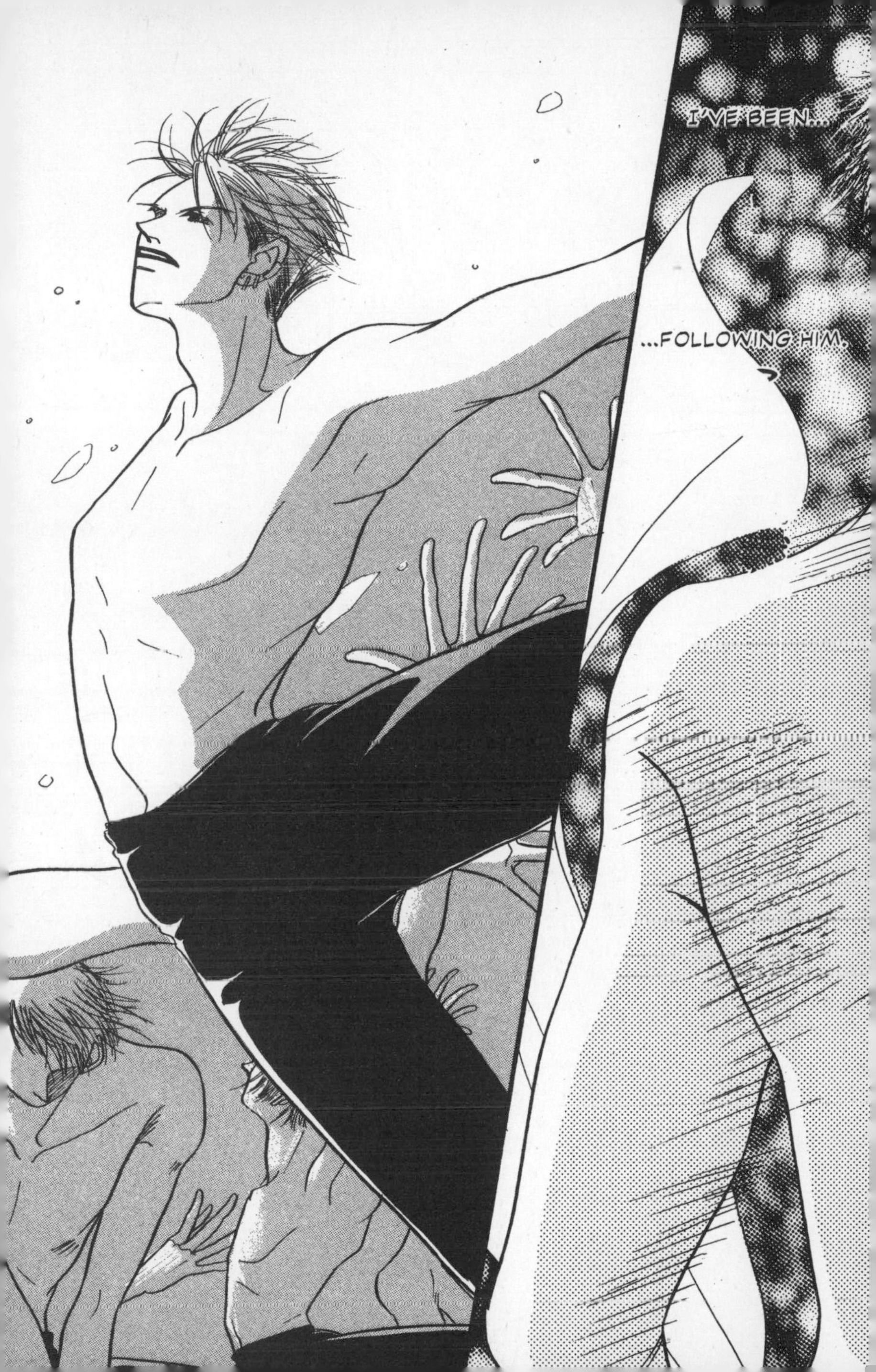
I'VE BEEN...
...FOLLOWING HIM.

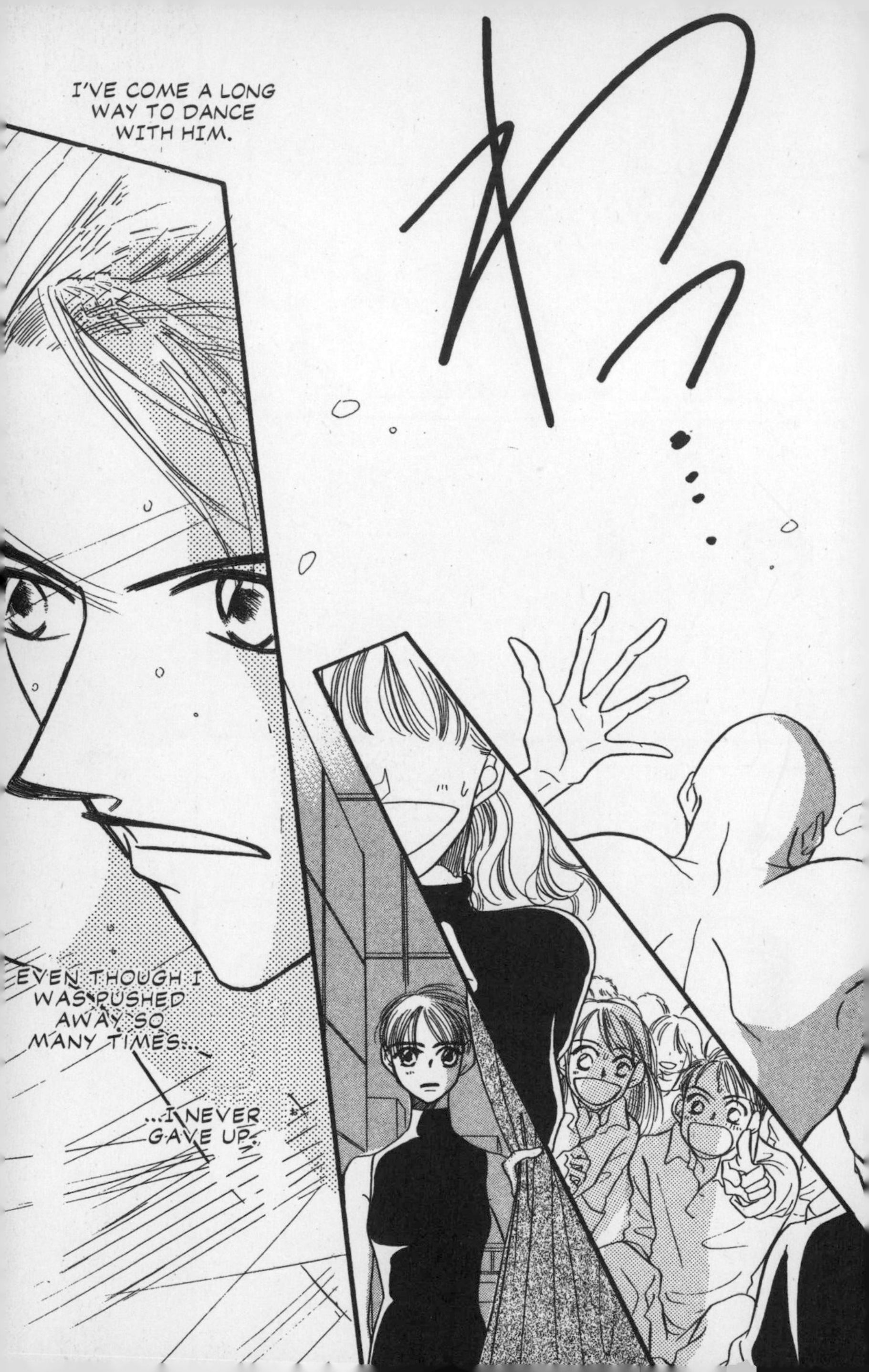
I'VE COME A LONG WAY TO DANCE WITH HIM.
EVEN THOUGH I WAS PUSHED AWAY SO MANY TIMES...
...I NEVER GAVE UP.

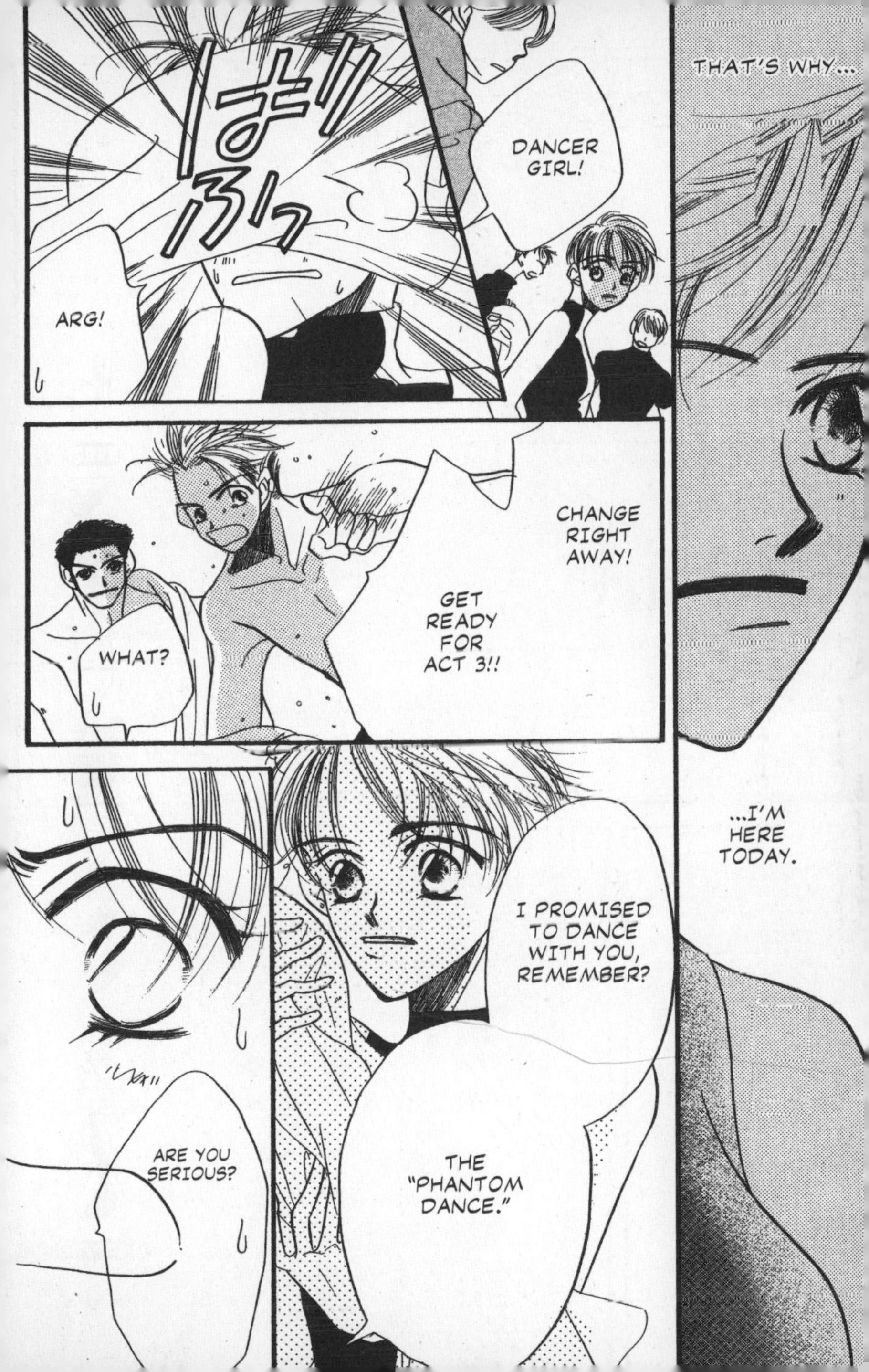
THAT'S WHY...
...I'M HERE TODAY.
DANCER GIRL!
はりふっ
ARG!
CHANGE RIGHT AWAY!
GET READY FOR ACT 3!!
WHAT?
I PROMISED TO DANCE WITH YOU, REMEMBER?
THE "PHANTOM DANCE."
ARE YOU SERIOUS?

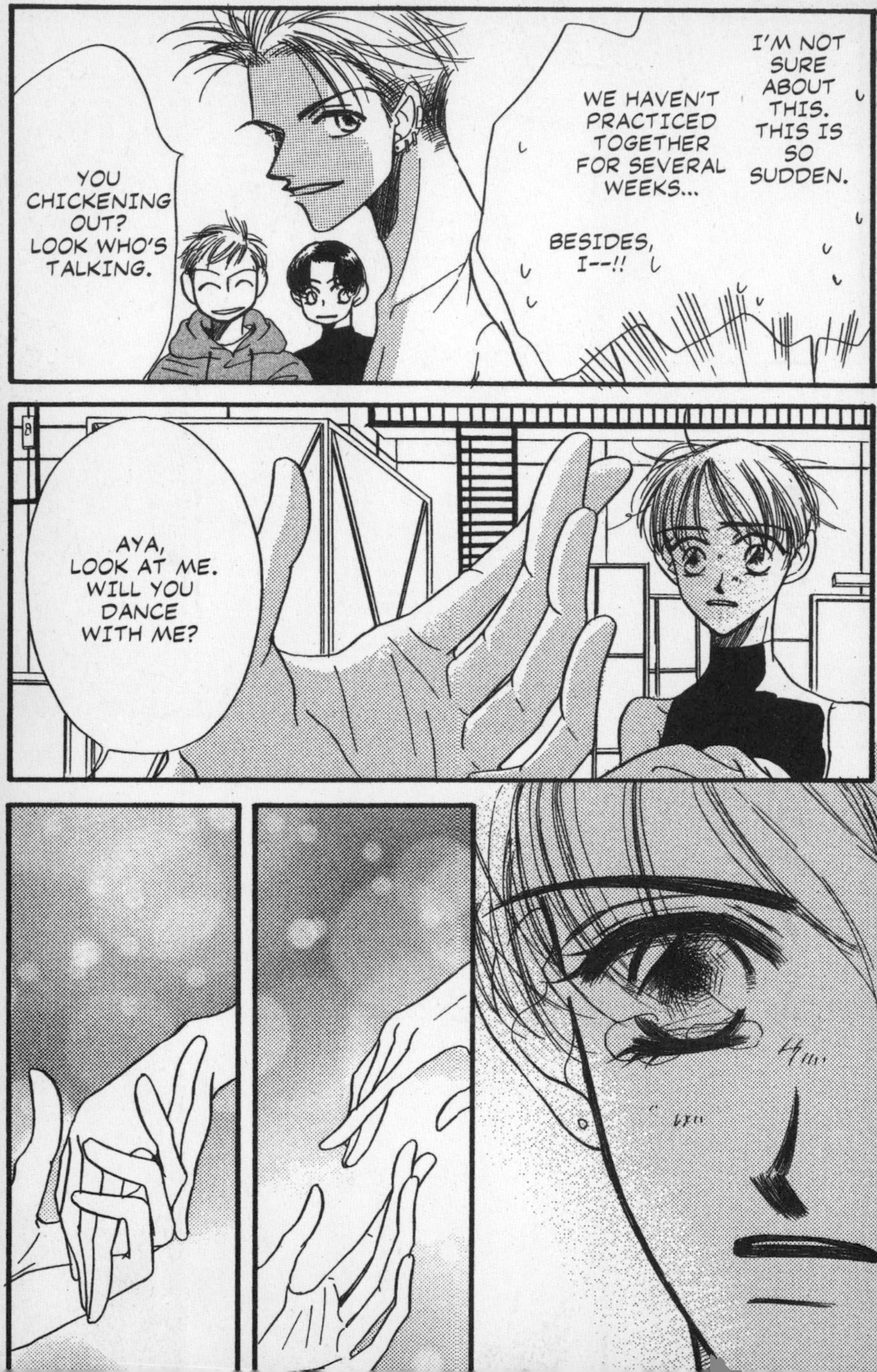
I'M NOT SURE ABOUT THIS. THIS IS SO SUDDEN.
WE HAVEN'T PRACTICED TOGETHER FOR SEVERAL WEEKS...
BESIDES, I--!!
YOU CHICKENING OUT? LOOK WHO'S TALKING.
AYA, LOOK AT ME. WILL YOU DANCE WITH ME?

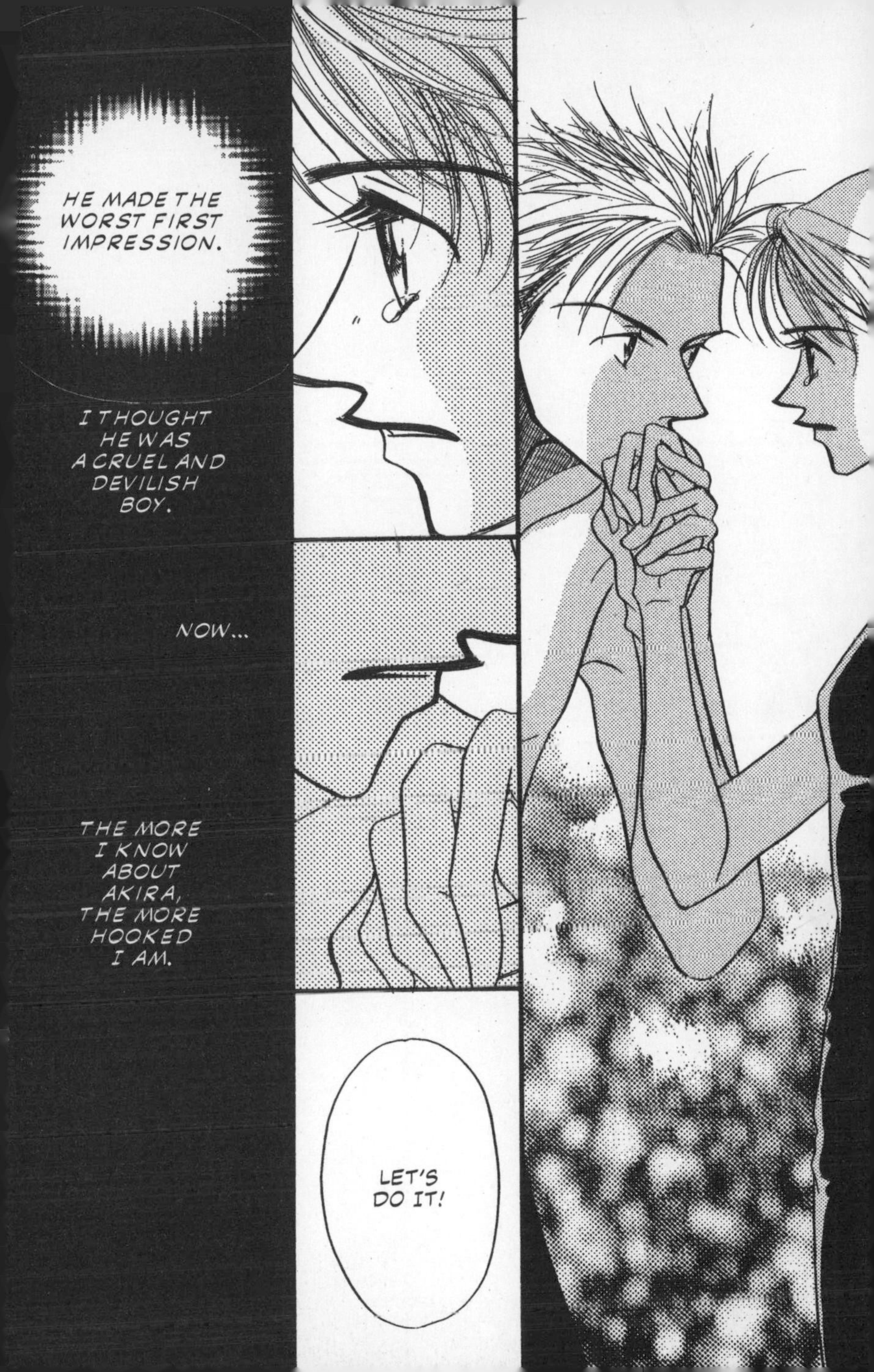
LET'S DO IT!
HE MADE THE WORST FIRST IMPRESSION.
I THOUGHT HE WAS A CRUEL AND DEVILISH BOY.
NOW...
THE MORE I KNOW ABOUT AKIRA, THE MORE HOOKED I AM.

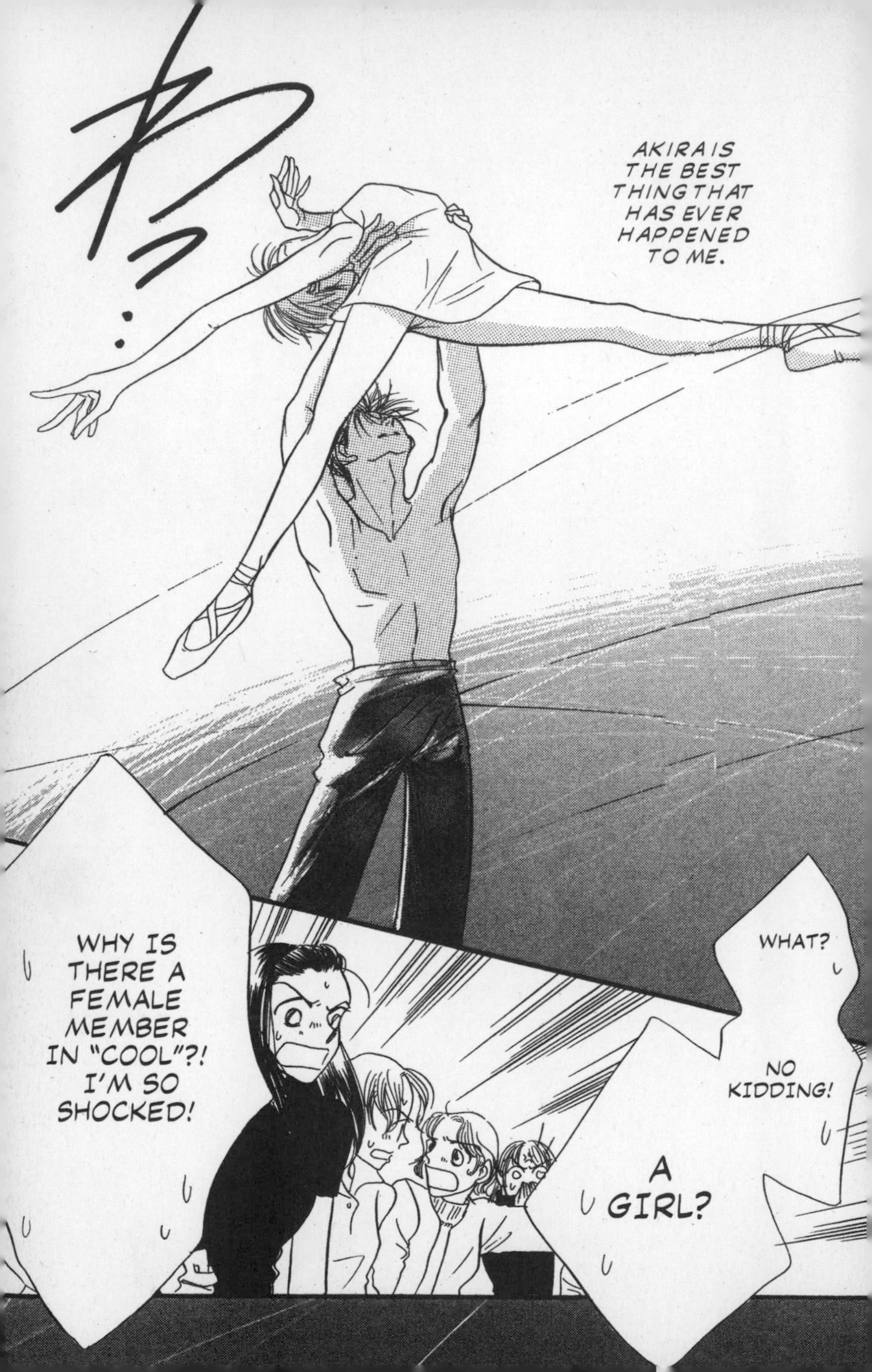
AKIRA IS THE BEST THING THAT HAS EVER HAPPENED TO ME.
WHAT?
NO KIDDING!
A GIRL?
WHY IS THERE A FEMALE MEMBER IN "COOL"?! I'M SO SHOCKED!

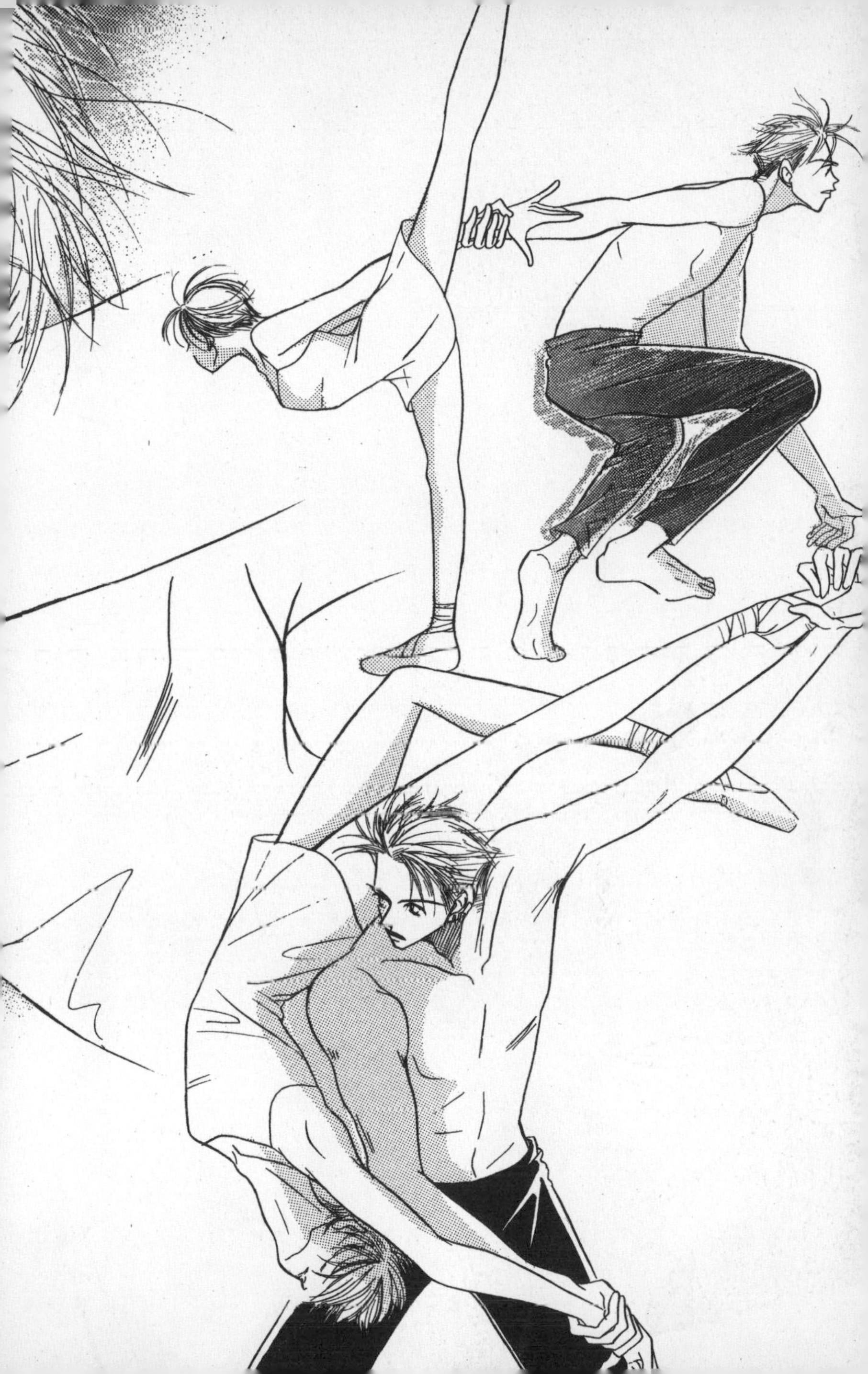

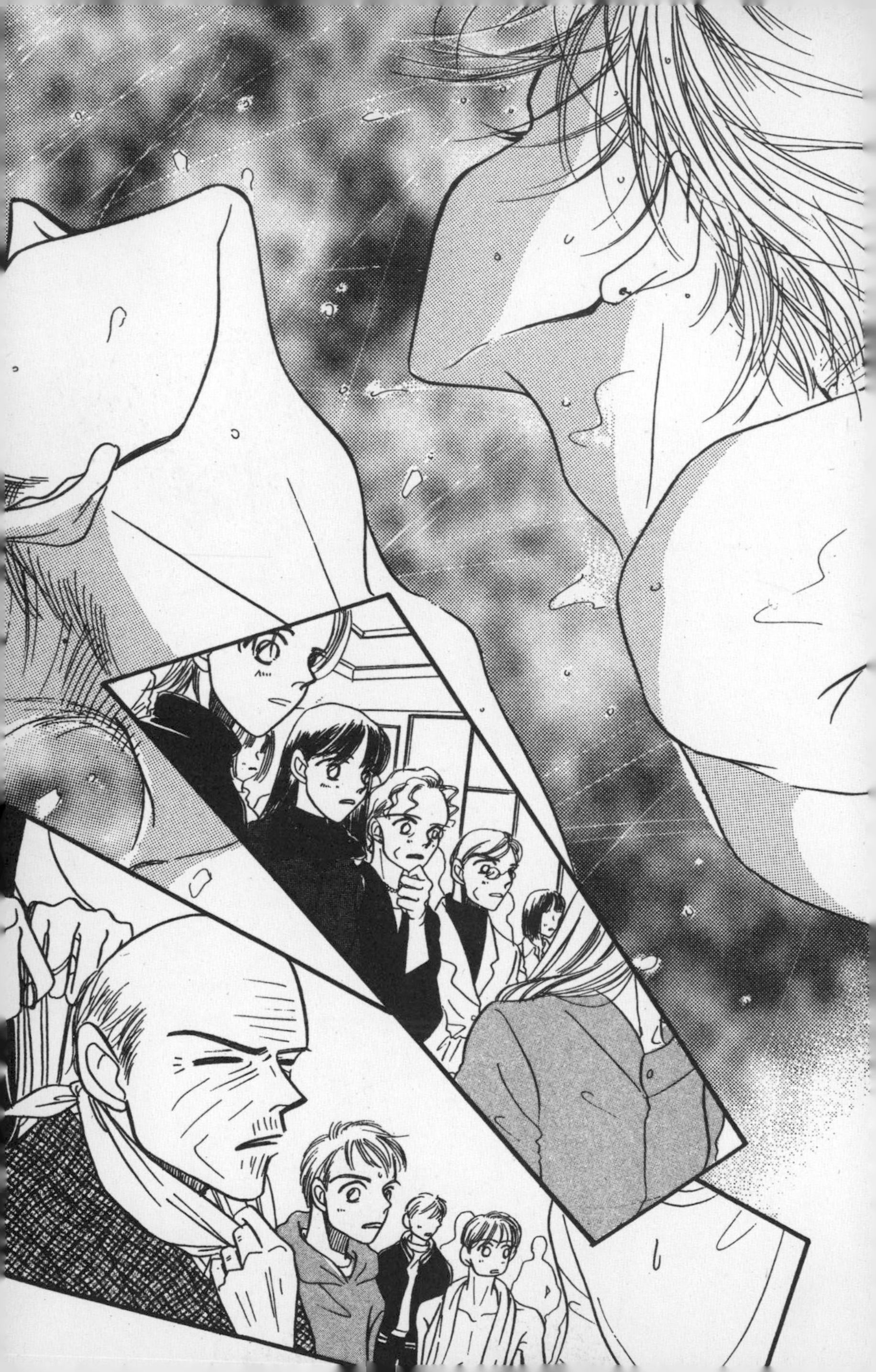

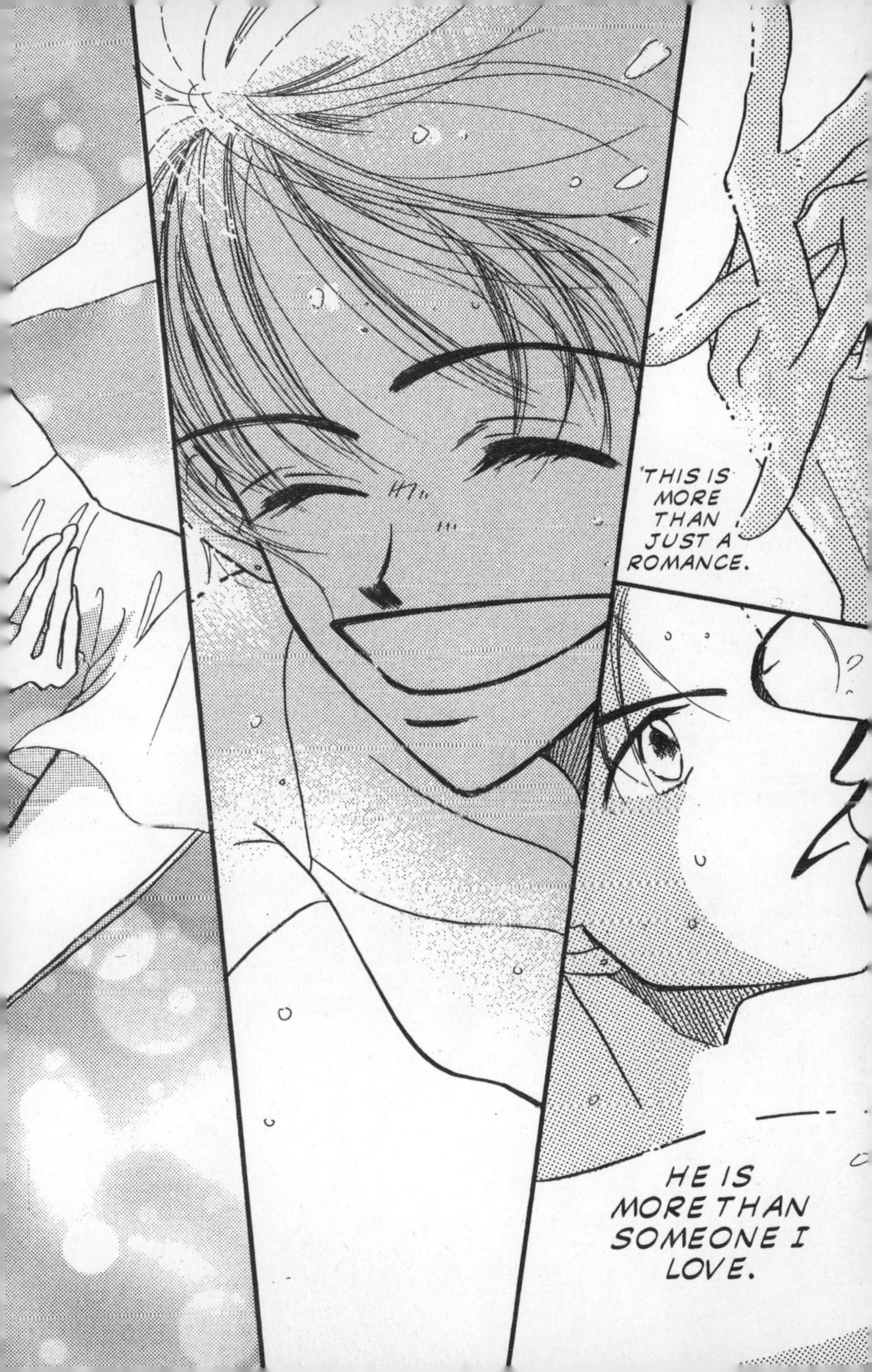
THIS IS MORE THAN JUST A ROMANCE.
HE IS MORE THAN SOMEONE I LOVE.

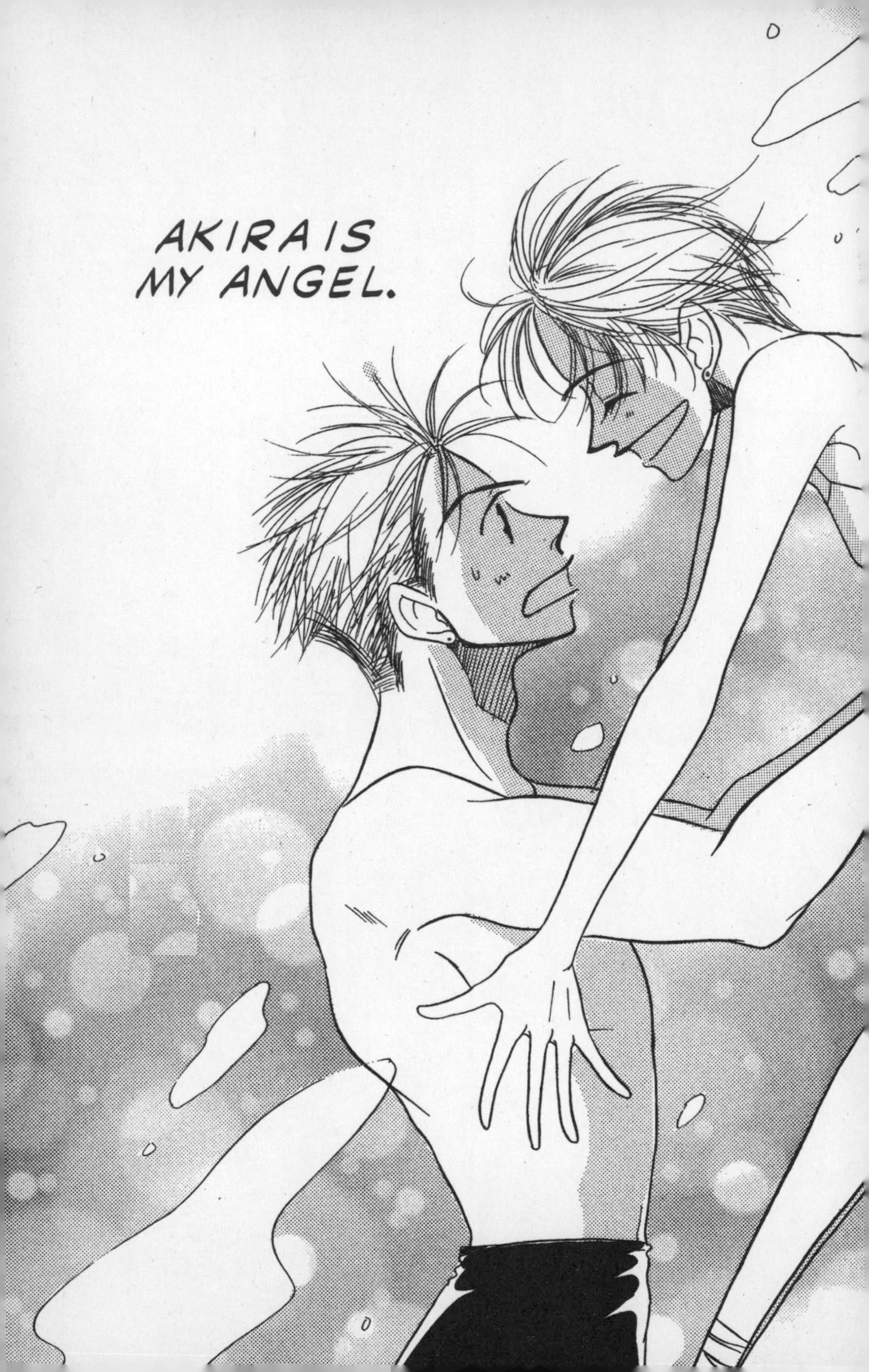
AKIRA IS
MY ANGEL.

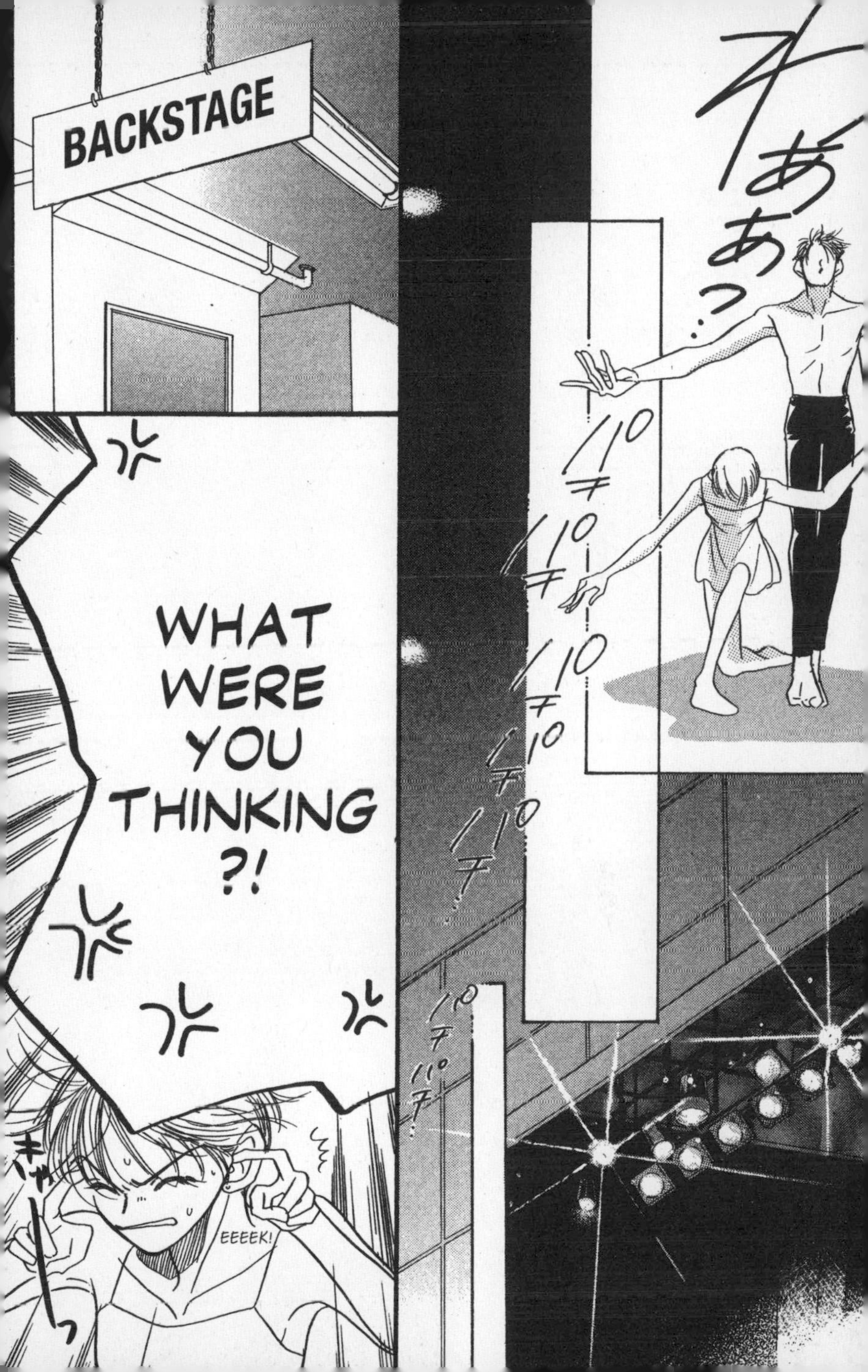
ああっ…
パチパチパチパチパチ…
パチパチ…
BACKSTAGE
WHAT WERE YOU THINKING?!
EEEEK!
きゃーっ

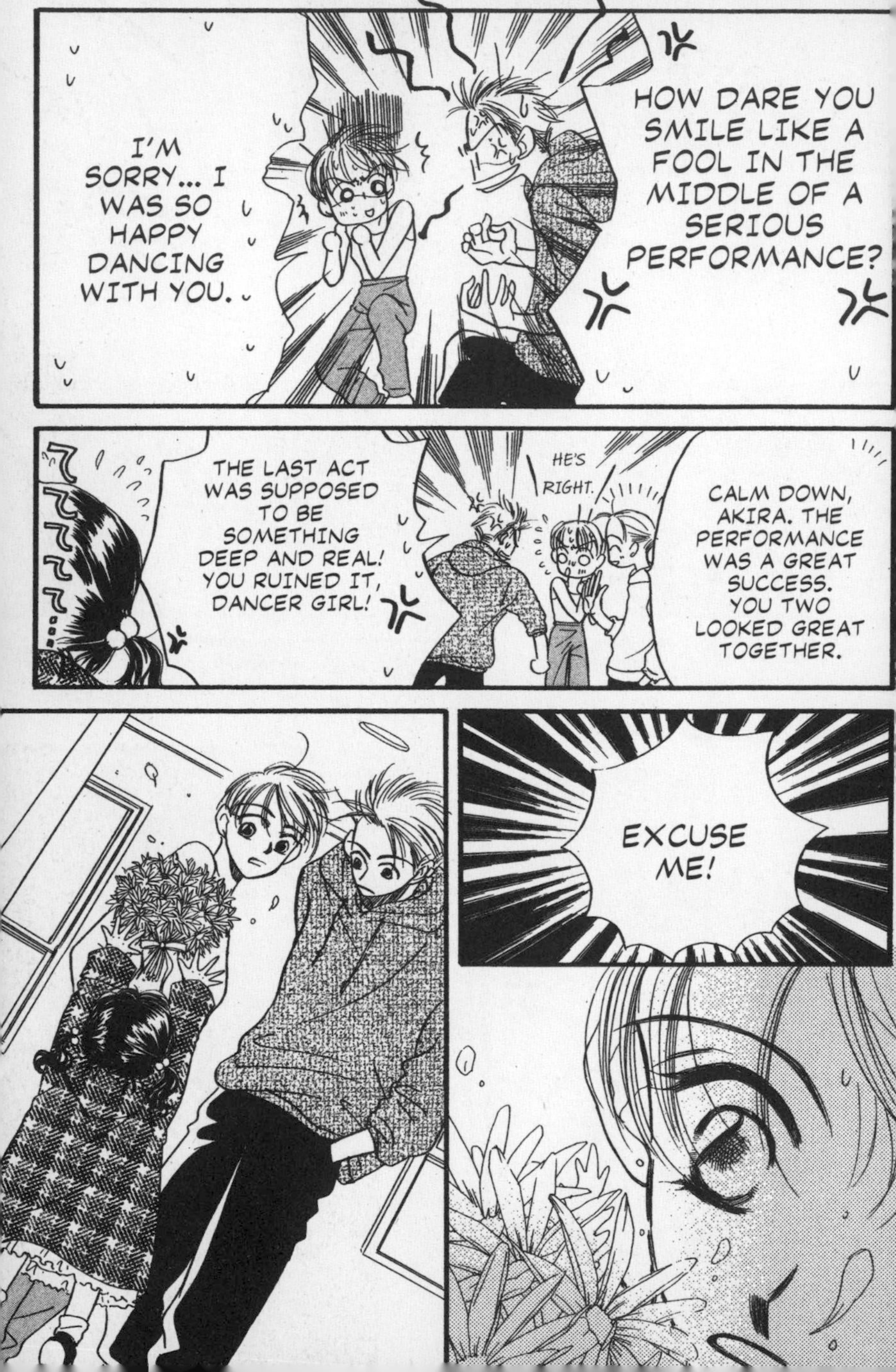
HOW DARE YOU SMILE LIKE A FOOL IN THE MIDDLE OF A SERIOUS PERFORMANCE?
I'M SORRY... I WAS SO HAPPY DANCING WITH YOU.
CALM DOWN, AKIRA. THE PERFORMANCE WAS A GREAT SUCCESS. YOU TWO LOOKED GREAT TOGETHER.
HE'S RIGHT.
THE LAST ACT WAS SUPPOSED TO BE SOMETHING DEEP AND REAL! YOU RUINED IT, DANCER GIRL!
EXCUSE ME!

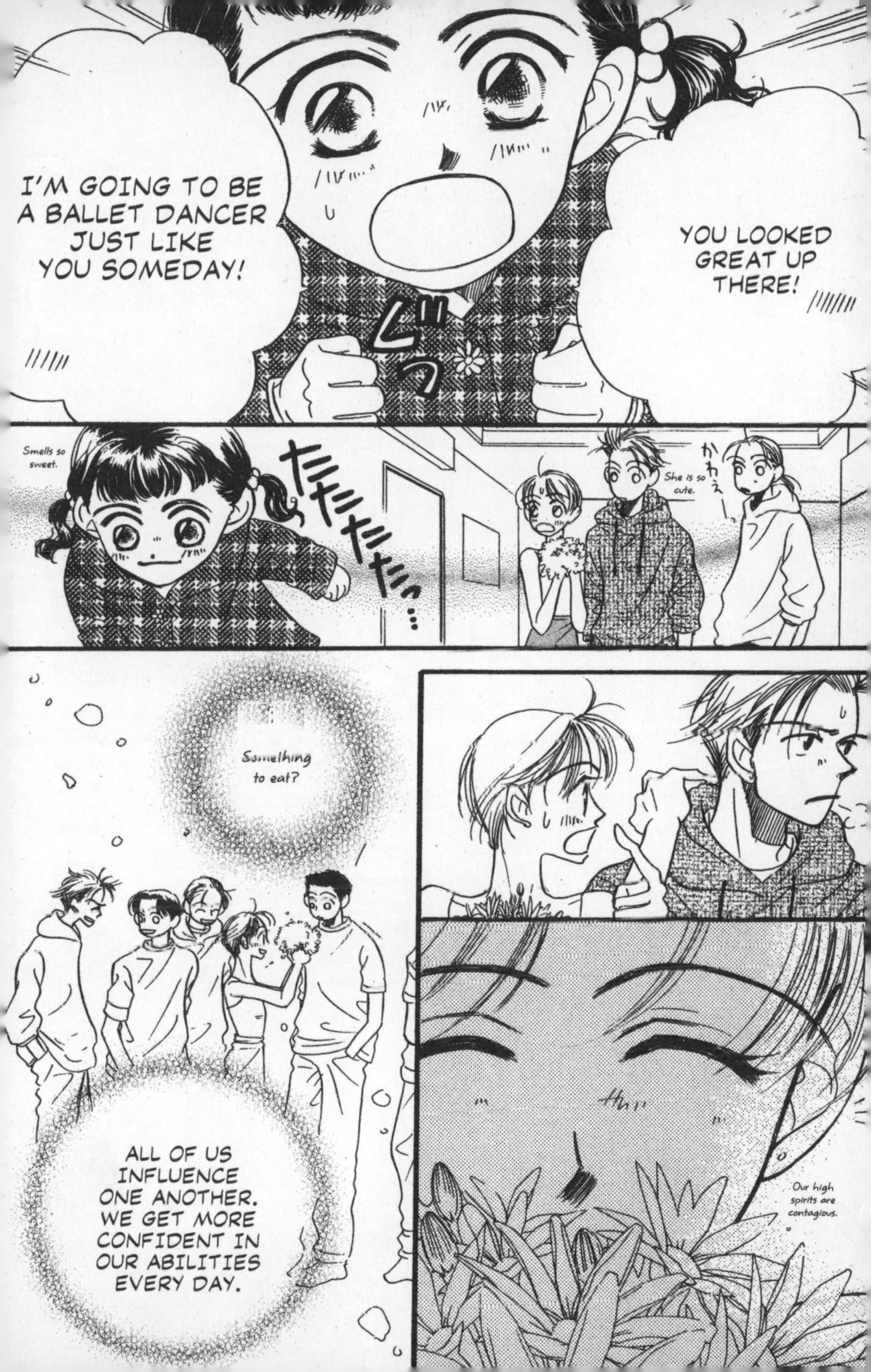
YOU LOOKED GREAT UP THERE!
I'M GOING TO BE A BALLET DANCER JUST LIKE YOU SOMEDAY!
ぐっ
かわえ～
She is so cute.
Smells so sweet.
たたたたっ…
Our high spirits are contagious.
Something to eat?
ALL OF US INFLUENCE ONE ANOTHER. WE GET MORE CONFIDENT IN OUR ABILITIES EVERY DAY.

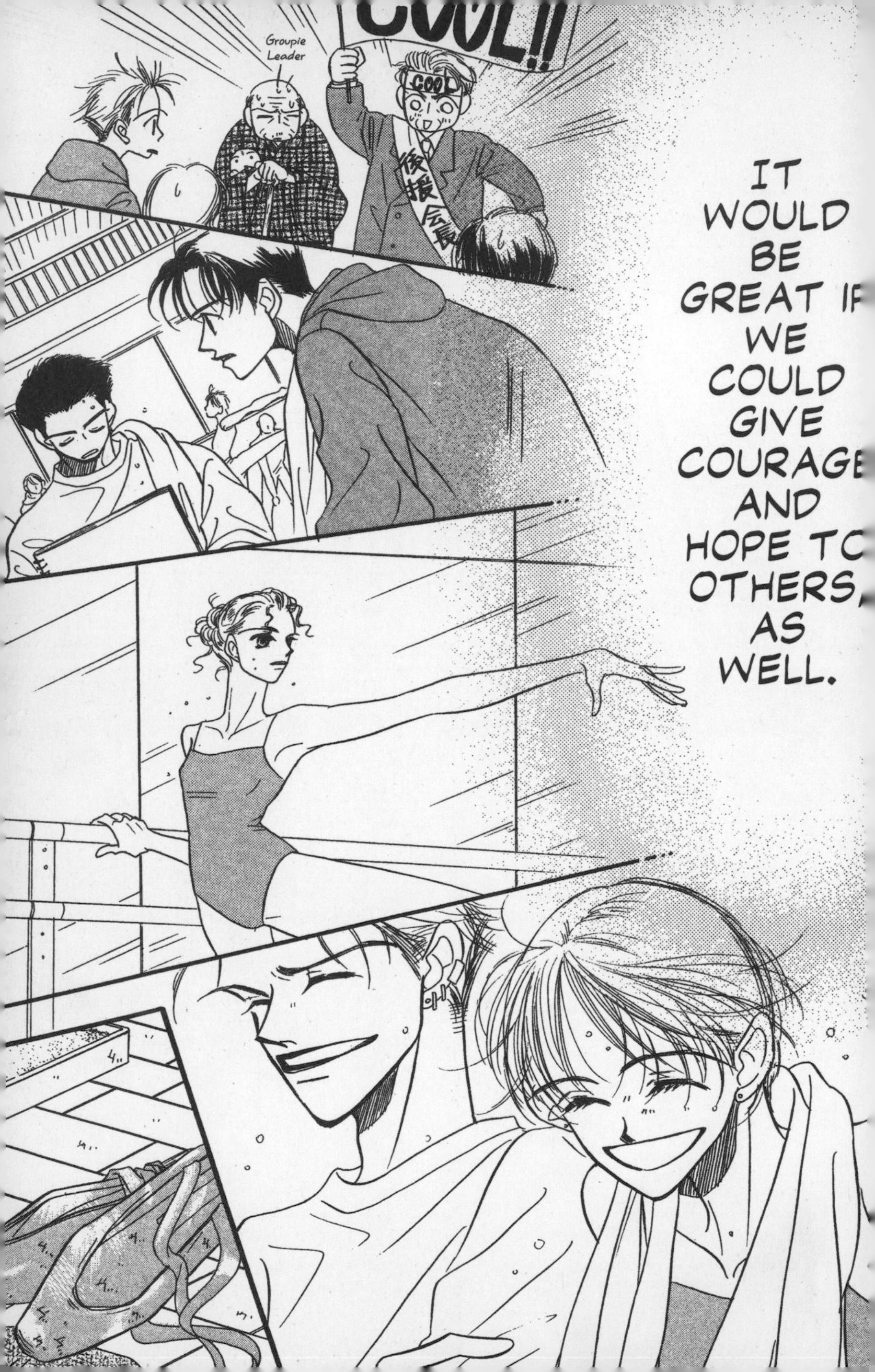
COOL!!
Groupie Leader
COOL
後援会長
IT WOULD BE GREAT IF WE COULD GIVE COURAGE AND HOPE TO OTHERS, AS WELL.

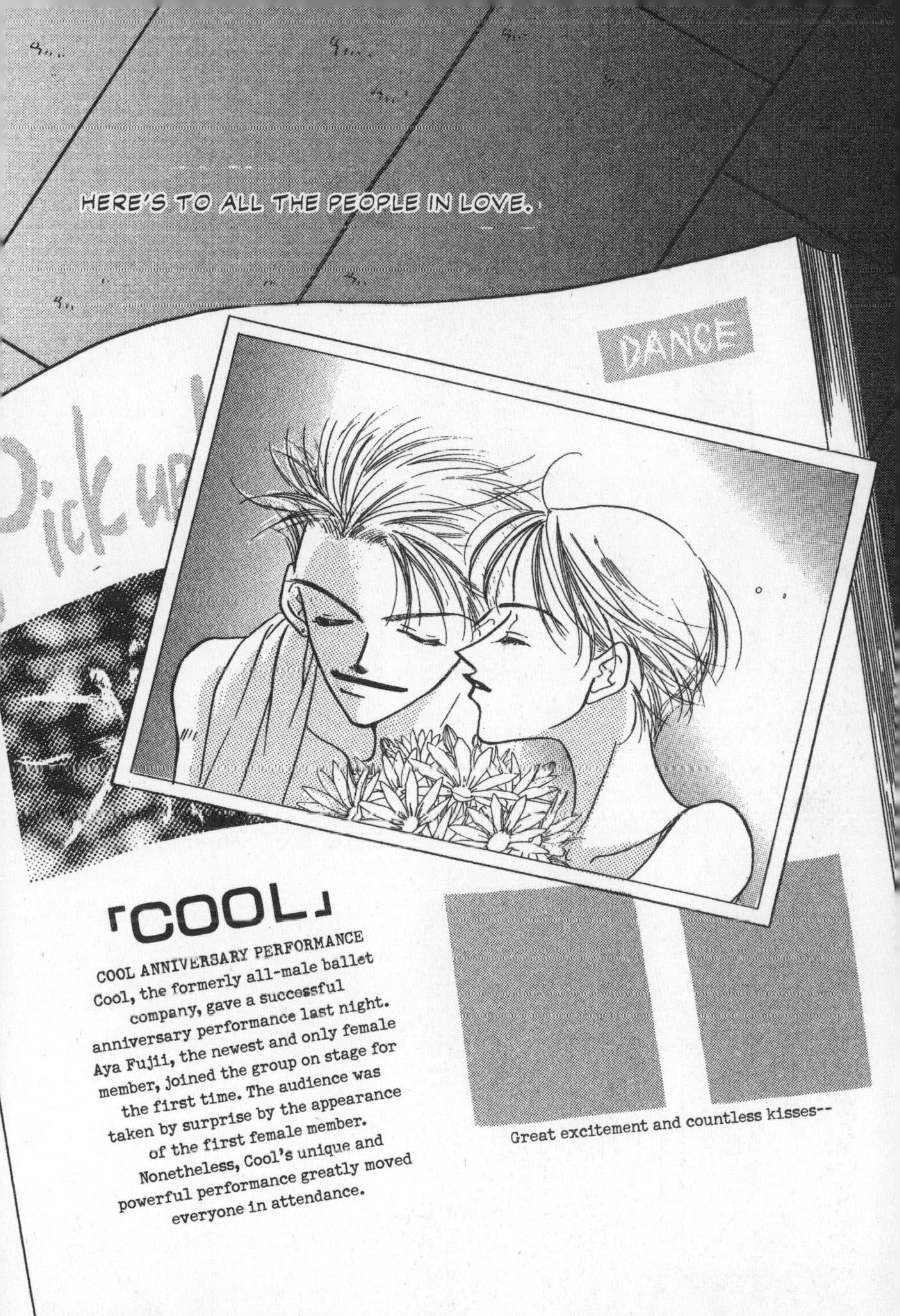
HERE'S TO ALL THE PEOPLE IN LOVE.
DANCE
Pick up
「COOL」
COOL ANNIVERSARY PERFORMANCE
Cool, the formerly all-male ballet company, gave a successful anniversary performance last night. Aya Fujii, the newest and only female member, joined the group on stage for the first time. The audience was taken by surprise by the appearance of the first female member. Nonetheless, Cool's unique and powerful performance greatly moved everyone in attendance.
Great excitement and countless kisses--

(FORBIDDEN DANCE VOL.4) * THE END * PUBLISHED IN BESSATSU SHOJO COMIC AUGUST ISSUE - SEPTEMBER ISSUE, 1998

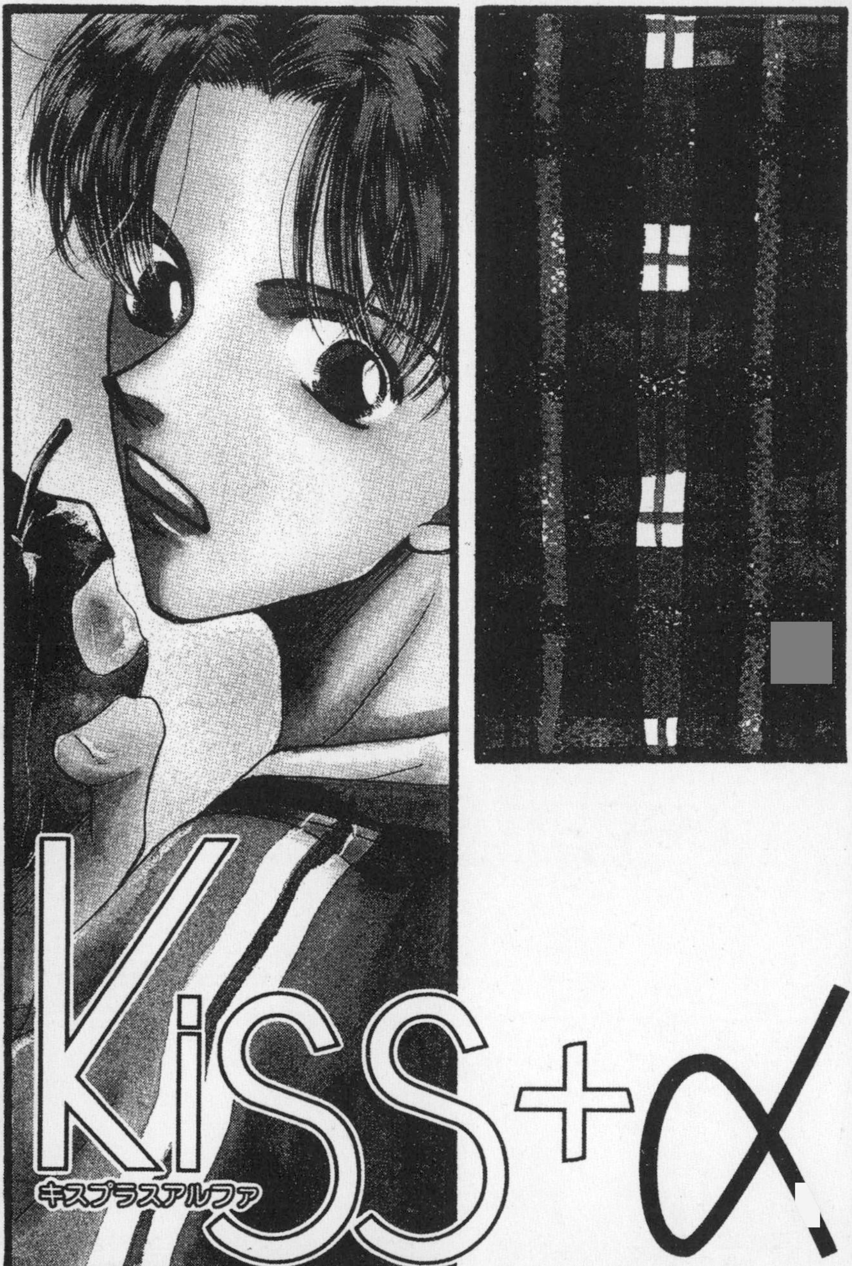
KiSS+α
キスプラスアルファ

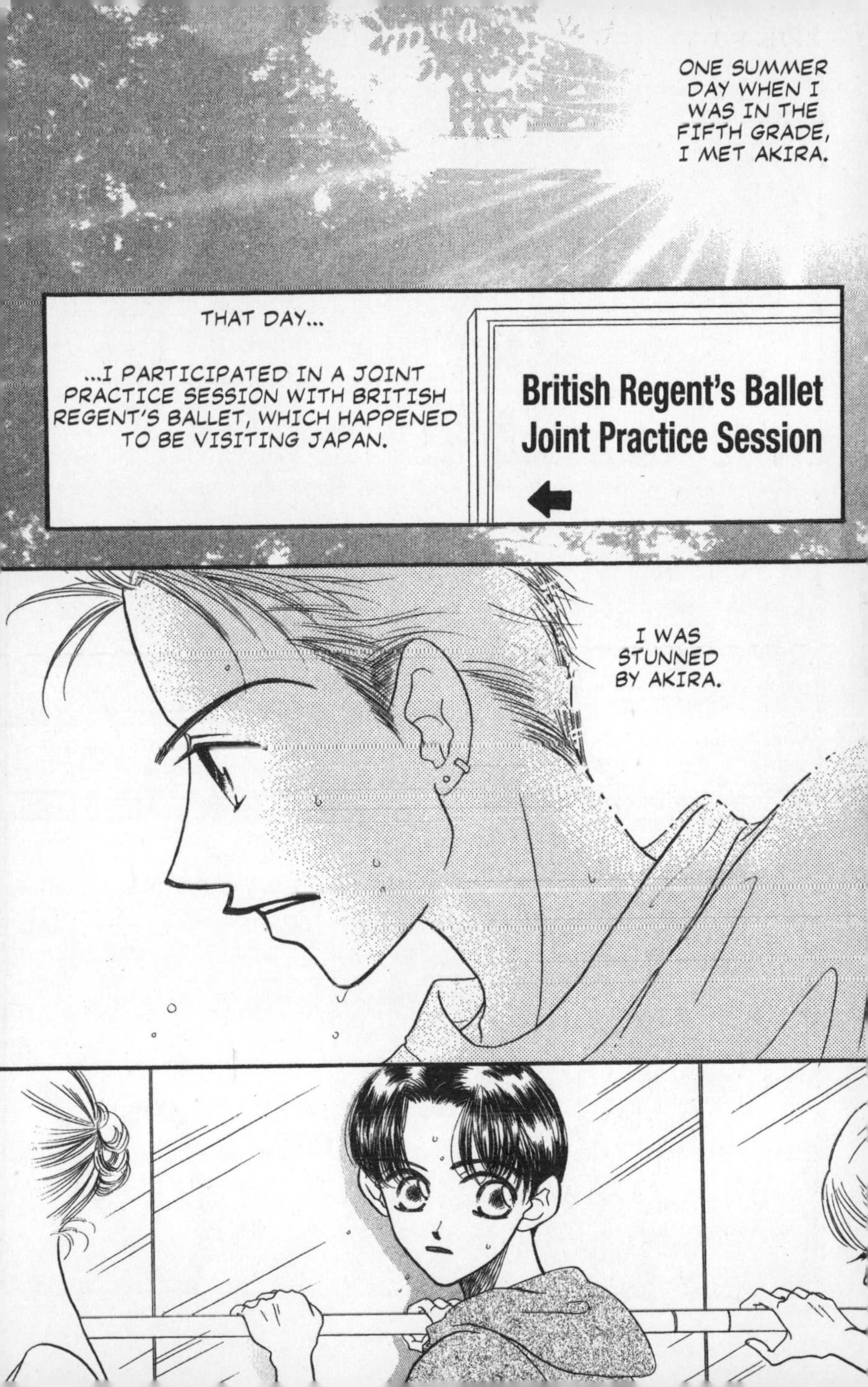
ONE SUMMER DAY WHEN I WAS IN THE FIFTH GRADE, I MET AKIRA.
British Regent's Ballet Joint Practice Session
THAT DAY...
...I PARTICIPATED IN A JOINT PRACTICE SESSION WITH BRITISH REGENT'S BALLET, WHICH HAPPENED TO BE VISITING JAPAN.
I WAS STUNNED BY AKIRA.

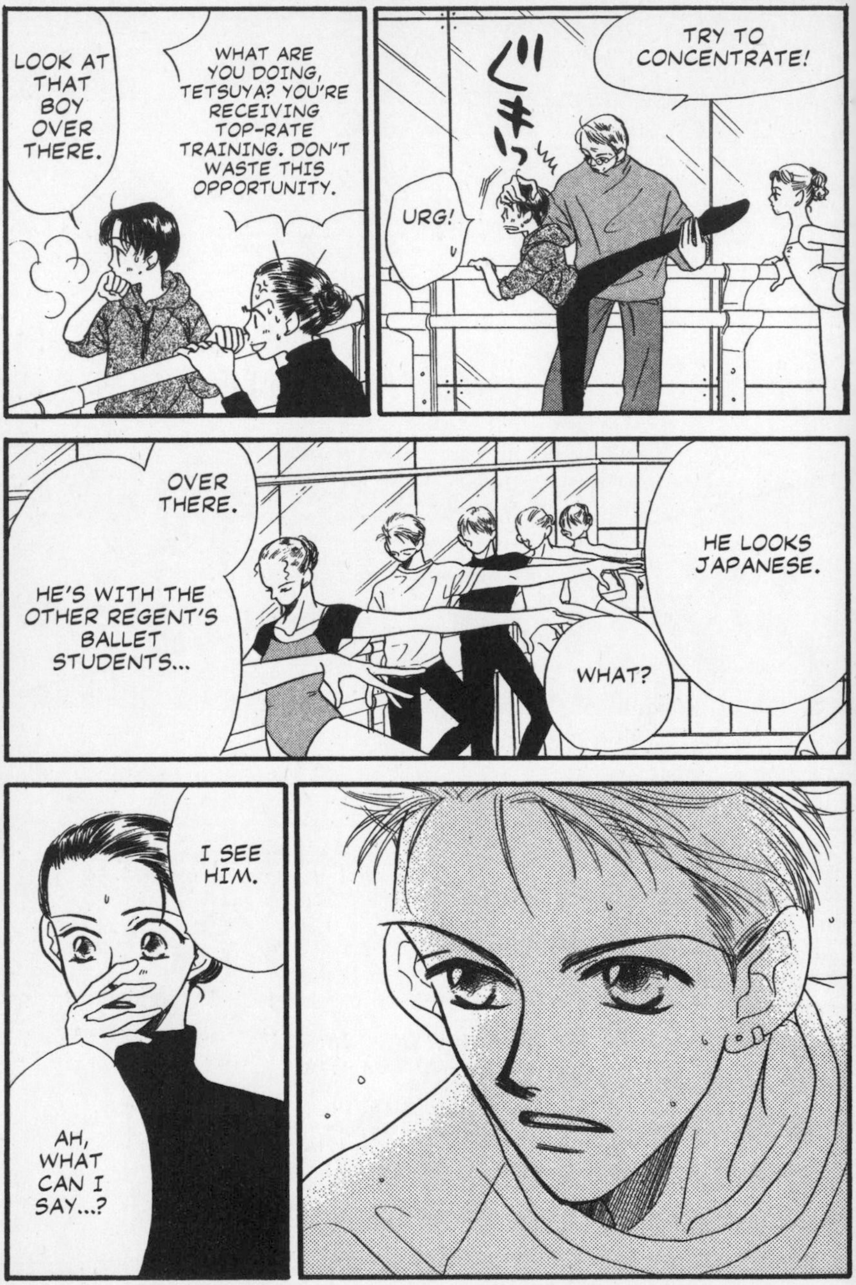
TRY TO CONCENTRATE!
ぐきっ
URG!
WHAT ARE YOU DOING, TETSUYA? YOU'RE RECEIVING TOP-RATE TRAINING. DON'T WASTE THIS OPPORTUNITY.
LOOK AT THAT BOY OVER THERE.
HE LOOKS JAPANESE.
WHAT?
OVER THERE.
HE'S WITH THE OTHER REGENT'S BALLET STUDENTS...
I SEE HIM.
AH, WHAT CAN I SAY...?

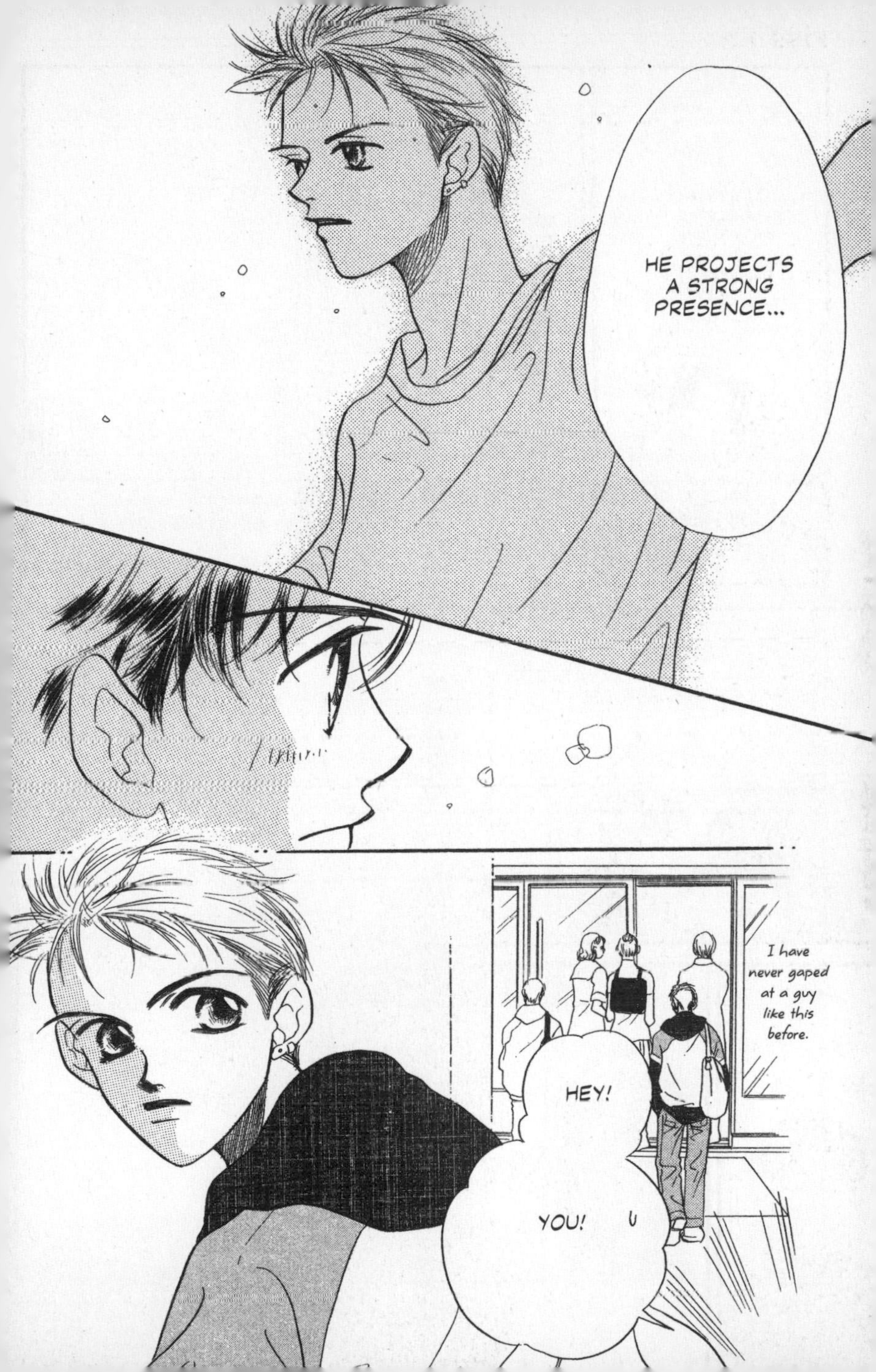
HE PROJECTS A STRONG PRESENCE...
I have never gaped at a guy like this before.
HEY!
YOU!

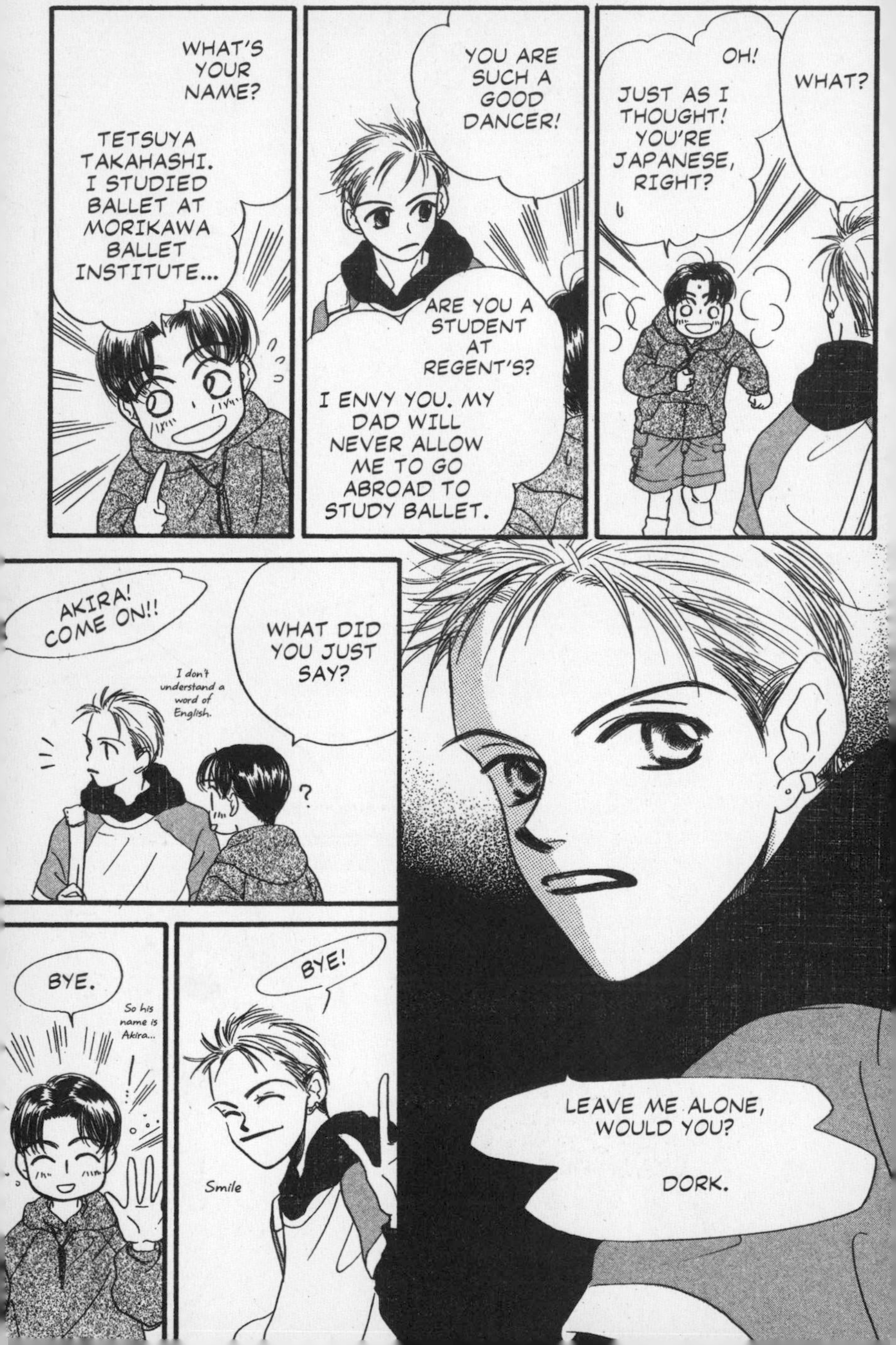
WHAT?
OH!
JUST AS I THOUGHT! YOU'RE JAPANESE, RIGHT?
YOU ARE SUCH A GOOD DANCER!
ARE YOU A STUDENT AT REGENT'S?
I ENVY YOU. MY DAD WILL NEVER ALLOW ME TO GO ABROAD TO STUDY BALLET.
WHAT'S YOUR NAME?
TETSUYA TAKAHASHI. I STUDIED BALLET AT MORIKAWA BALLET INSTITUTE...
LEAVE ME ALONE, WOULD YOU?
DORK.
WHAT DID YOU JUST SAY?
AKIRA! COME ON!!
I don't understand a word of English.
BYE!
Smile
BYE.
So his name is Akira...

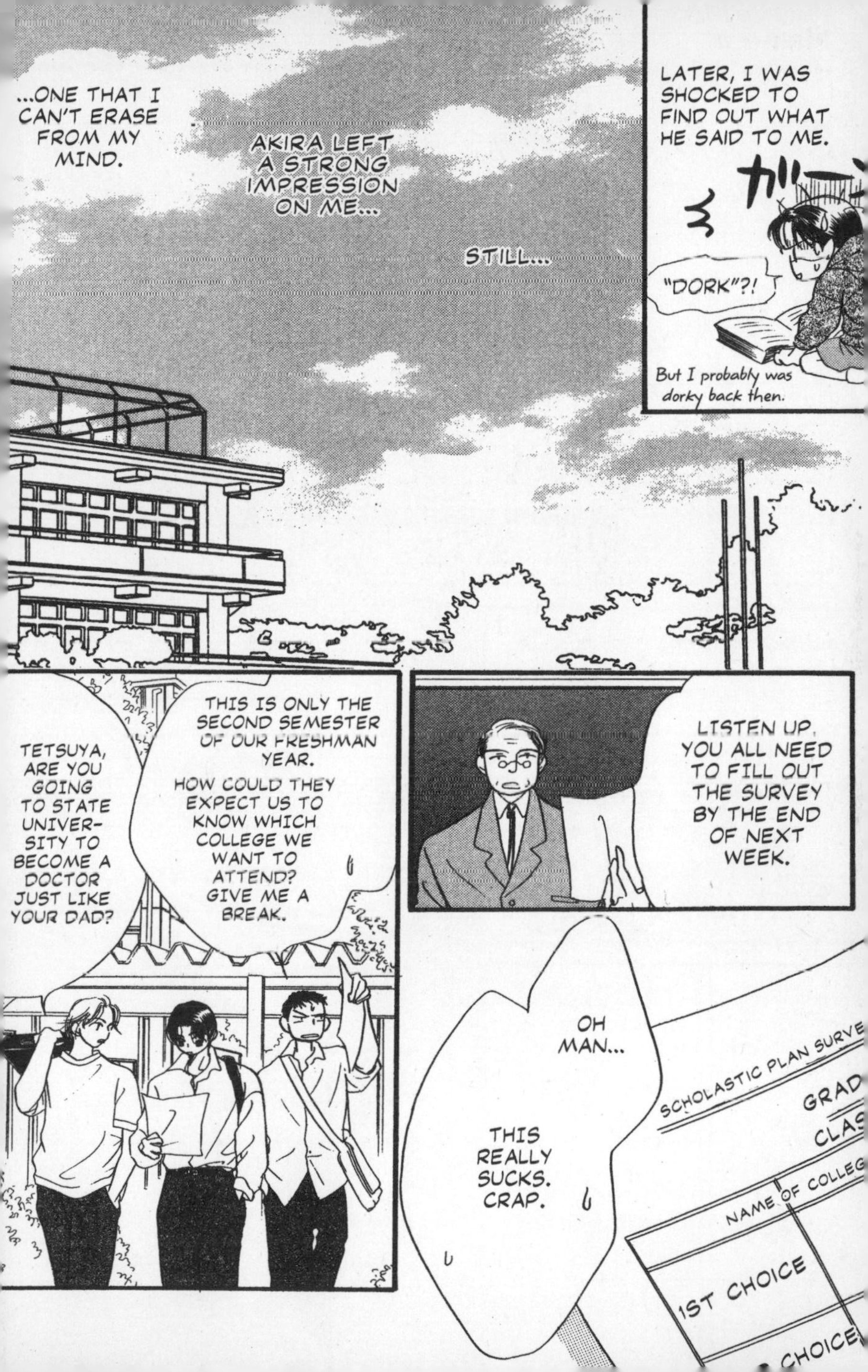

LATER, I WAS SHOCKED TO FIND OUT WHAT HE SAID TO ME.
"DORK"?!
But I probably was dorky back then.
AKIRA LEFT A STRONG IMPRESSION ON ME...
...ONE THAT I CAN'T ERASE FROM MY MIND.
STILL...
LISTEN UP. YOU ALL NEED TO FILL OUT THE SURVEY BY THE END OF NEXT WEEK.
OH MAN...
THIS REALLY SUCKS. CRAP.
SCHOLASTIC PLAN SURVE
GRAD
CLAS
NAME OF COLLEG
1ST CHOICE
CHOICE
THIS IS ONLY THE SECOND SEMESTER OF OUR FRESHMAN YEAR.
HOW COULD THEY EXPECT US TO KNOW WHICH COLLEGE WE WANT TO ATTEND? GIVE ME A BREAK.
TETSUYA, ARE YOU GOING TO STATE UNIVERSITY TO BECOME A DOCTOR JUST LIKE YOUR DAD?

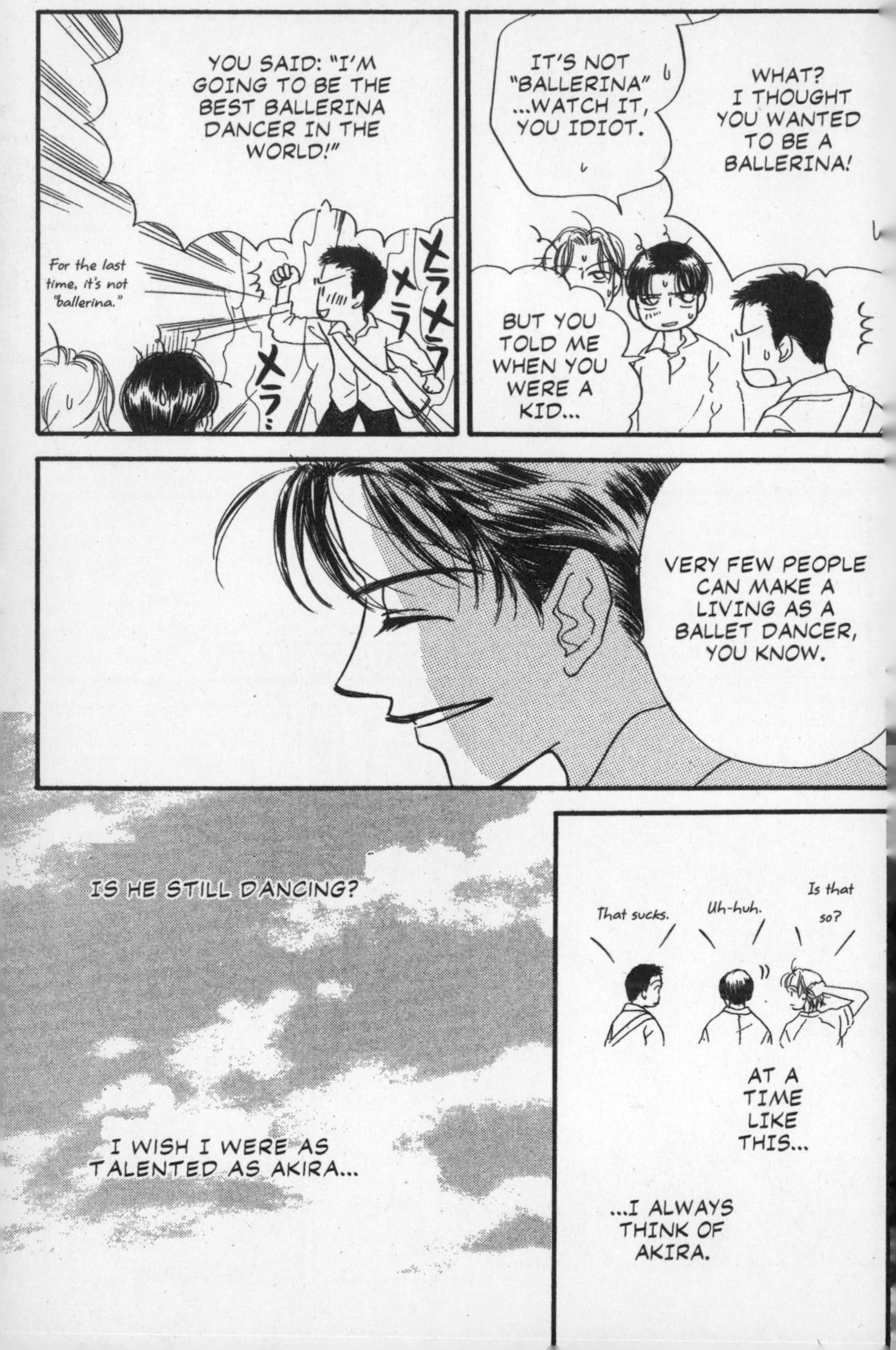
WHAT? I THOUGHT YOU WANTED TO BE A BALLERINA!
IT'S NOT "BALLERINA" ...WATCH IT, YOU IDIOT.
BUT YOU TOLD ME WHEN YOU WERE A KID...
YOU SAID: "I'M GOING TO BE THE BEST BALLERINA DANCER IN THE WORLD!"
メラメラ
メラ
メラ
For the last time, it's not "ballerina."
VERY FEW PEOPLE CAN MAKE A LIVING AS A BALLET DANCER, YOU KNOW.
Is that so?
Uh-huh.
That sucks.
AT A TIME LIKE THIS...
...I ALWAYS THINK OF AKIRA.
IS HE STILL DANCING?
I WISH I WERE AS TALENTED AS AKIRA...

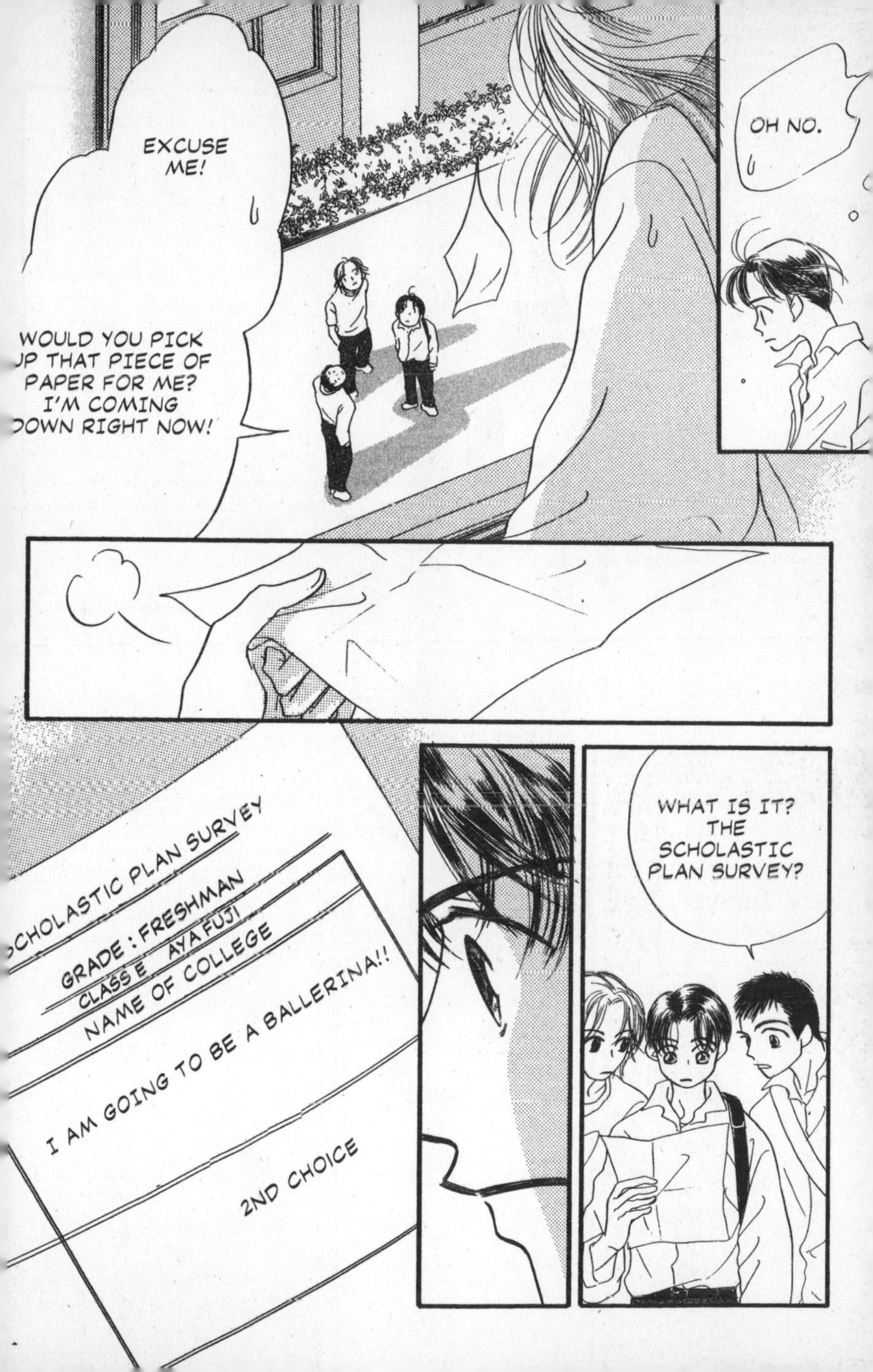
OH NO.
EXCUSE ME!
WOULD YOU PICK UP THAT PIECE OF PAPER FOR ME? I'M COMING DOWN RIGHT NOW!
WHAT IS IT? THE SCHOLASTIC PLAN SURVEY?
SCHOLASTIC PLAN SURVEY
GRADE : FRESHMAN
CLASS E AYA FUJI
NAME OF COLLEGE
I AM GOING TO BE A BALLERINA!!
2ND CHOICE

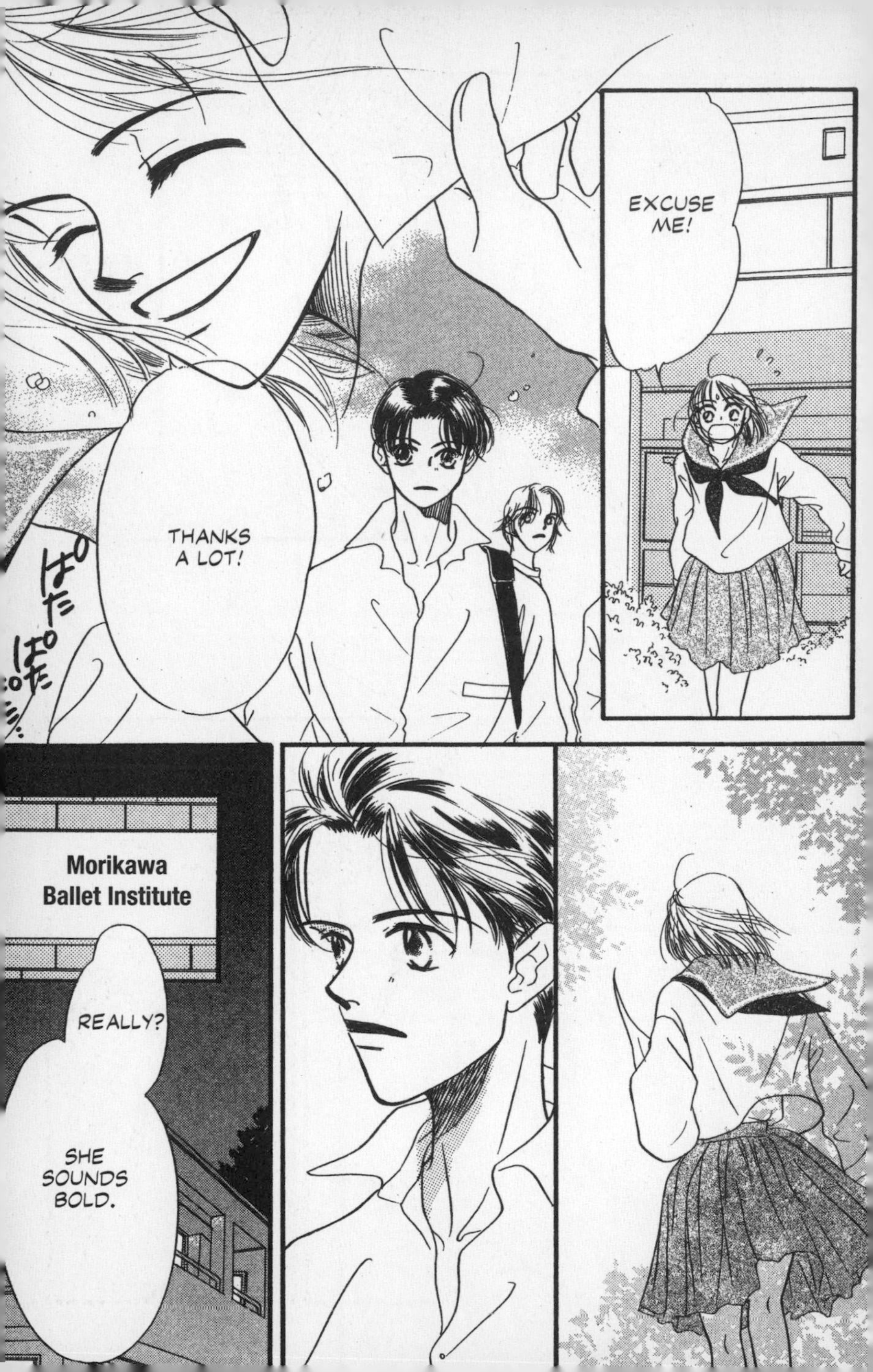
EXCUSE ME!
THANKS A LOT!
ぱたぱた
Morikawa Ballet Institute
REALLY?
SHE SOUNDS BOLD.

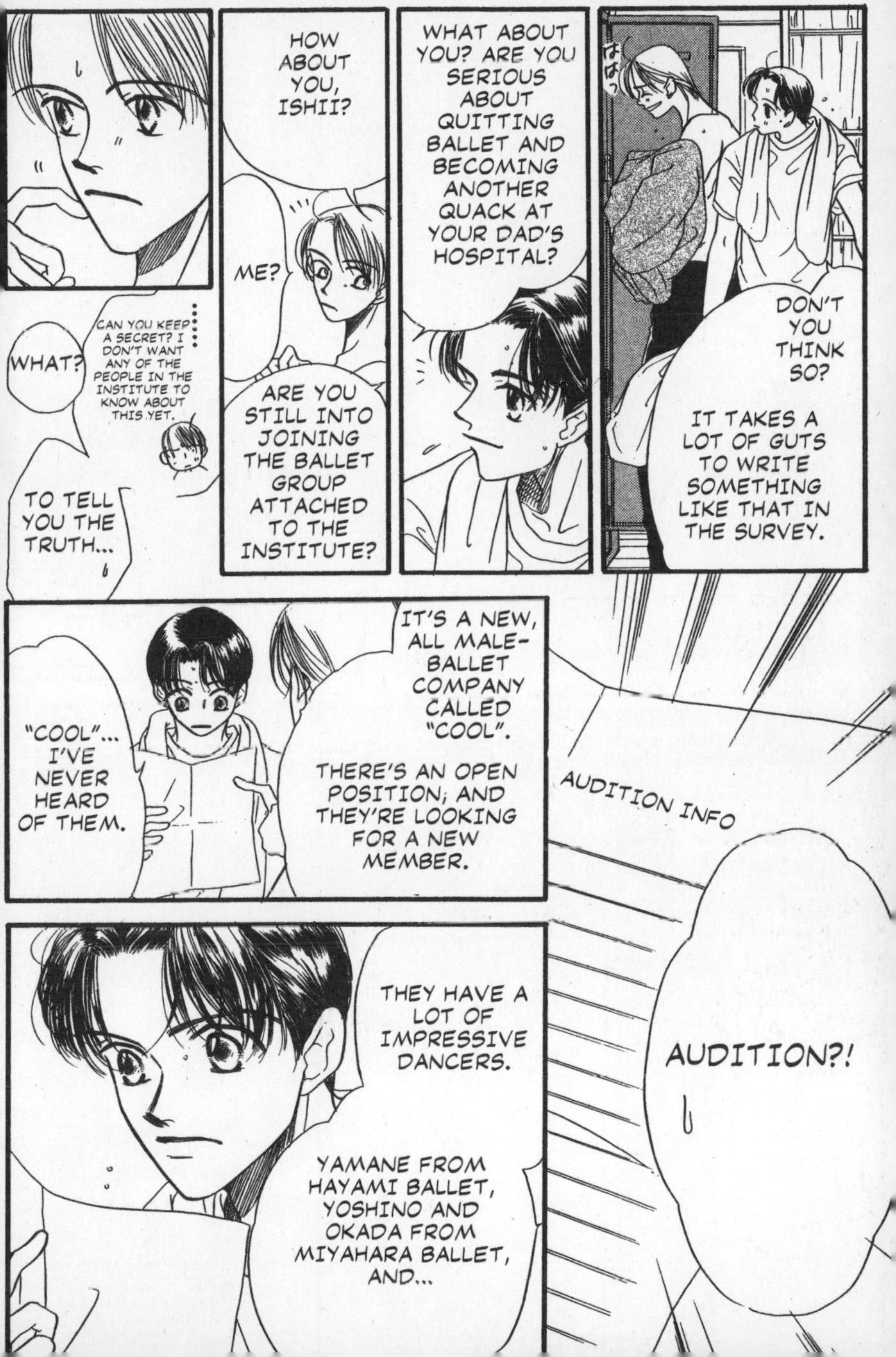
はは
DON'T YOU THINK SO?
IT TAKES A LOT OF GUTS TO WRITE SOMETHING LIKE THAT IN THE SURVEY.
WHAT ABOUT YOU? ARE YOU SERIOUS ABOUT QUITTING BALLET AND BECOMING ANOTHER QUACK AT YOUR DAD'S HOSPITAL?
HOW ABOUT YOU, ISHII?
ME?
ARE YOU STILL INTO JOINING THE BALLET GROUP ATTACHED TO THE INSTITUTE?
CAN YOU KEEP A SECRET? I DON'T WANT ANY OF THE PEOPLE IN THE INSTITUTE TO KNOW ABOUT THIS YET.
WHAT?
TO TELL YOU THE TRUTH...
AUDITION INFO
AUDITION?!
IT'S A NEW, ALL MALE-BALLET COMPANY CALLED "COOL".
THERE'S AN OPEN POSITION; AND THEY'RE LOOKING FOR A NEW MEMBER.
"COOL"... I'VE NEVER HEARD OF THEM.
THEY HAVE A LOT OF IMPRESSIVE DANCERS.
YAMANE FROM HAYAMI BALLET, YOSHINO AND OKADA FROM MIYAHARA BALLET, AND...

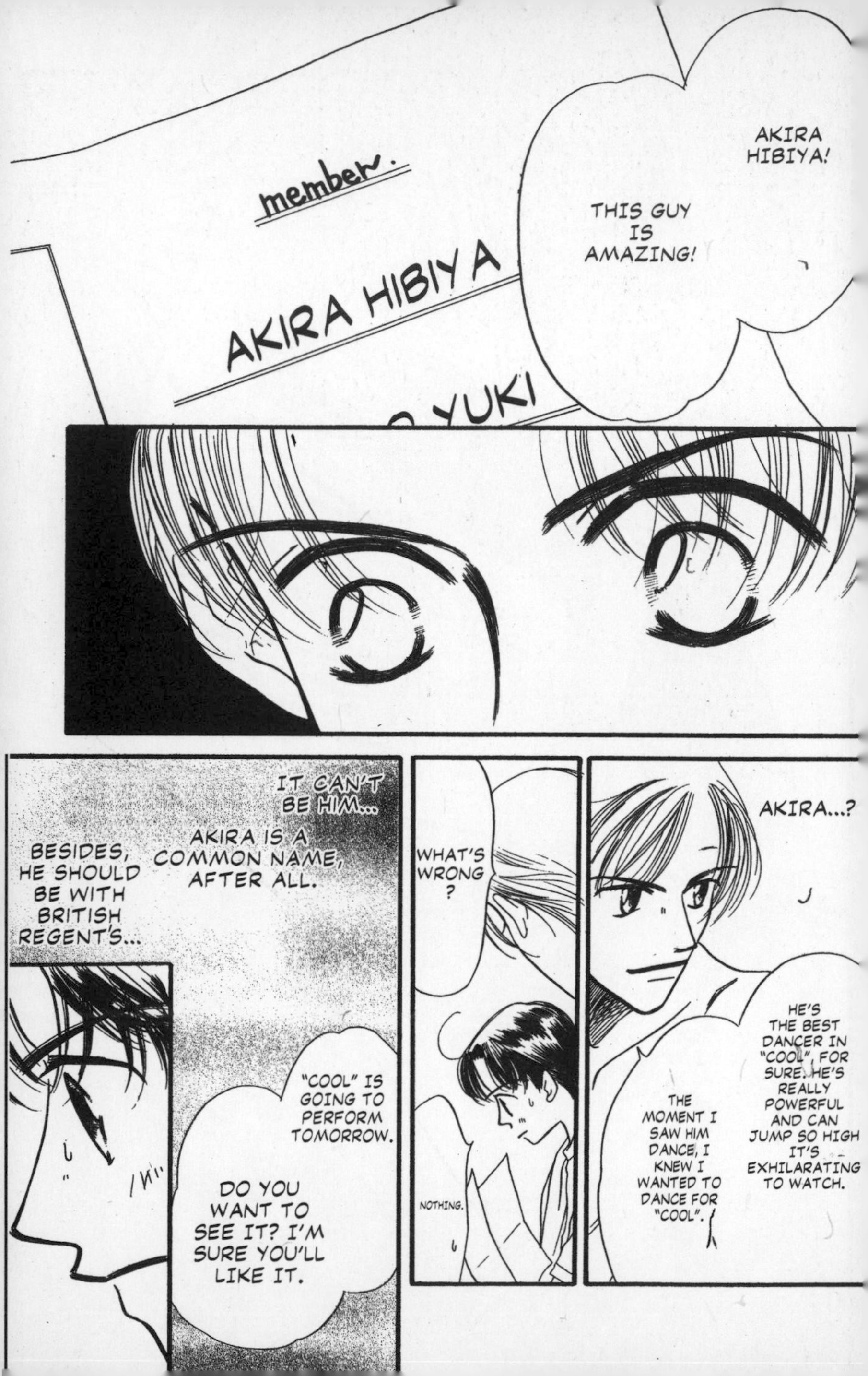

AKIRA HIBIYA! THIS GUY IS AMAZING!
member.
AKIRA HIBIYA
YUKI
AKIRA...?
HE'S THE BEST DANCER IN "COOL", FOR SURE. HE'S REALLY POWERFUL AND CAN JUMP SO HIGH IT'S EXHILARATING TO WATCH.
THE MOMENT I SAW HIM DANCE, I KNEW I WANTED TO DANCE FOR "COOL".
WHAT'S WRONG?
NOTHING.
IT CAN'T BE HIM...
AKIRA IS A COMMON NAME, AFTER ALL.
BESIDES, HE SHOULD BE WITH BRITISH REGENT'S...
"COOL" IS GOING TO PERFORM TOMORROW.
DO YOU WANT TO SEE IT? I'M SURE YOU'LL LIKE IT.

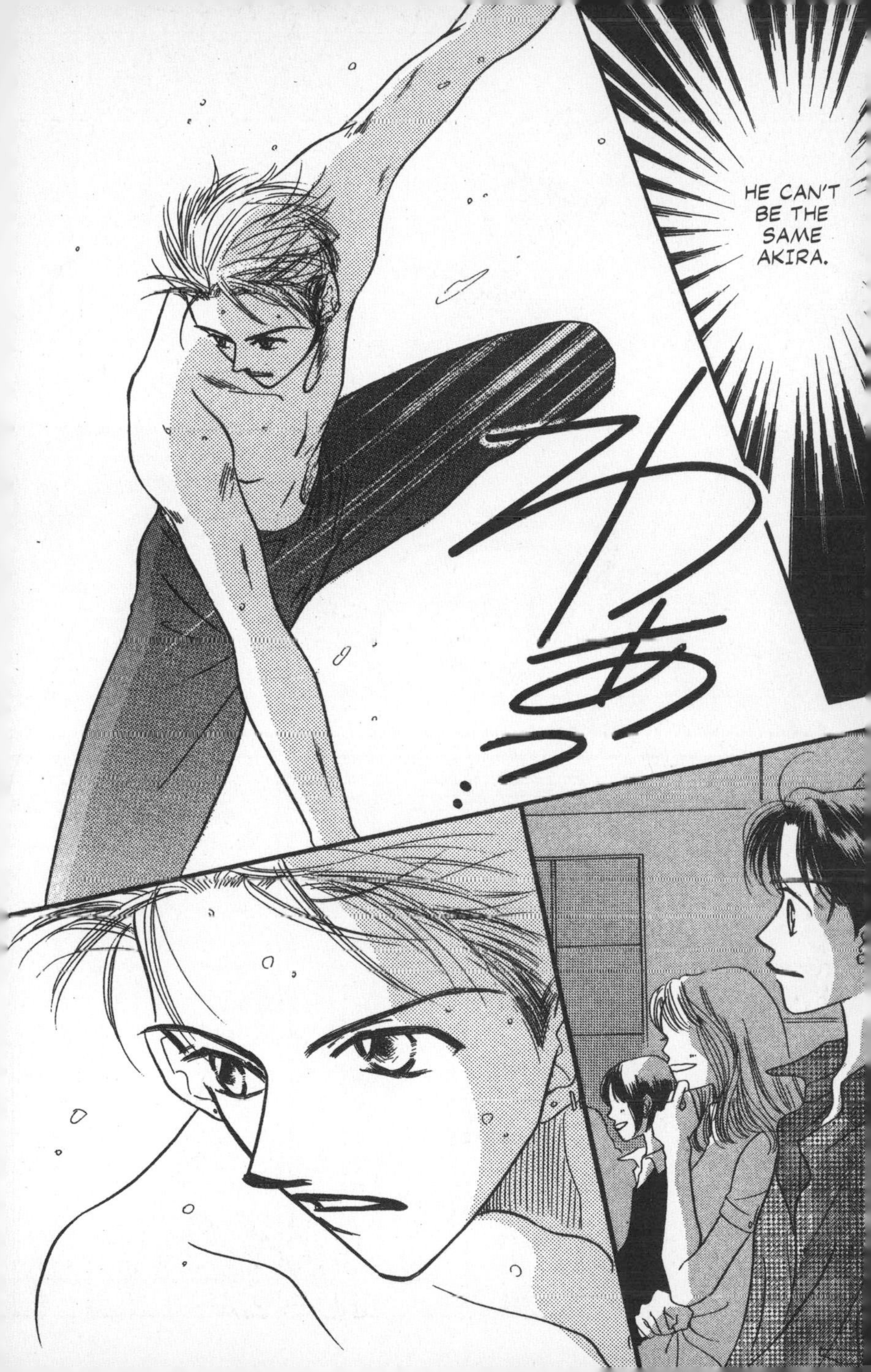
HE CAN'T BE THE SAME AKIRA.

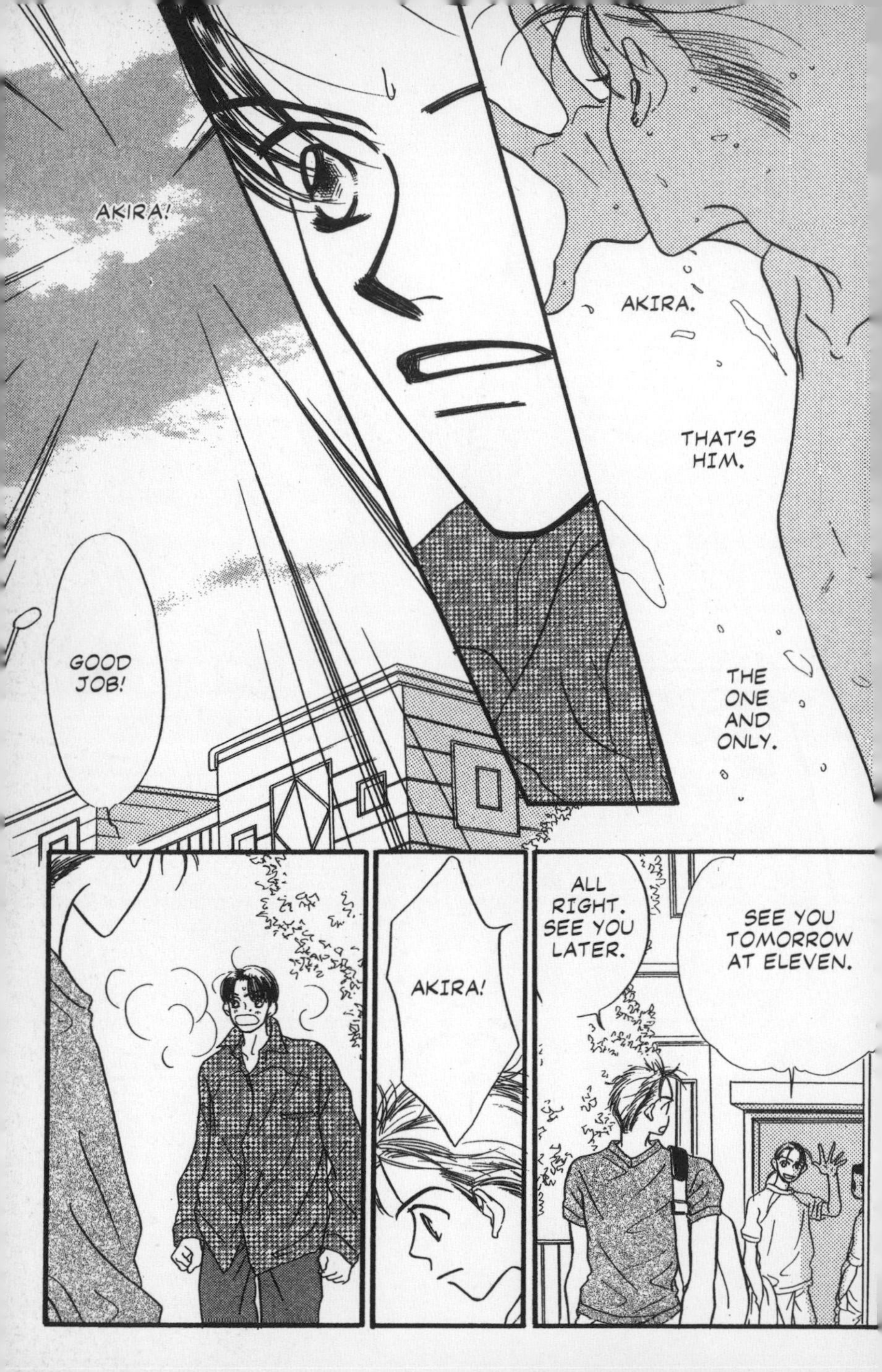
AKIRA.
THAT'S HIM.
THE ONE AND ONLY.
AKIRA!
GOOD JOB!
SEE YOU TOMORROW AT ELEVEN.
ALL RIGHT. SEE YOU LATER.
AKIRA!

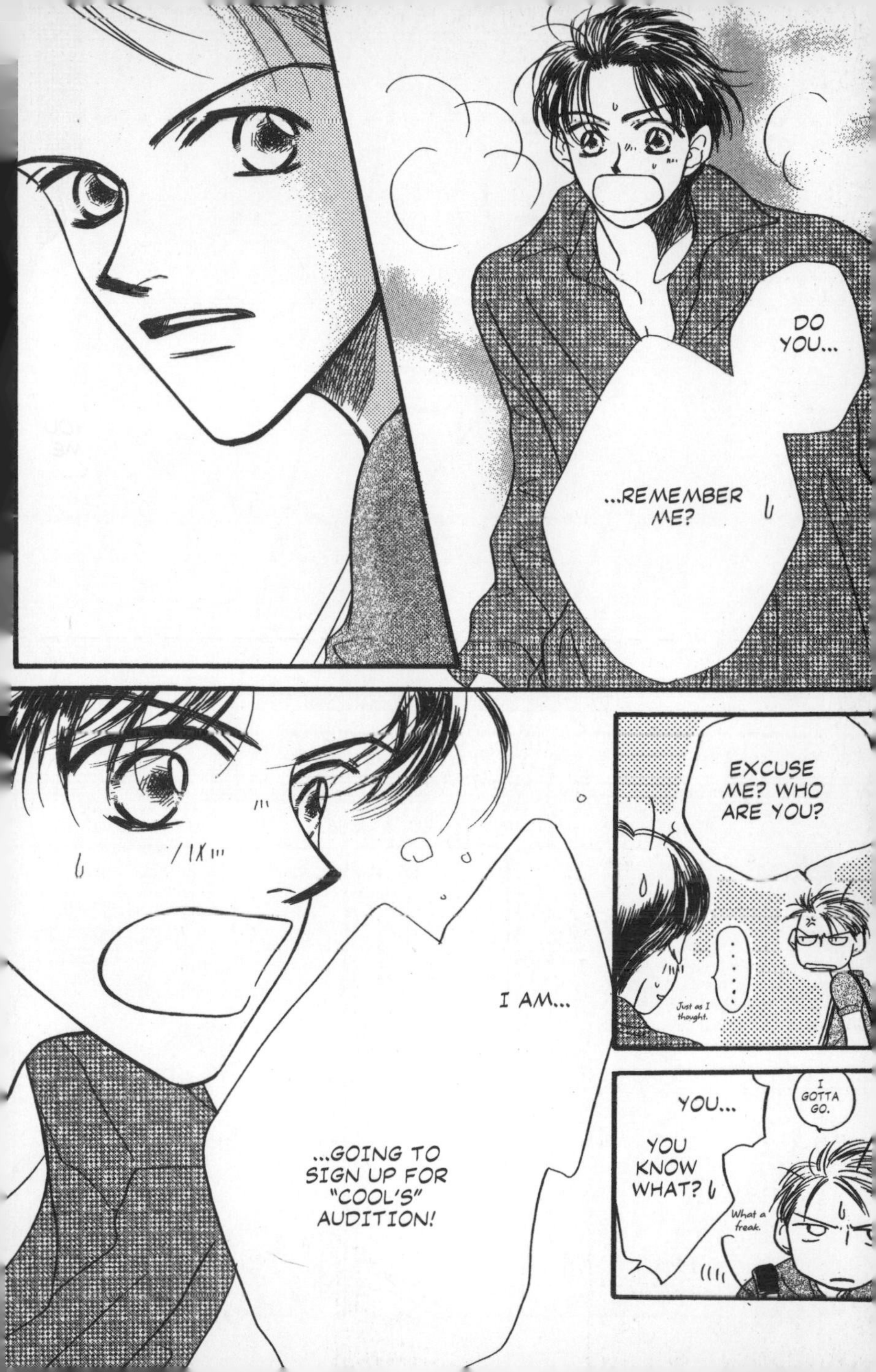
DO YOU...
...REMEMBER ME?
EXCUSE ME? WHO ARE YOU?
.....
Just as I thought.
I GOTTA GO.
YOU...
YOU KNOW WHAT?
What a freak.
I AM...
...GOING TO SIGN UP FOR "COOL'S" AUDITION!

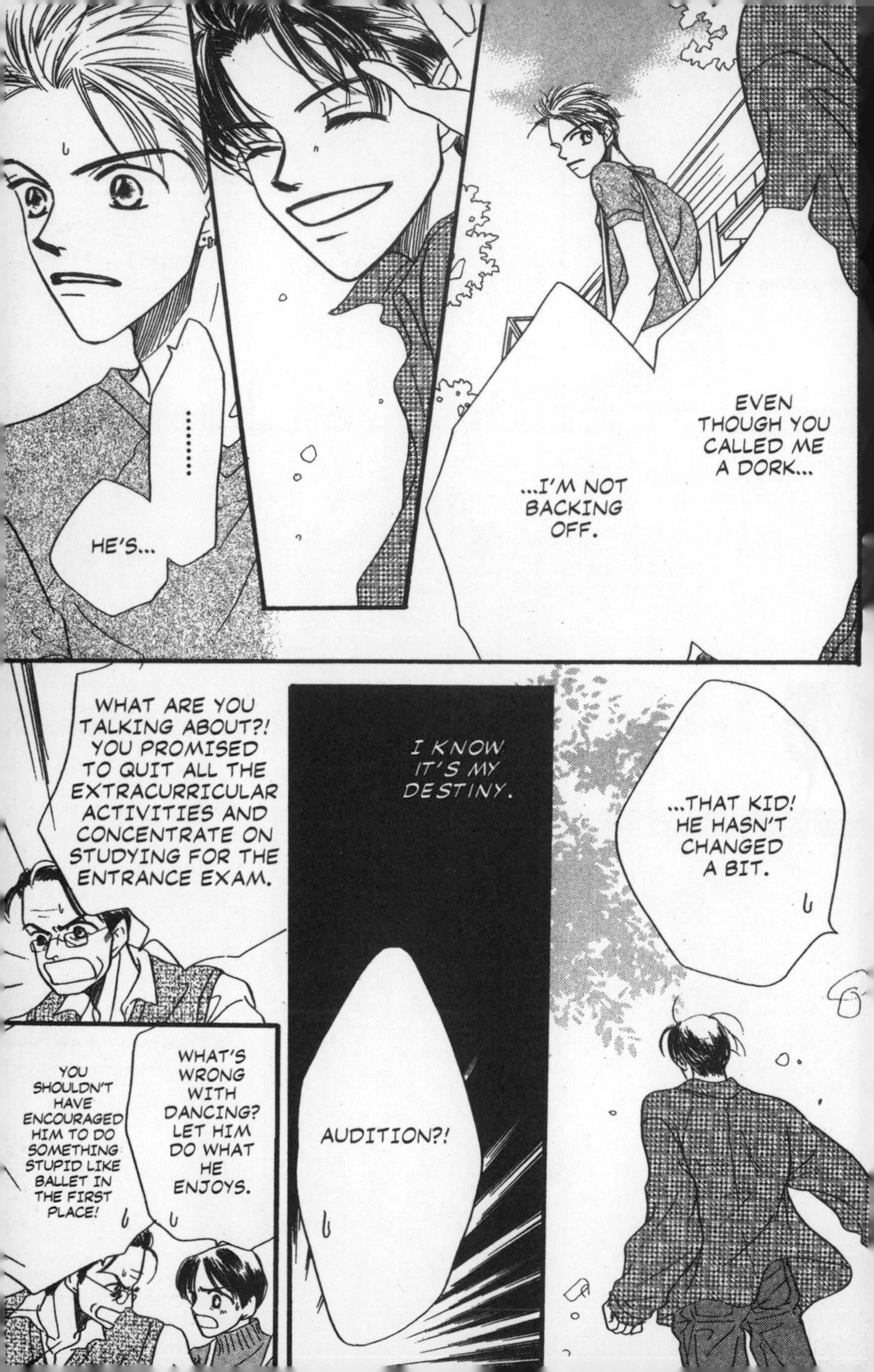
EVEN THOUGH YOU CALLED ME A DORK...
...I'M NOT BACKING OFF.
......
HE'S...
...THAT KID! HE HASN'T CHANGED A BIT.
I KNOW IT'S MY DESTINY.
AUDITION?!
WHAT ARE YOU TALKING ABOUT?! YOU PROMISED TO QUIT ALL THE EXTRACURRICULAR ACTIVITIES AND CONCENTRATE ON STUDYING FOR THE ENTRANCE EXAM.
WHAT'S WRONG WITH DANCING? LET HIM DO WHAT HE ENJOYS.
YOU SHOULDN'T HAVE ENCOURAGED HIM TO DO SOMETHING STUPID LIKE BALLET IN THE FIRST PLACE!

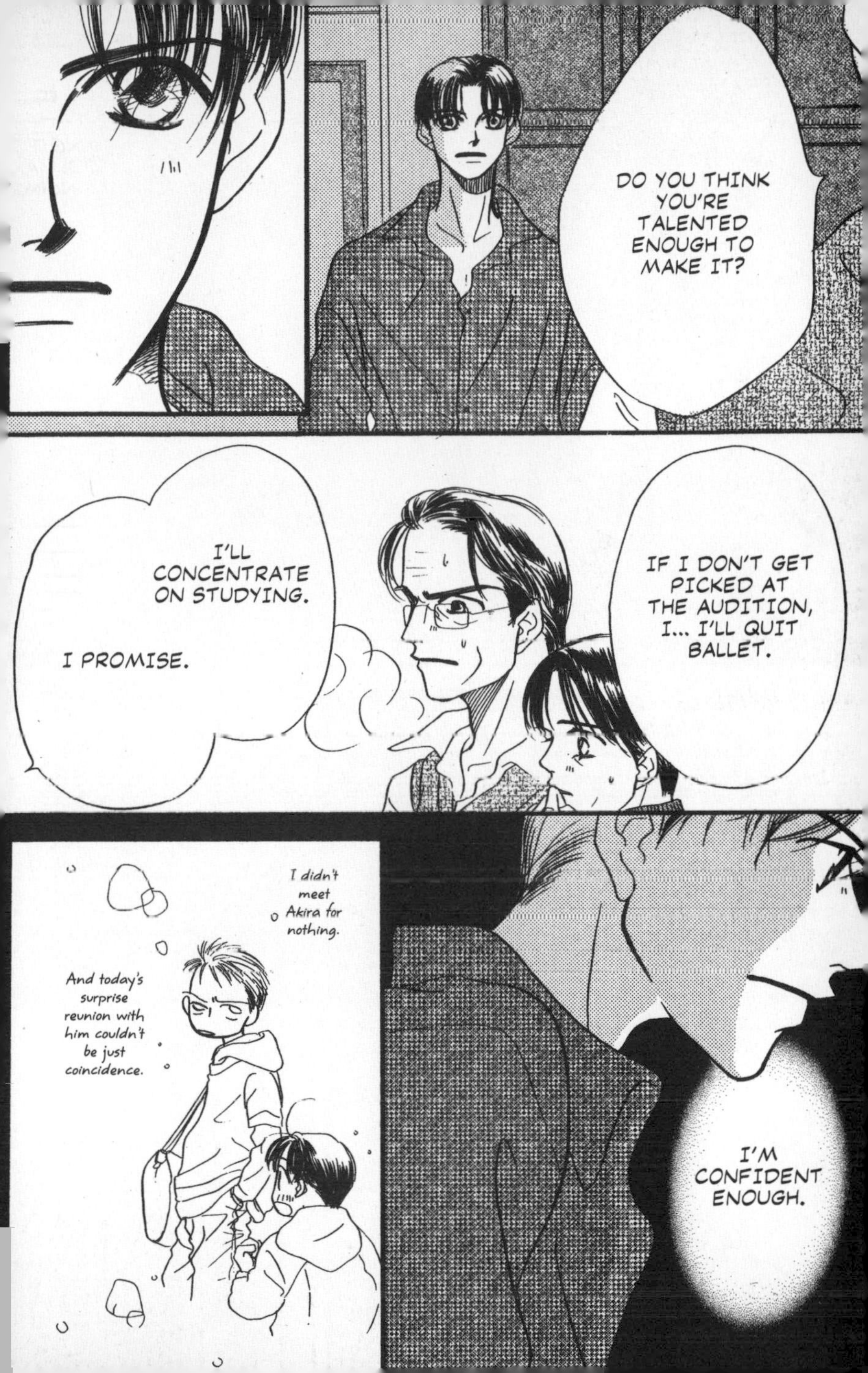
DO YOU THINK YOU'RE TALENTED ENOUGH TO MAKE IT?
IF I DON'T GET PICKED AT THE AUDITION, I... I'LL QUIT BALLET.
I'LL CONCENTRATE ON STUDYING.
I PROMISE.
I'M CONFIDENT ENOUGH.
I didn't meet Akira for nothing.
And today's surprise reunion with him couldn't be just coincidence.

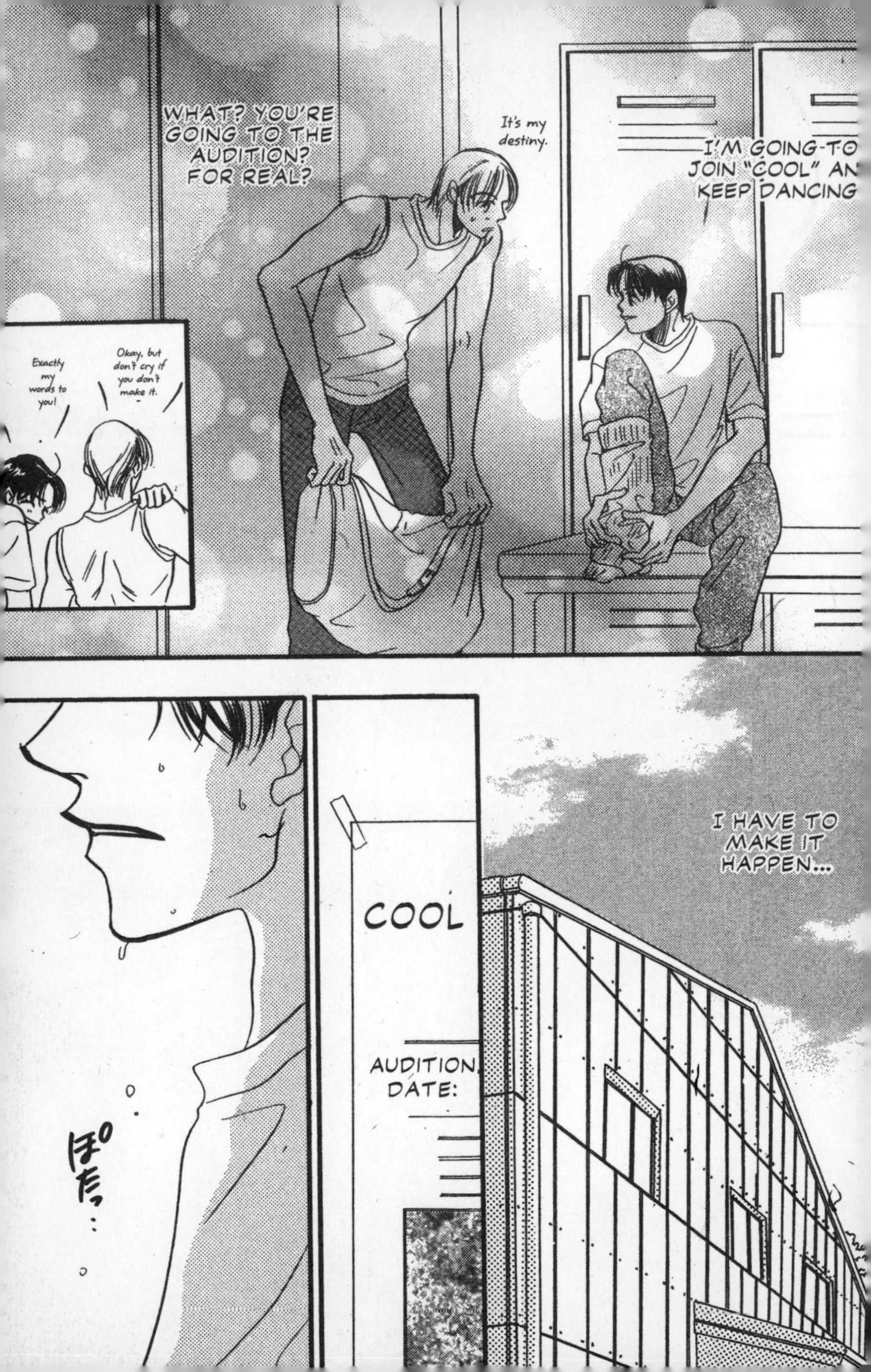
I'M GOING TO JOIN "COOL" AN KEEP DANCING
It's my destiny.
WHAT? YOU'RE GOING TO THE AUDITION? FOR REAL?
Okay, but don't cry if you don't make it.
Exactly my words to you!
I HAVE TO MAKE IT HAPPEN...
COOL
AUDITION DATE:
ぽたっ…

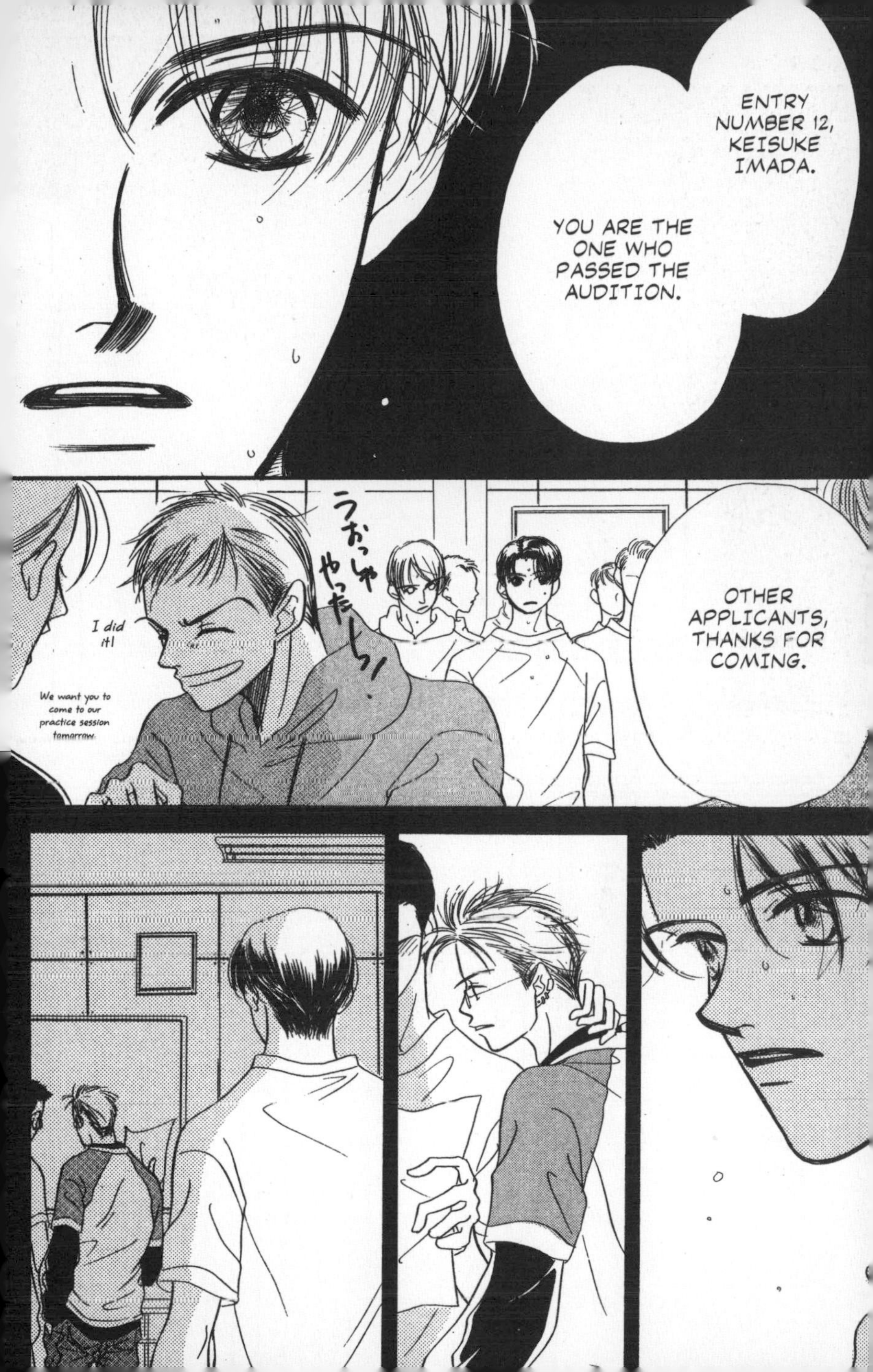
ENTRY NUMBER 12, KEISUKE IMADA.
YOU ARE THE ONE WHO PASSED THE AUDITION.
OTHER APPLICANTS, THANKS FOR COMING.
うおっしゃやったーっ!
I did it!
We want you to come to our practice session tomorrow.

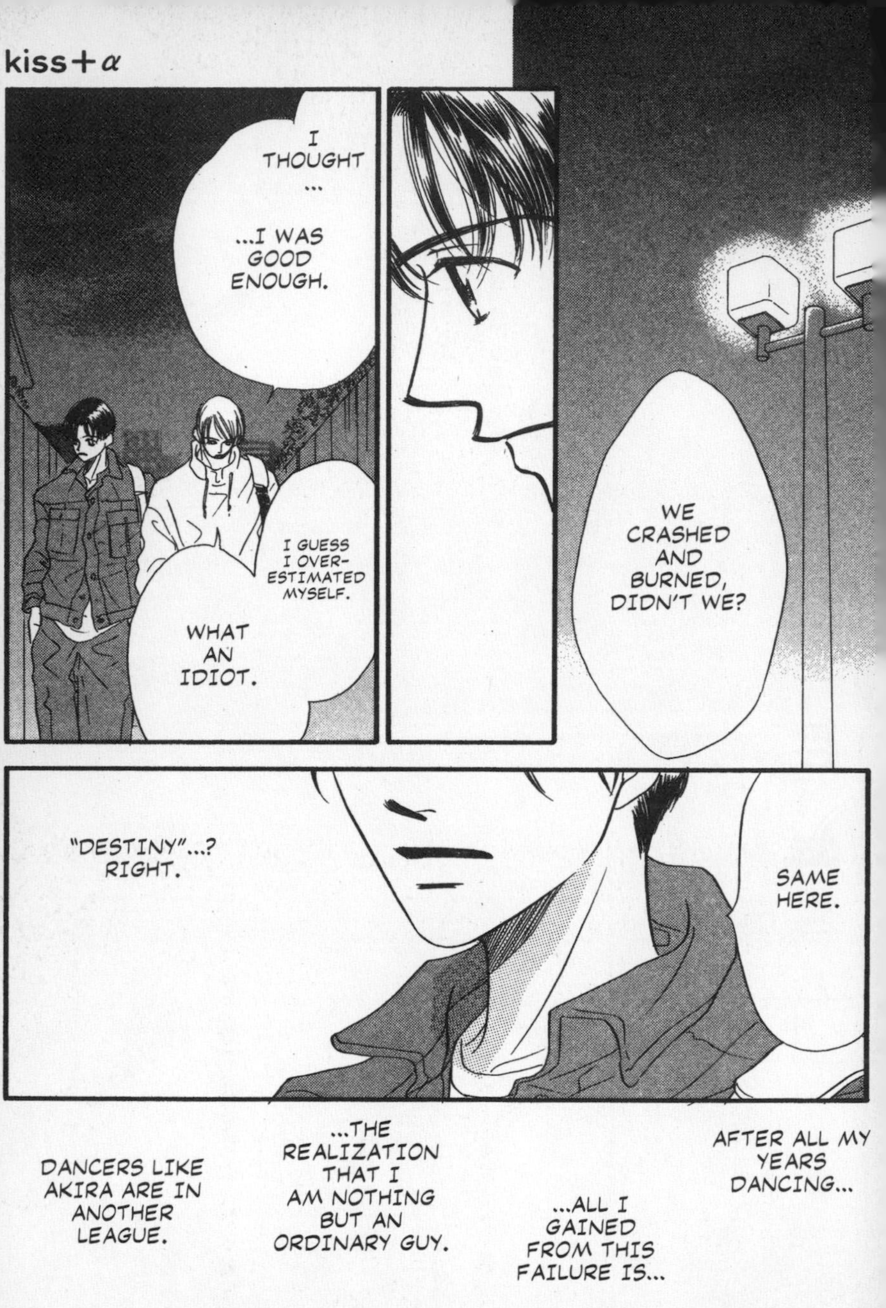
WE CRASHED AND BURNED, DIDN'T WE?
I THOUGHT ...
...I WAS GOOD ENOUGH.
I GUESS I OVER-ESTIMATED MYSELF.
WHAT AN IDIOT.
SAME HERE.
"DESTINY"...? RIGHT.
AFTER ALL MY YEARS DANCING...
...ALL I GAINED FROM THIS FAILURE IS...
...THE REALIZATION THAT I AM NOTHING BUT AN ORDINARY GUY.
DANCERS LIKE AKIRA ARE IN ANOTHER LEAGUE.

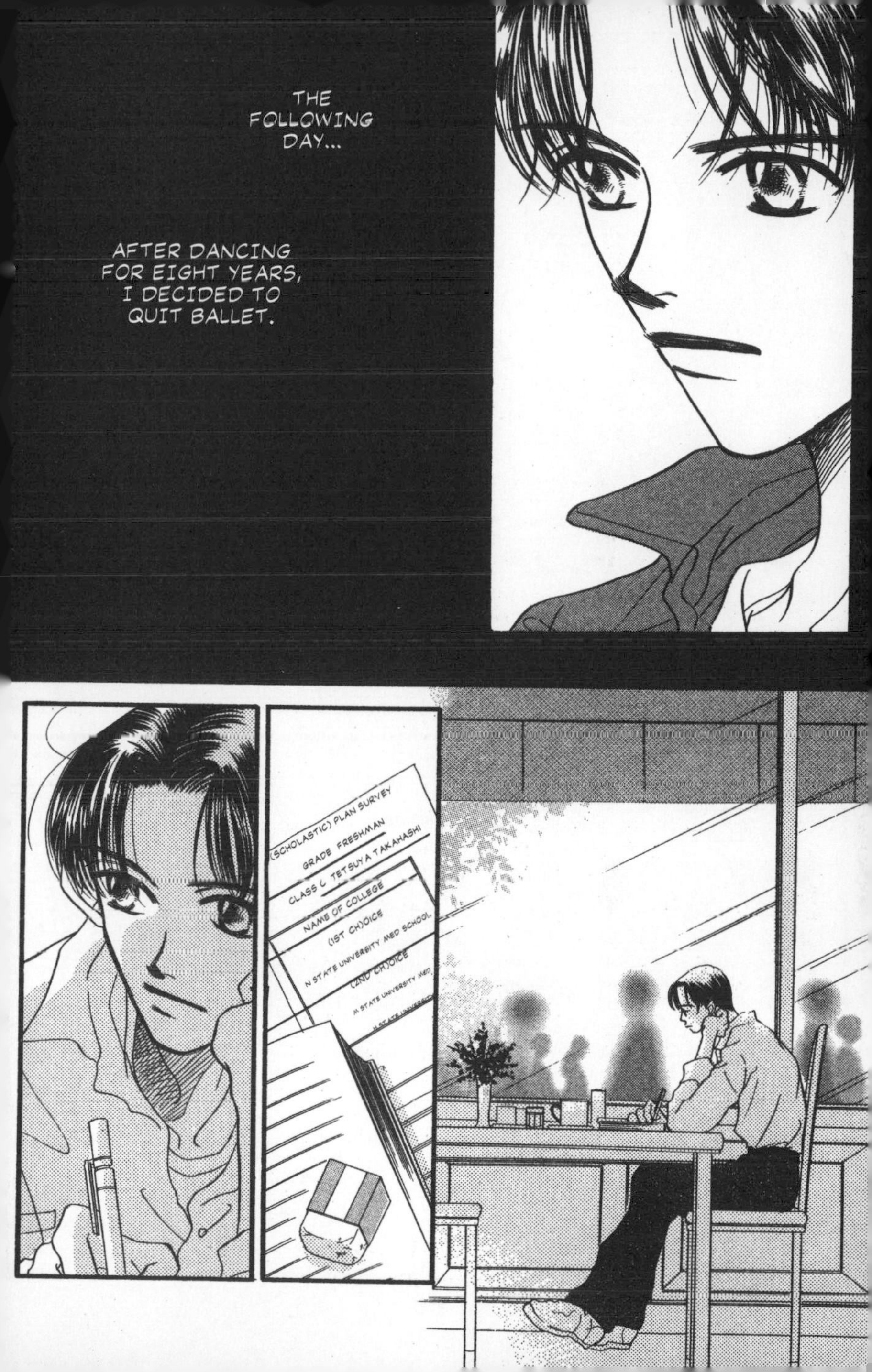
THE FOLLOWING DAY...
AFTER DANCING FOR EIGHT YEARS, I DECIDED TO QUIT BALLET.
(SCHOLASTIC) PLAN SURVEY
GRADE FRESHMAN
CLASS 6 TETSUYA TAKAHASHI
NAME OF COLLEGE
(1ST CH)OICE
N STATE UNIVERSITY MED SCHOOL
(2ND CH)OICE
M STATE UNIVERSITY MED

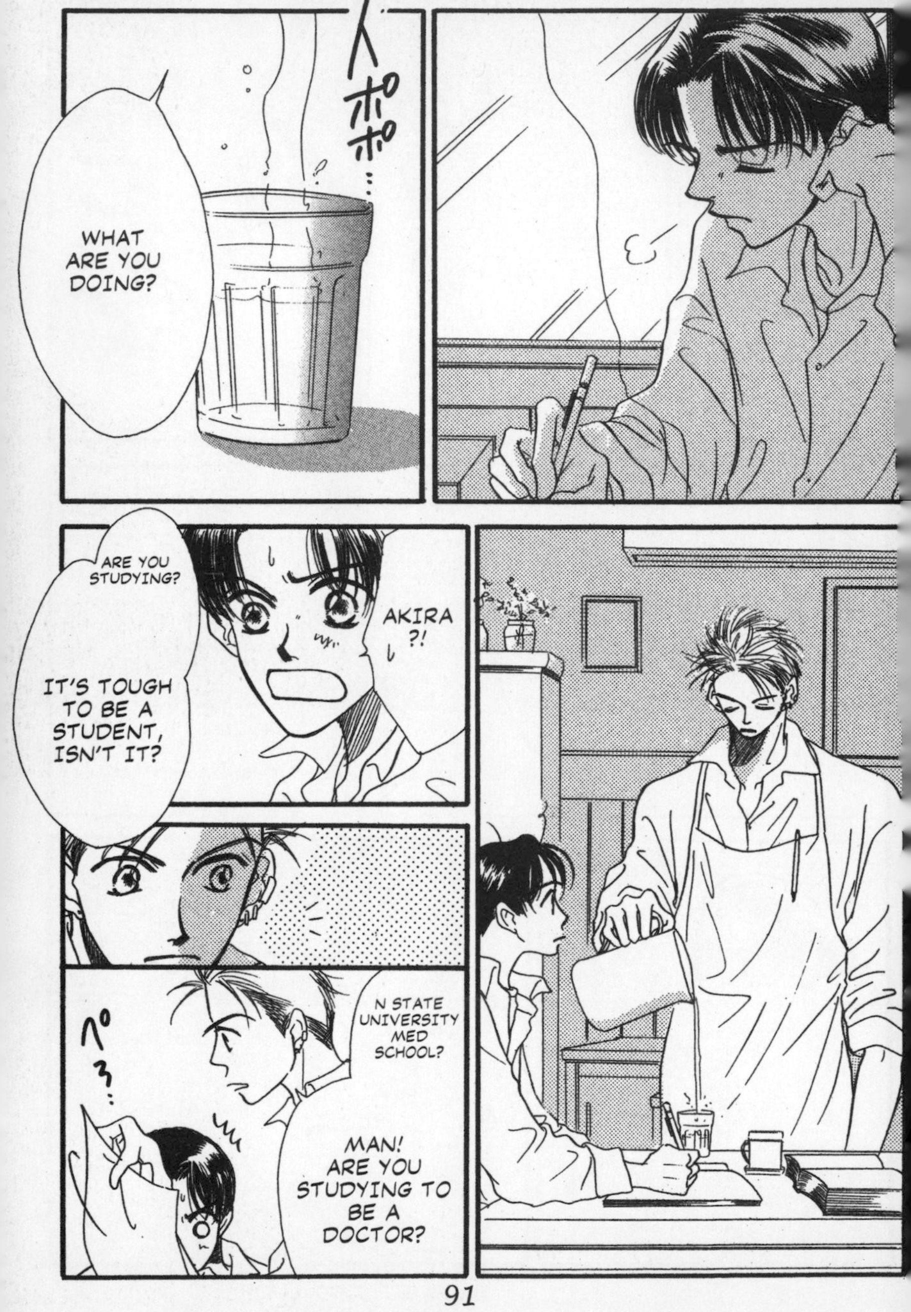
ポポ…
WHAT ARE YOU DOING?
ARE YOU STUDYING?
IT'S TOUGH TO BE A STUDENT, ISN'T IT?
AKIRA ?!
N STATE UNIVERSITY MED SCHOOL?
MAN! ARE YOU STUDYING TO BE A DOCTOR?
ぺろ…

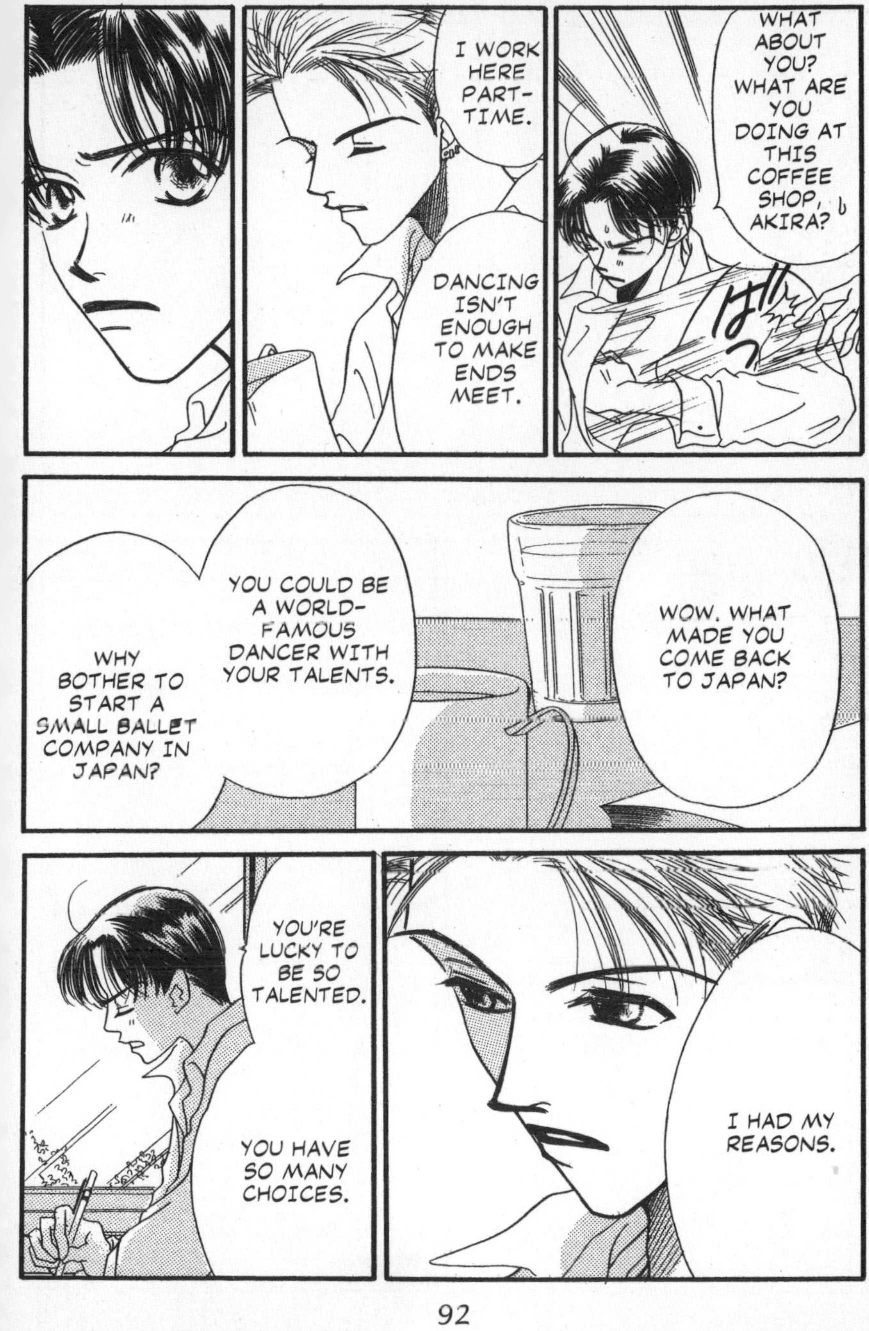
WHAT ABOUT YOU? WHAT ARE YOU DOING AT THIS COFFEE SHOP, AKIRA?
はっ
I WORK HERE PART-TIME.
DANCING ISN'T ENOUGH TO MAKE ENDS MEET.
WOW. WHAT MADE YOU COME BACK TO JAPAN?
YOU COULD BE A WORLD-FAMOUS DANCER WITH YOUR TALENTS.
WHY BOTHER TO START A SMALL BALLET COMPANY IN JAPAN?
I HAD MY REASONS.
YOU'RE LUCKY TO BE SO TALENTED.
YOU HAVE SO MANY CHOICES.

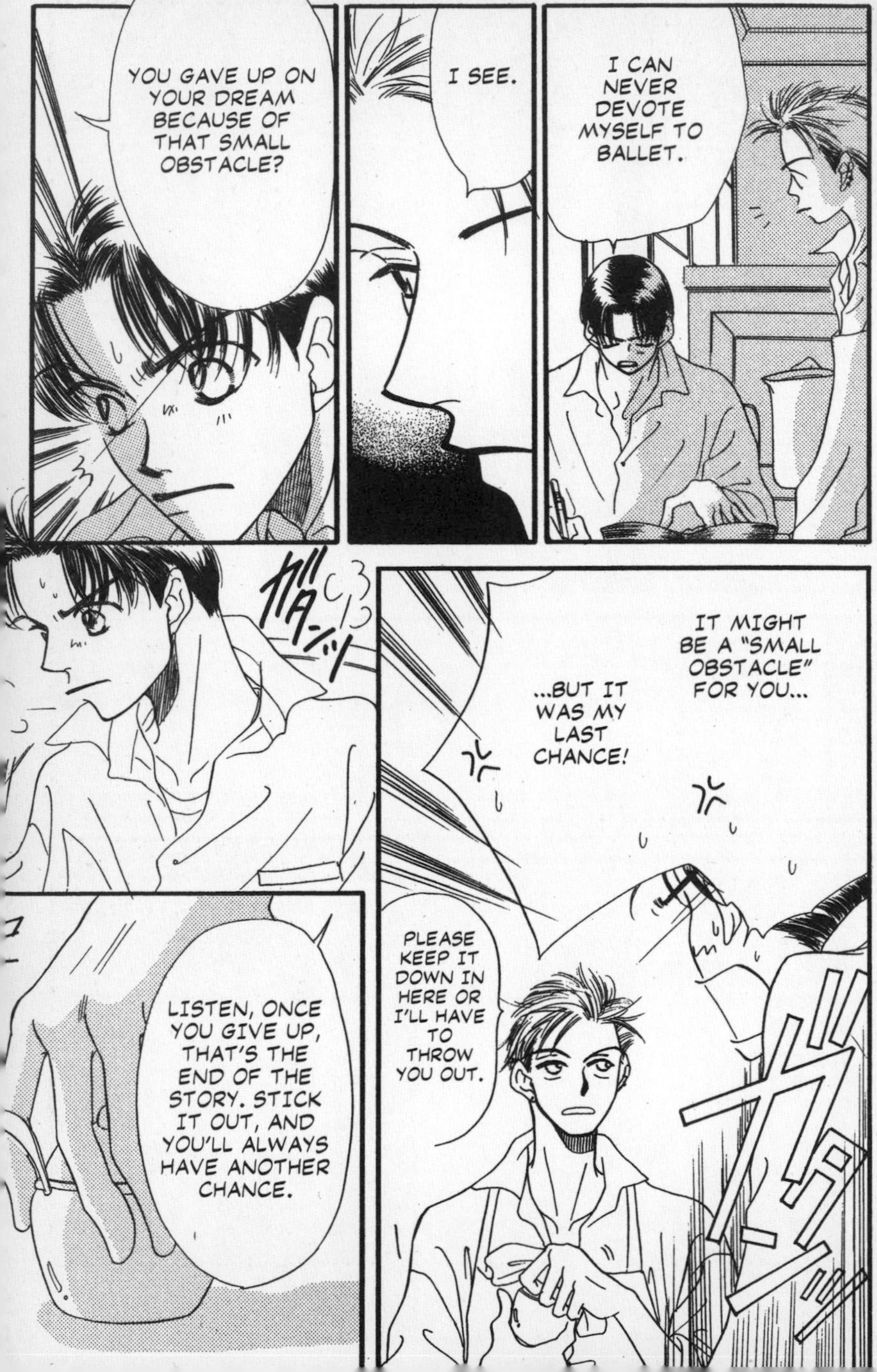
I CAN NEVER DEVOTE MYSELF TO BALLET.
I SEE.
YOU GAVE UP ON YOUR DREAM BECAUSE OF THAT SMALL OBSTACLE?
IT MIGHT BE A "SMALL OBSTACLE" FOR YOU...
...BUT IT WAS MY LAST CHANCE!
PLEASE KEEP IT DOWN IN HERE OR I'LL HAVE TO THROW YOU OUT.
LISTEN, ONCE YOU GIVE UP, THAT'S THE END OF THE STORY. STICK IT OUT, AND YOU'LL ALWAYS HAVE ANOTHER CHANCE.

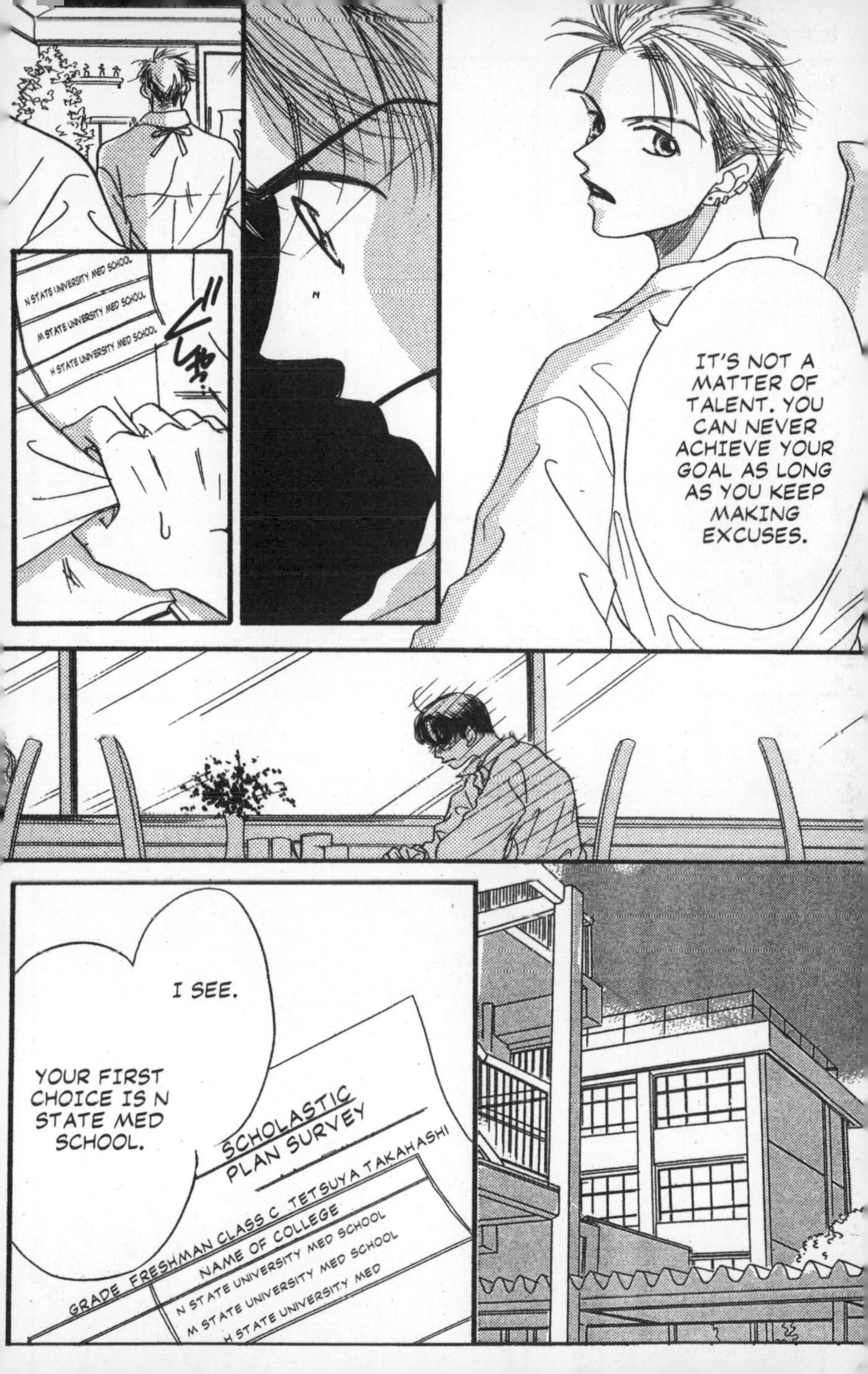
IT'S NOT A MATTER OF TALENT. YOU CAN NEVER ACHIEVE YOUR GOAL AS LONG AS YOU KEEP MAKING EXCUSES.
N STATE UNIVERSITY MED SCHOOL
M STATE UNIVERSITY MED SCHOOL
H STATE UNIVERSITY MED SCHOOL
I SEE.
YOUR FIRST CHOICE IS N STATE MED SCHOOL.
SCHOLASTIC PLAN SURVEY
GRADE FRESHMAN CLASS C TETSUYA TAKAHASHI
NAME OF COLLEGE
N STATE UNIVERSITY MED SCHOOL
M STATE UNIVERSITY MED SCHOOL
H STATE UNIVERSITY MED

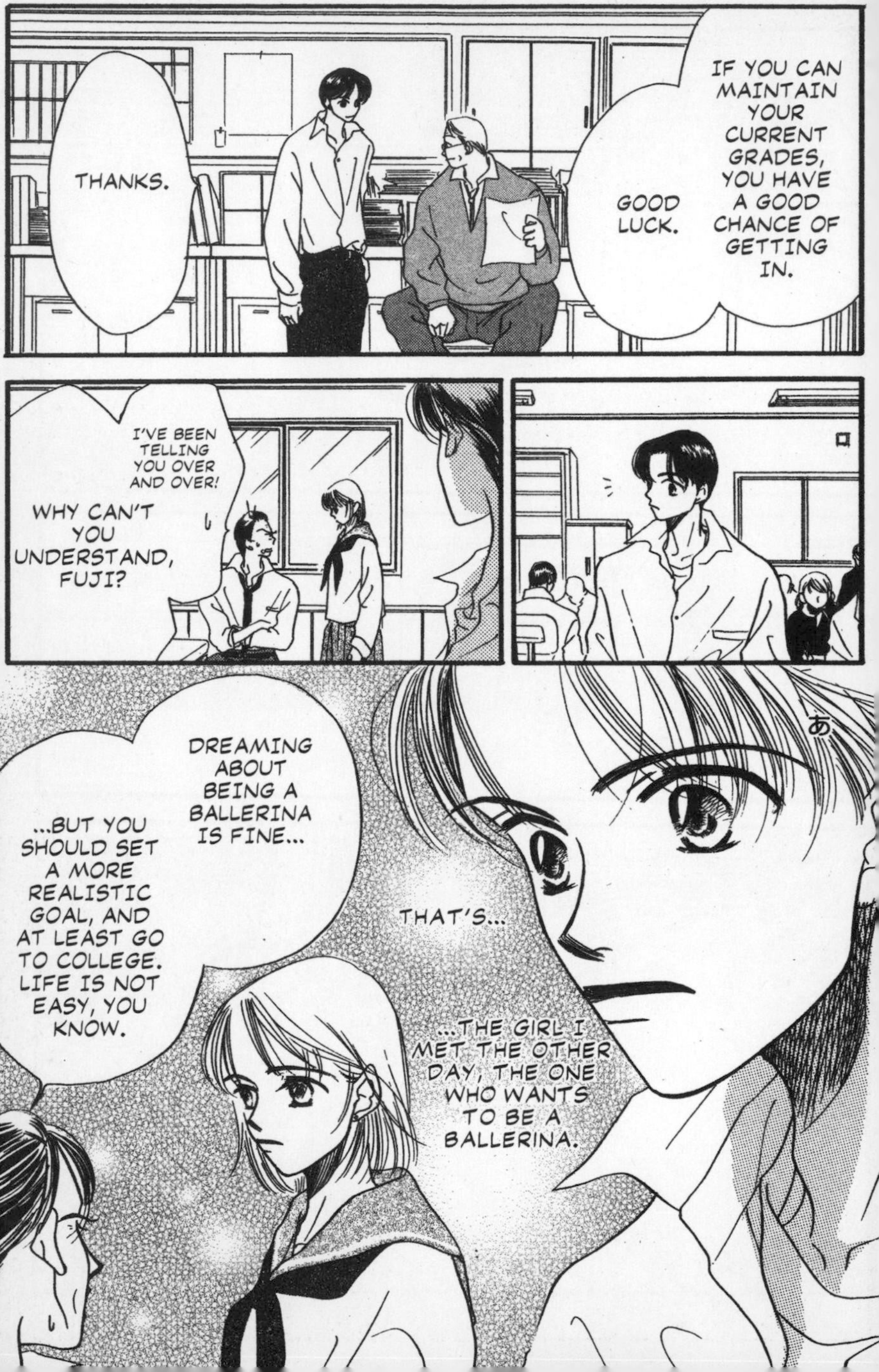
IF YOU CAN MAINTAIN YOUR CURRENT GRADES, YOU HAVE A GOOD CHANCE OF GETTING IN.
GOOD LUCK.
THANKS.
I'VE BEEN TELLING YOU OVER AND OVER!
WHY CAN'T YOU UNDERSTAND, FUJI?
あ
DREAMING ABOUT BEING A BALLERINA IS FINE...
...BUT YOU SHOULD SET A MORE REALISTIC GOAL, AND AT LEAST GO TO COLLEGE. LIFE IS NOT EASY, YOU KNOW.
THAT'S...
...THE GIRL I MET THE OTHER DAY, THE ONE WHO WANTS TO BE A BALLERINA.

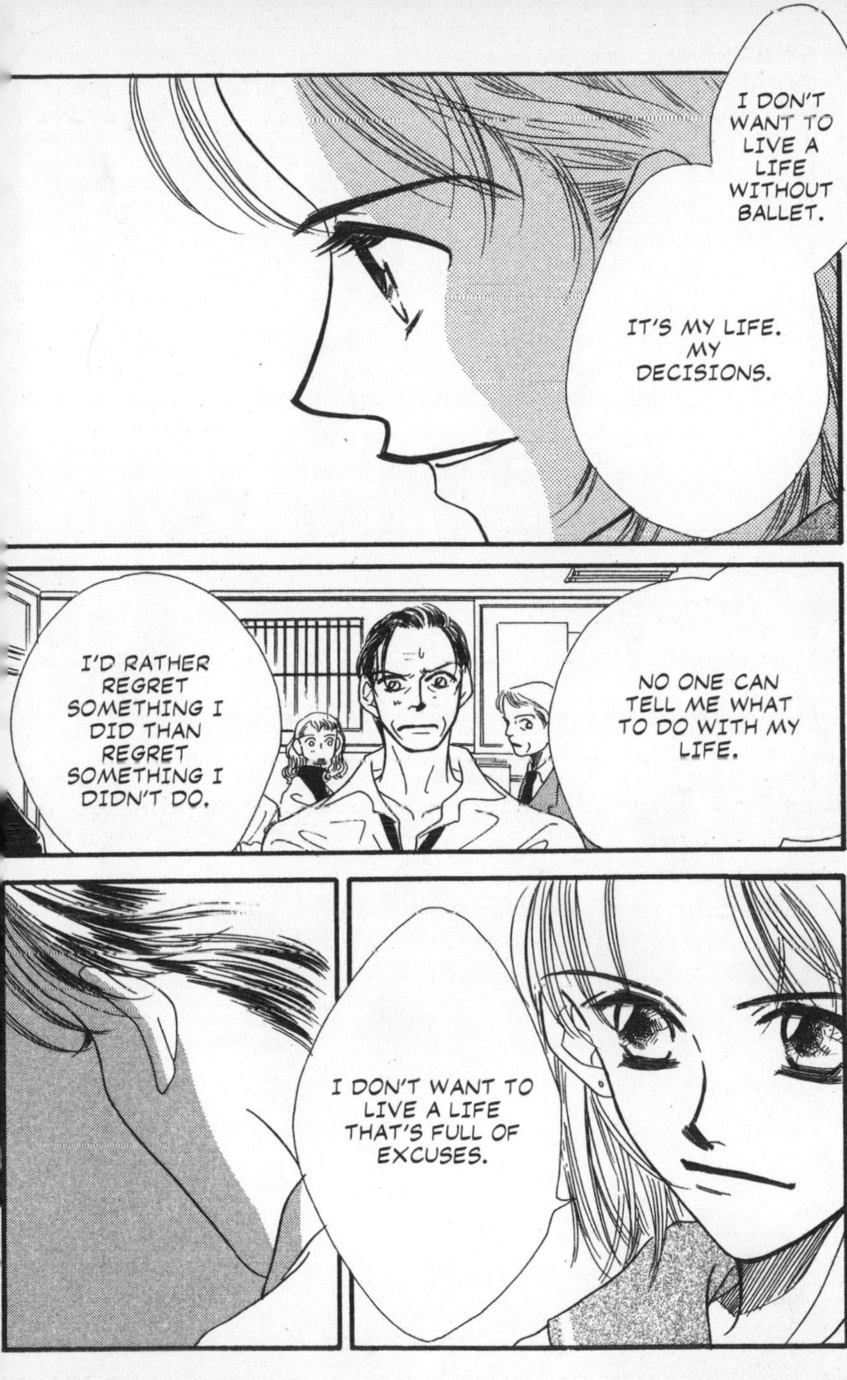
I DON'T WANT TO LIVE A LIFE WITHOUT BALLET.
IT'S MY LIFE. MY DECISIONS.
NO ONE CAN TELL ME WHAT TO DO WITH MY LIFE.
I'D RATHER REGRET SOMETHING I DID THAN REGRET SOMETHING I DIDN'T DO.
I DON'T WANT TO LIVE A LIFE THAT'S FULL OF EXCUSES.

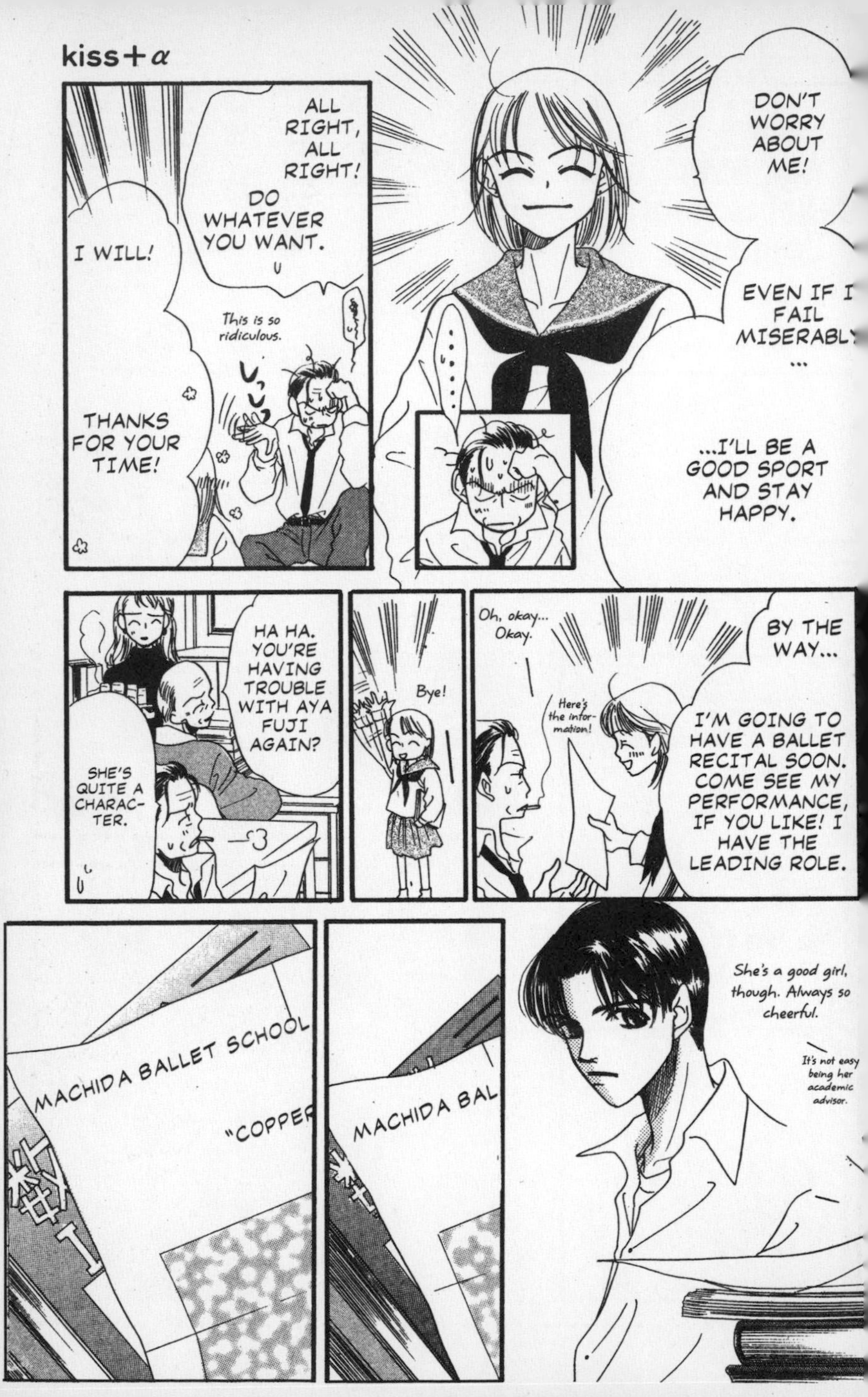
DON'T WORRY ABOUT ME!
EVEN IF I FAIL MISERABLY...
...I'LL BE A GOOD SPORT AND STAY HAPPY.
ALL RIGHT, ALL RIGHT! DO WHATEVER YOU WANT.
This is so ridiculous.
I WILL!
THANKS FOR YOUR TIME!
BY THE WAY...
I'M GOING TO HAVE A BALLET RECITAL SOON. COME SEE MY PERFORMANCE, IF YOU LIKE! I HAVE THE LEADING ROLE.
Here's the information!
Oh, okay... Okay.
Bye!
HA HA. YOU'RE HAVING TROUBLE WITH AYA FUJI AGAIN?
SHE'S QUITE A CHARACTER.
She's a good girl, though. Always so cheerful.
It's not easy being her academic advisor.
MACHIDA BAL
MACHIDA BALLET SCHOOL
"COPPER

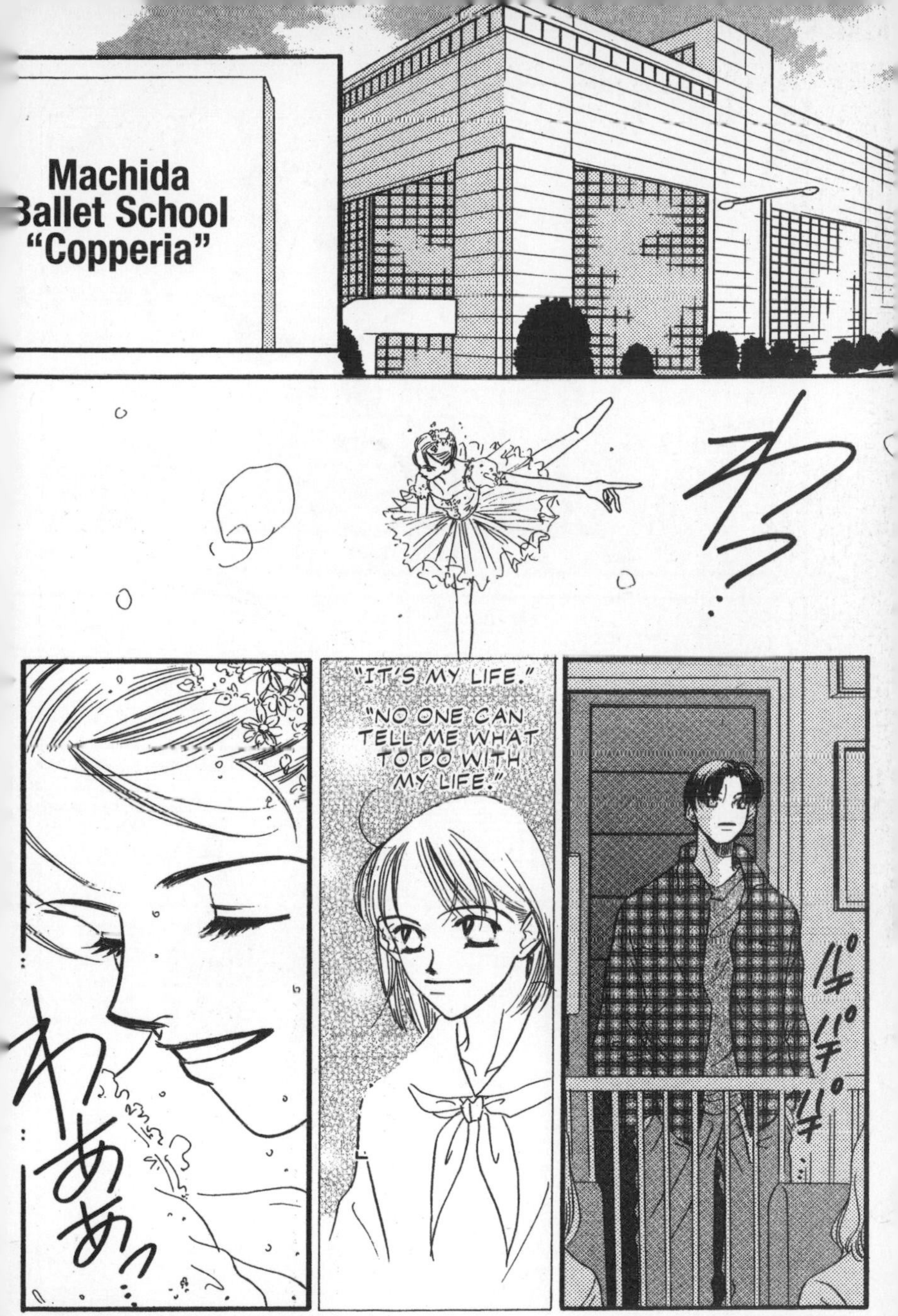
Machida Ballet School "Copperia"
わっ
パチパチパチ
"IT'S MY LIFE."
"NO ONE CAN TELL ME WHAT TO DO WITH MY LIFE."
わああっ

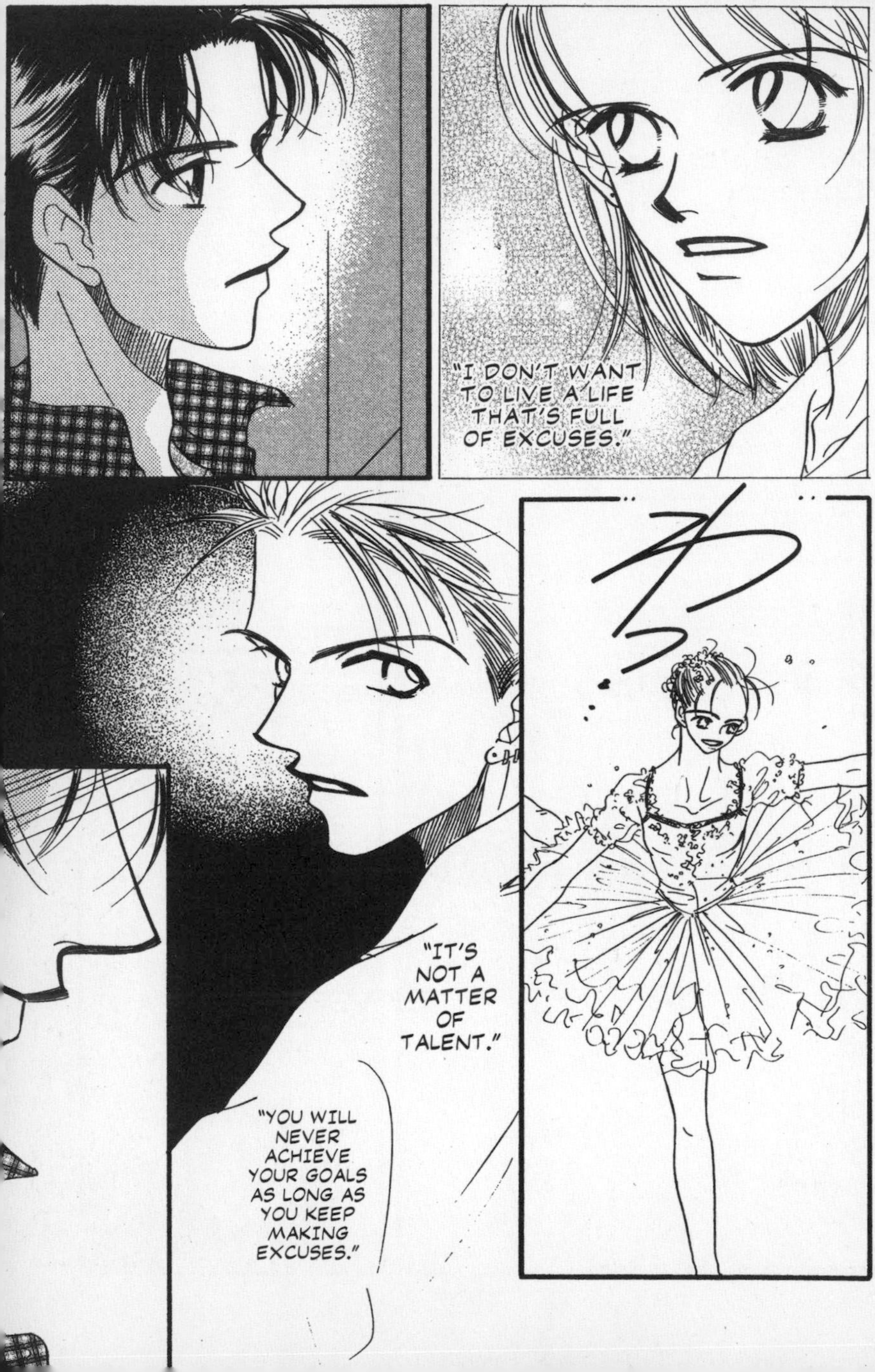
"I DON'T WANT TO LIVE A LIFE THAT'S FULL OF EXCUSES."
"IT'S NOT A MATTER OF TALENT."
"YOU WILL NEVER ACHIEVE YOUR GOALS AS LONG AS YOU KEEP MAKING EXCUSES."

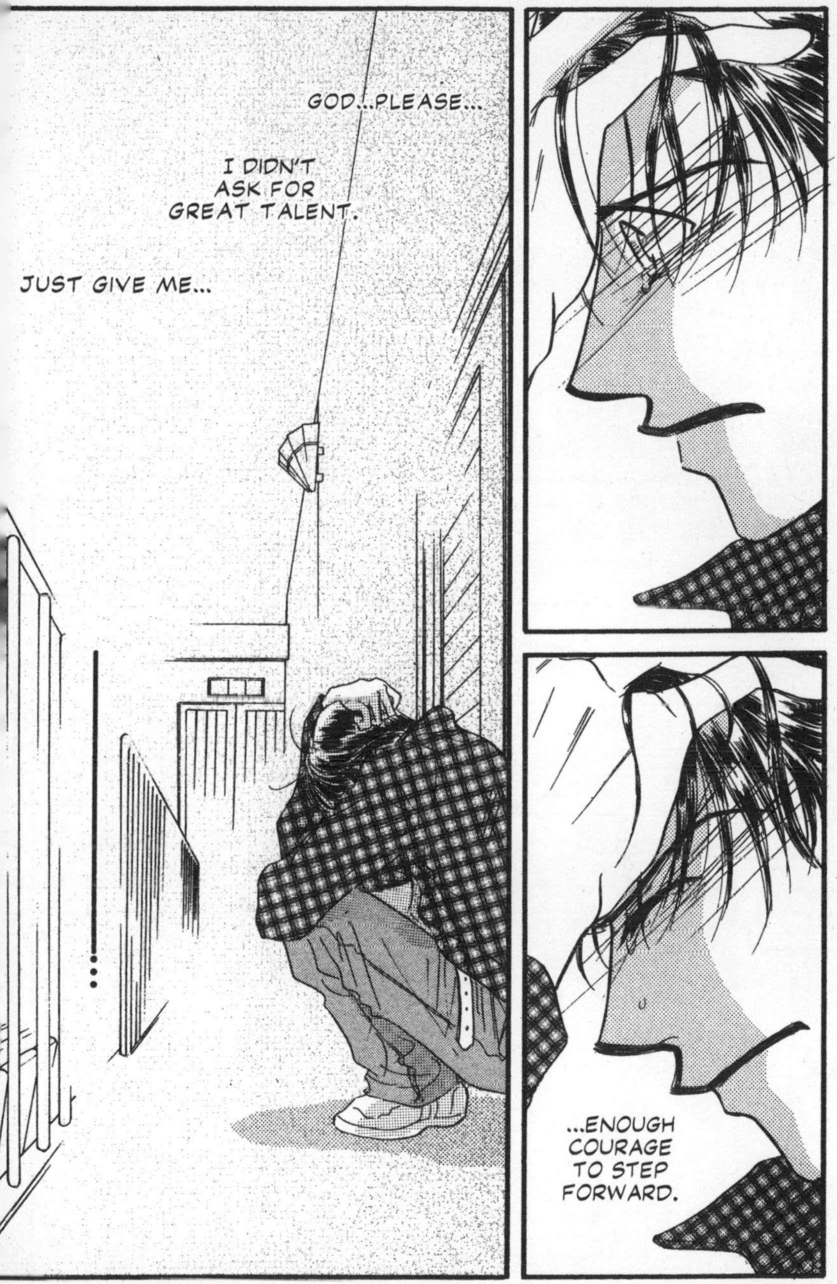
GOD...PLEASE...
I DIDN'T ASK FOR GREAT TALENT.
JUST GIVE ME...
.....
...ENOUGH COURAGE TO STEP FORWARD.

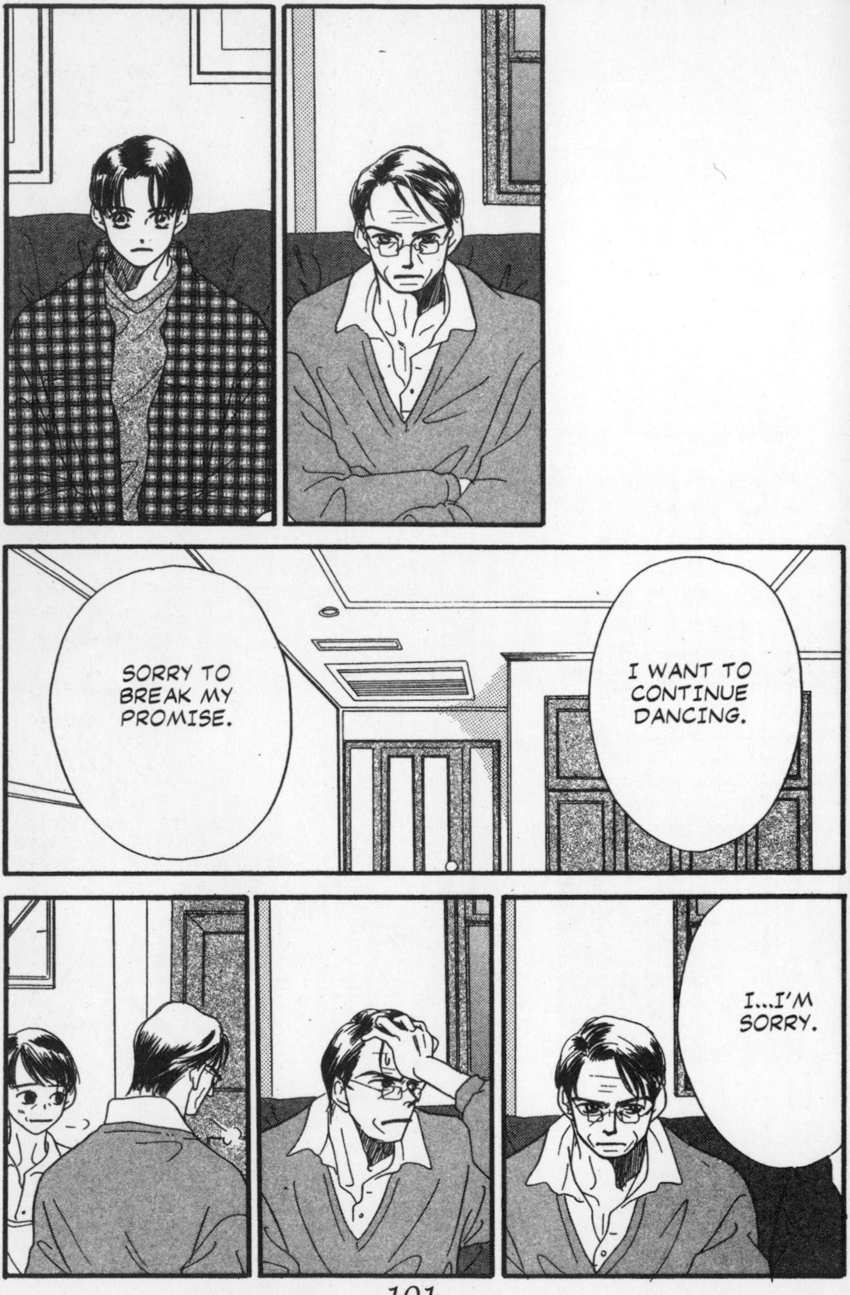
I WANT TO CONTINUE DANCING.
SORRY TO BREAK MY PROMISE.
I...I'M SORRY.

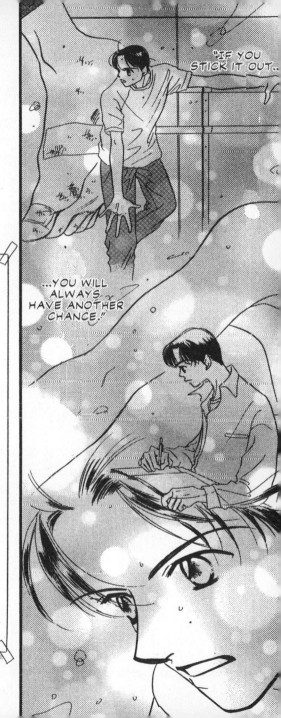

"IF YOU STICK IT OUT..

...YOU WILL ALWAYS HAVE ANOTHER CHANCE."

I WON'T GIVE UP!

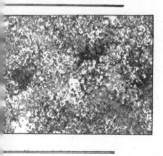

COOL
MEMBER WANTED
AUDITION DATE
APPLICANTS MUST
VE AT LEAST 5 YEARS
BALLET EXPERIENCE
ALE APPLICANTS ONLY

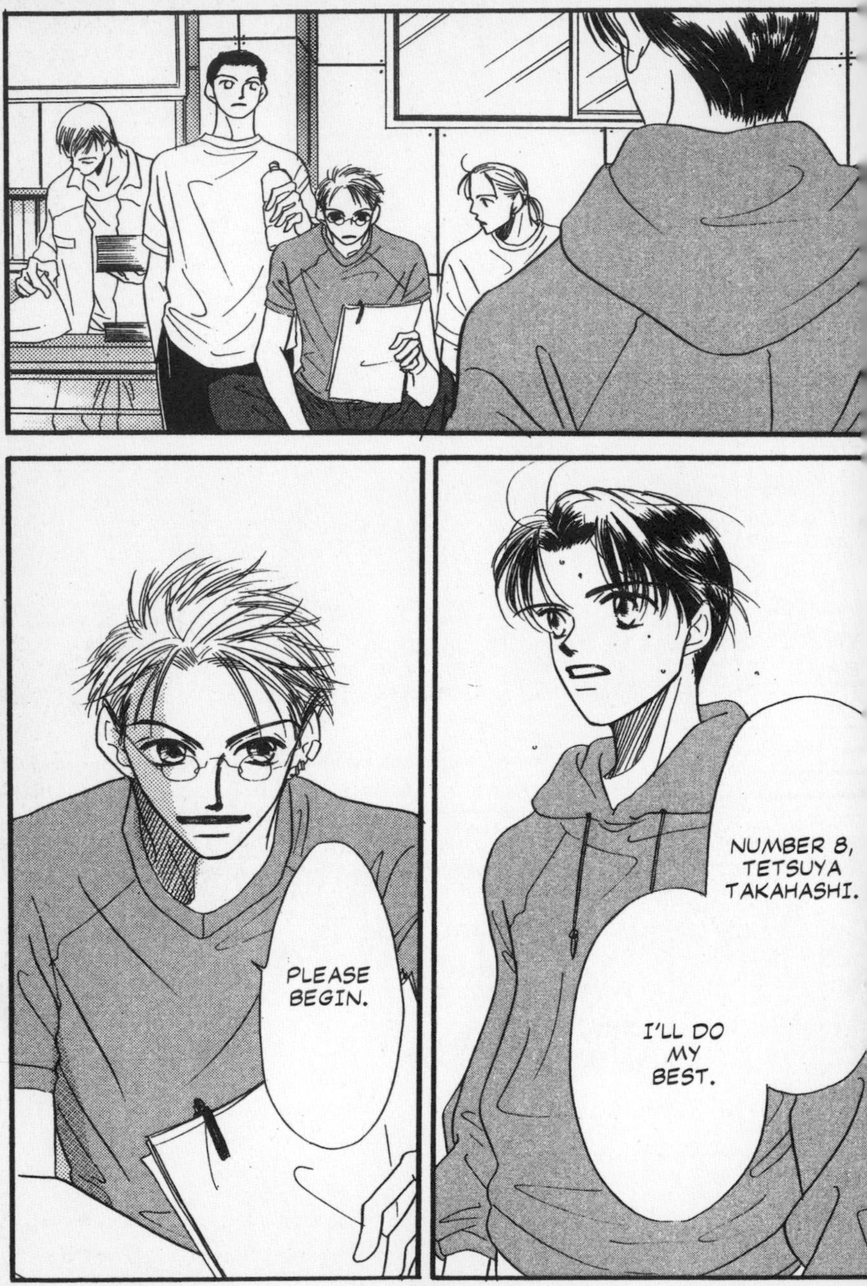
NUMBER 8, TETSUYA TAKAHASHI.
I'LL DO MY BEST.
PLEASE BEGIN.

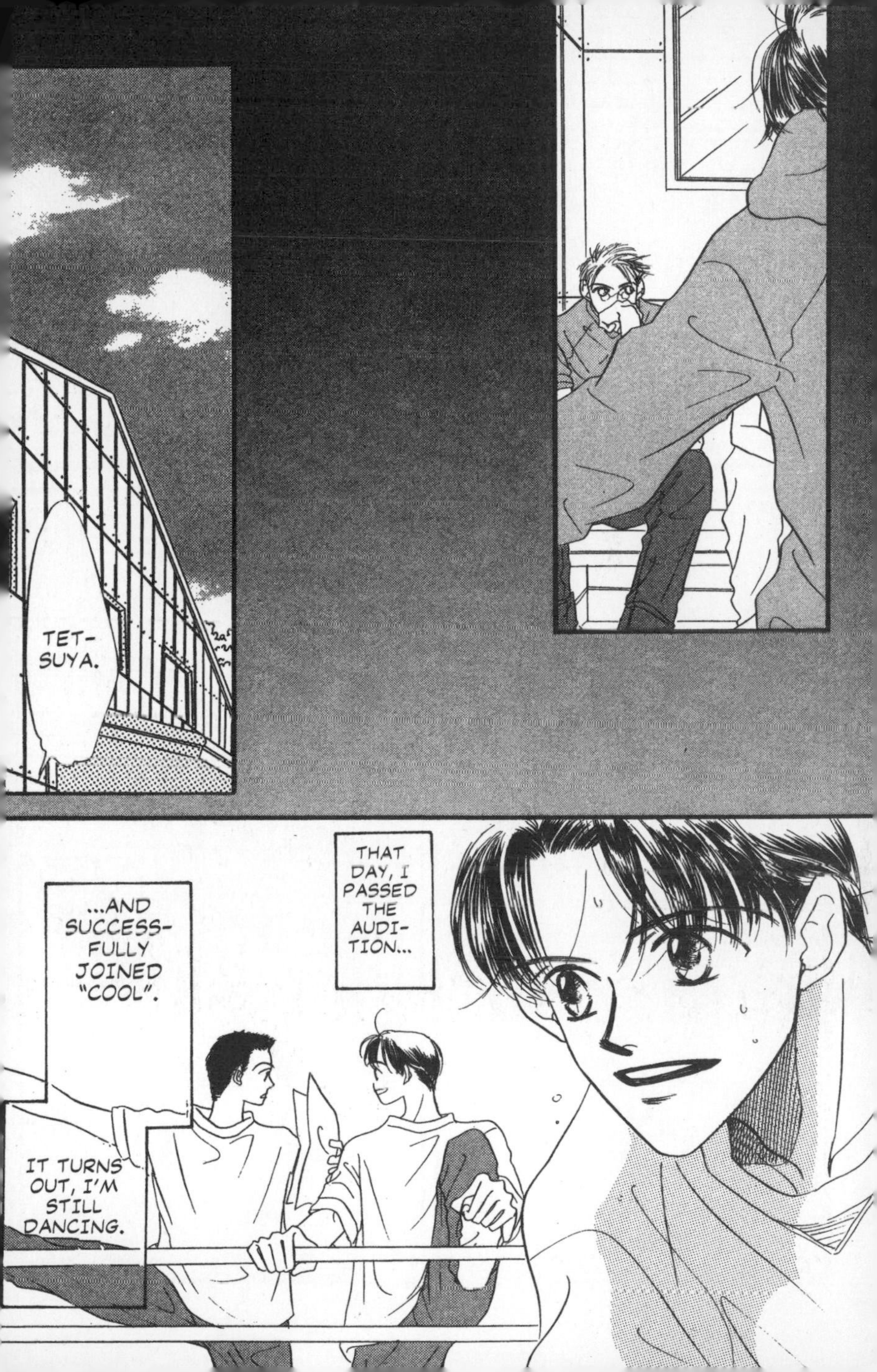
TET-SUYA.
THAT DAY, I PASSED THE AUDI-TION...
...AND SUCCESS-FULLY JOINED "COOL".
IT TURNS OUT, I'M STILL DANCING.

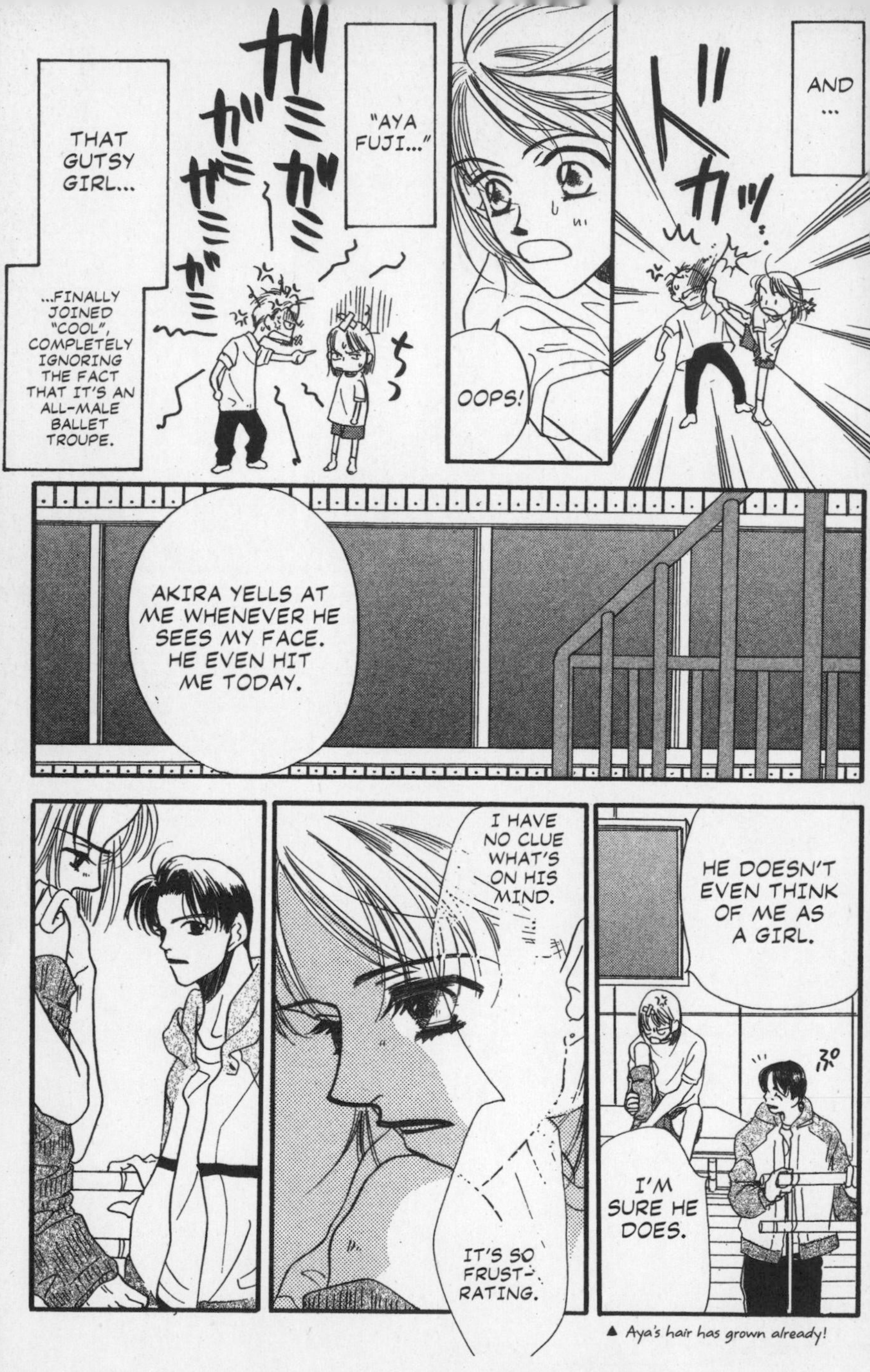
AND ...
ドカッ
OOPS!
"AYA FUJI..."
ガミガミ
ガミガミ
ガミガミ
THAT GUTSY GIRL...
...FINALLY JOINED "COOL", COMPLETELY IGNORING THE FACT THAT IT'S AN ALL-MALE BALLET TROUPE.
ちっ
AKIRA YELLS AT ME WHENEVER HE SEES MY FACE. HE EVEN HIT ME TODAY.
HE DOESN'T EVEN THINK OF ME AS A GIRL.
I'M SURE HE DOES.
I HAVE NO CLUE WHAT'S ON HIS MIND.
IT'S SO FRUST-RATING.

▲ Aya's hair has grown already!

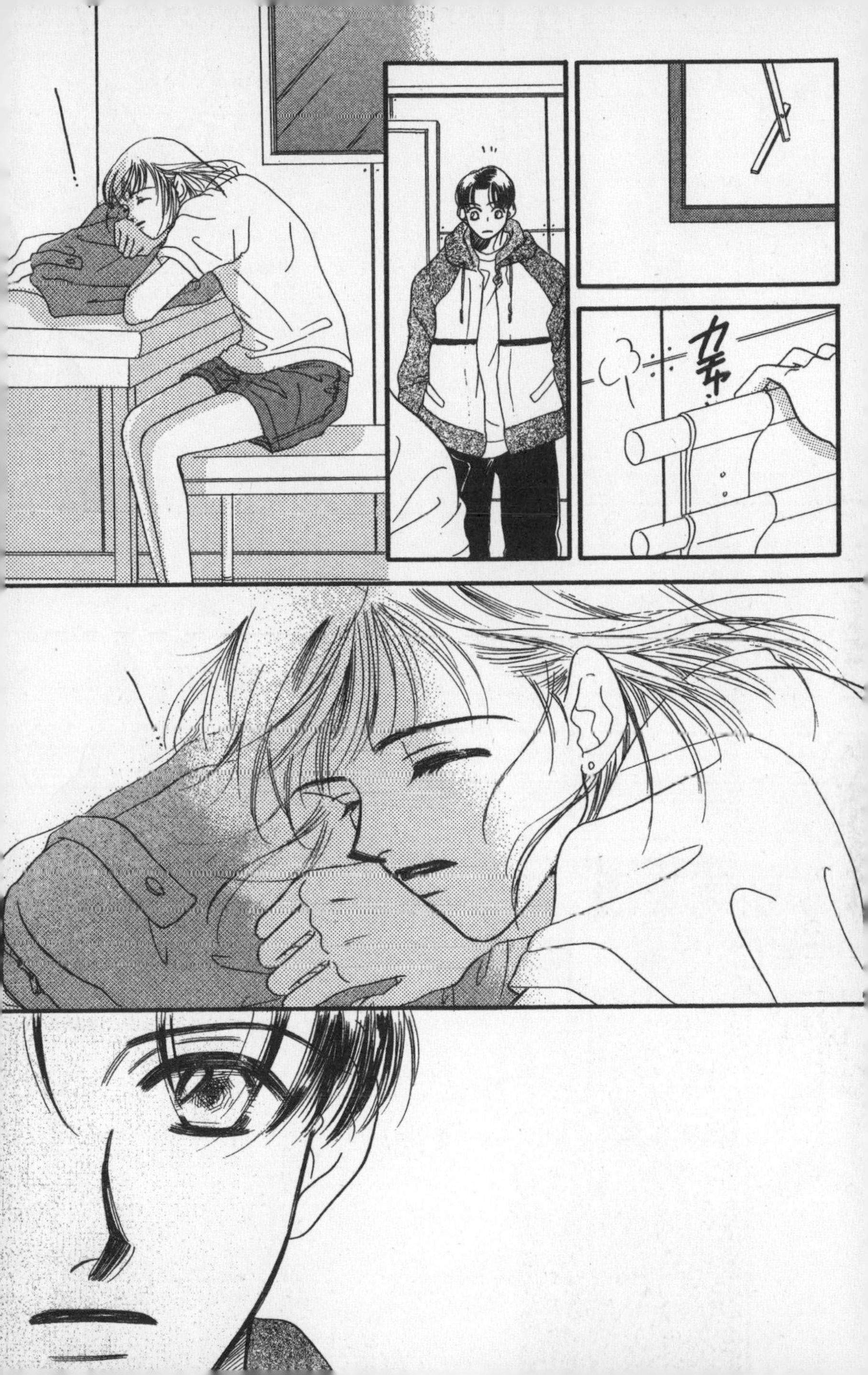
カチャ

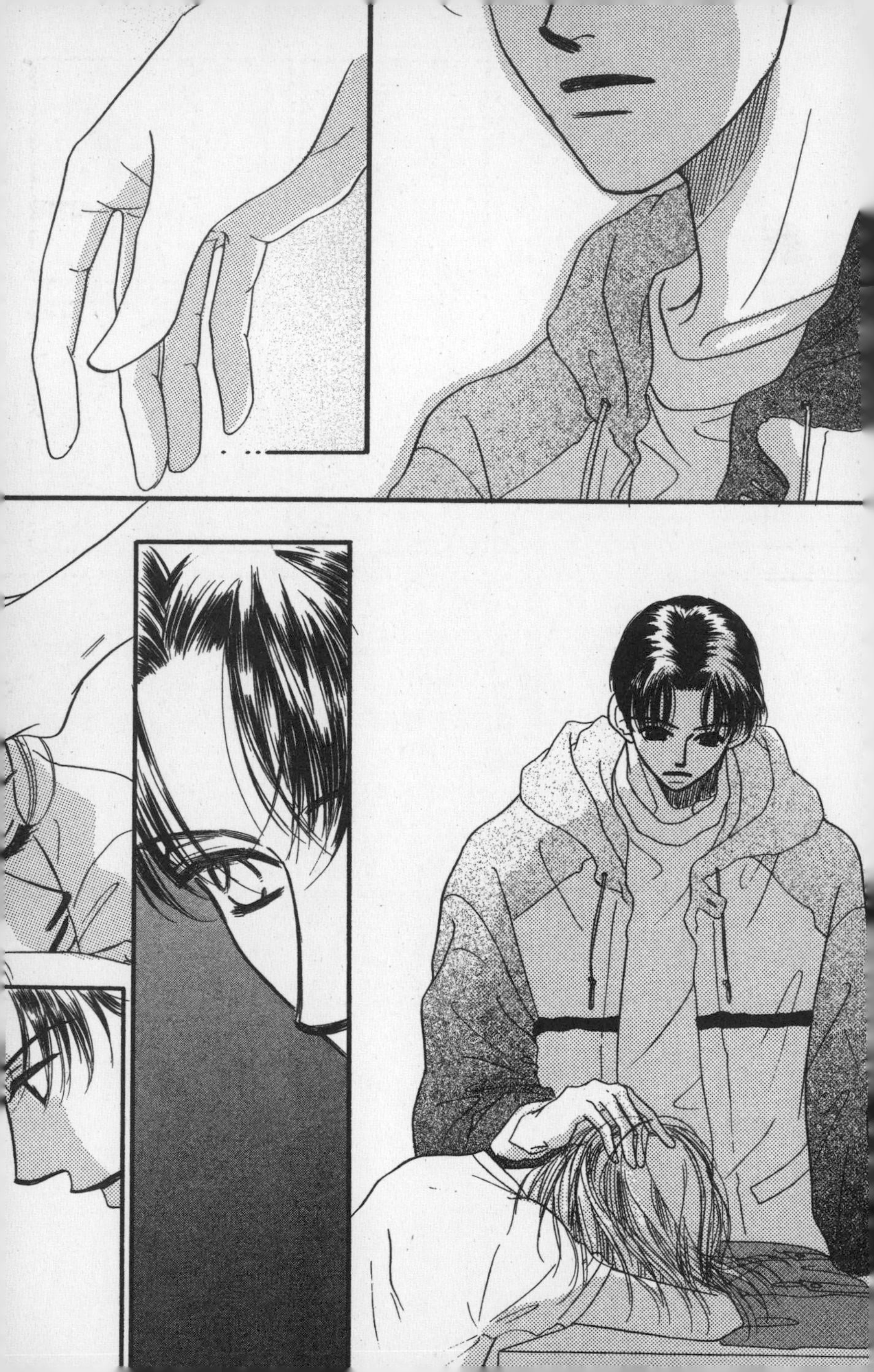
...

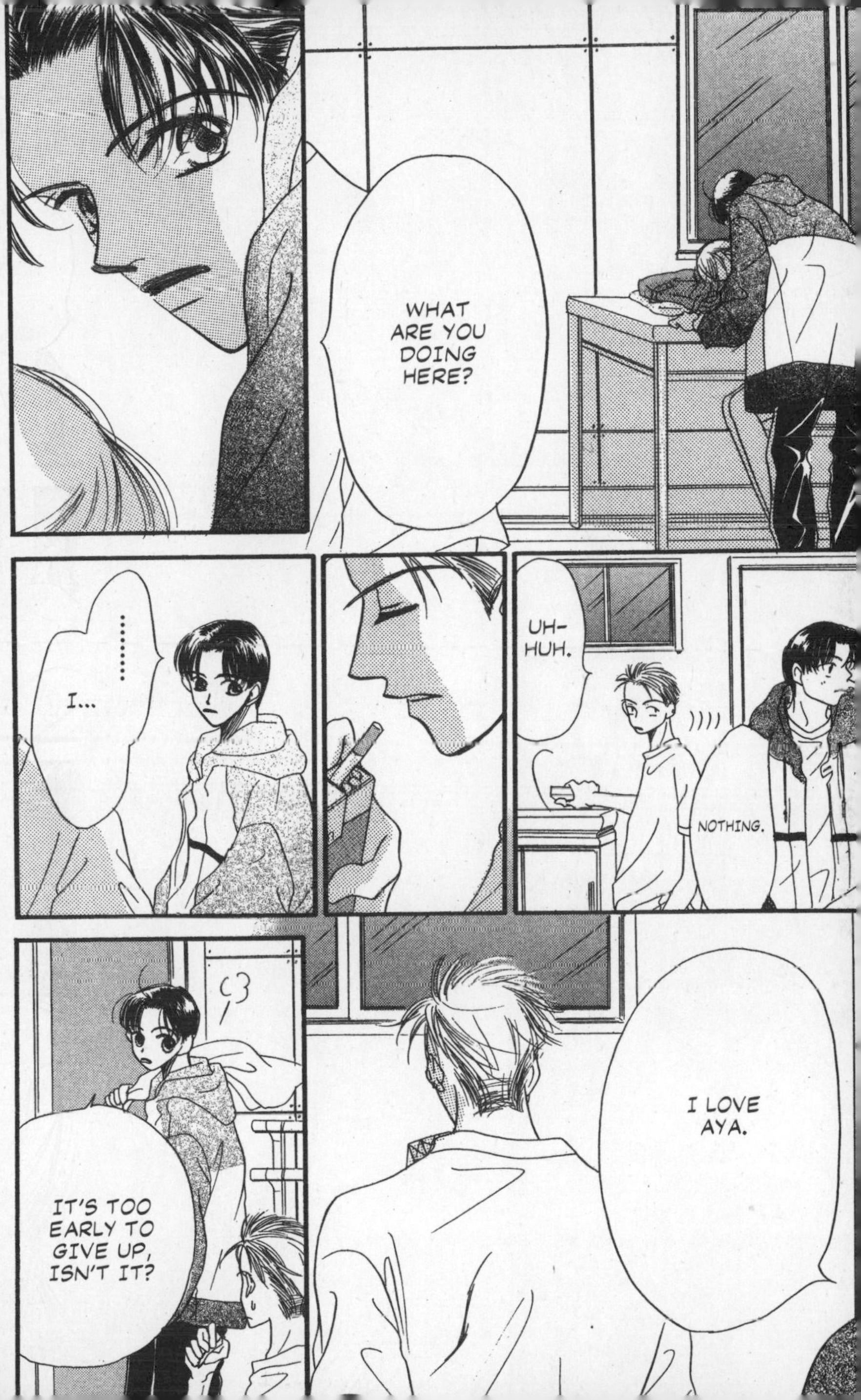
WHAT ARE YOU DOING HERE?
UH-HUH.
NOTHING.
......
I...
I LOVE AYA.
IT'S TOO EARLY TO GIVE UP, ISN'T IT?

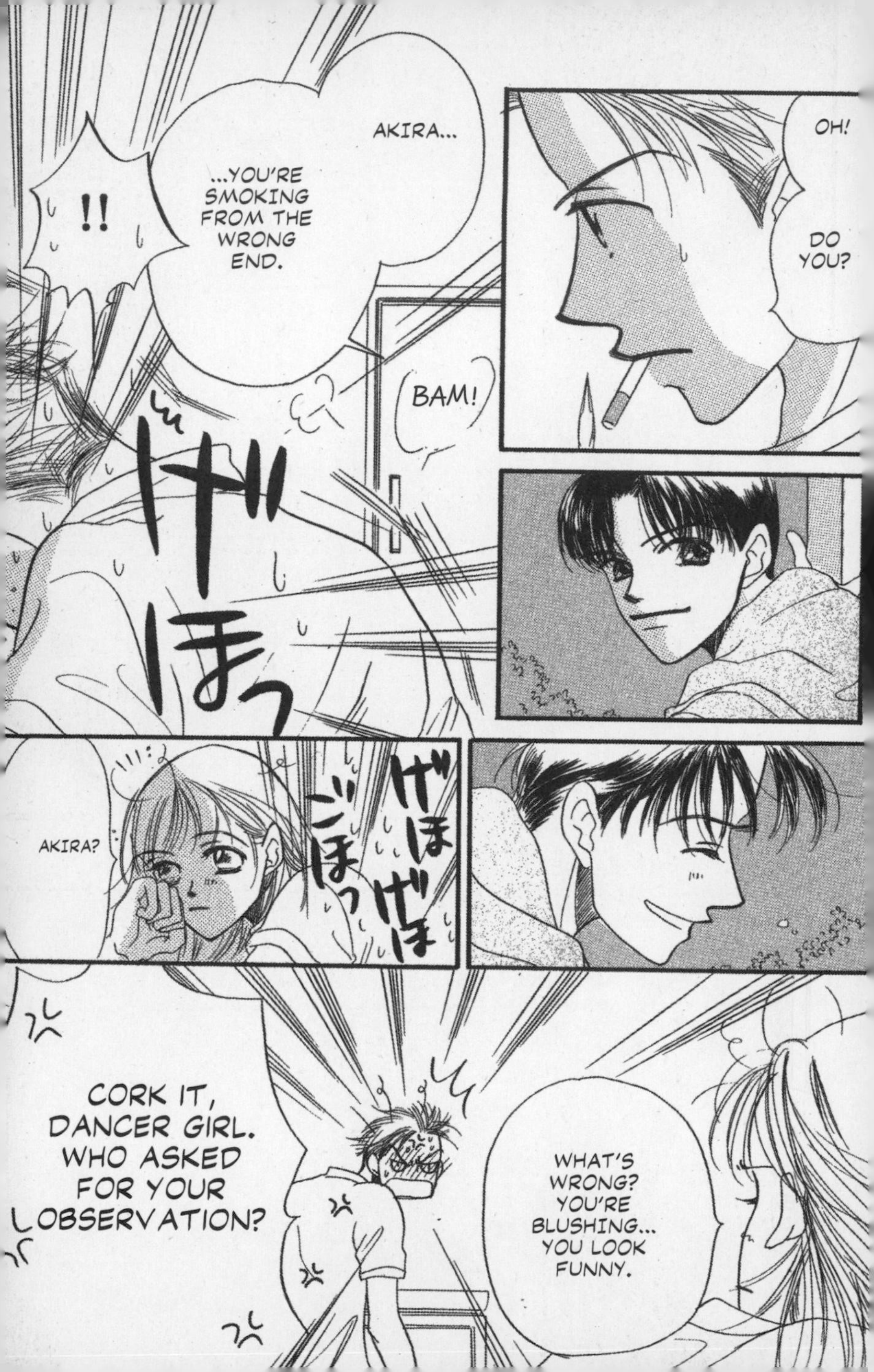
OH!
DO YOU?
AKIRA...
...YOU'RE SMOKING FROM THE WRONG END.
BAM!
!!
げほっ
AKIRA?
げほげほ
ごほっ
WHAT'S WRONG? YOU'RE BLUSHING... YOU LOOK FUNNY.
CORK IT, DANCER GIRL. WHO ASKED FOR YOUR OBSERVATION?

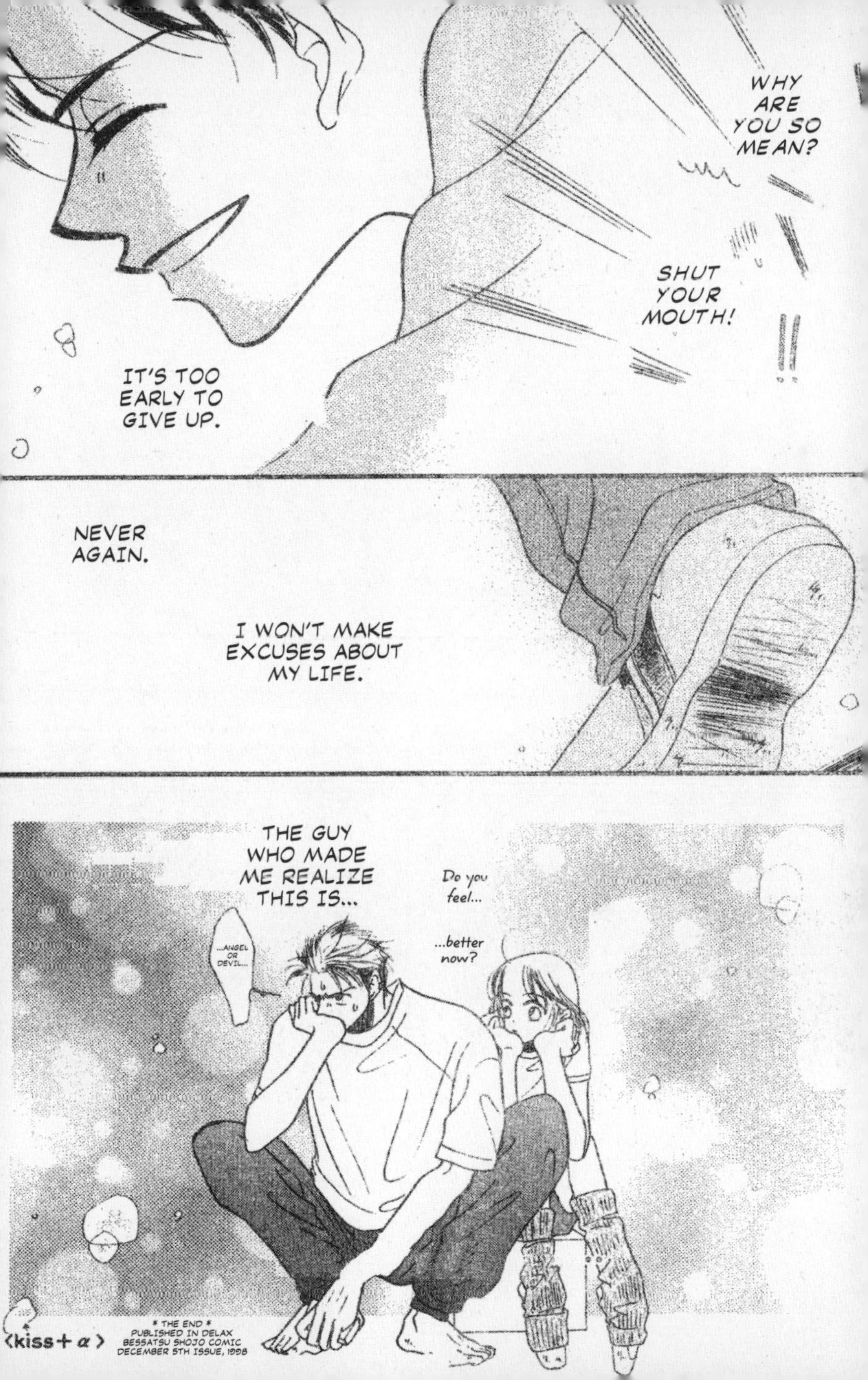
WHY ARE YOU SO MEAN?
SHUT YOUR MOUTH!
IT'S TOO EARLY TO GIVE UP.
NEVER AGAIN.
I WON'T MAKE EXCUSES ABOUT MY LIFE.
THE GUY WHO MADE ME REALIZE THIS IS...
Do you feel...
...better now?
...ANGEL OR DEVIL...
* THE END *
PUBLISHED IN DELAX BESSATSU SHOJO COMIC DECEMBER 5TH ISSUE, 1998
<kiss+α>

Land of Happiness

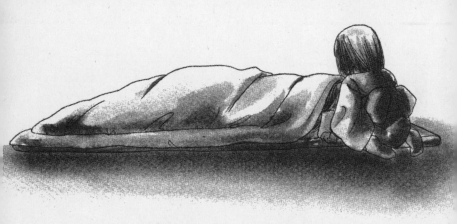

"SOME DAY YOU WILL MEET
SOMEONE SPECIAL AND HE WILL
TAKE YOU TO THE LAND OF
HAPPINESS." AFTER THOSE WORDS,
MY MOM DREW HER LAST BREATH.

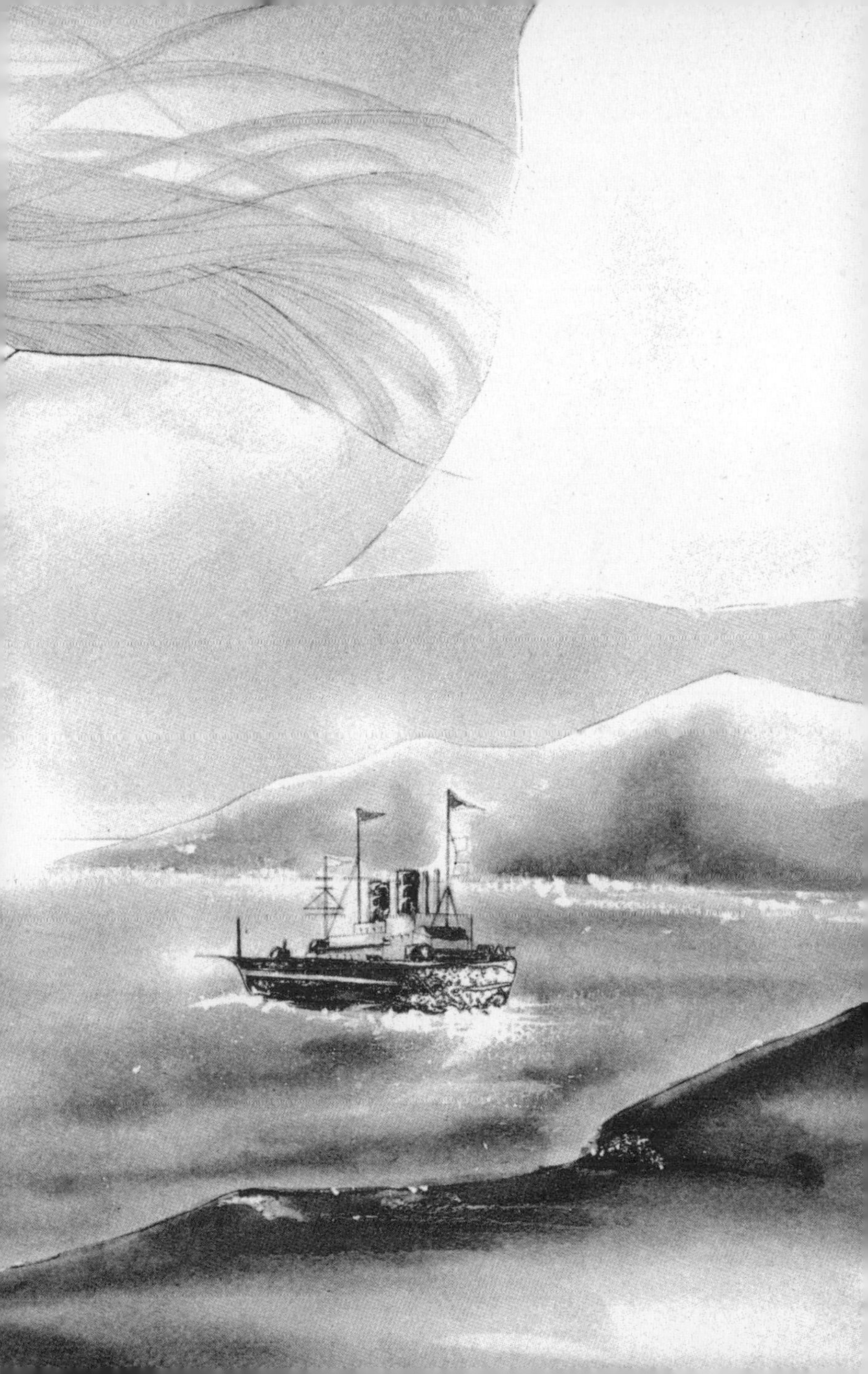

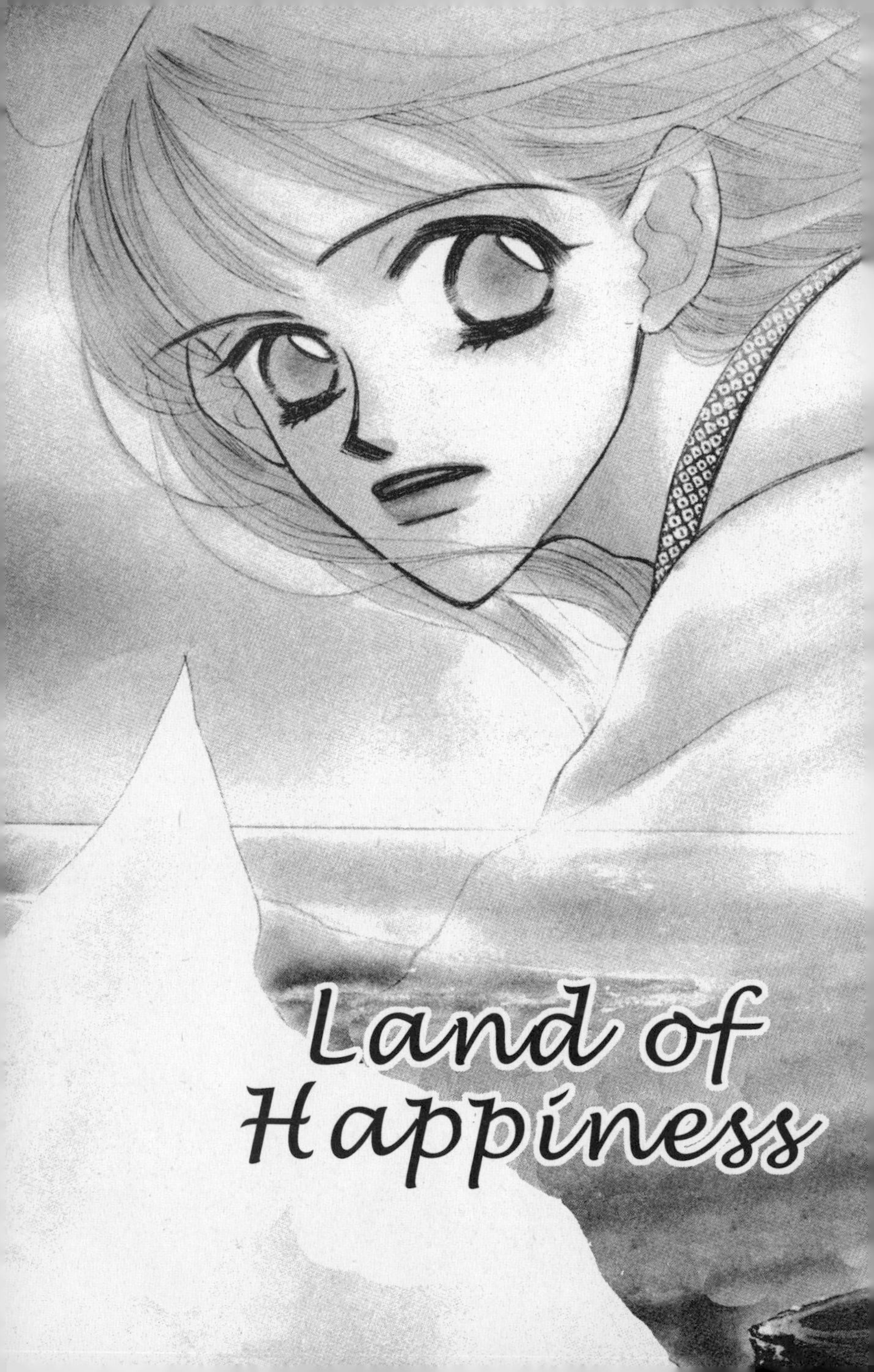
Land of
Happiness

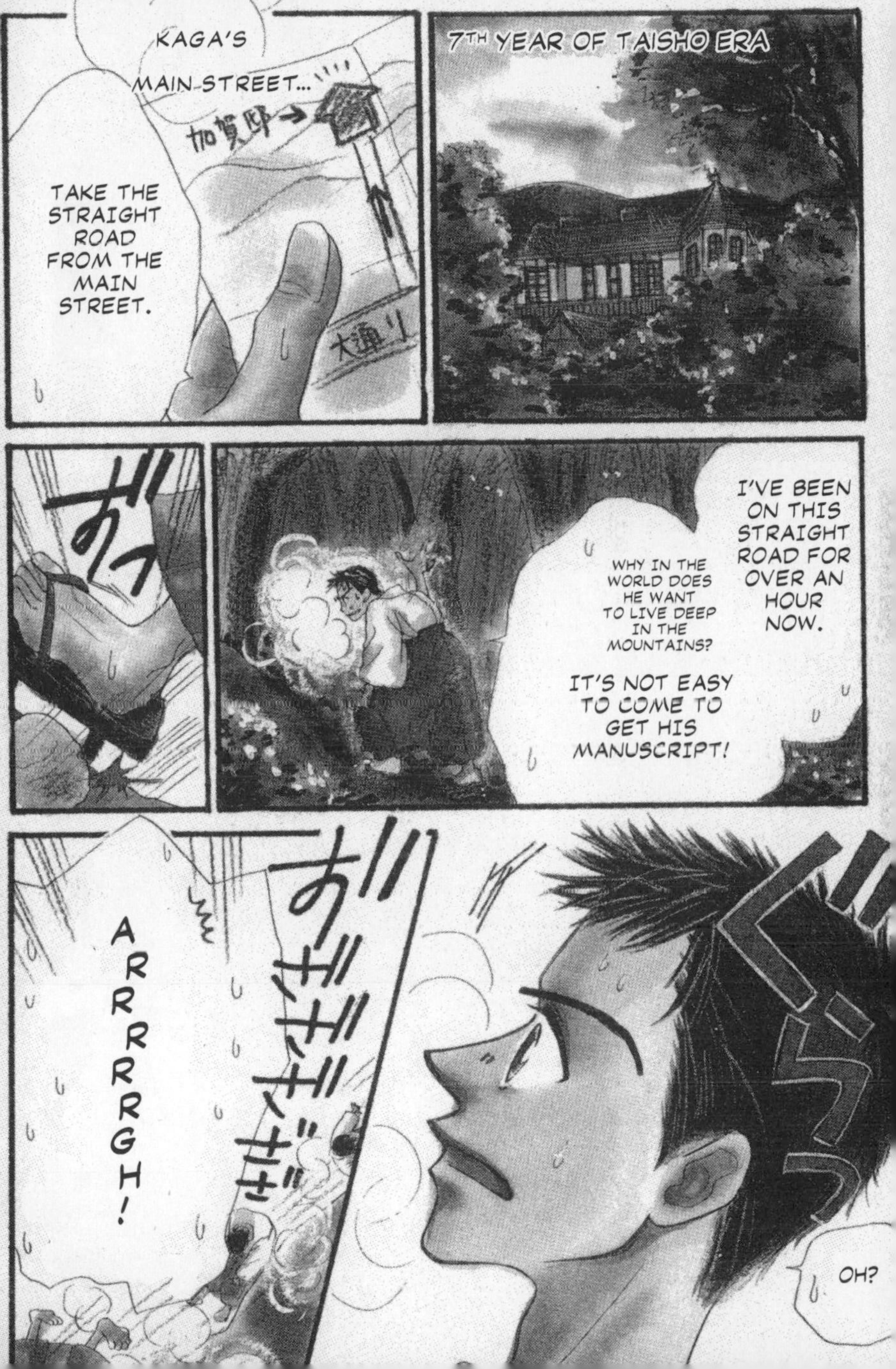
7TH YEAR OF TAISHO ERA
KAGA'S MAIN-STREET...
加賀邸→
TAKE THE STRAIGHT ROAD FROM THE MAIN STREET.
大通り
I'VE BEEN ON THIS STRAIGHT ROAD FOR OVER AN HOUR NOW.
WHY IN THE WORLD DOES HE WANT TO LIVE DEEP IN THE MOUNTAINS?
IT'S NOT EASY TO COME TO GET HIS MANUSCRIPT!
OH?
ARRRRGH!

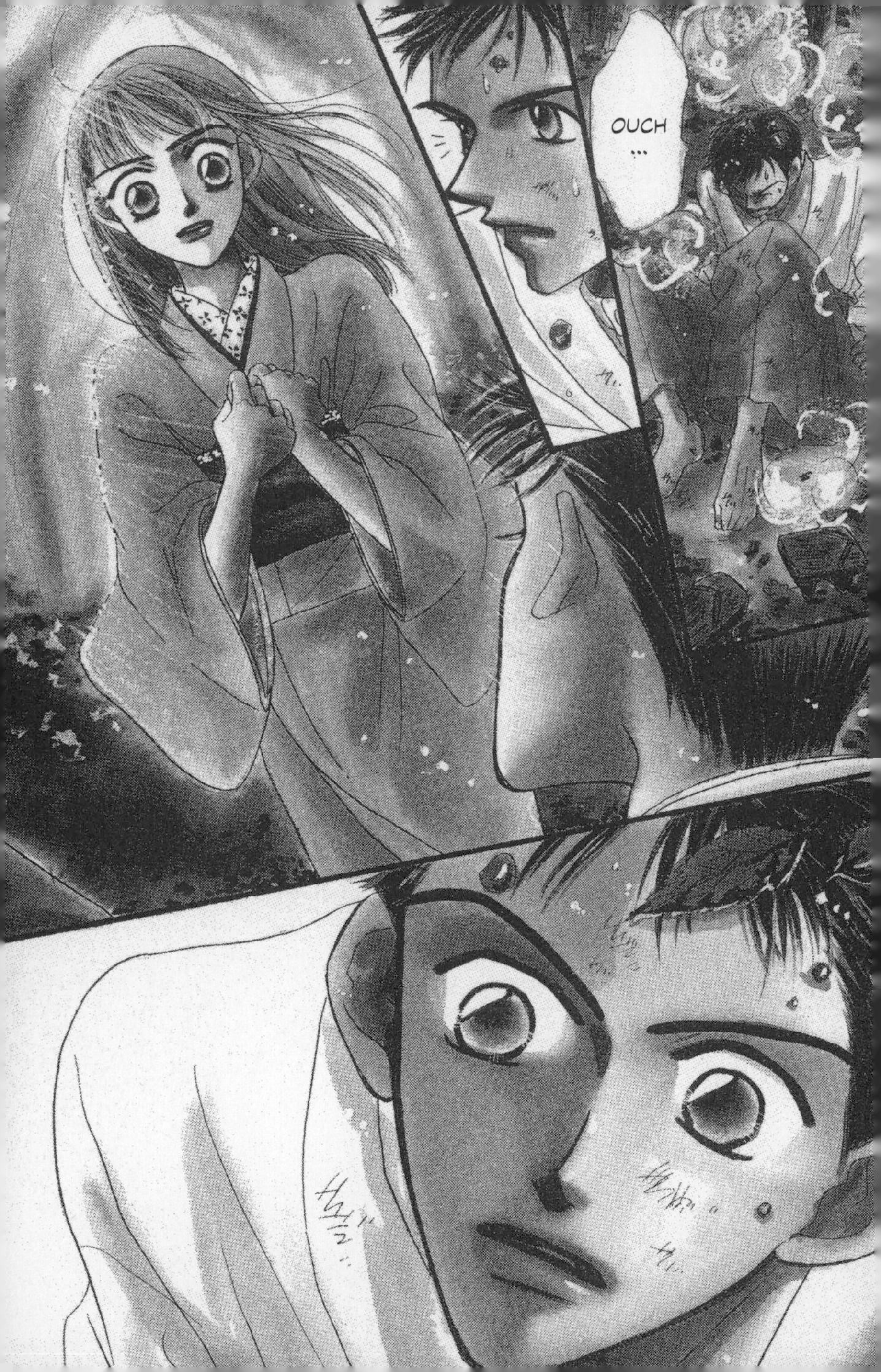
OUCH ...

「Kiss + α」のこと。

◆ About "Kiss + alpha" ◆

When I got a job to write a side story for Forbidden Dance, I first thought about writing a story about Akira's past. Then I realized 40 pages isn't long enough to write about such a deep character as Akira. I decided on a story about Tetsuya. His monologue sounds very personal. Tetsuya definitely loves Aya, but his feelings for Aya were never clearly depicted in Forbidden Dance. It's good that I could make his love for Aya clear to the reader in this side story. He is a very shy character, after all. What Akira is to Aya, Aya is to Tetsuya. Get it?

◆ About "Land of Happiness ◆

It was not an easy task to write an 80-page story in a short period of time. I had a story already thought out, so the only thing I had to do was "naming" (allocating frames, inserting lines in the bubbles etc. In a nutshell, it's a process of writing the story as manga). I thought it was going to be an easy job, but I had the hardest time to make the story fit into exactly 80 pages. I ended up making a lot of changes and had to make the story shorter. Shiro is my typical image of a "good boy." He is honest and sweet. It's always enjoyable to write a character like him. What about Kaga, you ask? I don't know what to say!

116

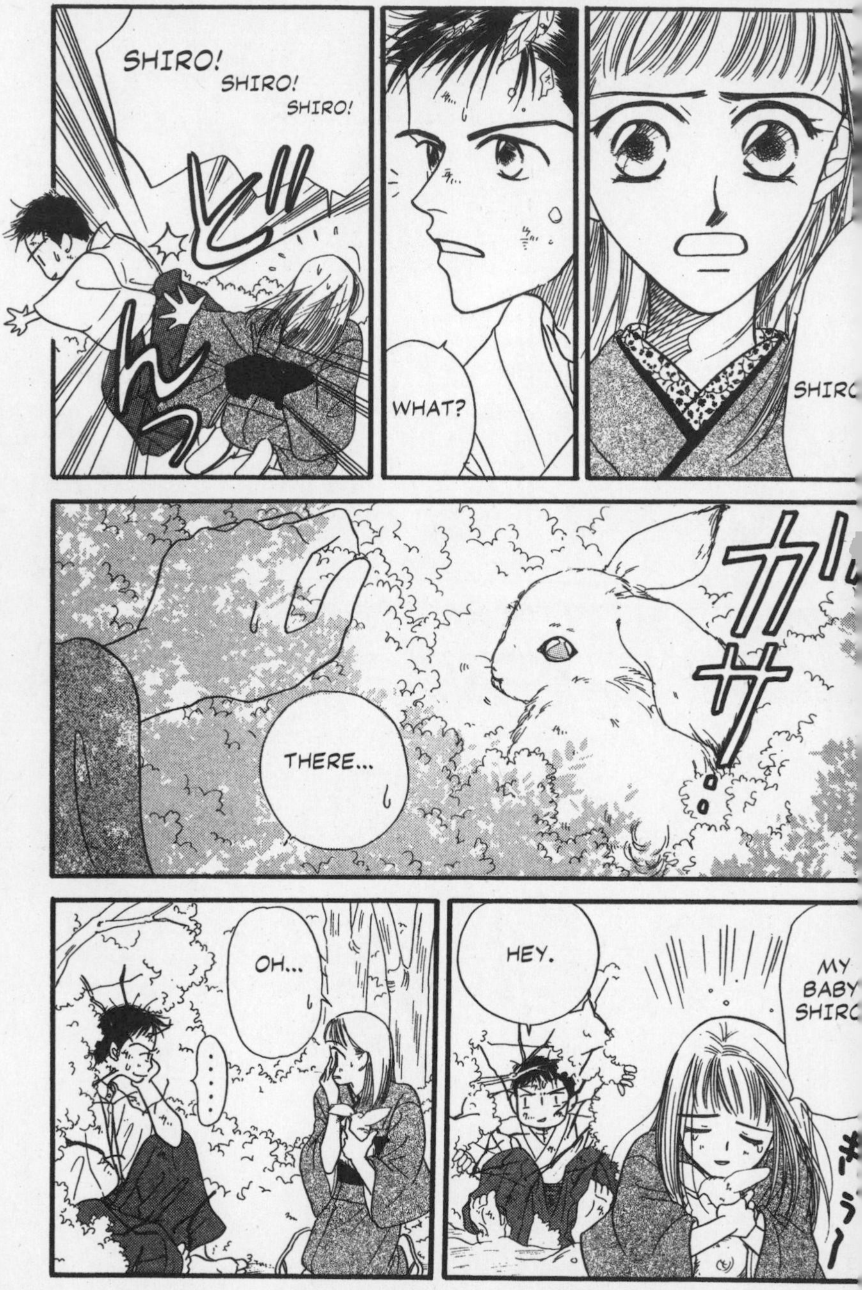
SHIRO
WHAT?
SHIRO!
SHIRO!
SHIRO!
THERE...
MY BABY SHIRO
HEY.
OH...
......

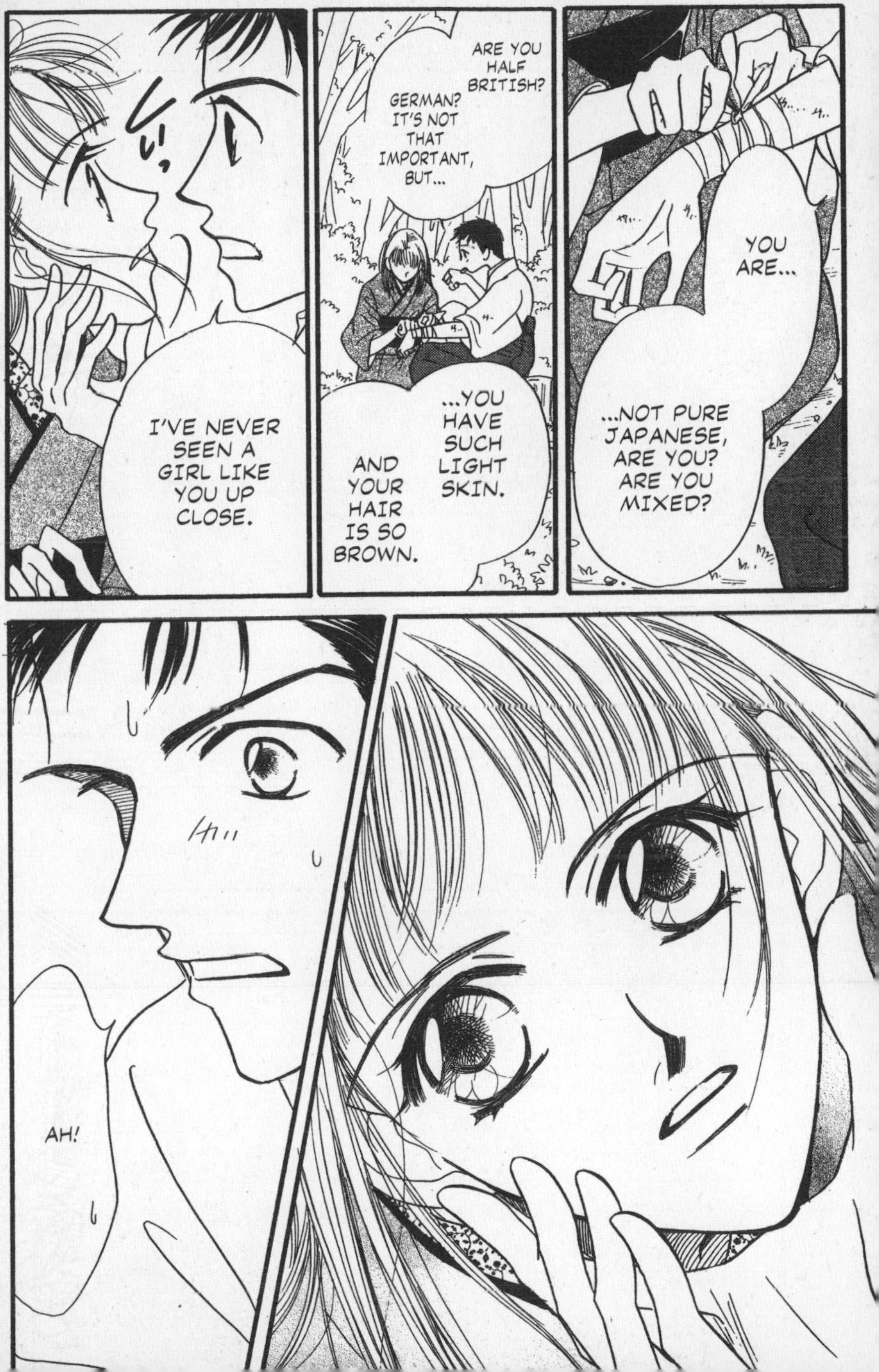
YOU ARE...
...NOT PURE JAPANESE, ARE YOU? ARE YOU MIXED?
ARE YOU HALF BRITISH?
GERMAN? IT'S NOT THAT IMPORTANT, BUT...
...YOU HAVE SUCH LIGHT SKIN.
AND YOUR HAIR IS SO BROWN.
I'VE NEVER SEEN A GIRL LIKE YOU UP CLOSE.
AH!

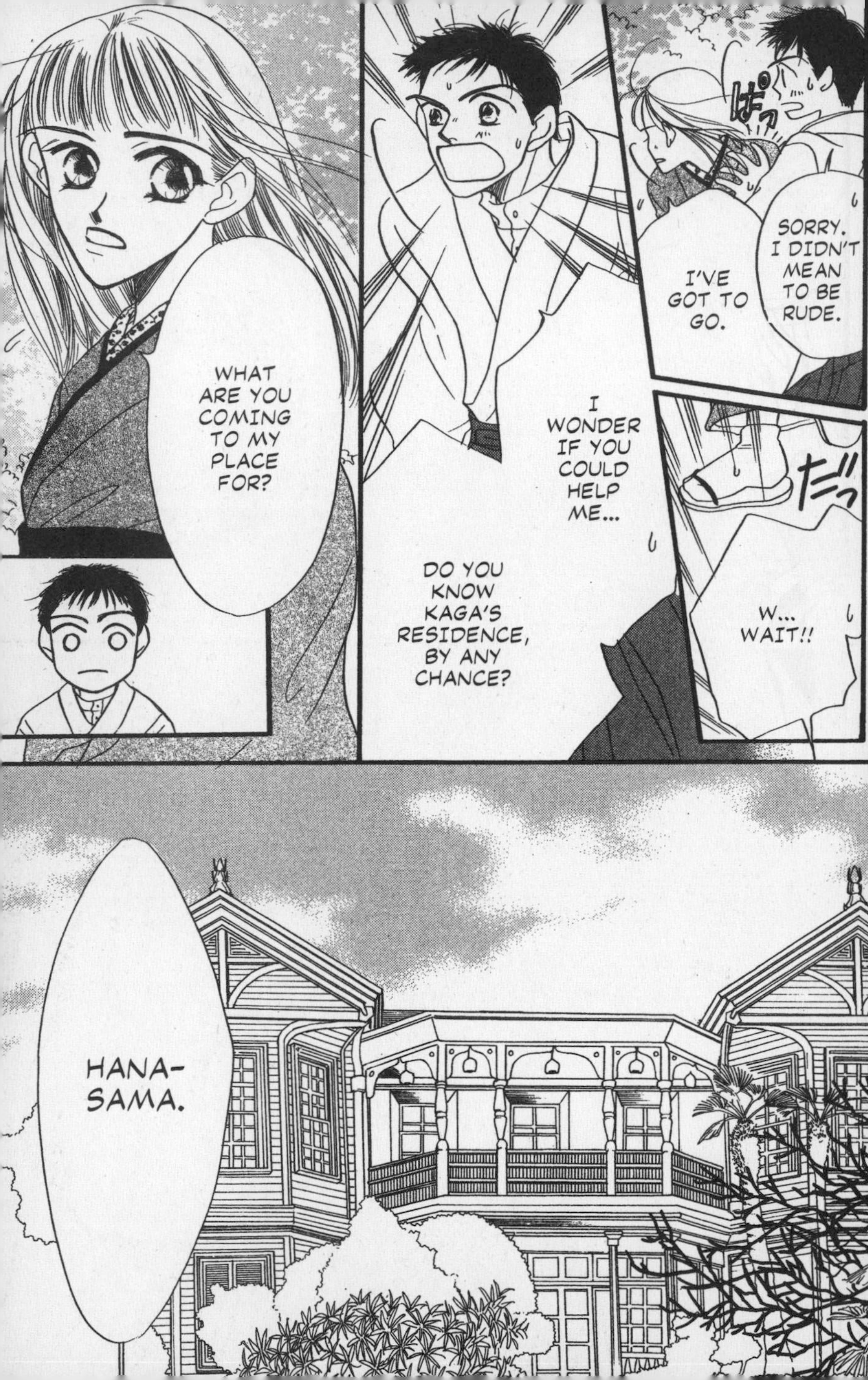
I WONDER IF YOU COULD HELP ME...
DO YOU KNOW KAGA'S RESIDENCE, BY ANY CHANCE?
WHAT ARE YOU COMING TO MY PLACE FOR?
ぱっ
SORRY. I DIDN'T MEAN TO BE RUDE.
I'VE GOT TO GO.
だっ
W... WAIT!!
HANA-SAMA.

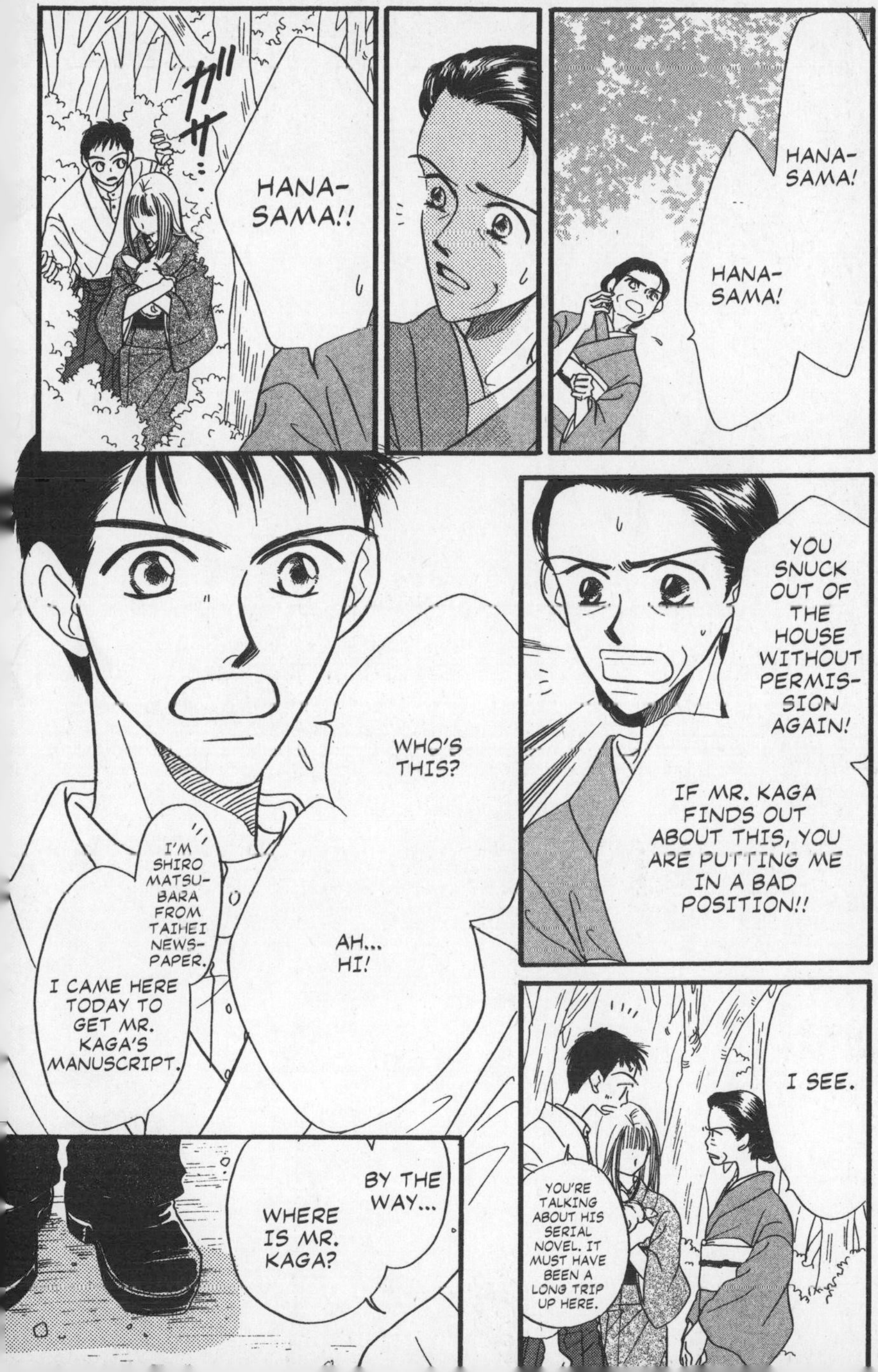
HANA-SAMA!
HANA-SAMA!
HANA-SAMA!!
ガサ
YOU SNUCK OUT OF THE HOUSE WITHOUT PERMIS-SION AGAIN!
IF MR. KAGA FINDS OUT ABOUT THIS, YOU ARE PUTTING ME IN A BAD POSITION!!
I SEE.
YOU'RE TALKING ABOUT HIS SERIAL NOVEL. IT MUST HAVE BEEN A LONG TRIP UP HERE.
WHO'S THIS?
AH... HI!
I'M SHIRO MATSU-BARA FROM TAIHEI NEWS-PAPER.
I CAME HERE TODAY TO GET MR. KAGA'S MANUSCRIPT.
BY THE WAY...
WHERE IS MR. KAGA?

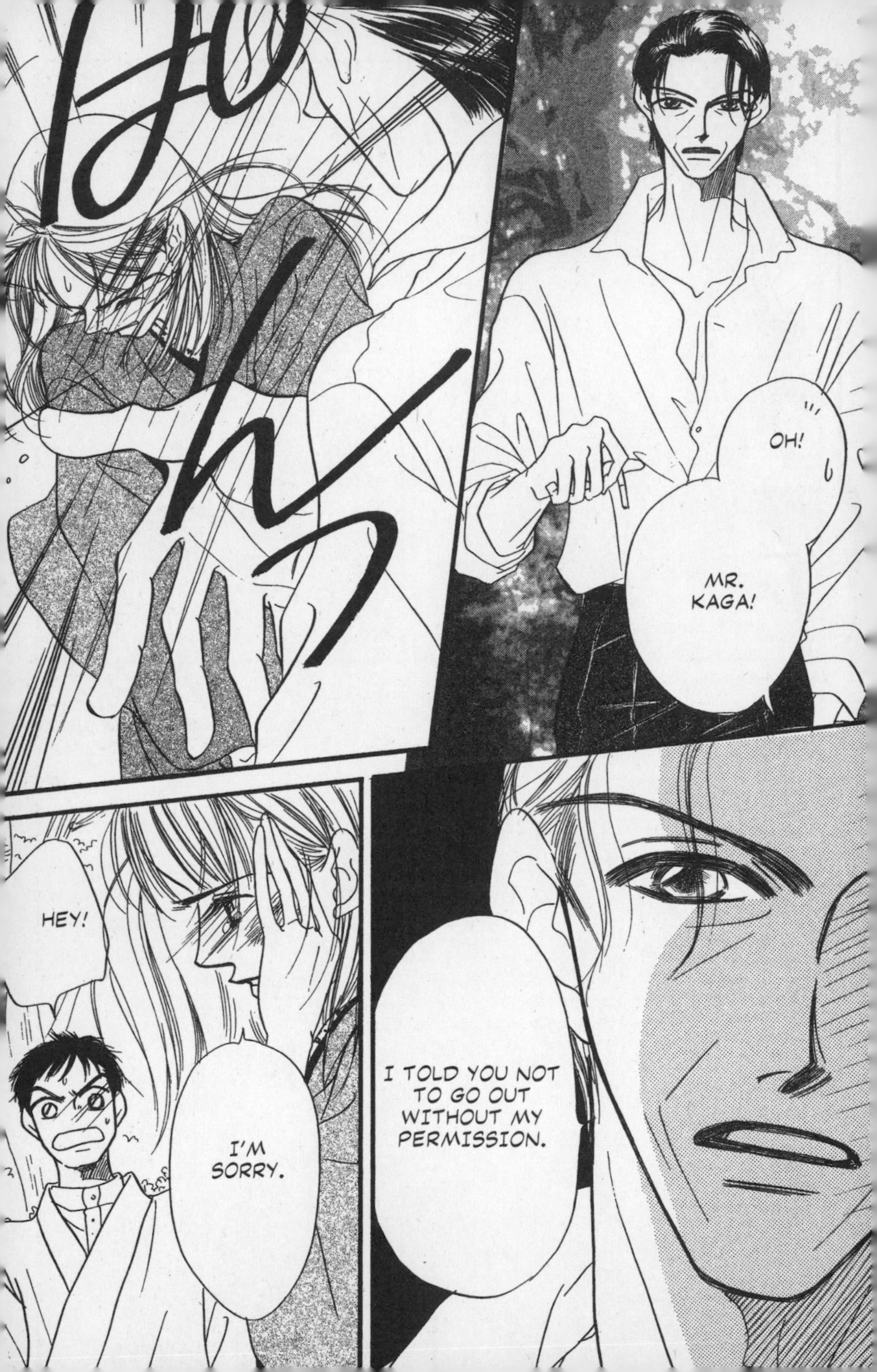
OH!
MR. KAGA!
I TOLD YOU NOT TO GO OUT WITHOUT MY PERMISSION.
I'M SORRY.
HEY!

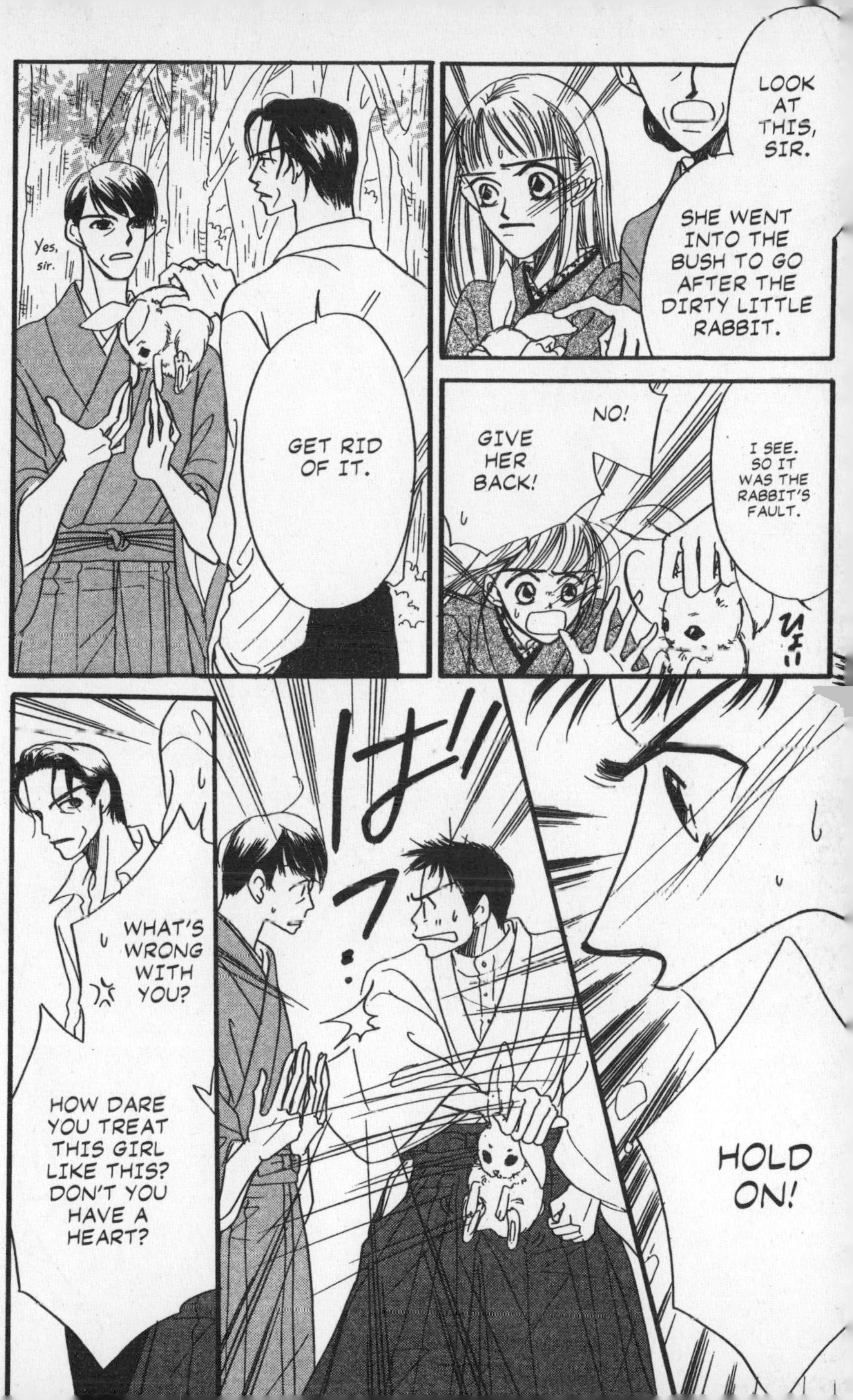
LOOK AT THIS, SIR.
SHE WENT INTO THE BUSH TO GO AFTER THE DIRTY LITTLE RABBIT.
I SEE. SO IT WAS THE RABBIT'S FAULT.
ひょい
NO!
GIVE HER BACK!
GET RID OF IT.
Yes, sir.
HOLD ON!
はっ
WHAT'S WRONG WITH YOU?
HOW DARE YOU TREAT THIS GIRL LIKE THIS? DON'T YOU HAVE A HEART?

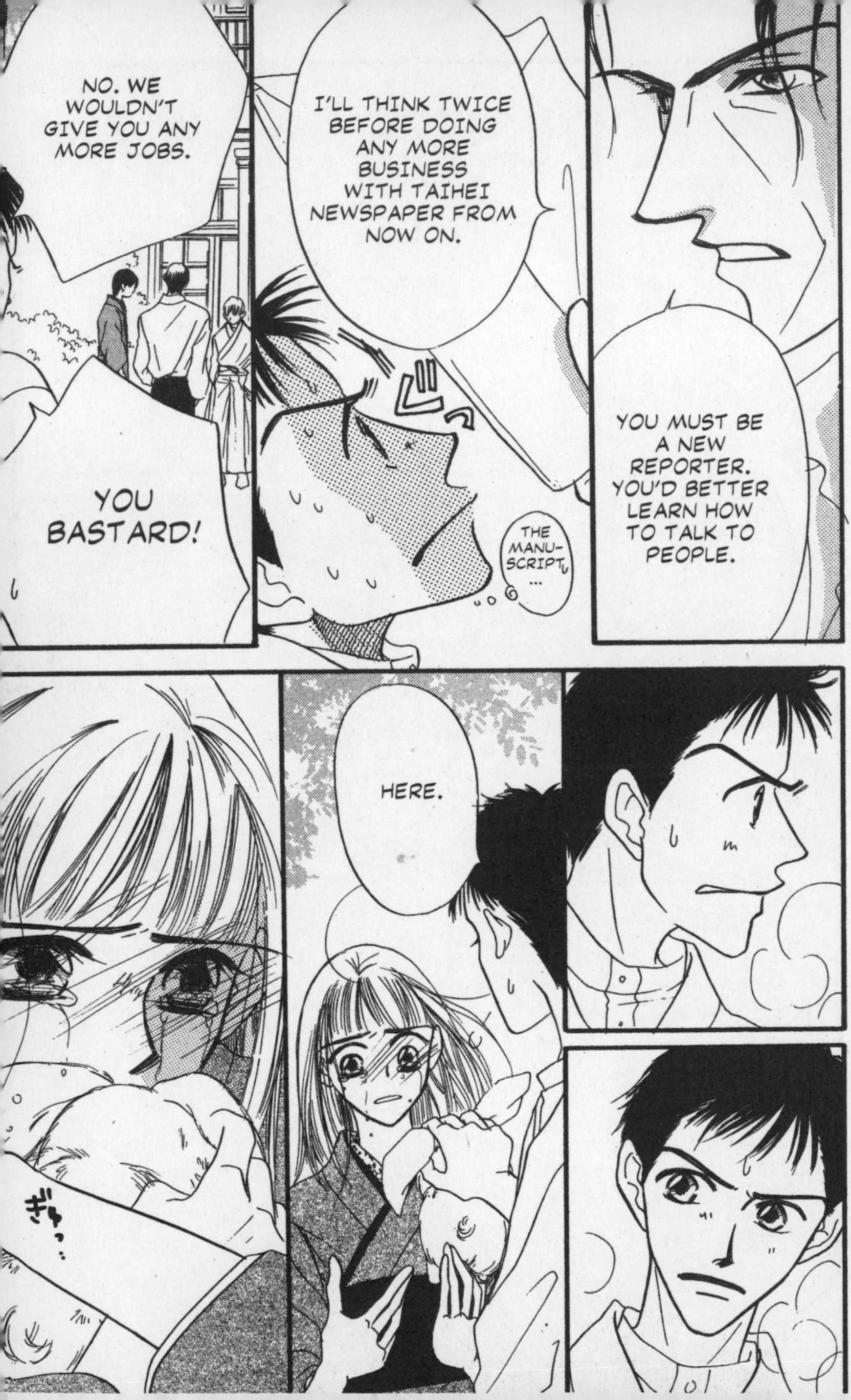
YOU MUST BE A NEW REPORTER. YOU'D BETTER LEARN HOW TO TALK TO PEOPLE.
I'LL THINK TWICE BEFORE DOING ANY MORE BUSINESS WITH TAIHEI NEWSPAPER FROM NOW ON.
THE MANU-SCRIPT...
NO. WE WOULDN'T GIVE YOU ANY MORE JOBS.
YOU BASTARD!
HERE.

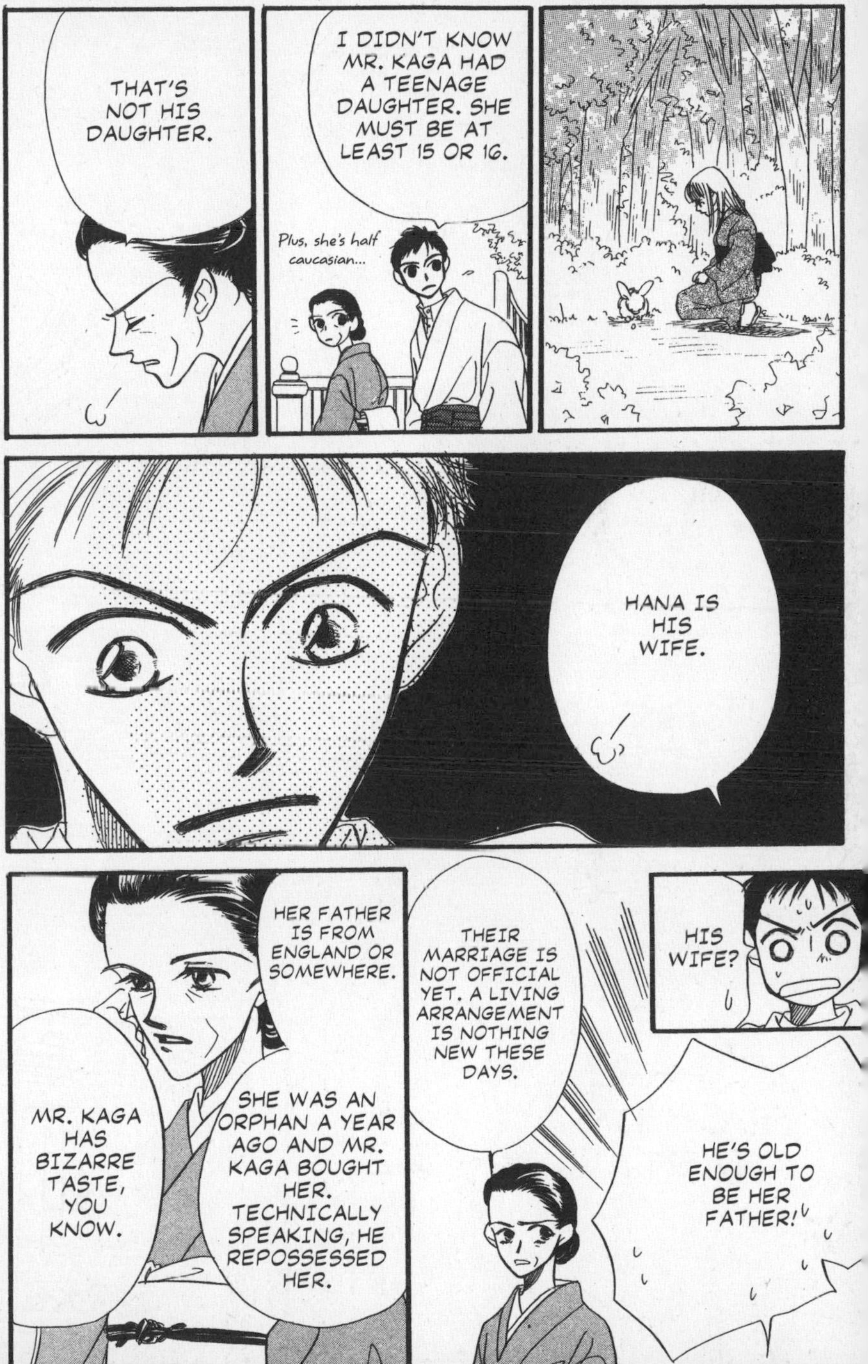
I DIDN'T KNOW MR. KAGA HAD A TEENAGE DAUGHTER. SHE MUST BE AT LEAST 15 OR 16.
Plus, she's half caucasian...
THAT'S NOT HIS DAUGHTER.
HANA IS HIS WIFE.
HIS WIFE?
HE'S OLD ENOUGH TO BE HER FATHER!
THEIR MARRIAGE IS NOT OFFICIAL YET. A LIVING ARRANGEMENT IS NOTHING NEW THESE DAYS.
HER FATHER IS FROM ENGLAND OR SOMEWHERE.
SHE WAS AN ORPHAN A YEAR AGO AND MR. KAGA BOUGHT HER. TECHNICALLY SPEAKING, HE REPOSSESSED HER.
MR. KAGA HAS BIZARRE TASTE, YOU KNOW.

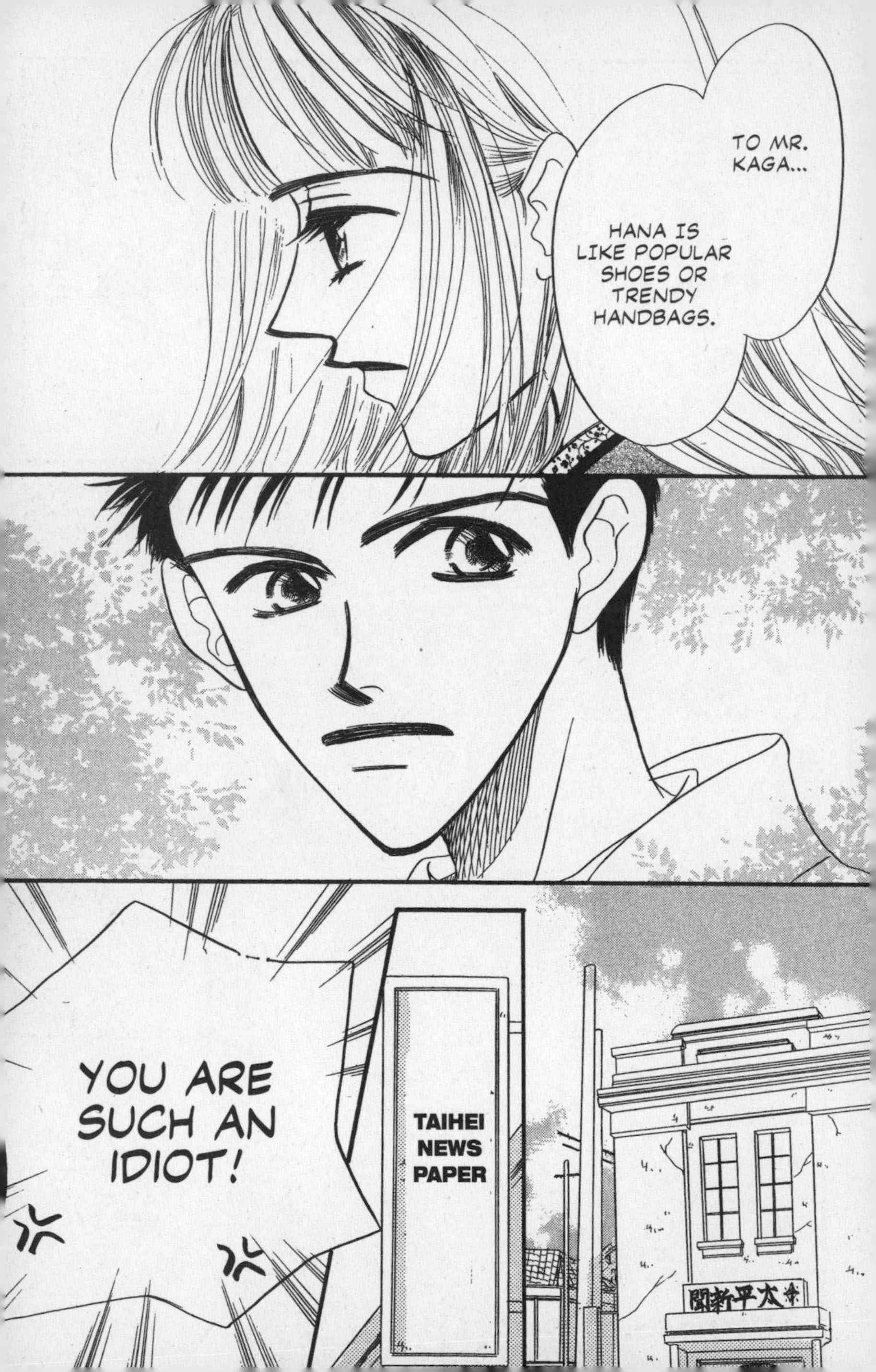
TO MR. KAGA...
HANA IS LIKE POPULAR SHOES OR TRENDY HANDBAGS.
太平新聞
TAIHEI NEWS PAPER
YOU ARE SUCH AN IDIOT!

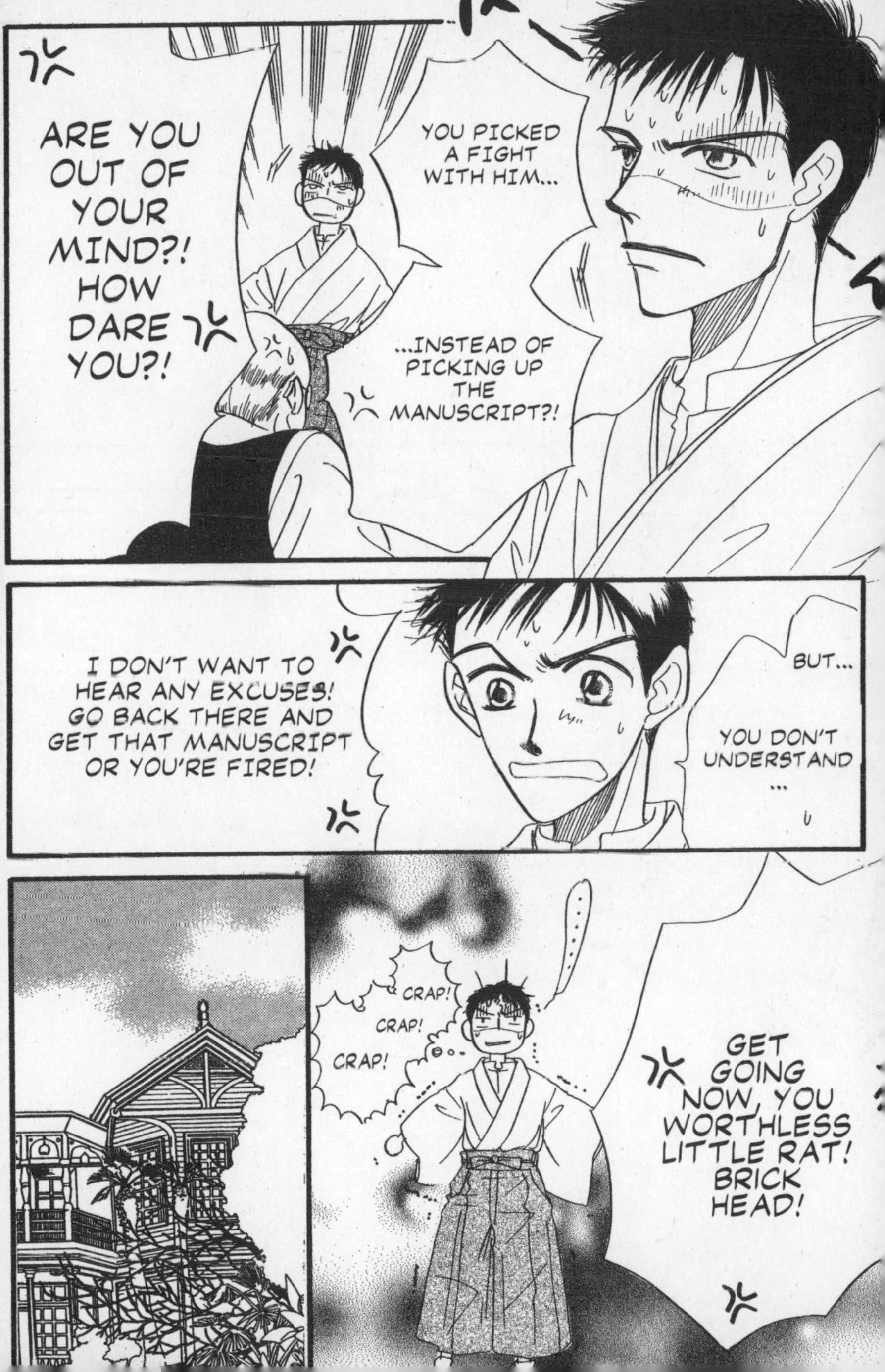
YOU PICKED A FIGHT WITH HIM...
...INSTEAD OF PICKING UP THE MANUSCRIPT?!
ARE YOU OUT OF YOUR MIND?! HOW DARE YOU?!
BUT...
YOU DON'T UNDERSTAND ...
I DON'T WANT TO HEAR ANY EXCUSES! GO BACK THERE AND GET THAT MANUSCRIPT OR YOU'RE FIRED!
GET GOING NOW, YOU WORTHLESS LITTLE RAT! BRICK HEAD!
CRAP!
CRAP!
CRAP!

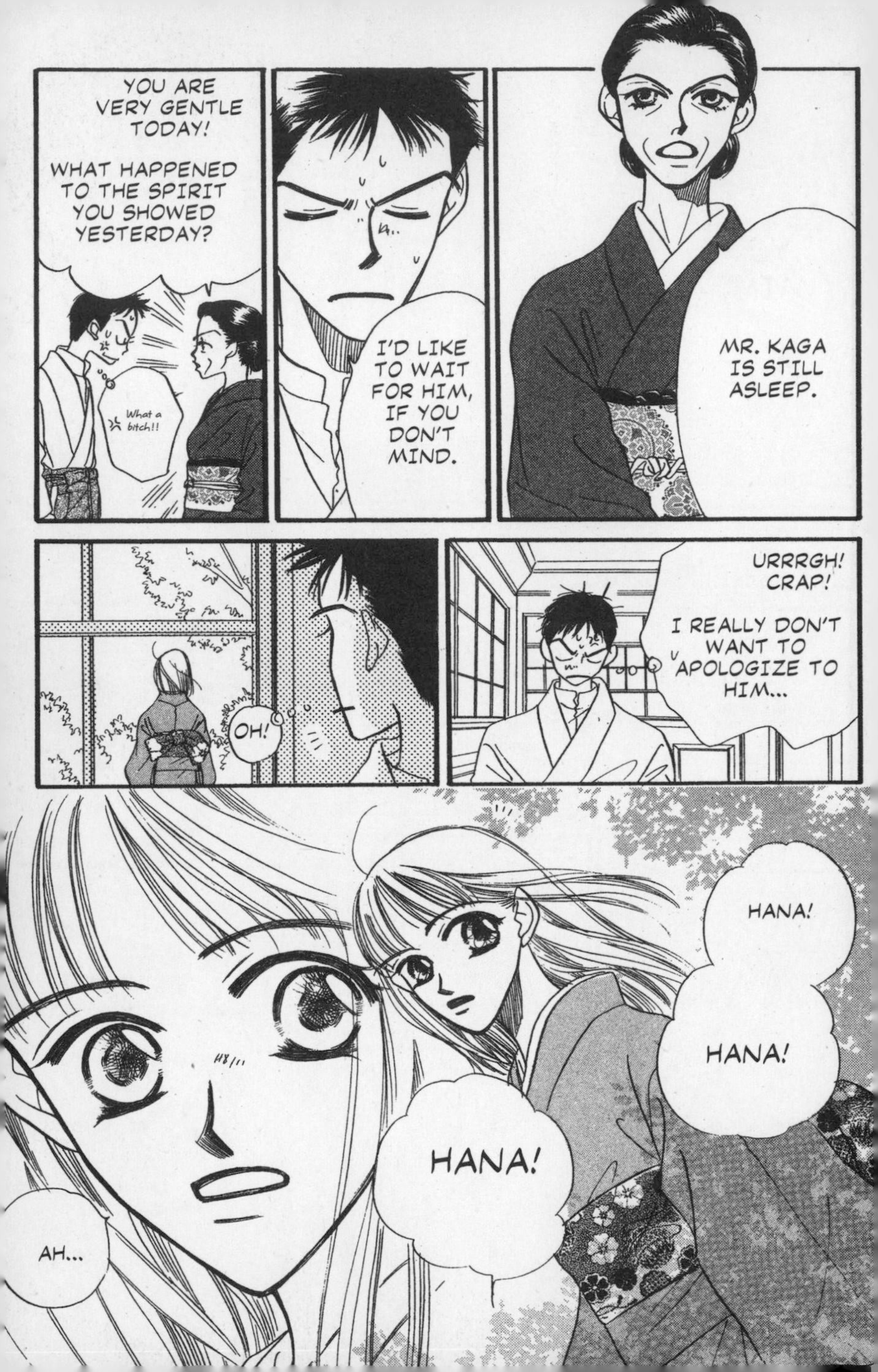
MR. KAGA IS STILL ASLEEP.
I'D LIKE TO WAIT FOR HIM, IF YOU DON'T MIND.
YOU ARE VERY GENTLE TODAY!
WHAT HAPPENED TO THE SPIRIT YOU SHOWED YESTERDAY?
What a bitch!!
URRRGH! CRAP!
I REALLY DON'T WANT TO APOLOGIZE TO HIM...
OH!
HANA!
HANA!
HANA!
AH...

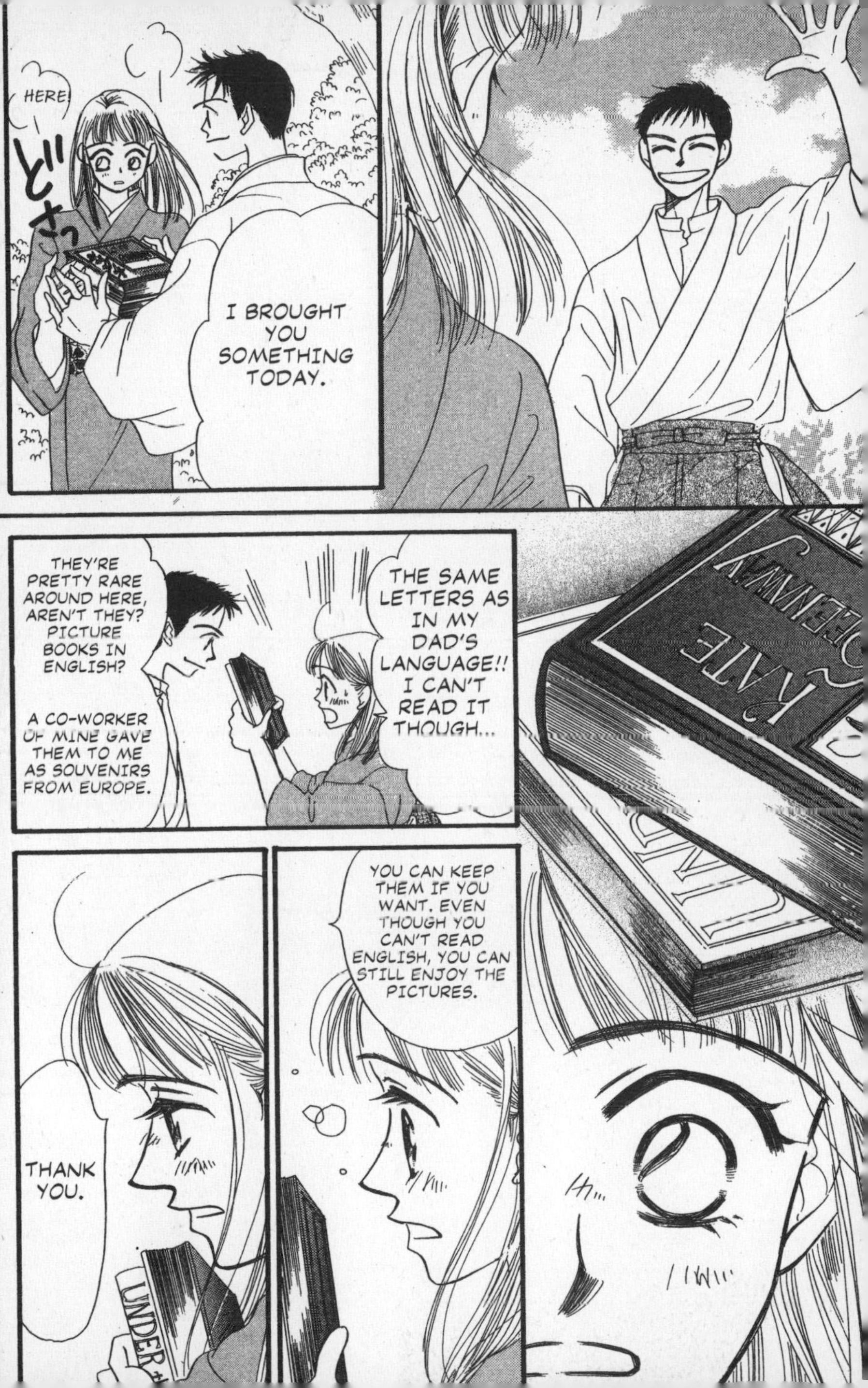
I BROUGHT YOU SOMETHING TODAY.
HERE!
どさっ
THE SAME LETTERS AS IN MY DAD'S LANGUAGE!! I CAN'T READ IT THOUGH...
THEY'RE PRETTY RARE AROUND HERE, AREN'T THEY? PICTURE BOOKS IN ENGLISH?
A CO-WORKER OF MINE GAVE THEM TO ME AS SOUVENIRS FROM EUROPE.
YOU CAN KEEP THEM IF YOU WANT. EVEN THOUGH YOU CAN'T READ ENGLISH, YOU CAN STILL ENJOY THE PICTURES.
THANK YOU.
UNDER

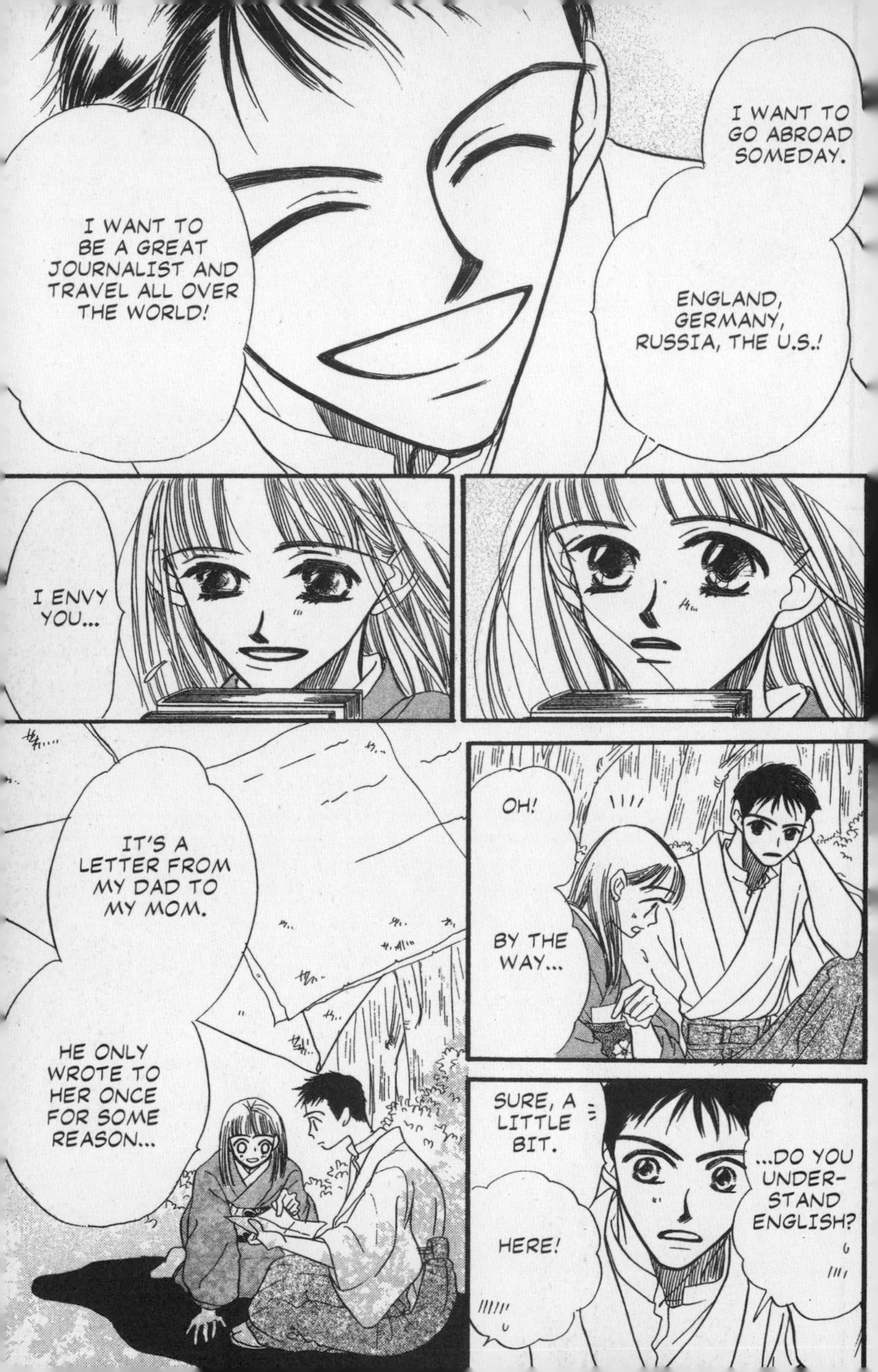

I WANT TO GO ABROAD SOMEDAY.
I WANT TO BE A GREAT JOURNALIST AND TRAVEL ALL OVER THE WORLD!
ENGLAND, GERMANY, RUSSIA, THE U.S.!
I ENVY YOU...
OH!
BY THE WAY...
...DO YOU UNDERSTAND ENGLISH?
SURE, A LITTLE BIT.
HERE!
IT'S A LETTER FROM MY DAD TO MY MOM.
HE ONLY WROTE TO HER ONCE FOR SOME REASON...

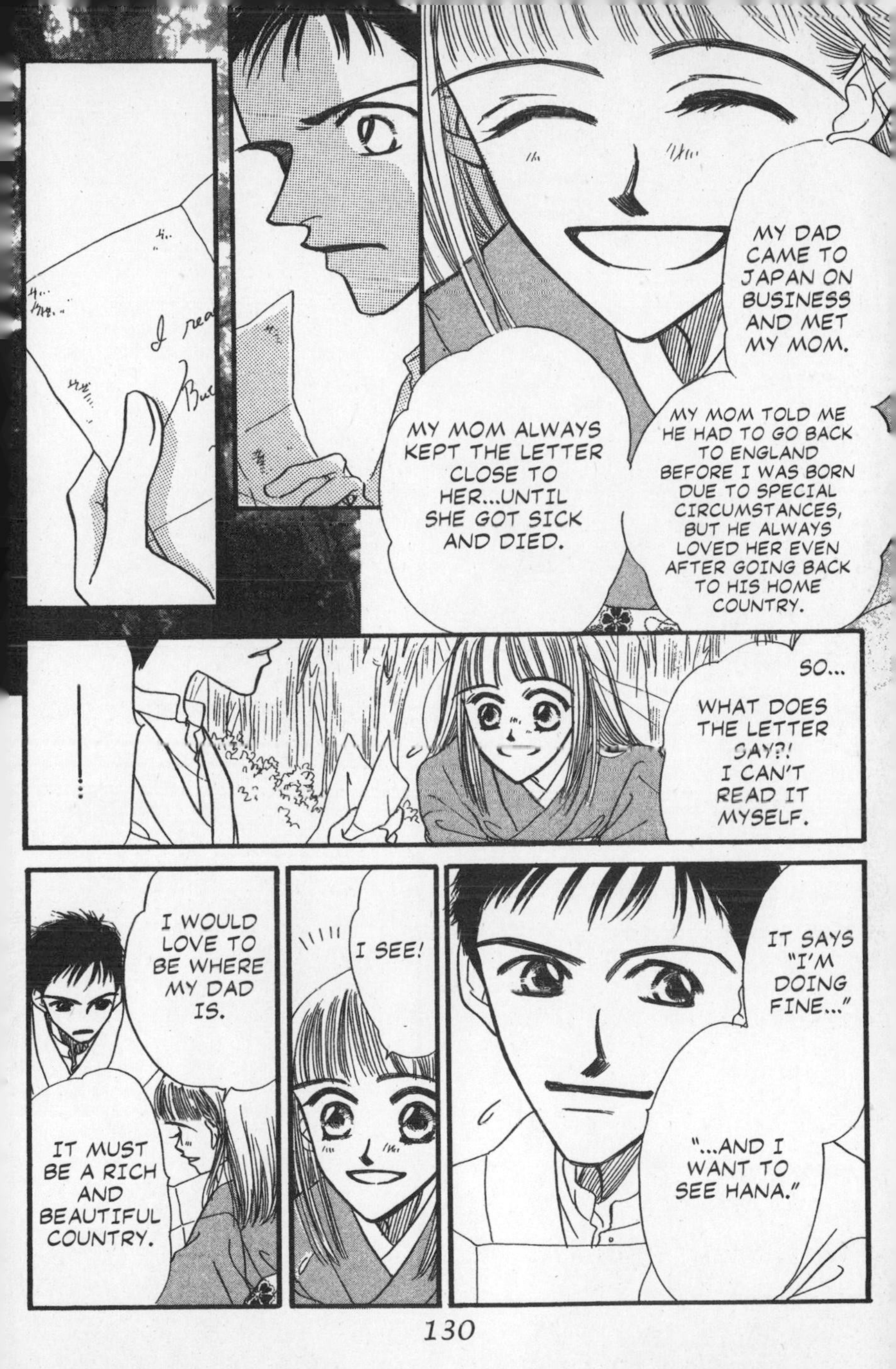
MY DAD CAME TO JAPAN ON BUSINESS AND MET MY MOM.
MY MOM TOLD ME HE HAD TO GO BACK TO ENGLAND BEFORE I WAS BORN DUE TO SPECIAL CIRCUMSTANCES, BUT HE ALWAYS LOVED HER EVEN AFTER GOING BACK TO HIS HOME COUNTRY.
MY MOM ALWAYS KEPT THE LETTER CLOSE TO HER...UNTIL SHE GOT SICK AND DIED.
SO...
WHAT DOES THE LETTER SAY?! I CAN'T READ IT MYSELF.
IT SAYS "I'M DOING FINE..."
"...AND I WANT TO SEE HANA."
I SEE!
I WOULD LOVE TO BE WHERE MY DAD IS.
IT MUST BE A RICH AND BEAUTIFUL COUNTRY.

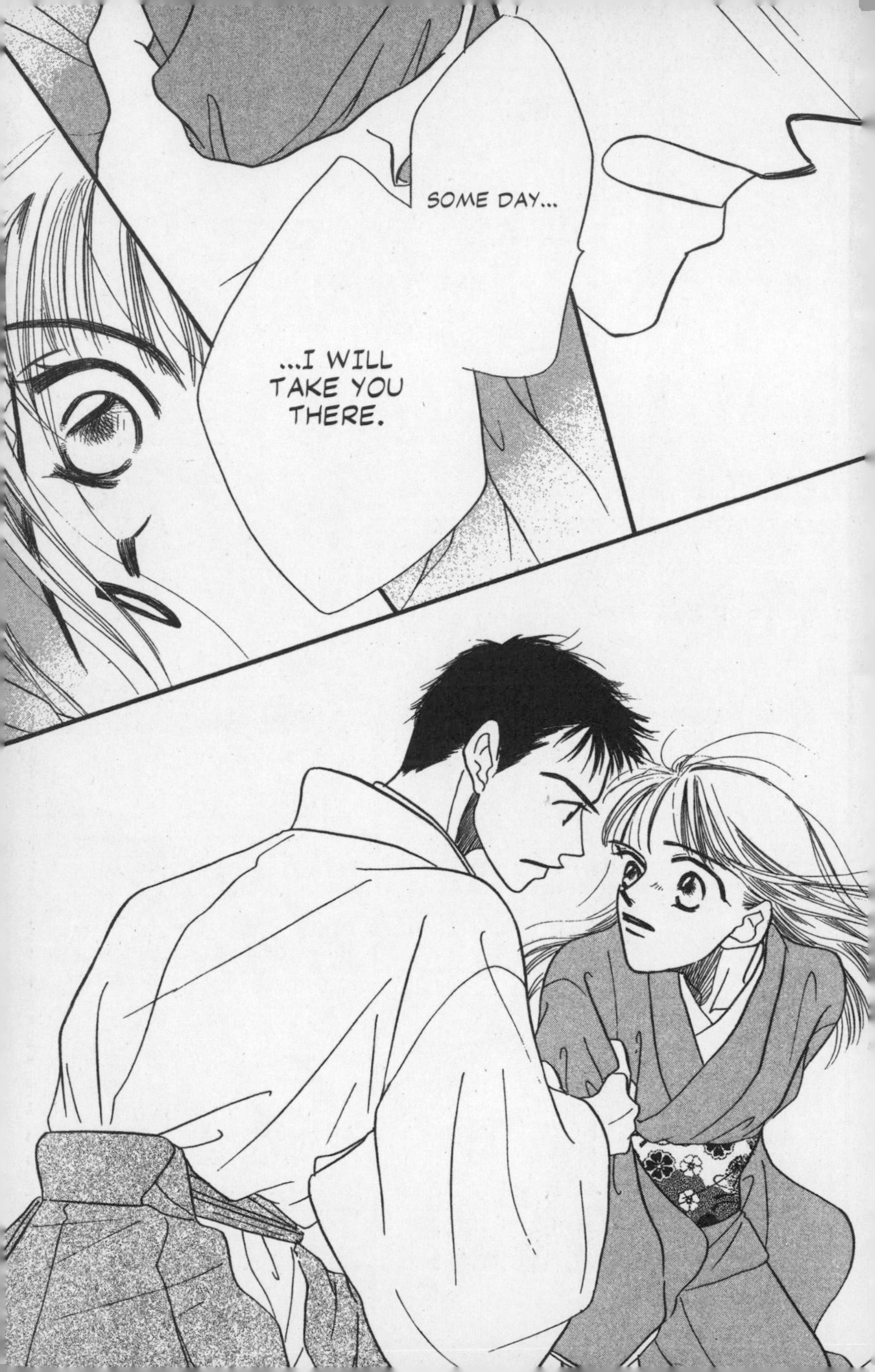
SOME DAY...
...I WILL TAKE YOU THERE.

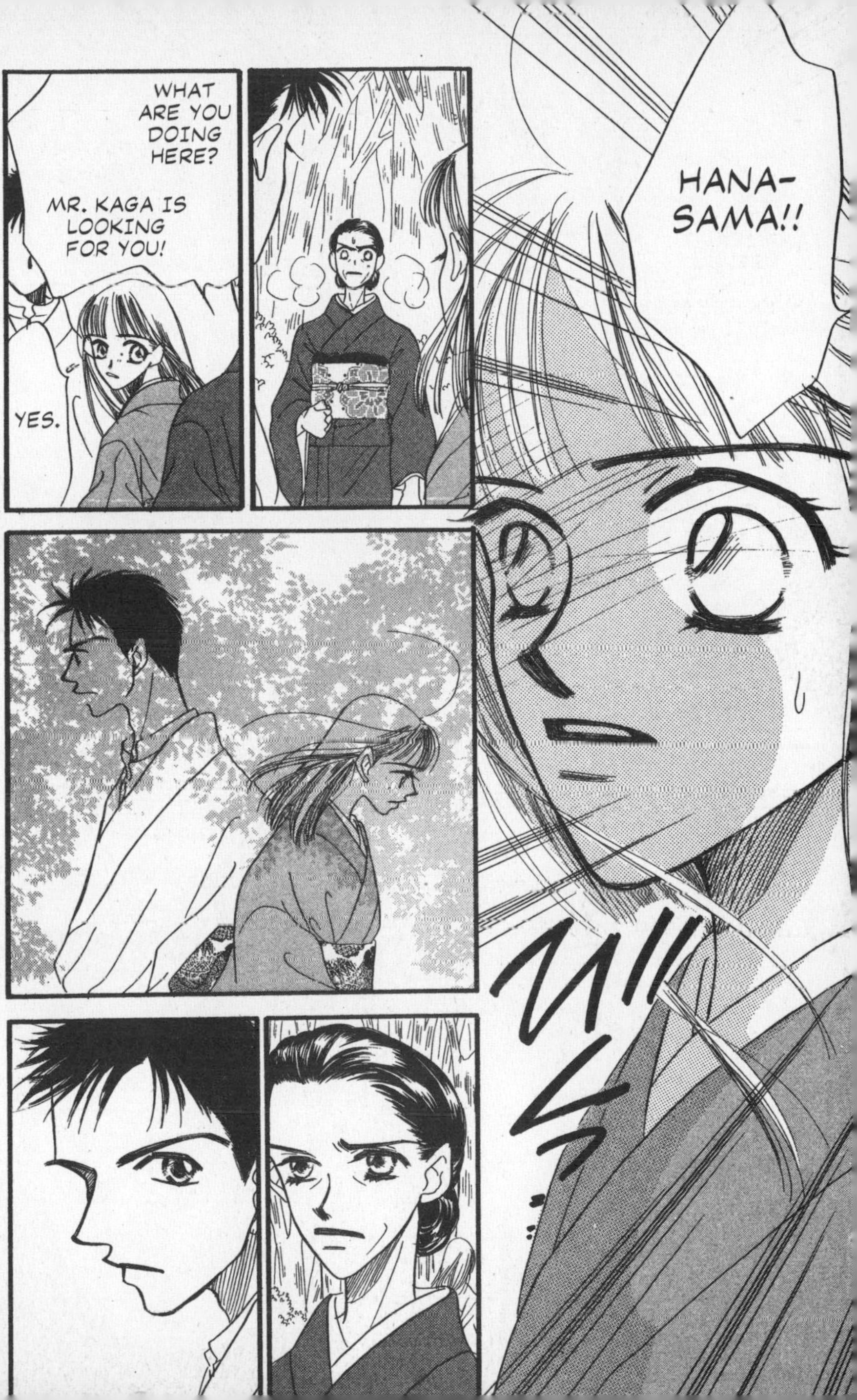
HANA-SAMA!!
WHAT ARE YOU DOING HERE?
MR. KAGA IS LOOKING FOR YOU!
YES.

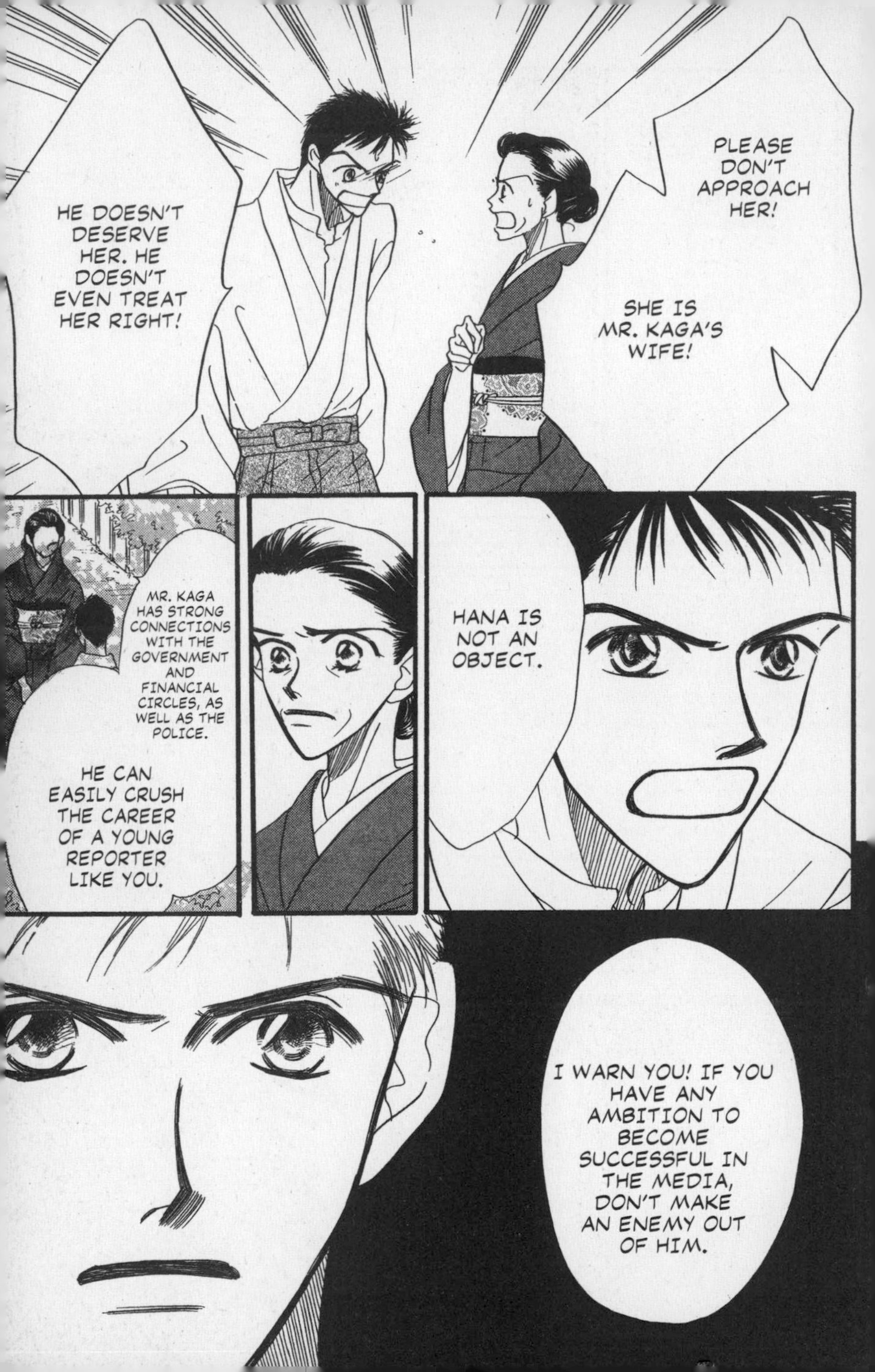
PLEASE DON'T APPROACH HER!
SHE IS MR. KAGA'S WIFE!
HE DOESN'T DESERVE HER. HE DOESN'T EVEN TREAT HER RIGHT!
HANA IS NOT AN OBJECT.
MR. KAGA HAS STRONG CONNECTIONS WITH THE GOVERNMENT AND FINANCIAL CIRCLES, AS WELL AS THE POLICE.
HE CAN EASILY CRUSH THE CAREER OF A YOUNG REPORTER LIKE YOU.
I WARN YOU! IF YOU HAVE ANY AMBITION TO BECOME SUCCESSFUL IN THE MEDIA, DON'T MAKE AN ENEMY OUT OF HIM.

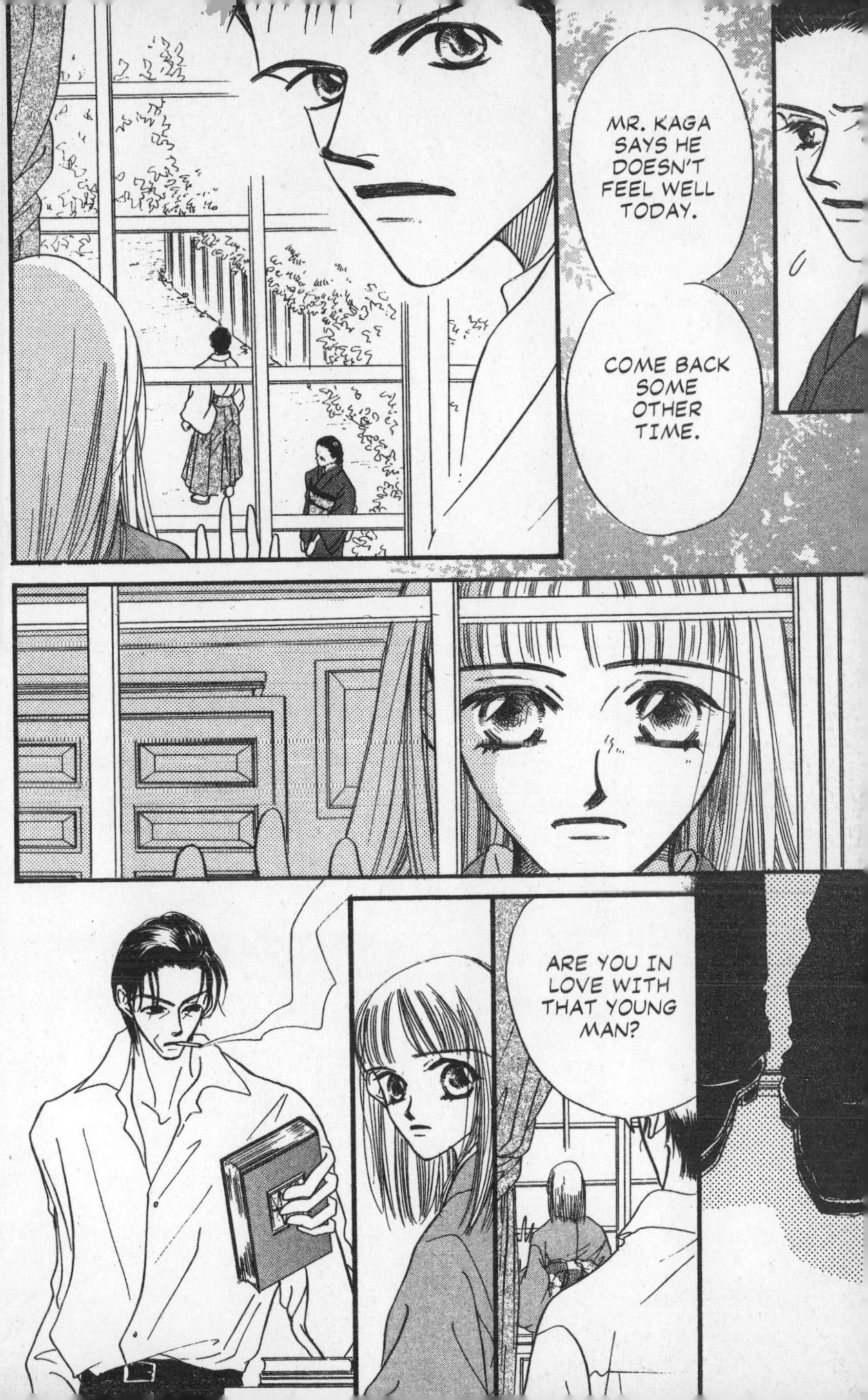
MR. KAGA SAYS HE DOESN'T FEEL WELL TODAY.
COME BACK SOME OTHER TIME.
ARE YOU IN LOVE WITH THAT YOUNG MAN?

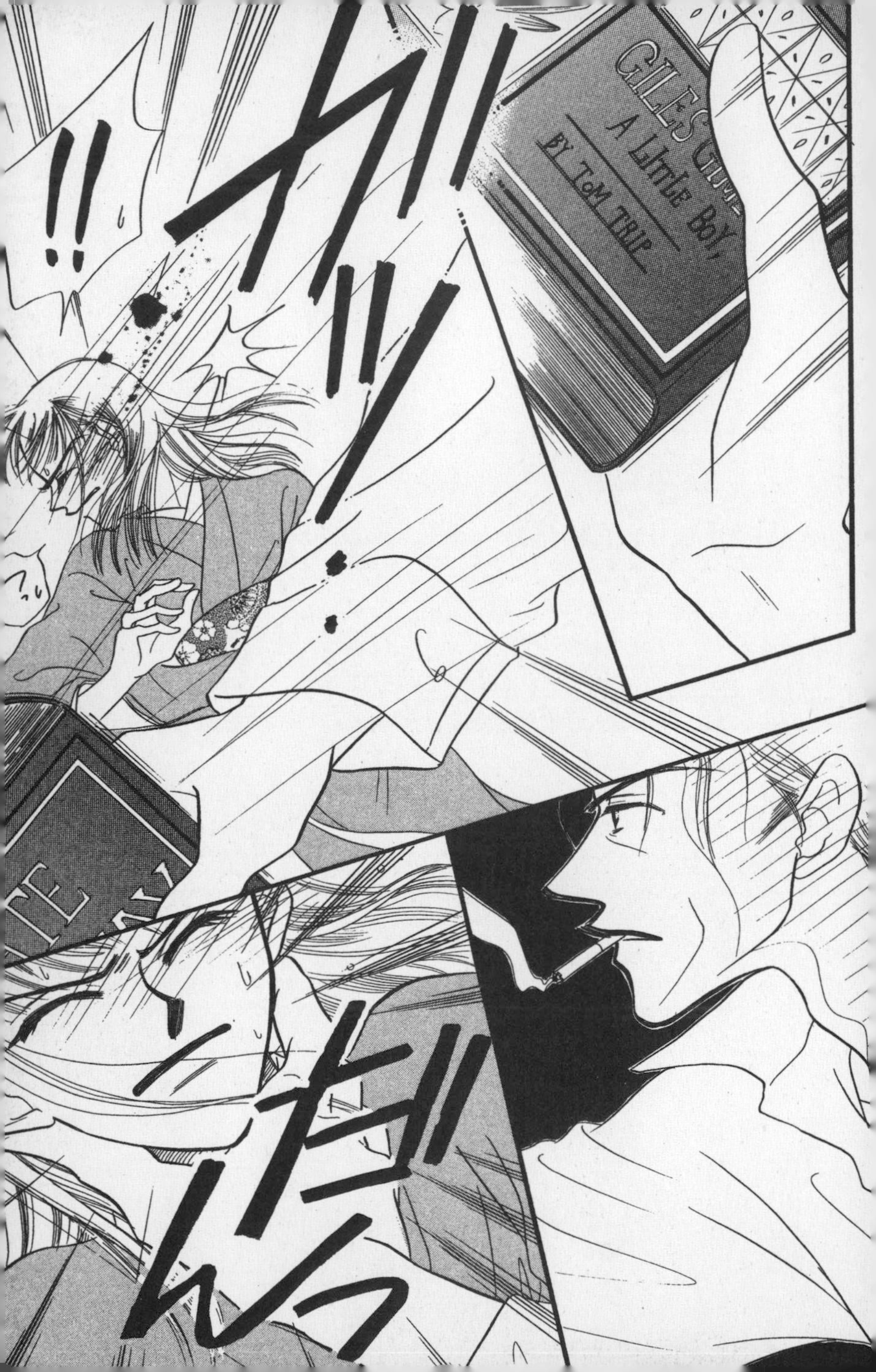
!!
ガッ
A LITTLE BOY,
BY TOM TRIP
ガんっ

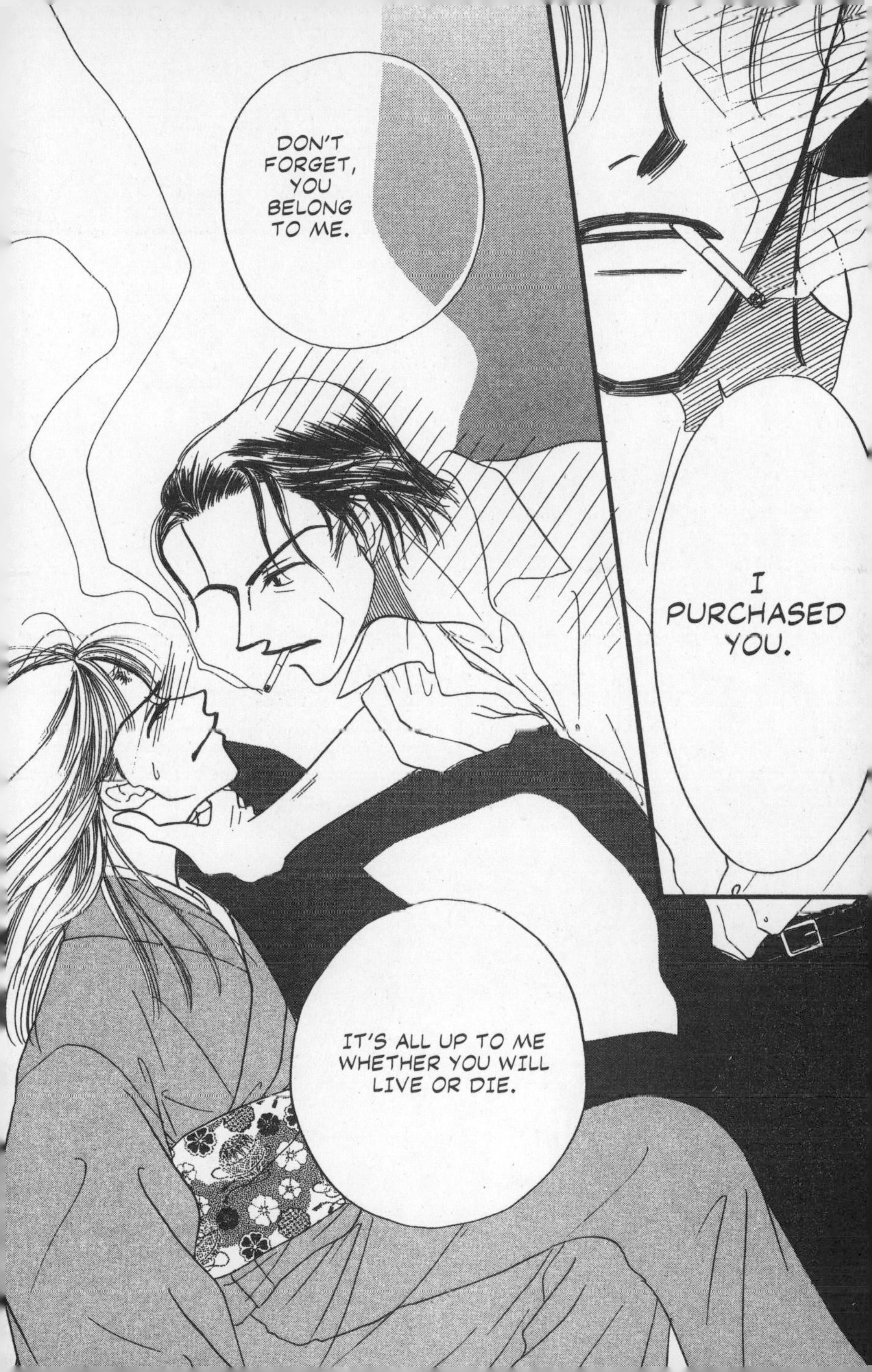
DON'T FORGET, YOU BELONG TO ME.
I PURCHASED YOU.
IT'S ALL UP TO ME WHETHER YOU WILL LIVE OR DIE.

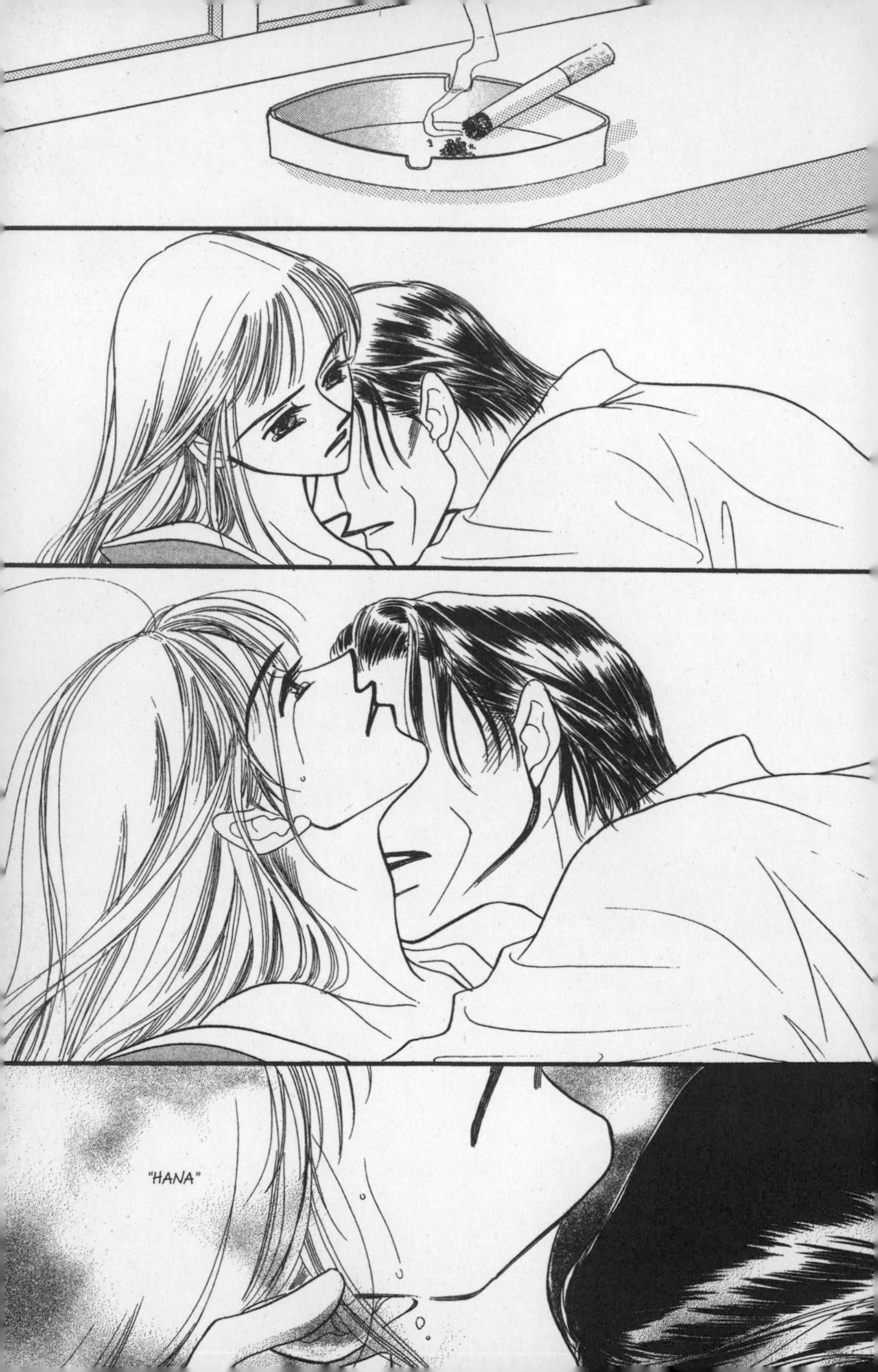
"HANA"

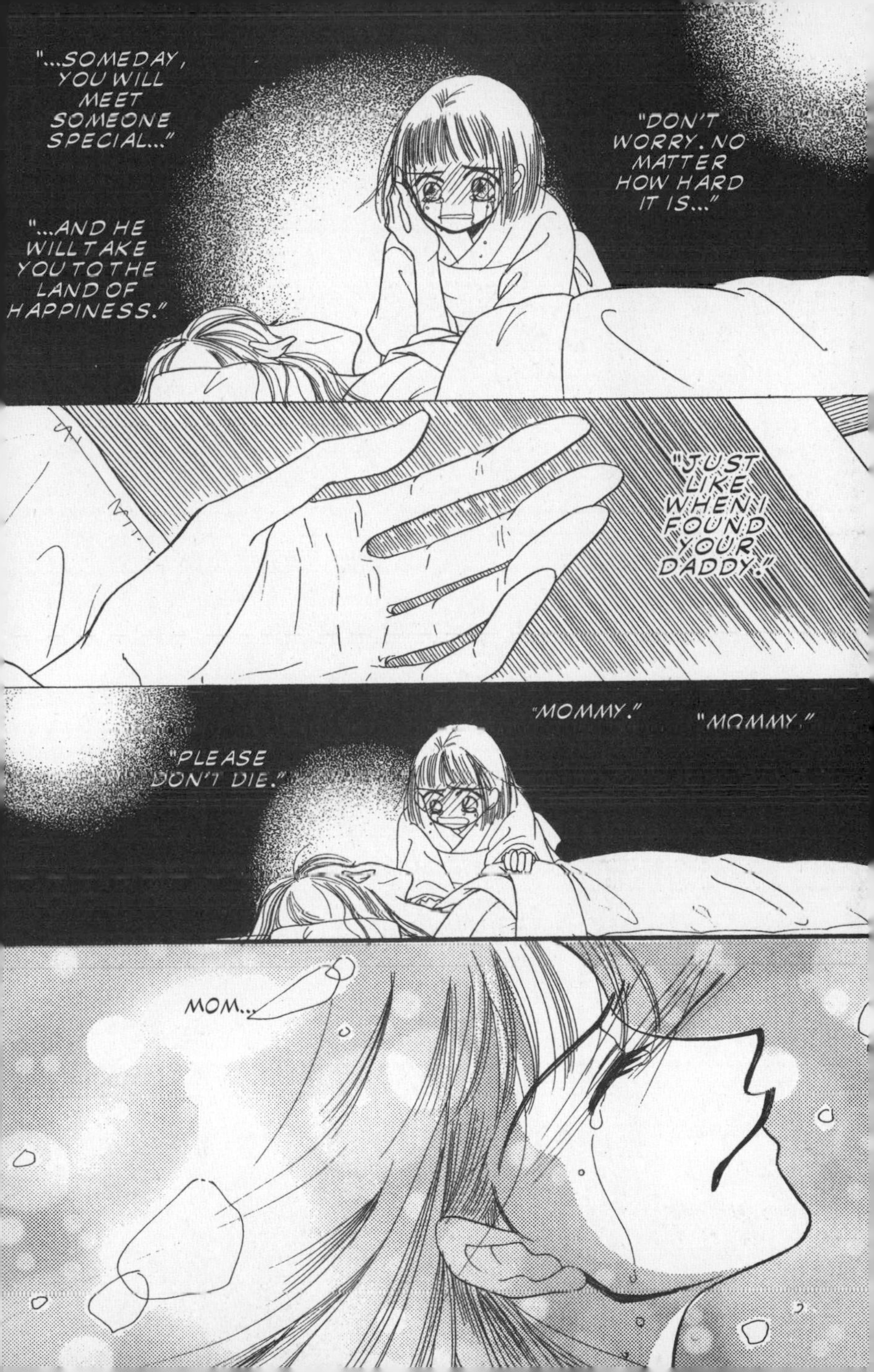
"...SOMEDAY, YOU WILL MEET SOMEONE SPECIAL..."
"...AND HE WILL TAKE YOU TO THE LAND OF HAPPINESS."
"DON'T WORRY. NO MATTER HOW HARD IT IS..."
"JUST LIKE WHEN I FOUND YOUR DADDY!"
"MOMMY."
"MOMMY."
"PLEASE DON'T DIE."
MOM...

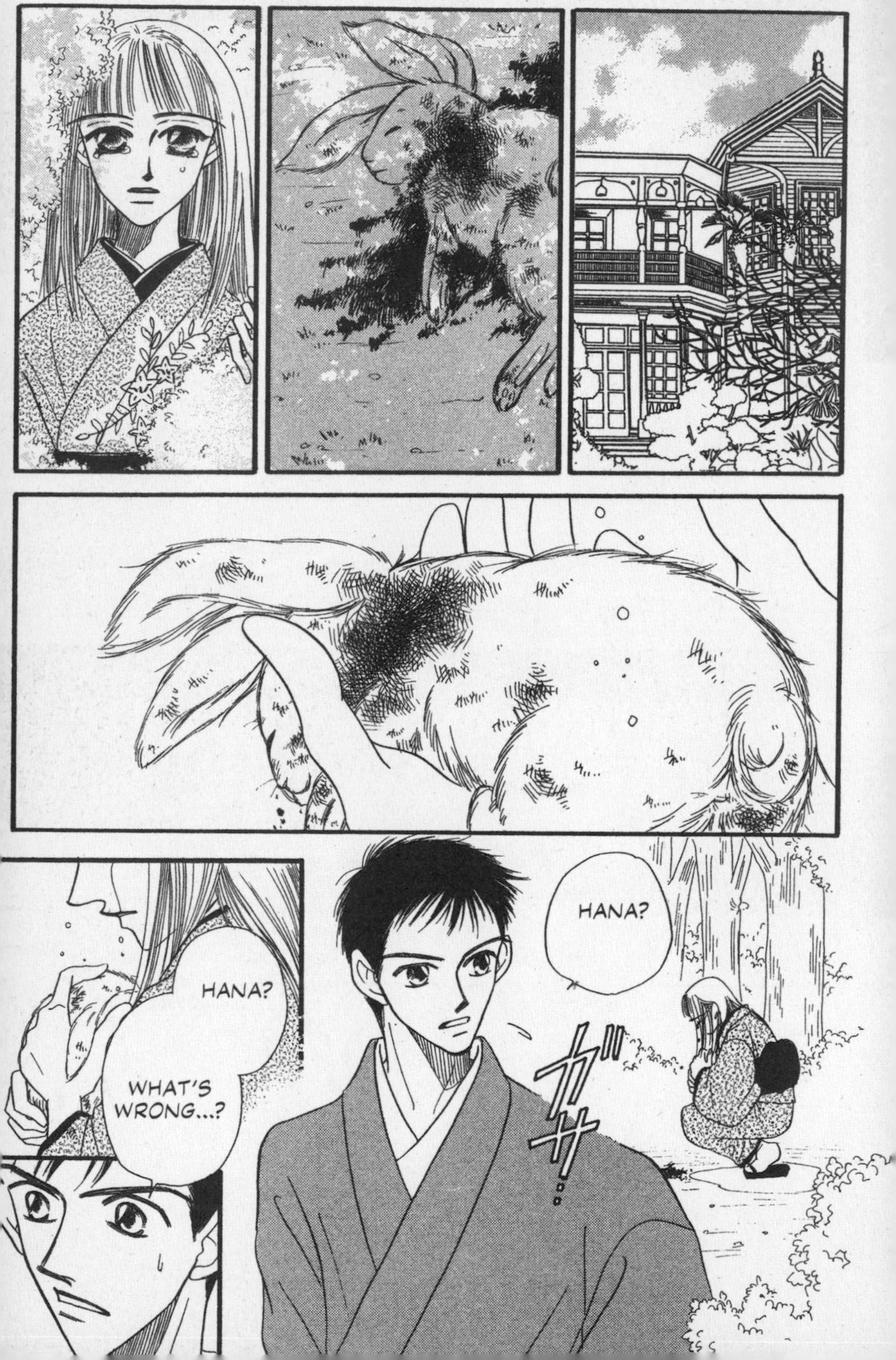
HANA?
HANA?
WHAT'S WRONG...?

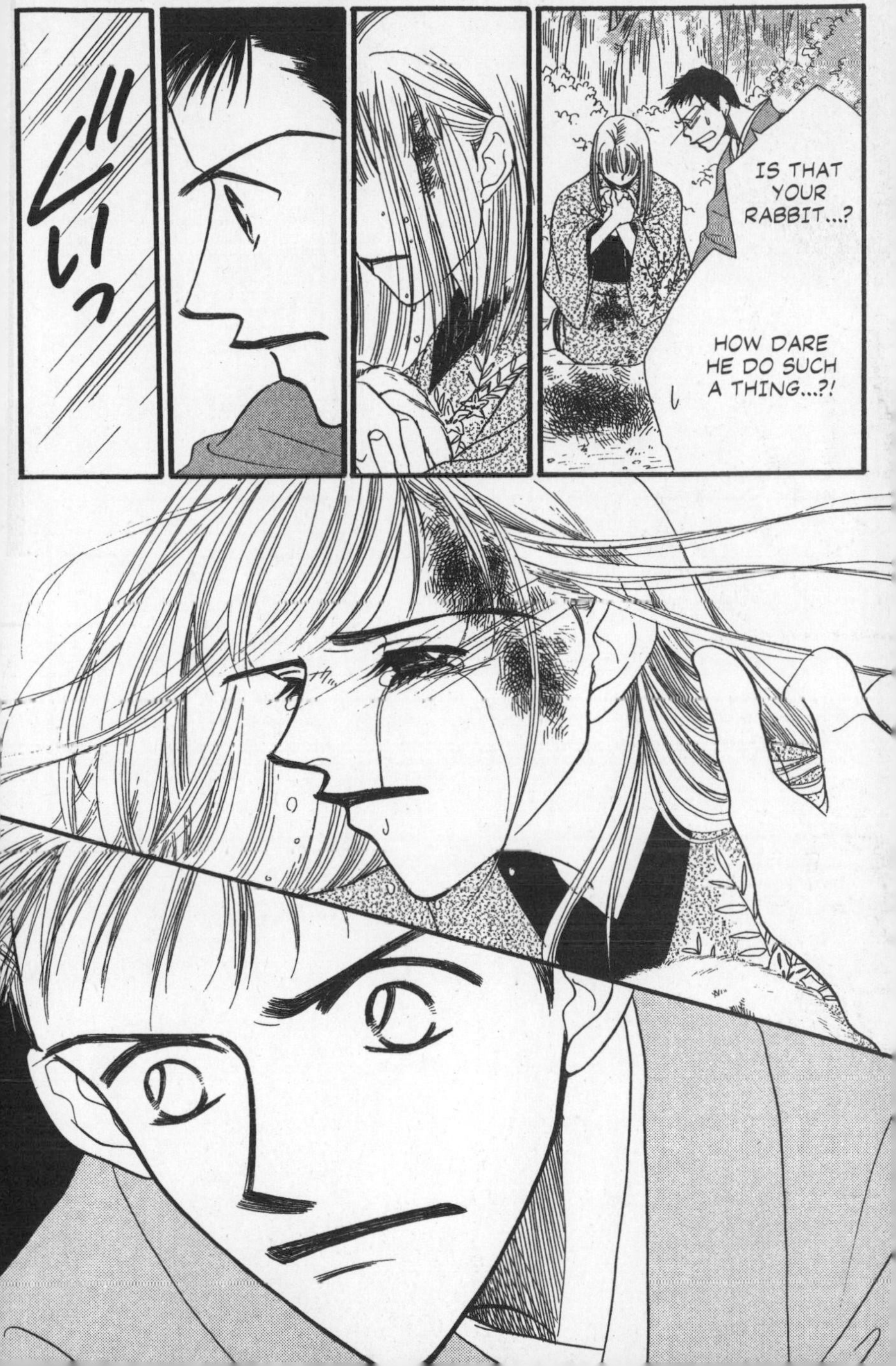
IS THAT YOUR RABBIT...?
HOW DARE HE DO SUCH A THING...?!
じいっ

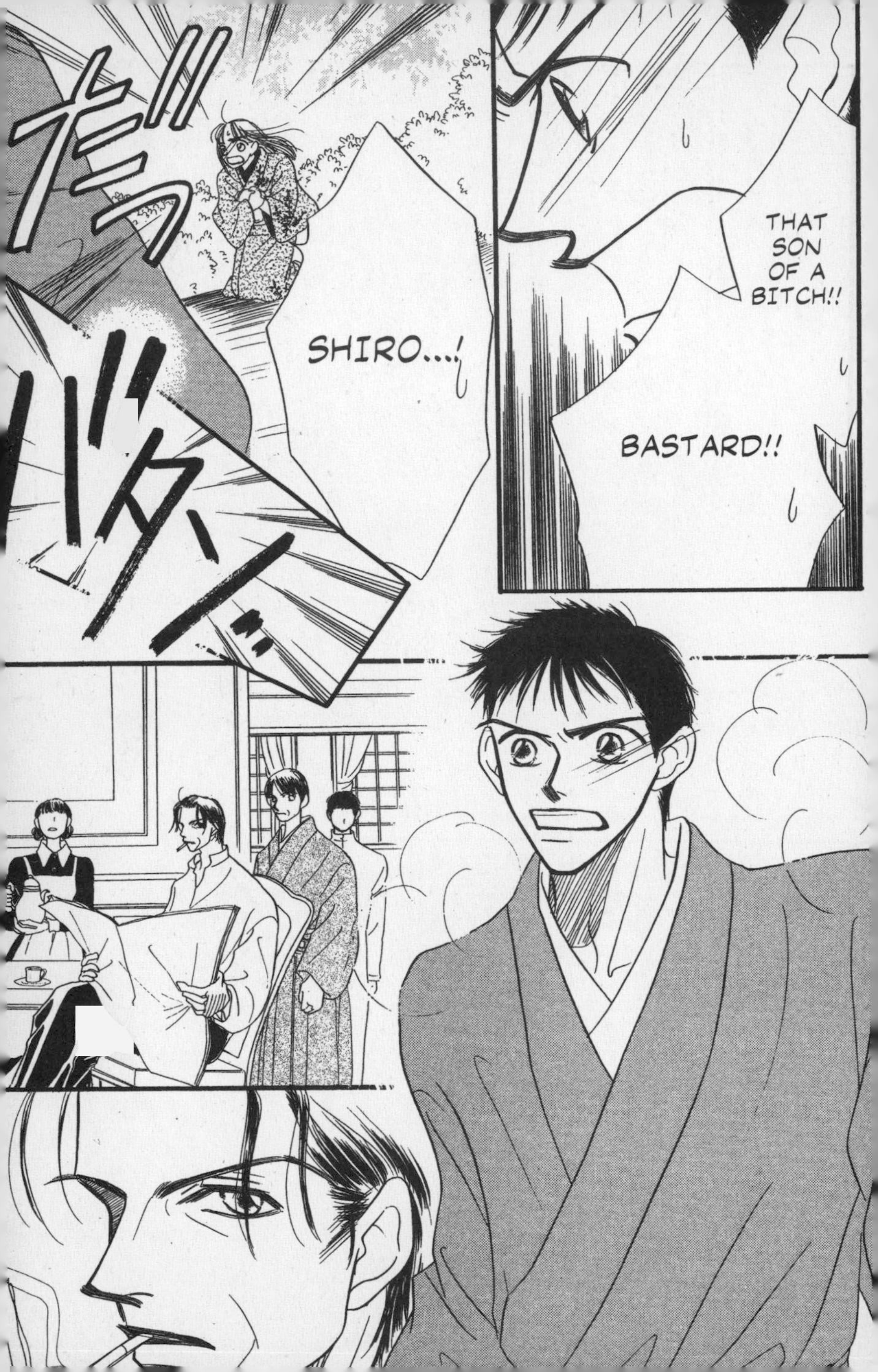
THAT SON OF A BITCH!!
BASTARD!!
だっ
SHIRO...!
バタン

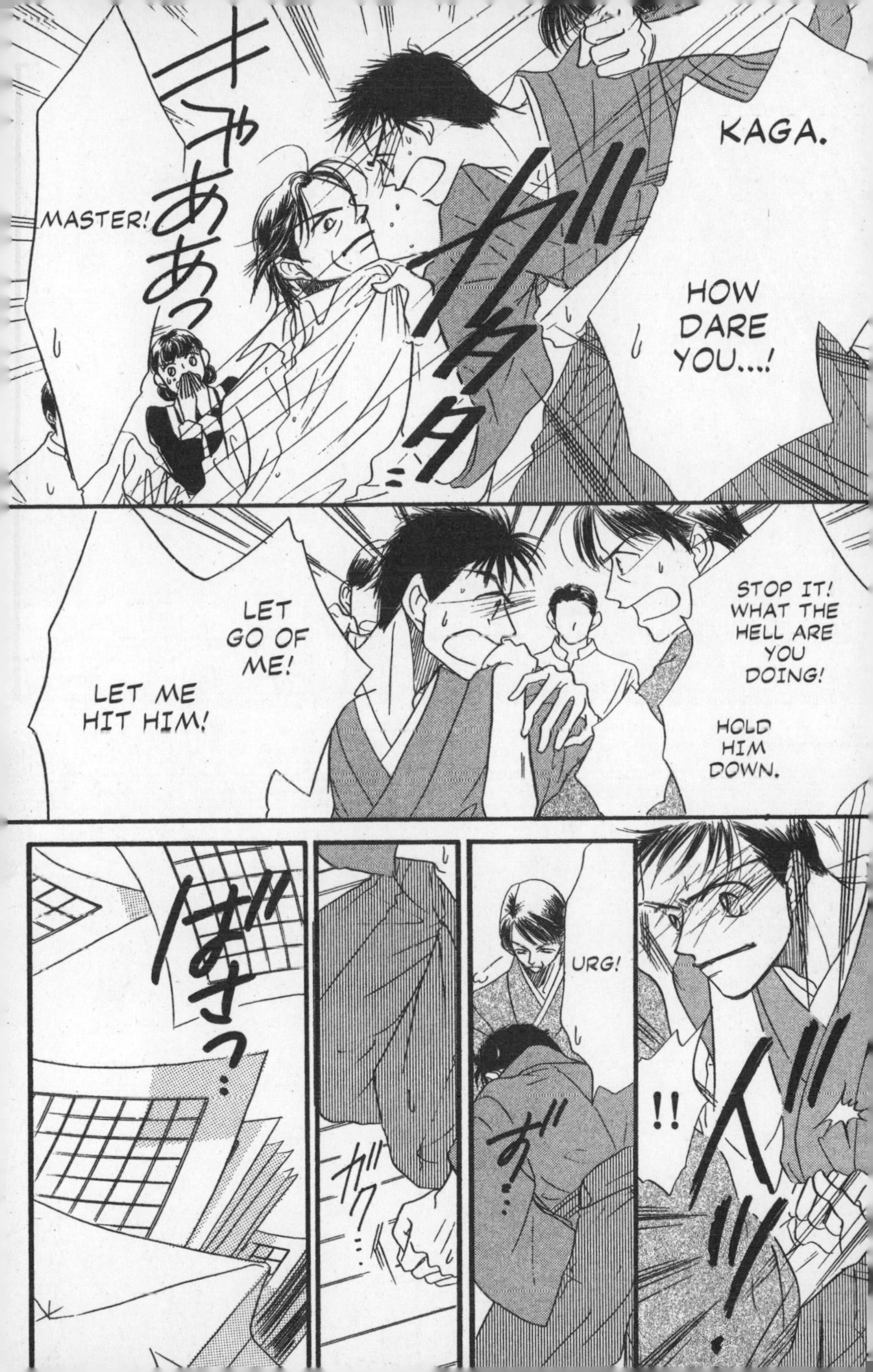
KAGA.
HOW DARE YOU...!
ガタ
MASTER!
ぎゃああっ
STOP IT! WHAT THE HELL ARE YOU DOING!
HOLD HIM DOWN.
LET GO OF ME!
LET ME HIT HIM!
!!
URG!
ずっ
ガク

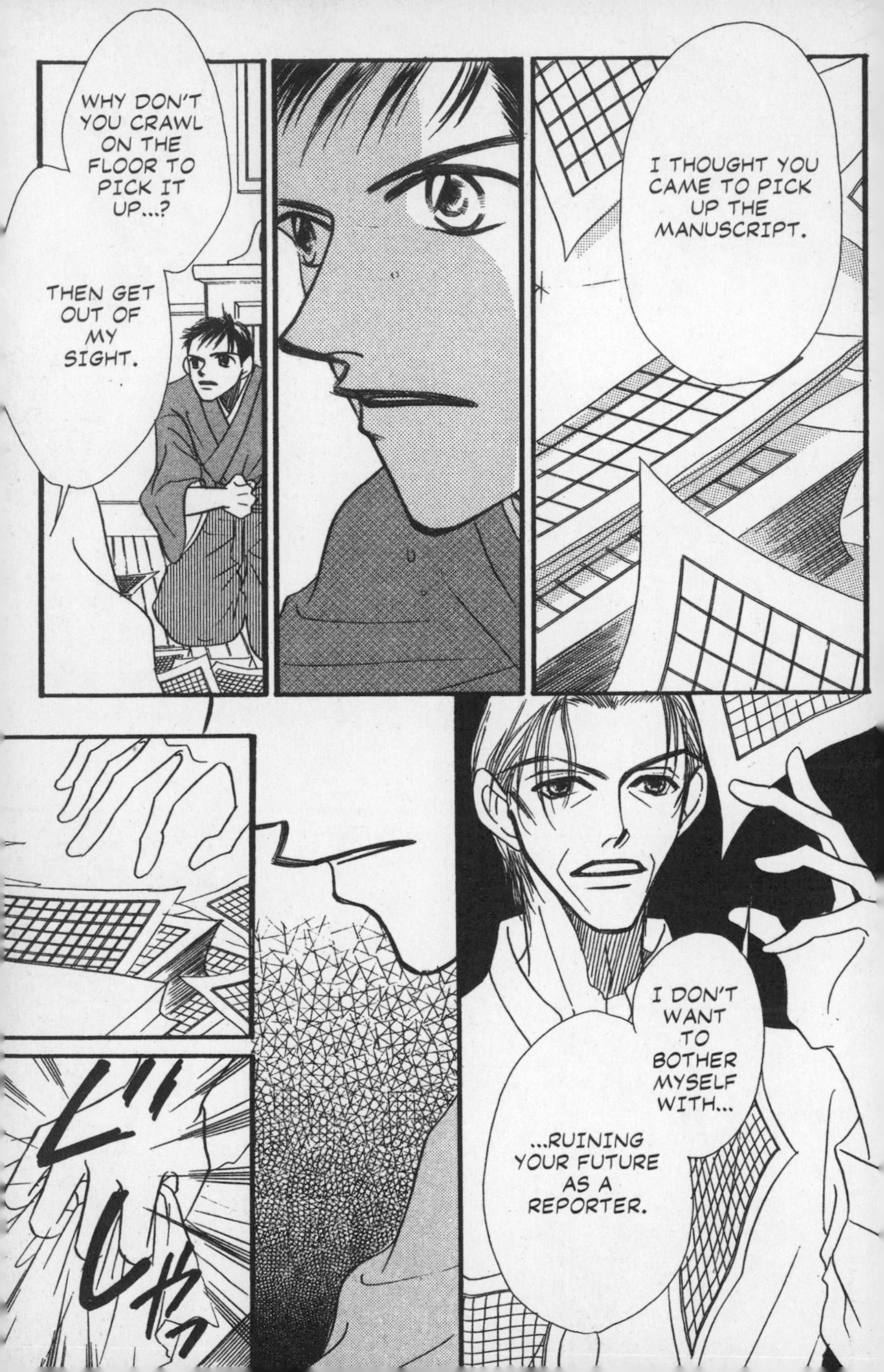
I THOUGHT YOU CAME TO PICK UP THE MANUSCRIPT.
WHY DON'T YOU CRAWL ON THE FLOOR TO PICK IT UP...?
THEN GET OUT OF MY SIGHT.
I DON'T WANT TO BOTHER MYSELF WITH...
...RUINING YOUR FUTURE AS A REPORTER.

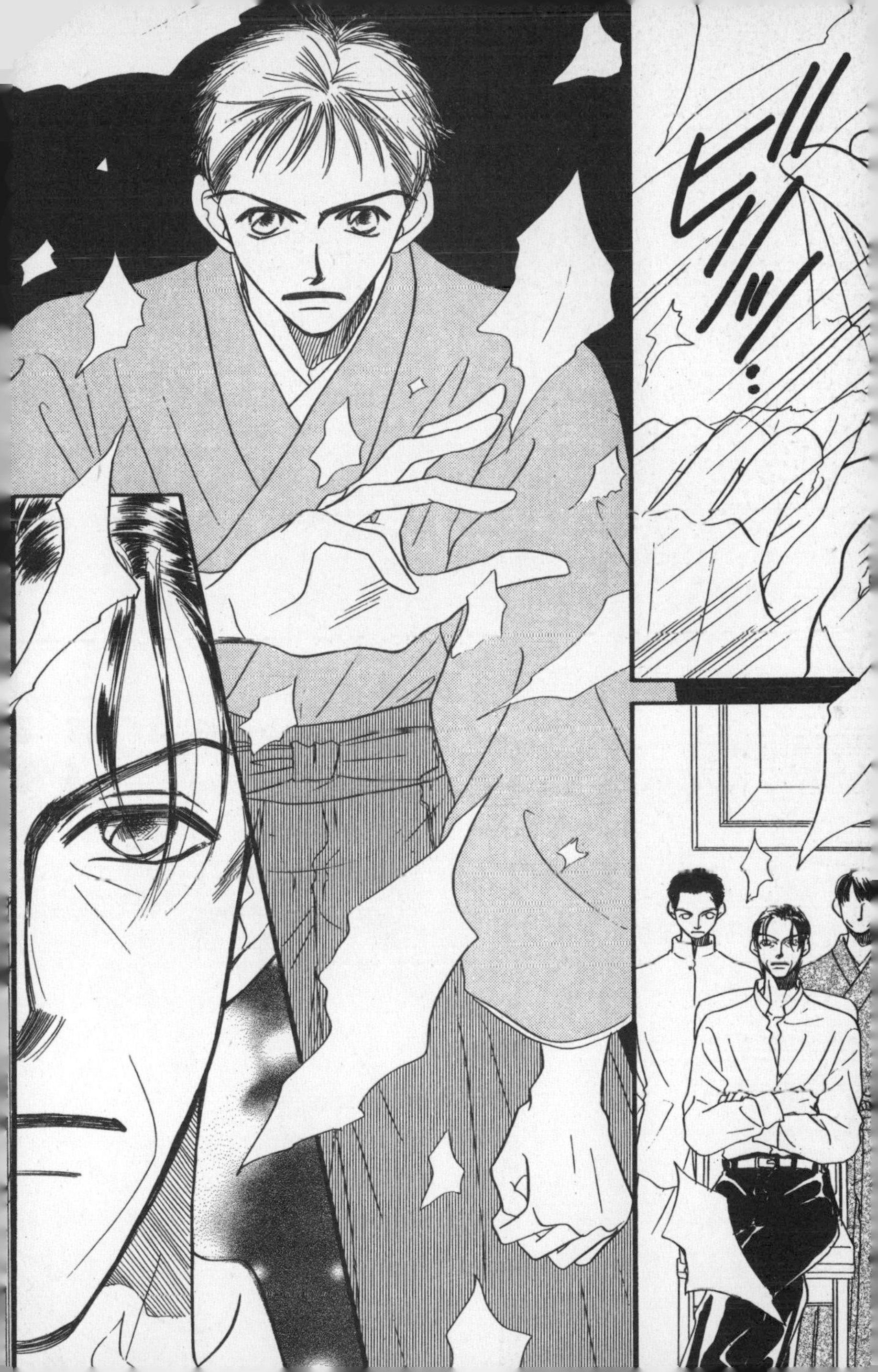
ビリッ!!

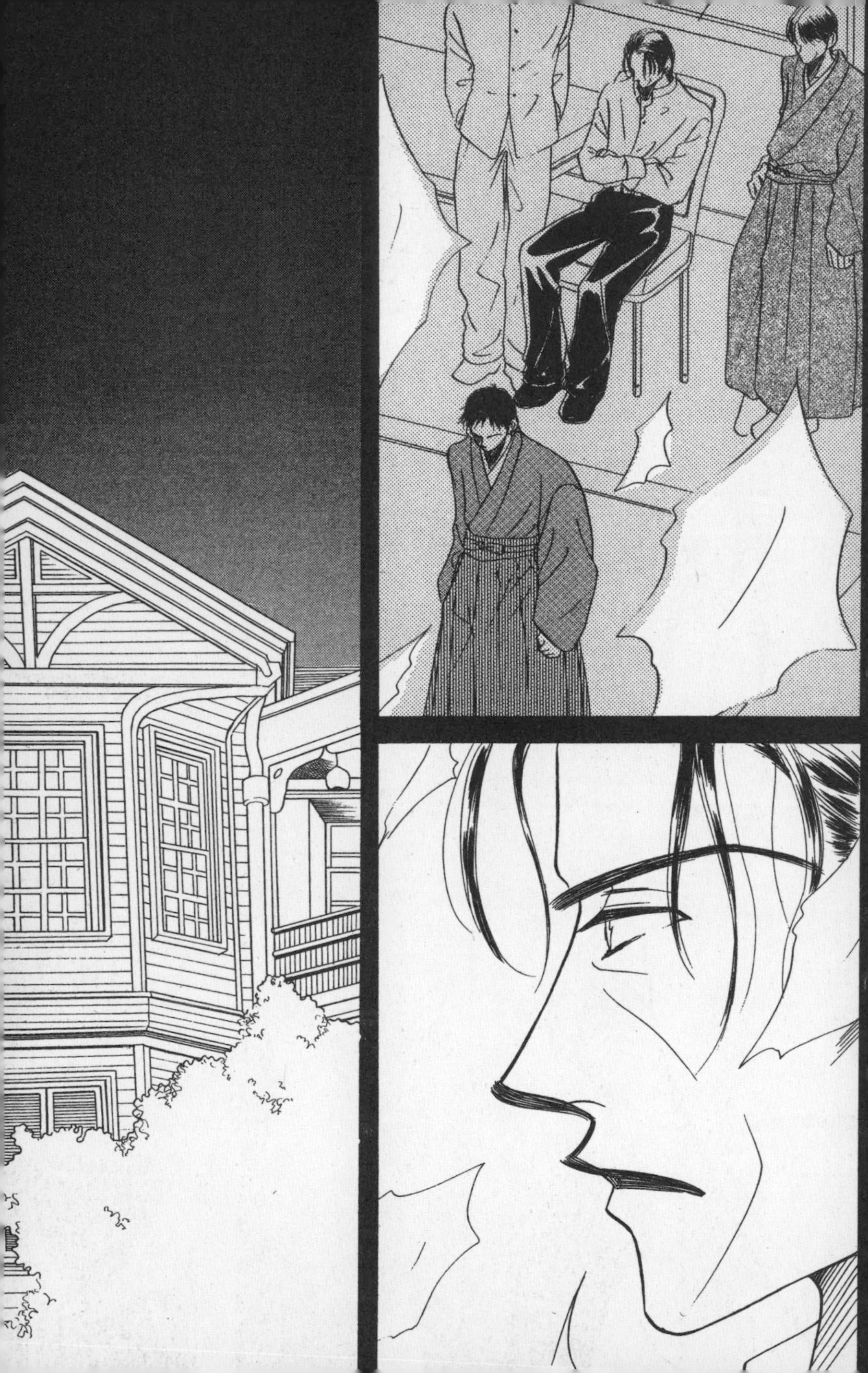

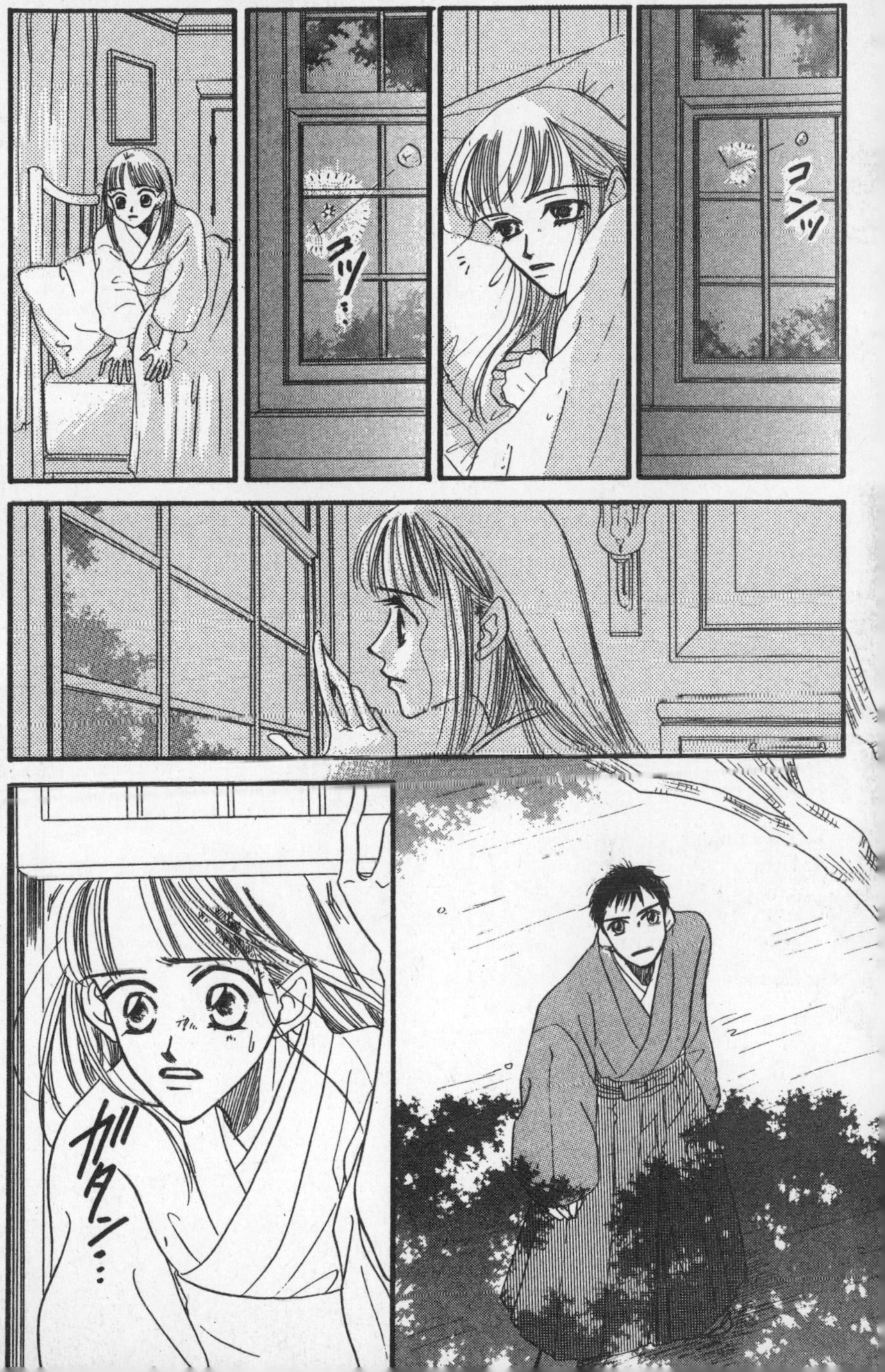
コンッ
コツッ…
ガタン…

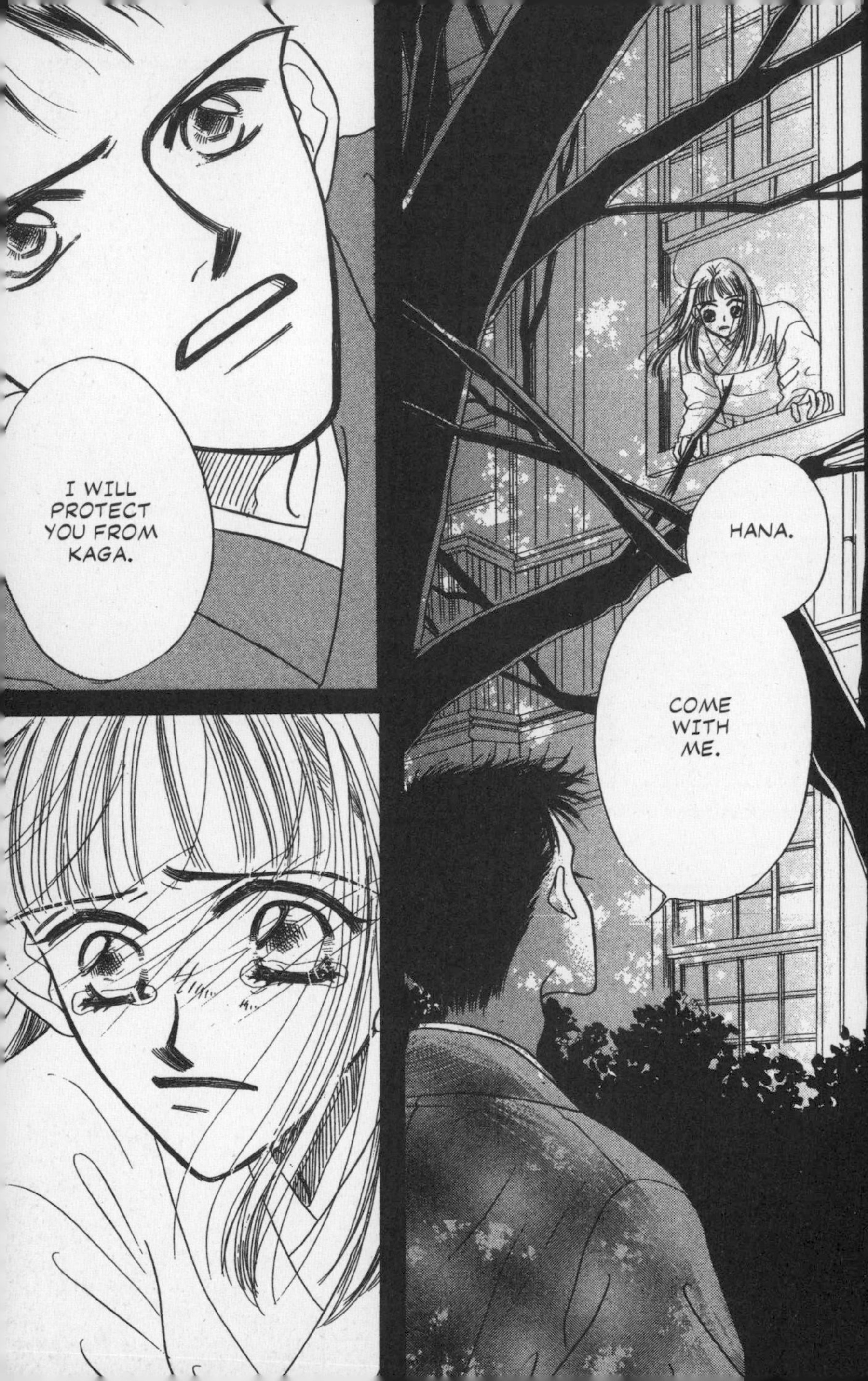
HANA.
COME WITH ME.
I WILL PROTECT YOU FROM KAGA.

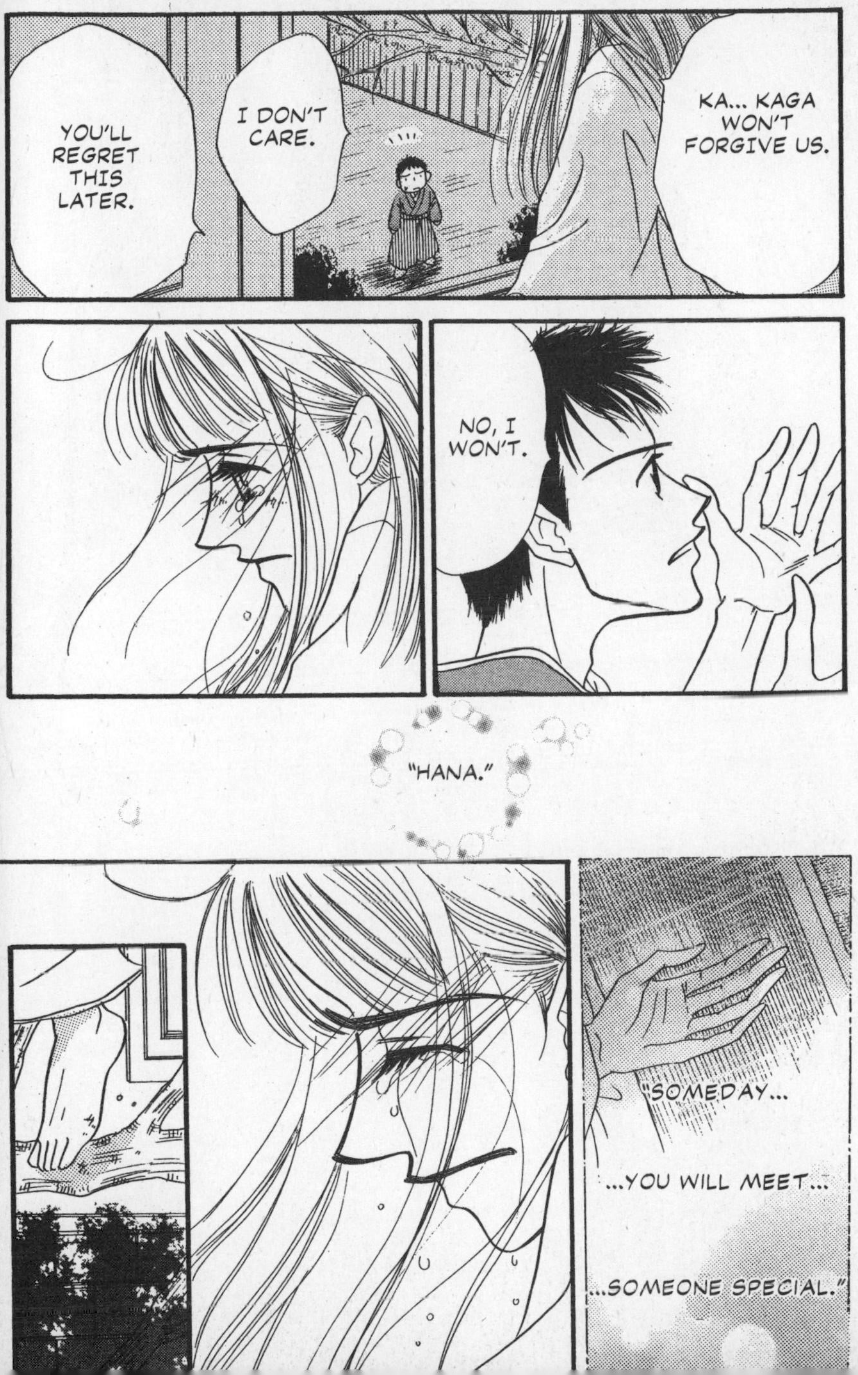
KA... KAGA WON'T FORGIVE US.
I DON'T CARE.
YOU'LL REGRET THIS LATER.
NO, I WON'T.
"HANA."
"SOMEDAY...
...YOU WILL MEET...
...SOMEONE SPECIAL."

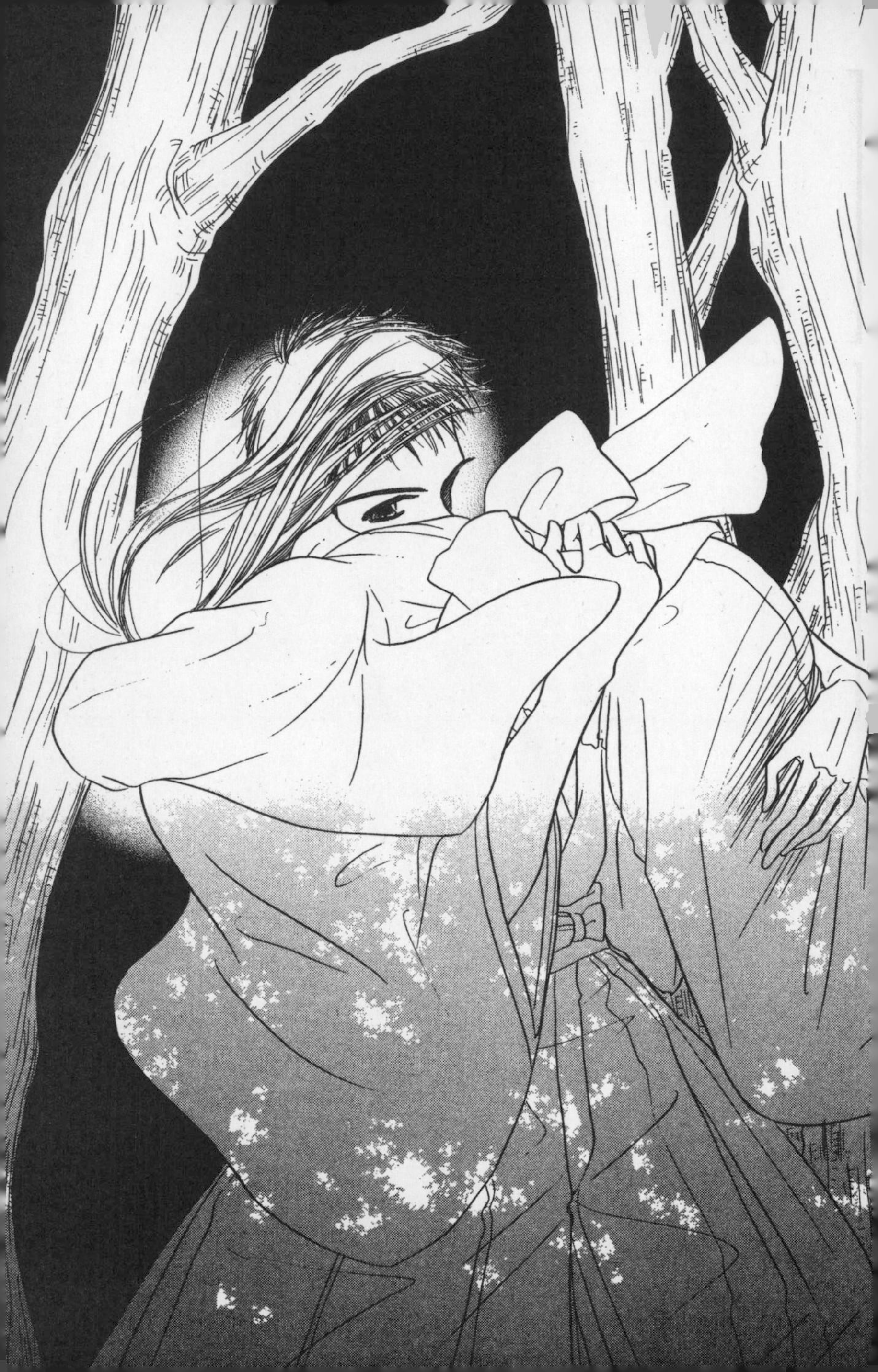

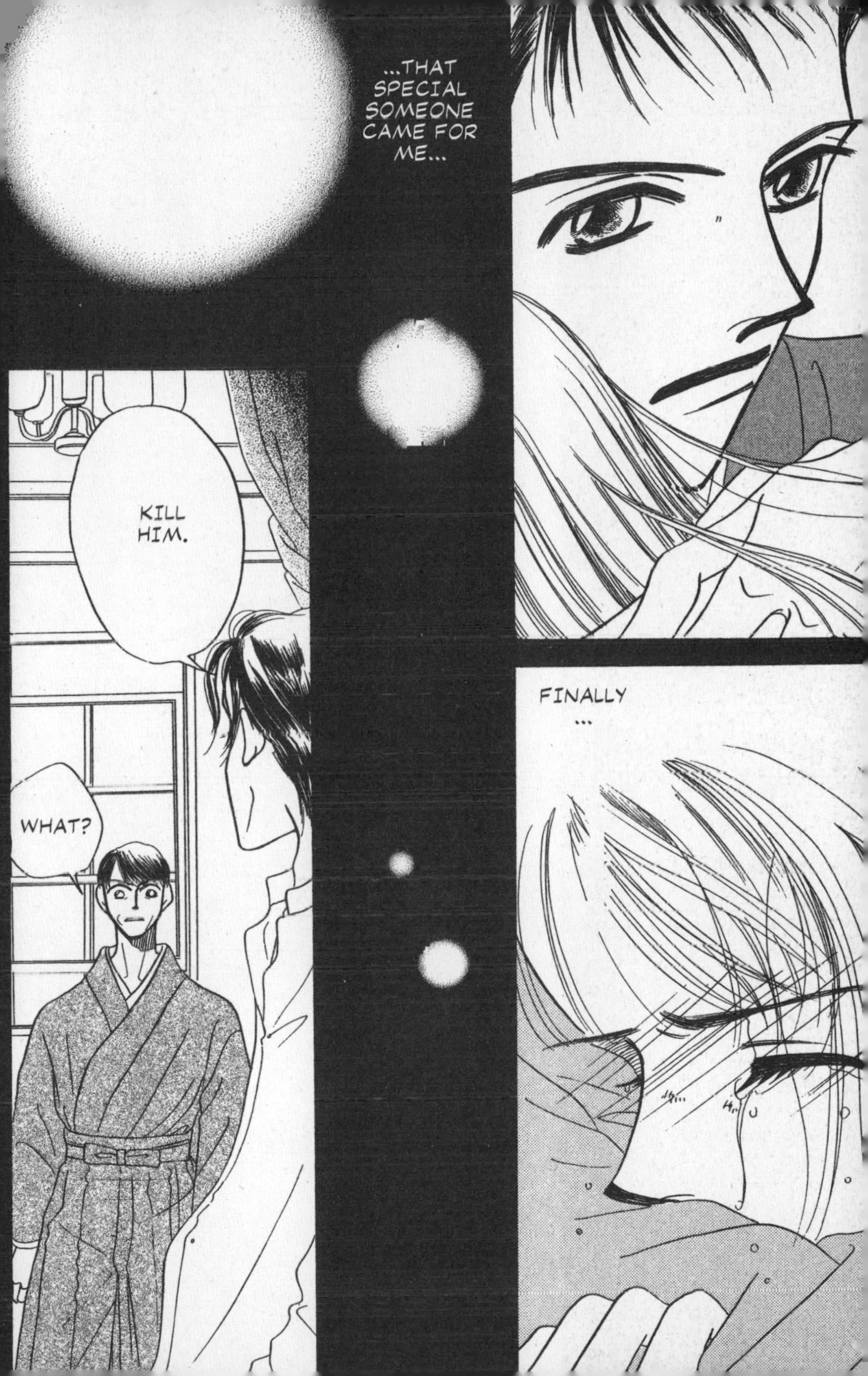
...THAT SPECIAL SOMEONE CAME FOR ME...
FINALLY ...
KILL HIM.
WHAT?

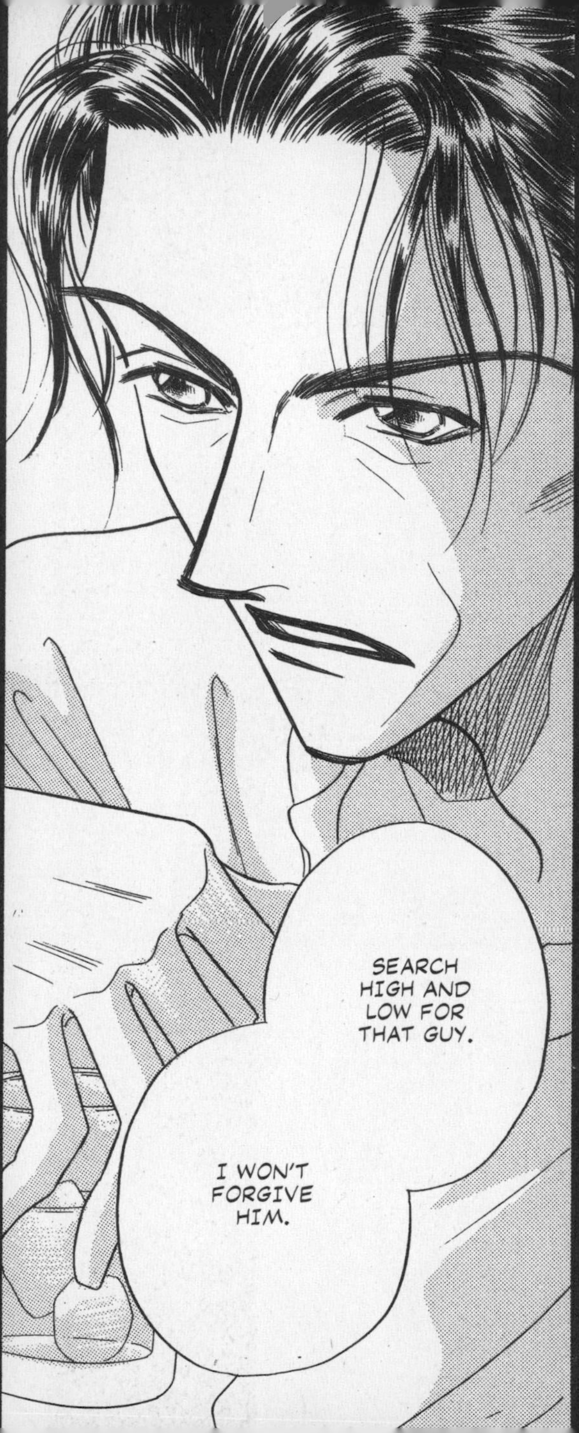
SEARCH HIGH AND LOW FOR THAT GUY.
I WON'T FORGIVE HIM.

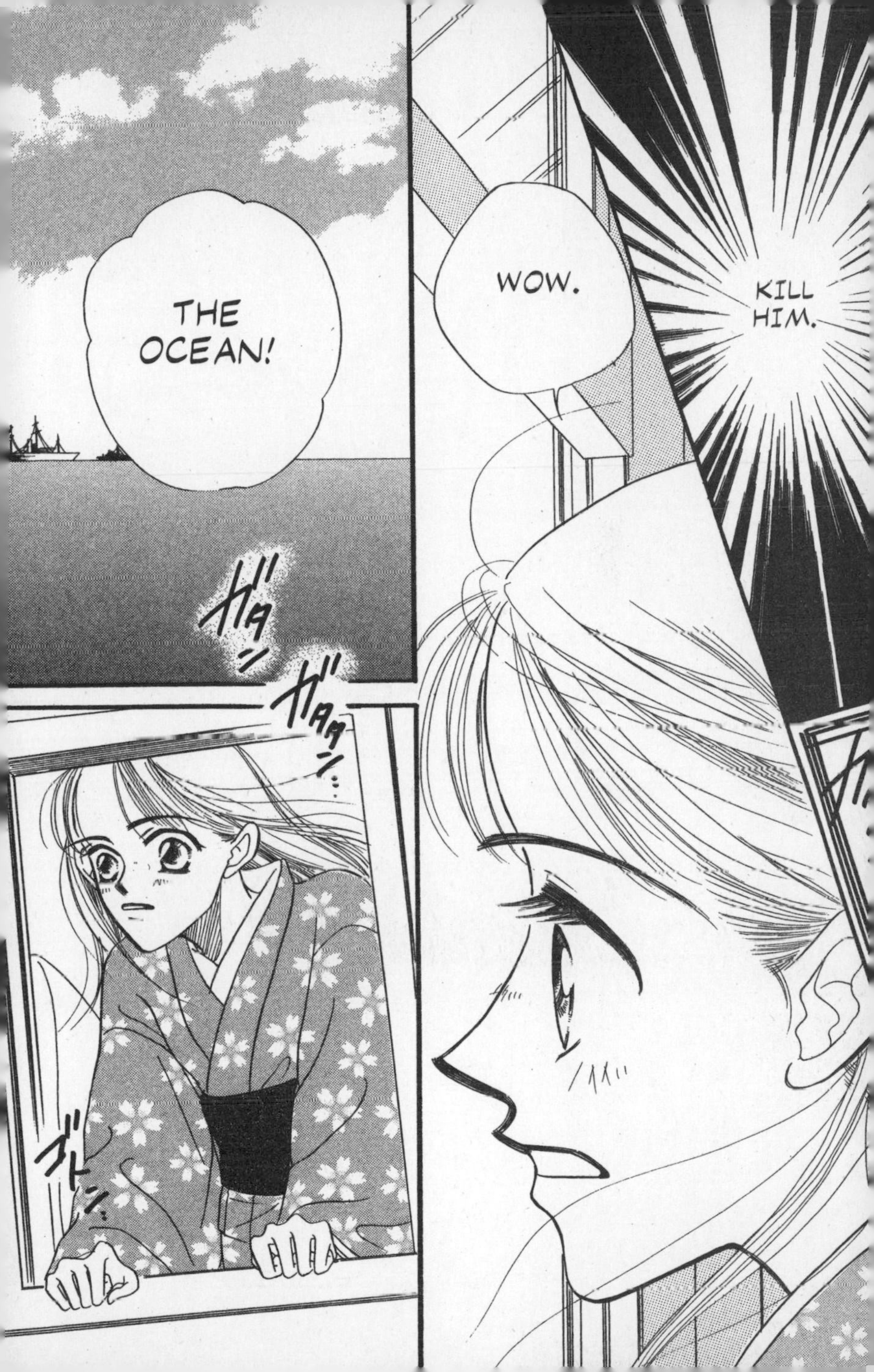
KILL HIM.
WOW.
THE OCEAN!

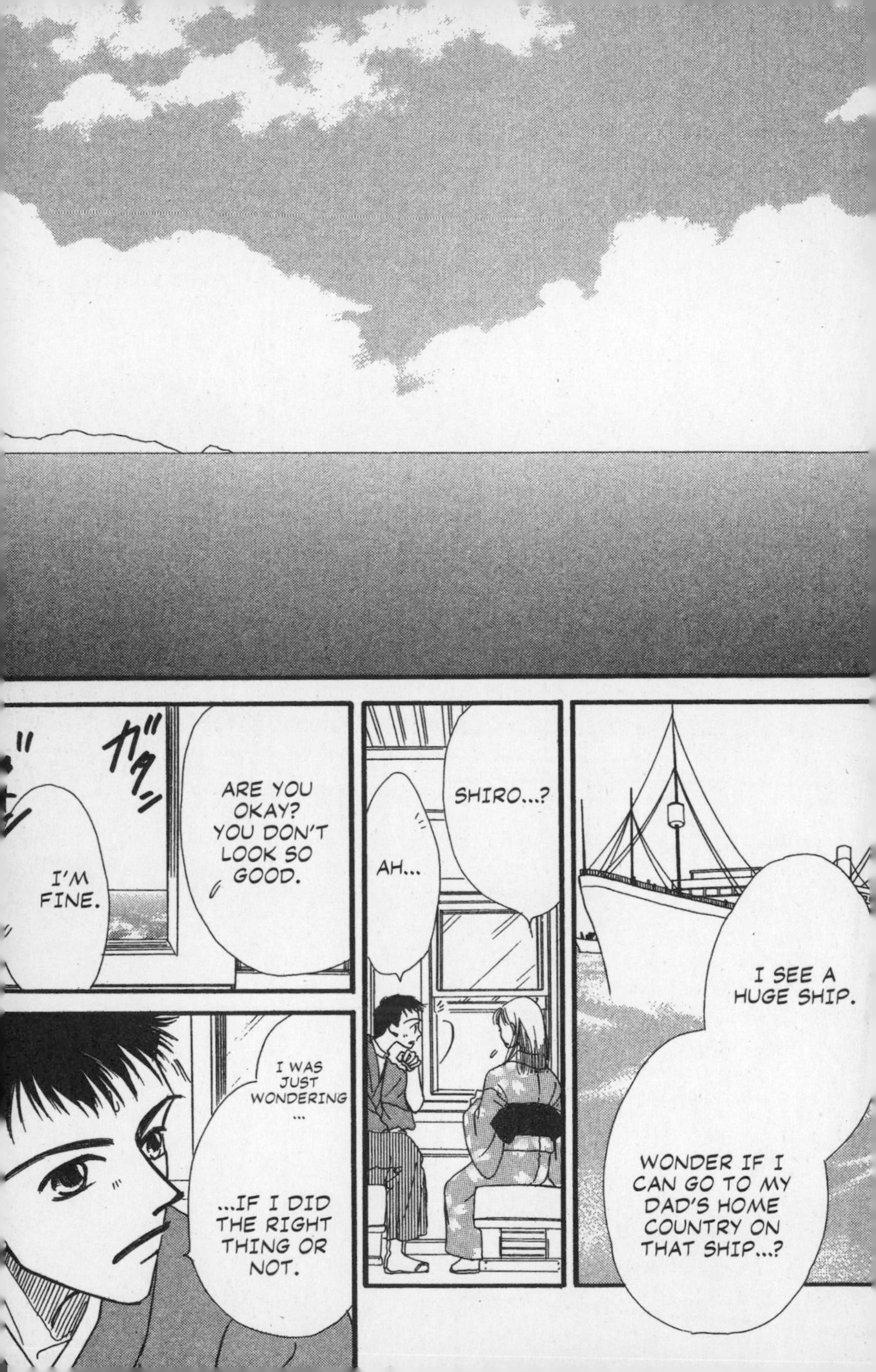
I SEE A HUGE SHIP.
WONDER IF I CAN GO TO MY DAD'S HOME COUNTRY ON THAT SHIP...?
SHIRO...?
AH...
ARE YOU OKAY? YOU DON'T LOOK SO GOOD.
ガタッ
I'M FINE.
I WAS JUST WONDERING...
...IF I DID THE RIGHT THING OR NOT.

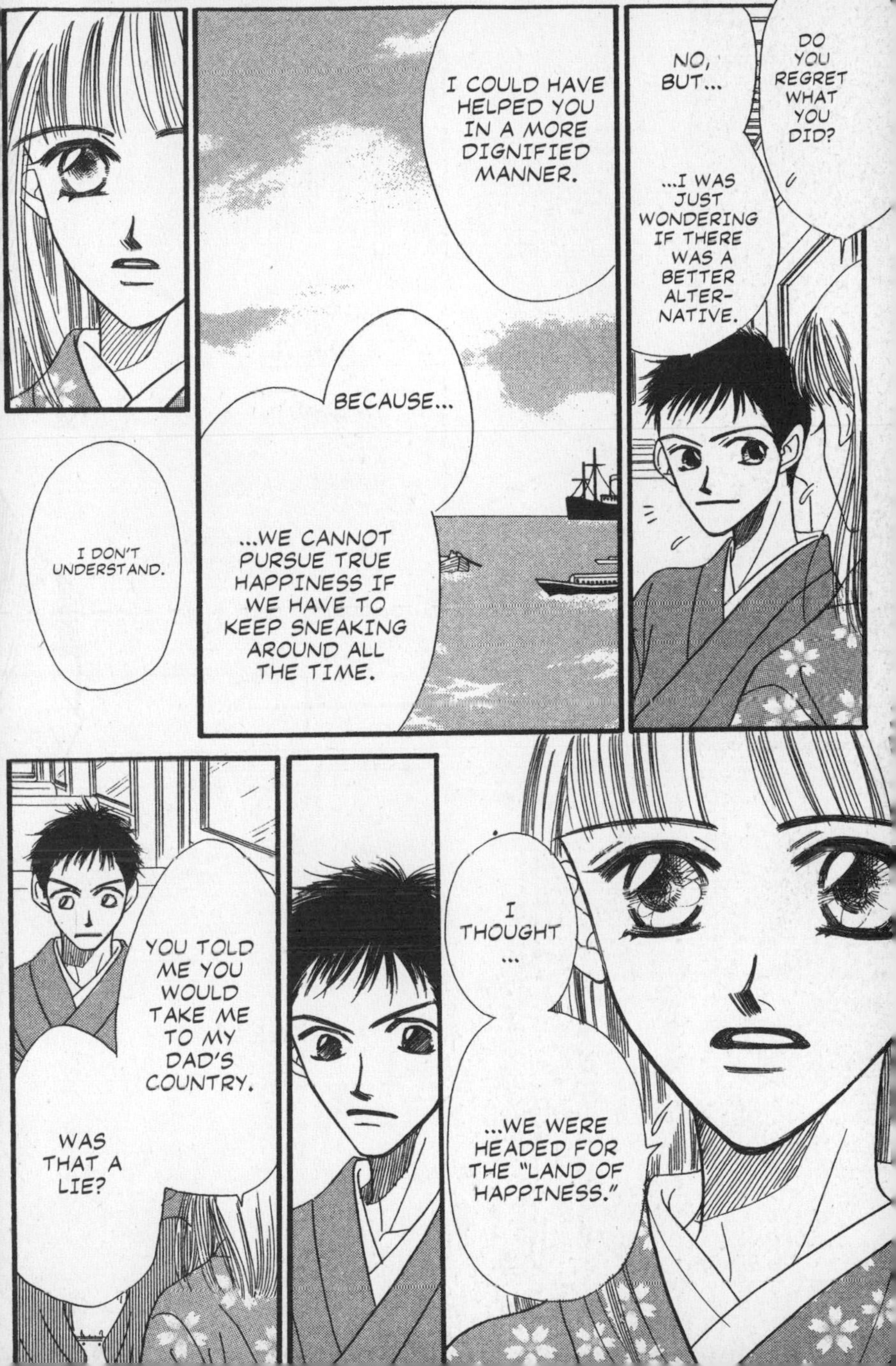
DO YOU REGRET WHAT YOU DID?
NO, BUT...
...I WAS JUST WONDERING IF THERE WAS A BETTER ALTER-NATIVE.
I COULD HAVE HELPED YOU IN A MORE DIGNIFIED MANNER.
BECAUSE...
...WE CANNOT PURSUE TRUE HAPPINESS IF WE HAVE TO KEEP SNEAKING AROUND ALL THE TIME.
I DON'T UNDERSTAND.
I THOUGHT...
...WE WERE HEADED FOR THE "LAND OF HAPPINESS."
YOU TOLD ME YOU WOULD TAKE ME TO MY DAD'S COUNTRY.
WAS THAT A LIE?

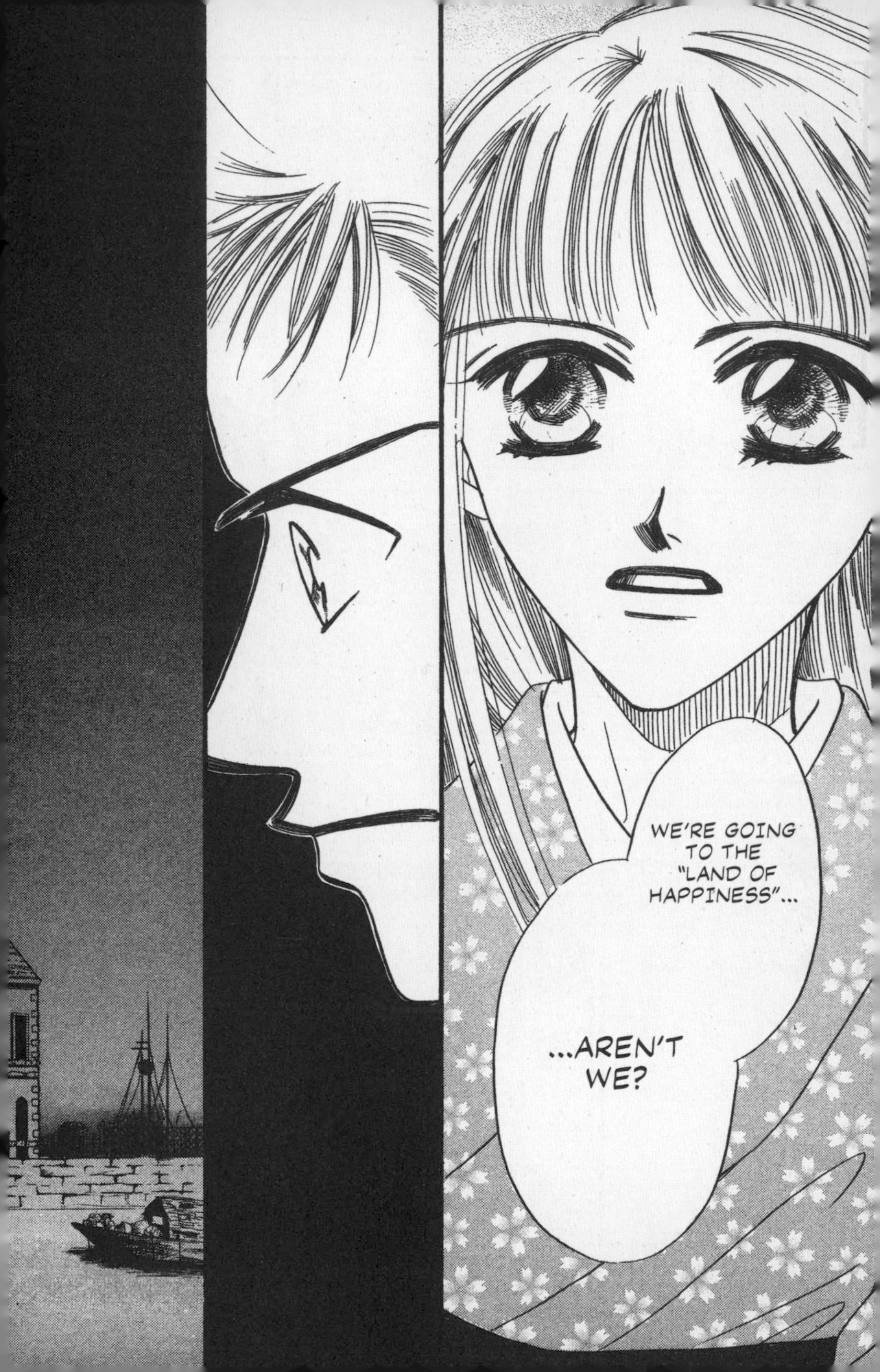
WE'RE GOING TO THE "LAND OF HAPPINESS"...
...AREN'T WE?

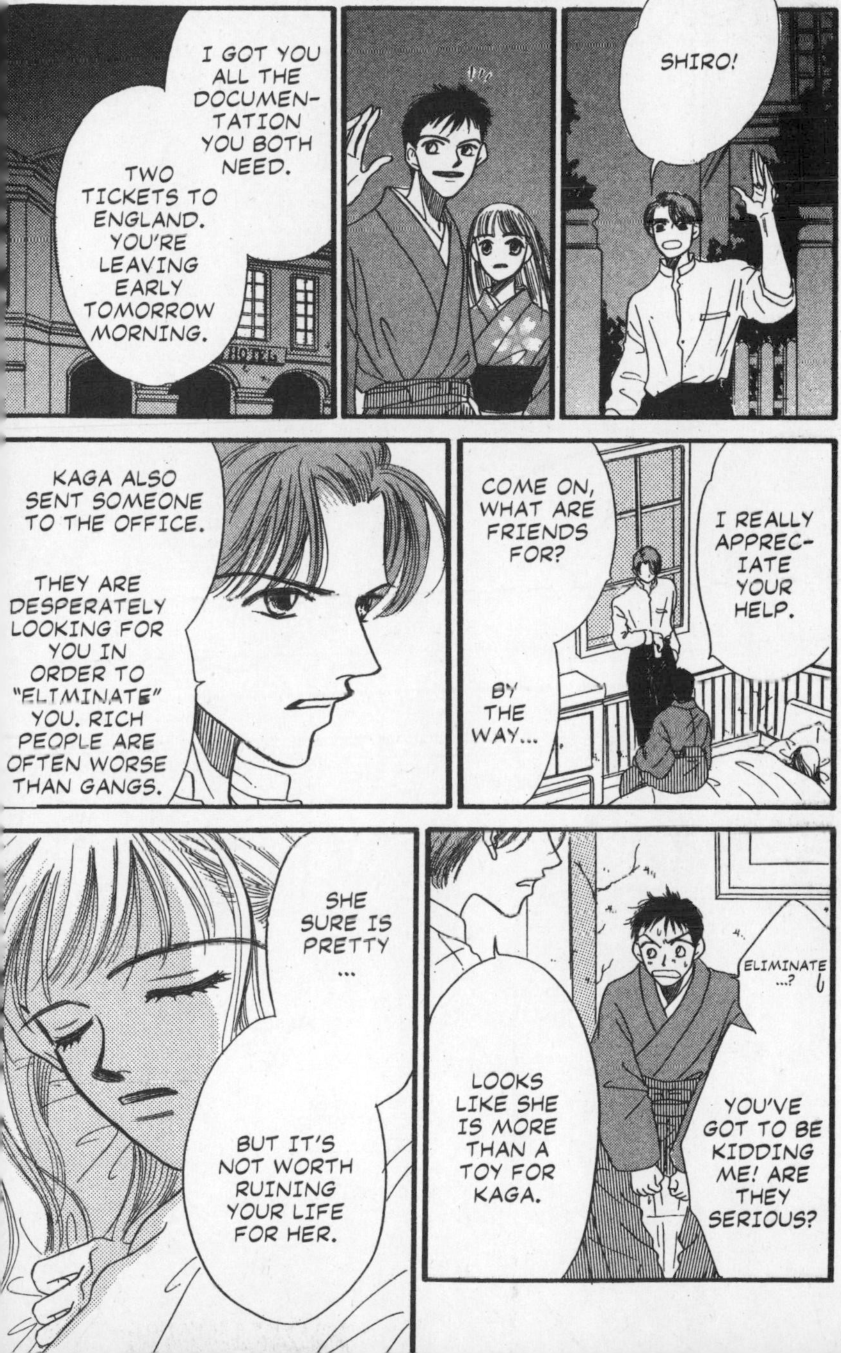
SHIRO!
I GOT YOU ALL THE DOCUMENTATION YOU BOTH NEED.
TWO TICKETS TO ENGLAND. YOU'RE LEAVING EARLY TOMORROW MORNING.
HOTEL
I REALLY APPRECIATE YOUR HELP.
COME ON, WHAT ARE FRIENDS FOR?
BY THE WAY...
KAGA ALSO SENT SOMEONE TO THE OFFICE.
THEY ARE DESPERATELY LOOKING FOR YOU IN ORDER TO "ELIMINATE" YOU. RICH PEOPLE ARE OFTEN WORSE THAN GANGS.
ELIMINATE ...?
YOU'VE GOT TO BE KIDDING ME! ARE THEY SERIOUS?
LOOKS LIKE SHE IS MORE THAN A TOY FOR KAGA.
SHE SURE IS PRETTY ...
BUT IT'S NOT WORTH RUINING YOUR LIFE FOR HER.

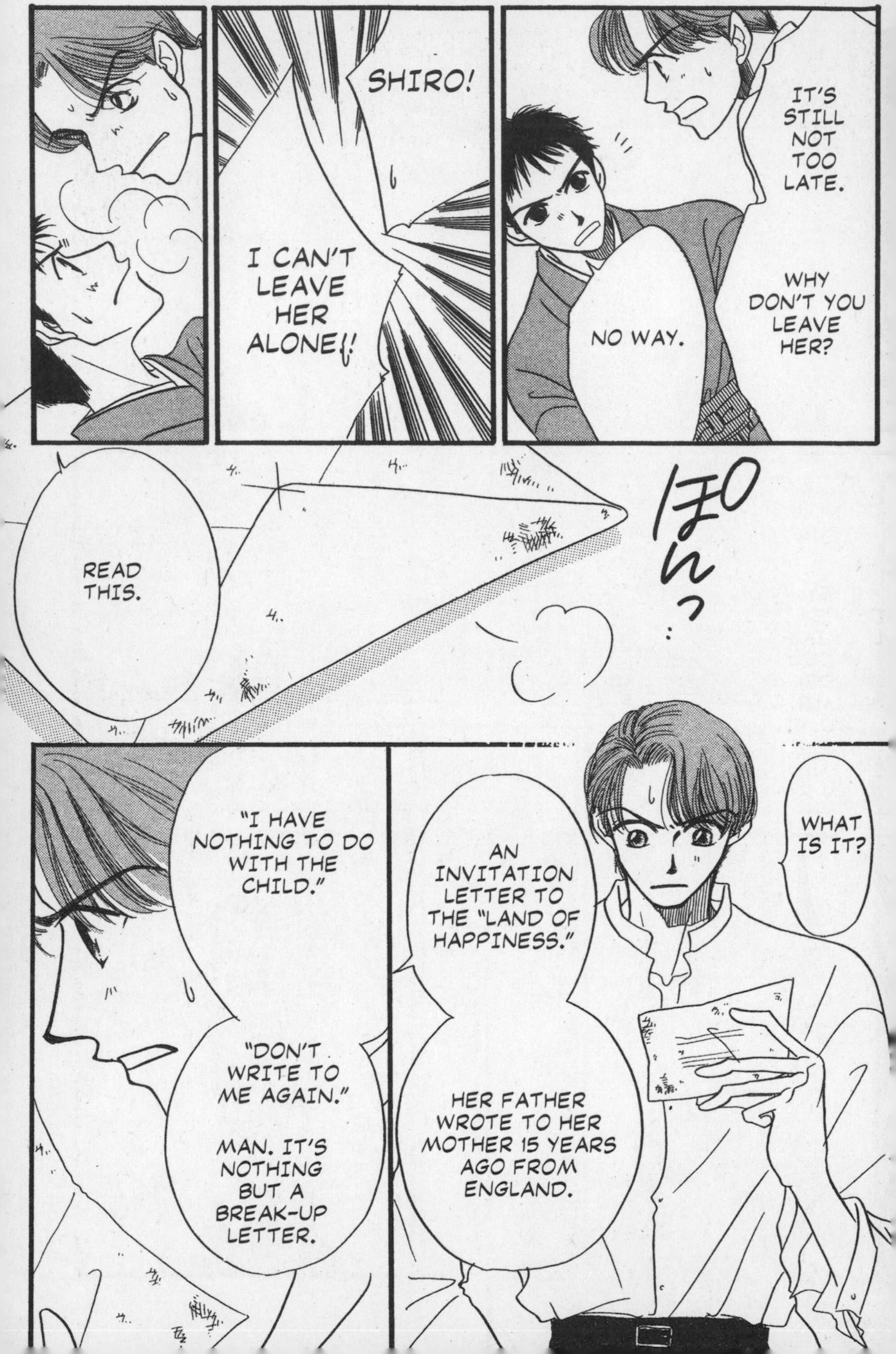
IT'S STILL NOT TOO LATE.
WHY DON'T YOU LEAVE HER?
NO WAY.
SHIRO!
I CAN'T LEAVE HER ALONE!!
ぽんっ
READ THIS.
WHAT IS IT?
AN INVITATION LETTER TO THE "LAND OF HAPPINESS."
HER FATHER WROTE TO HER MOTHER 15 YEARS AGO FROM ENGLAND.
"I HAVE NOTHING TO DO WITH THE CHILD."
"DON'T WRITE TO ME AGAIN."
MAN. IT'S NOTHING BUT A BREAK-UP LETTER.

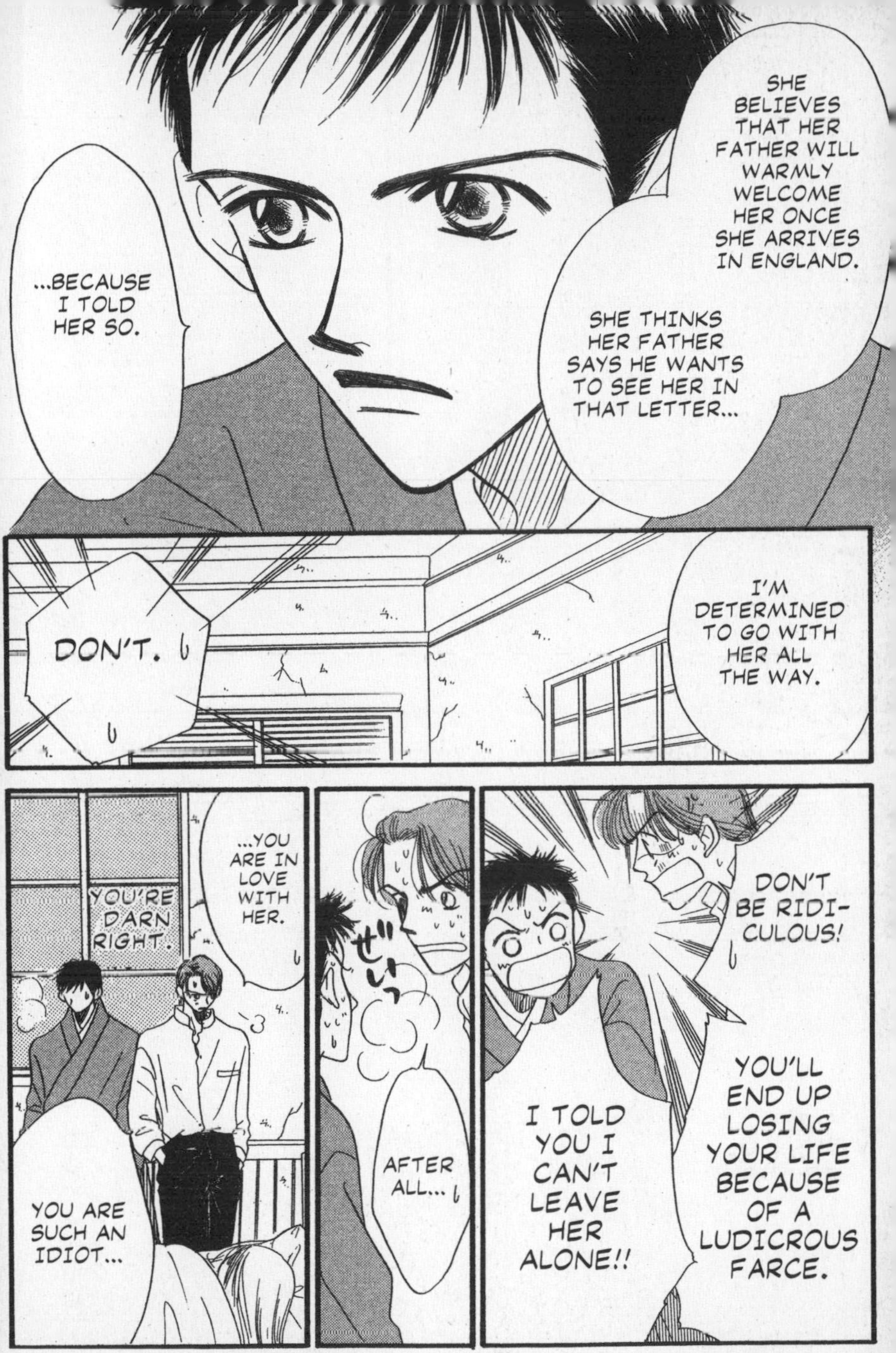
SHE BELIEVES THAT HER FATHER WILL WARMLY WELCOME HER ONCE SHE ARRIVES IN ENGLAND.
SHE THINKS HER FATHER SAYS HE WANTS TO SEE HER IN THAT LETTER...
...BECAUSE I TOLD HER SO.
I'M DETERMINED TO GO WITH HER ALL THE WAY.
DON'T.
DON'T BE RIDI- CULOUS!
YOU'LL END UP LOSING YOUR LIFE BECAUSE OF A LUDICROUS FARCE.
I TOLD YOU I CAN'T LEAVE HER ALONE!!
ぜいっ
AFTER ALL...
...YOU ARE IN LOVE WITH HER.
YOU'RE DARN RIGHT.
YOU ARE SUCH AN IDIOT...

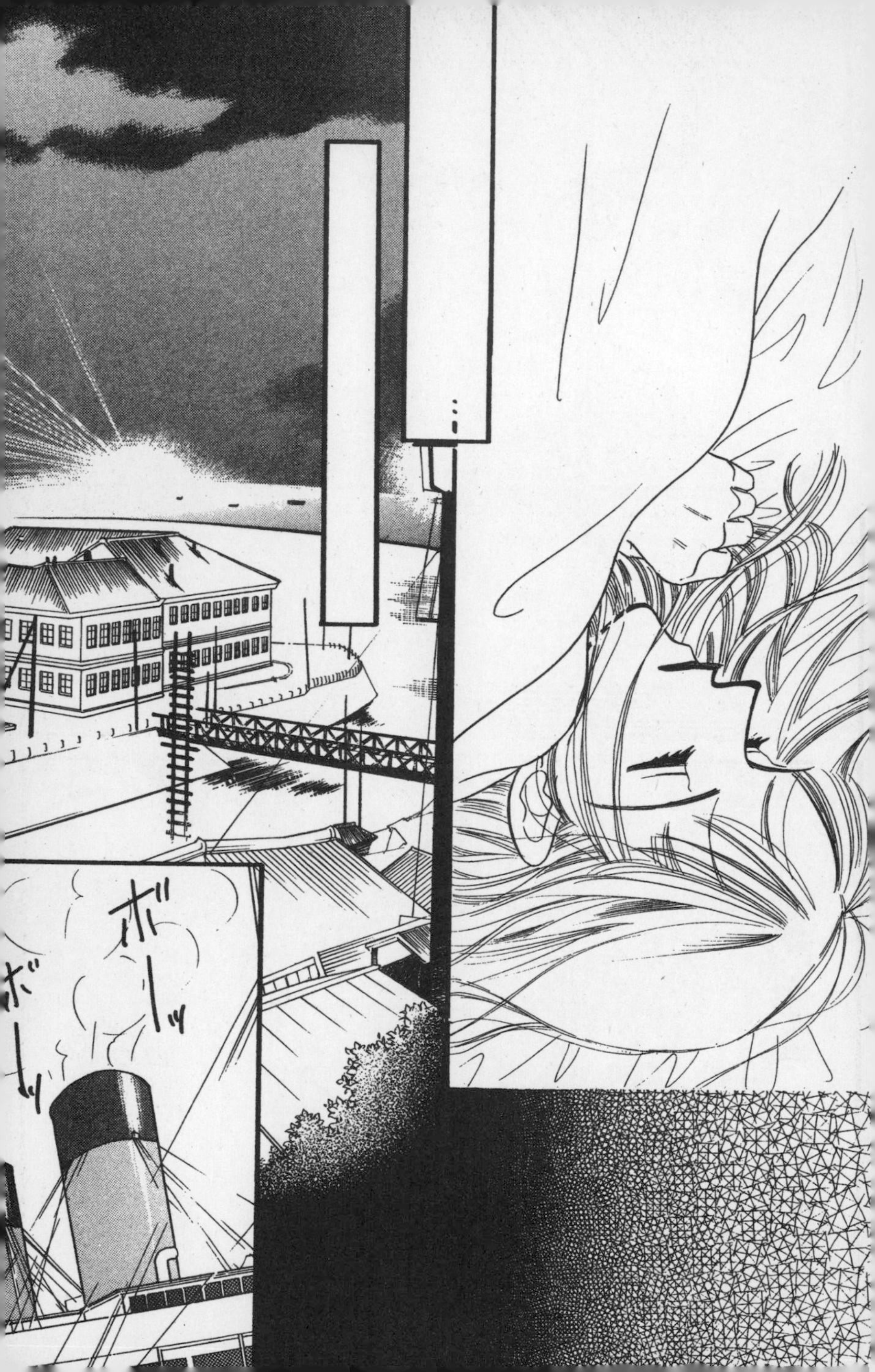
ボーッ
ボーッ

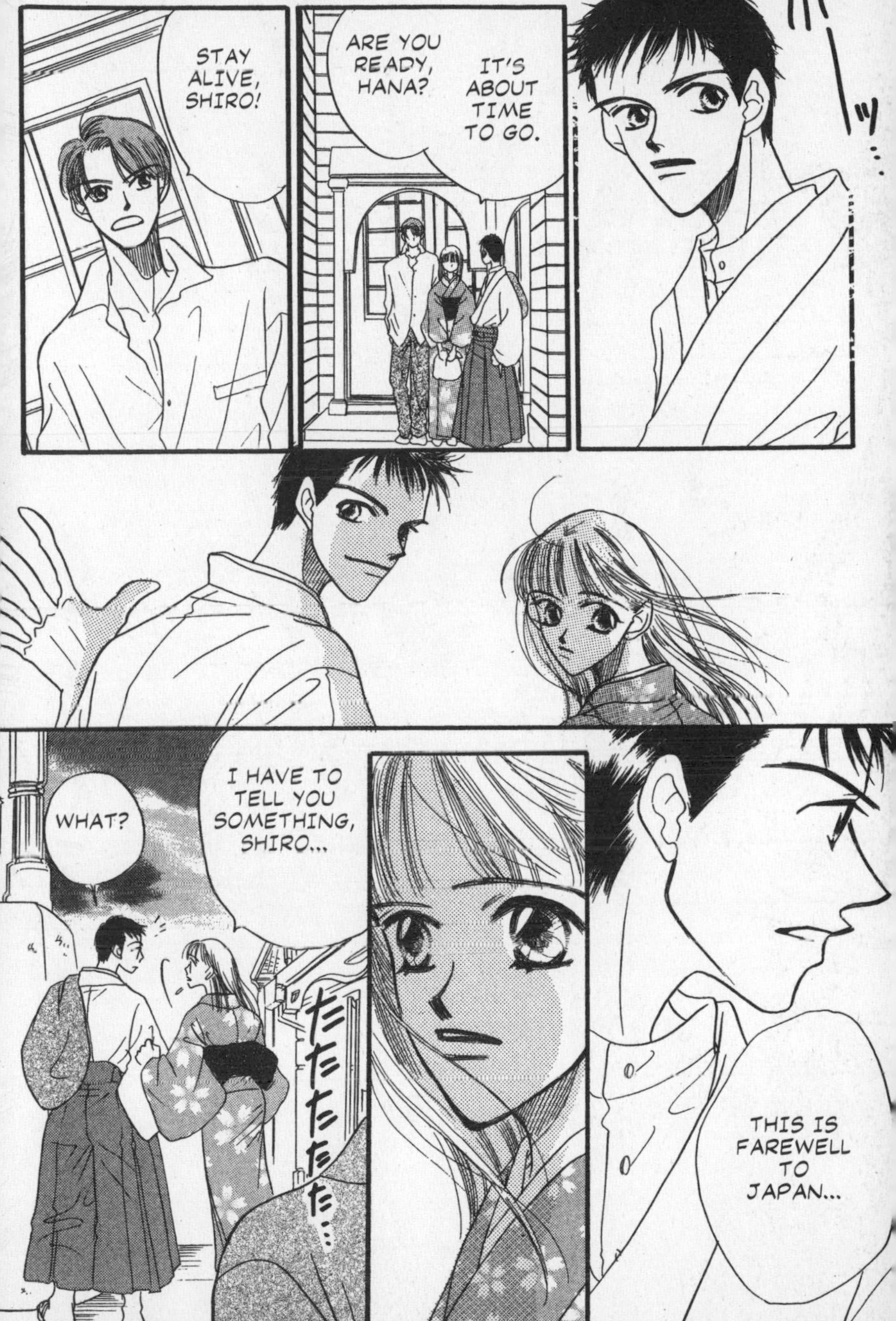
ボーッ…
ARE YOU READY, HANA?
IT'S ABOUT TIME TO GO.
STAY ALIVE, SHIRO!
THIS IS FAREWELL TO JAPAN...
I HAVE TO TELL YOU SOMETHING, SHIRO...
WHAT?
たたたたた…

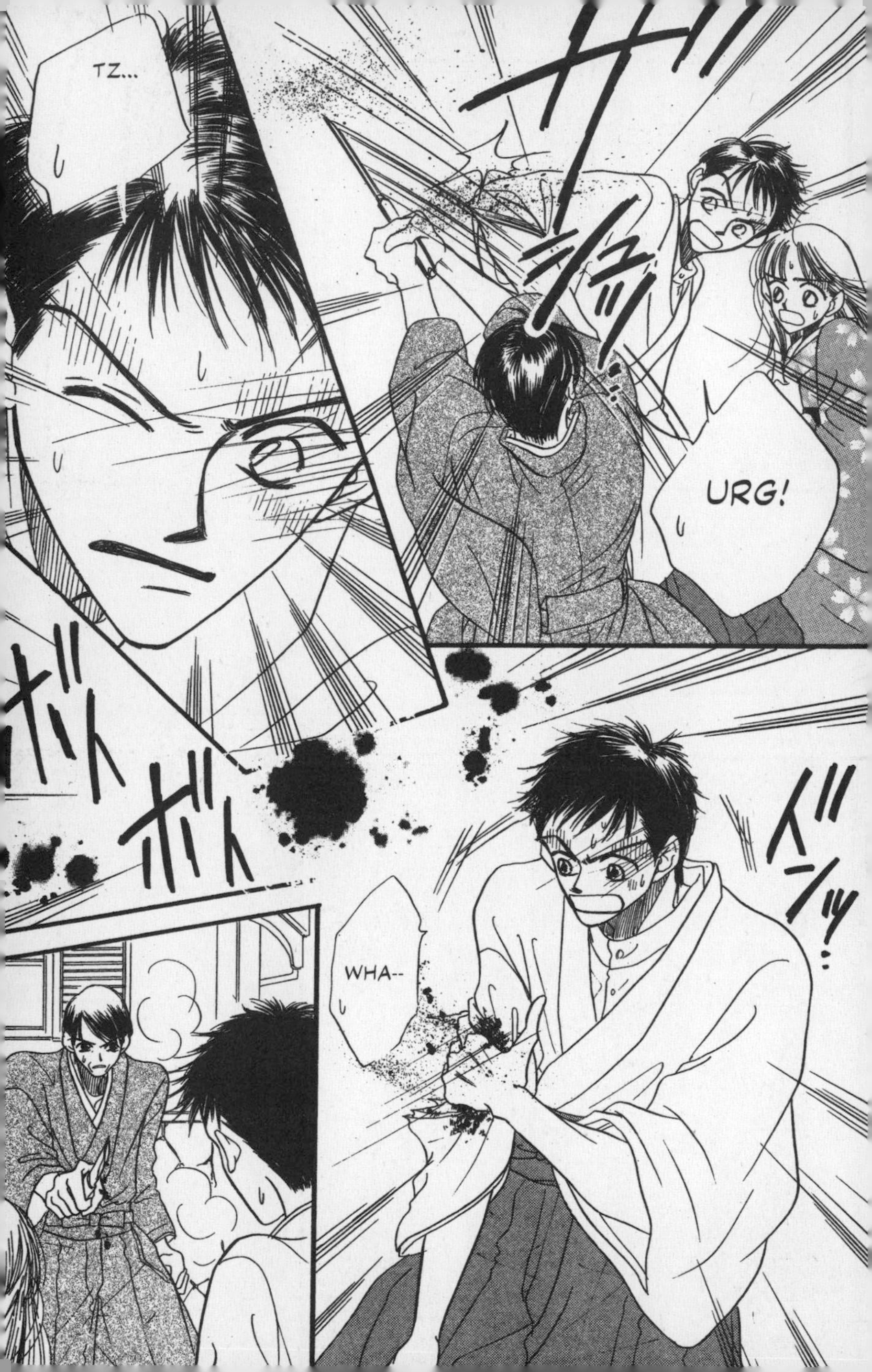
URG!
TZ...
WHA--

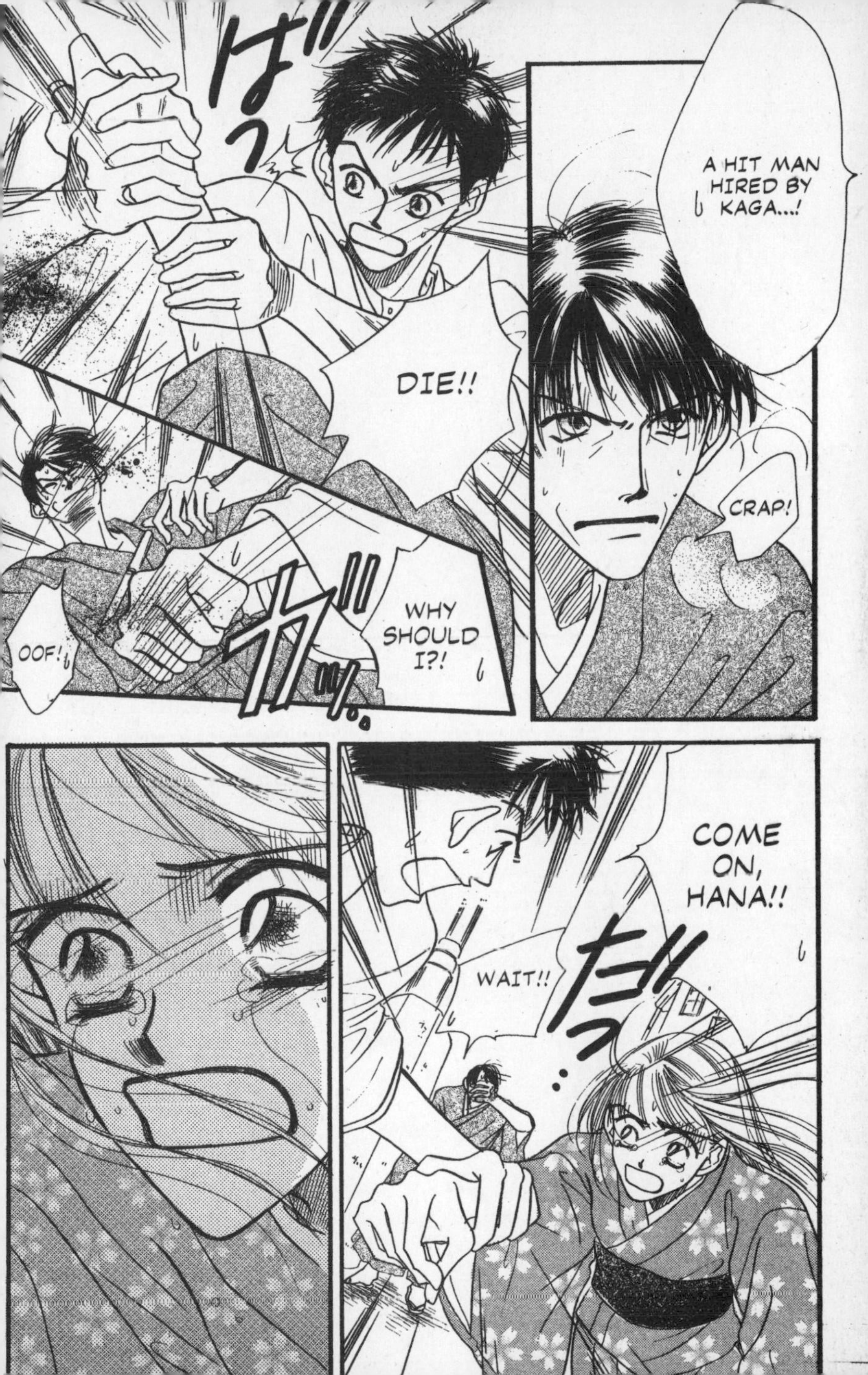
A HIT MAN HIRED BY KAGA...!
CRAP!
ばっ
DIE!!
ガッ
WHY SHOULD I?!
OOF!
COME ON, HANA!!
たっ
WAIT!!

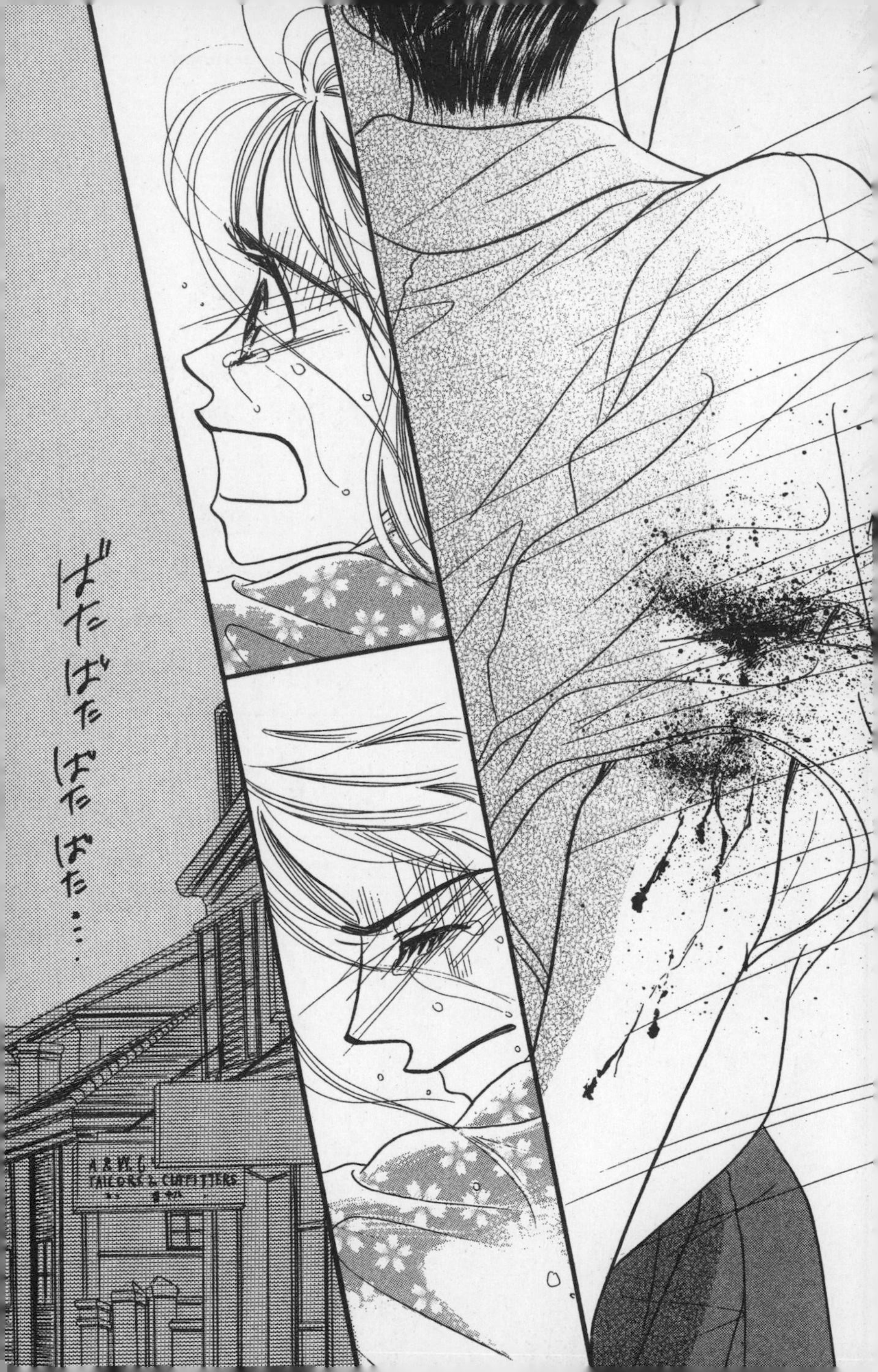
ぱたぱた ぱた ぱた…

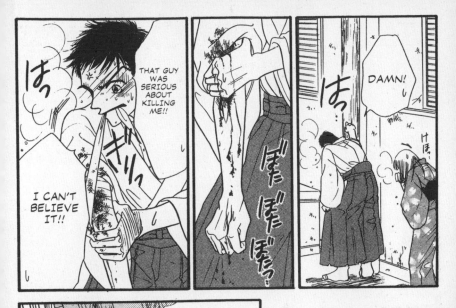

THAT GUY WAS SERIOUS ABOUT KILLING ME!!

I CAN'T BELIEVE IT!!

DAMN!

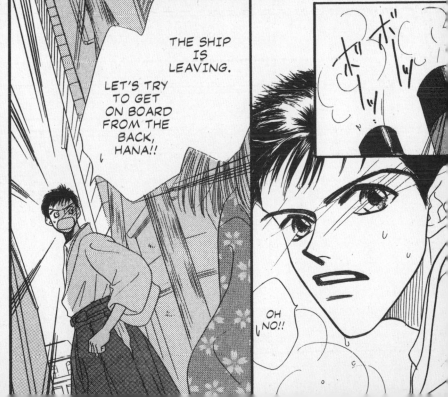

THE SHIP IS LEAVING.

LET'S TRY TO GET ON BOARD FROM THE BACK, HANA!!

OH NO!!

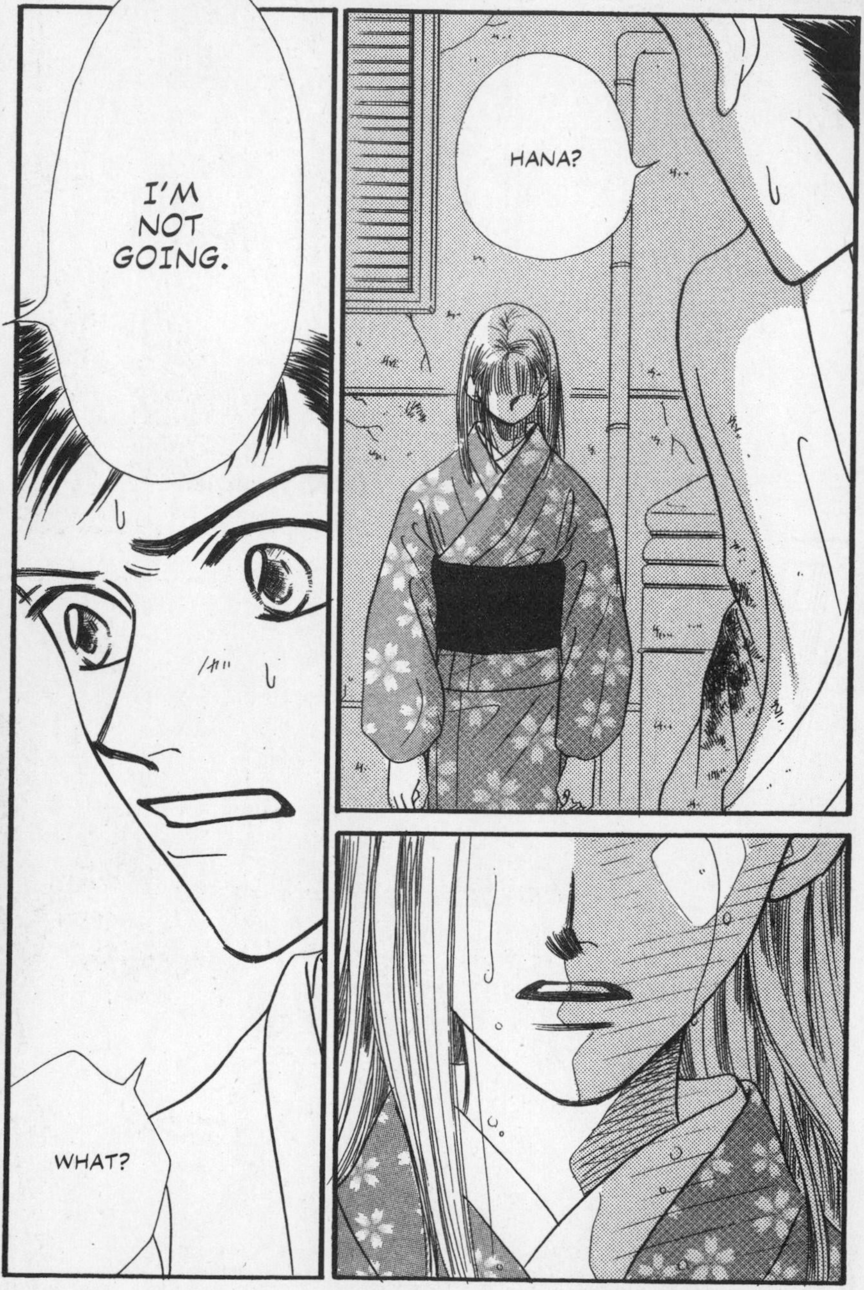
HANA?
I'M NOT GOING.
WHAT?

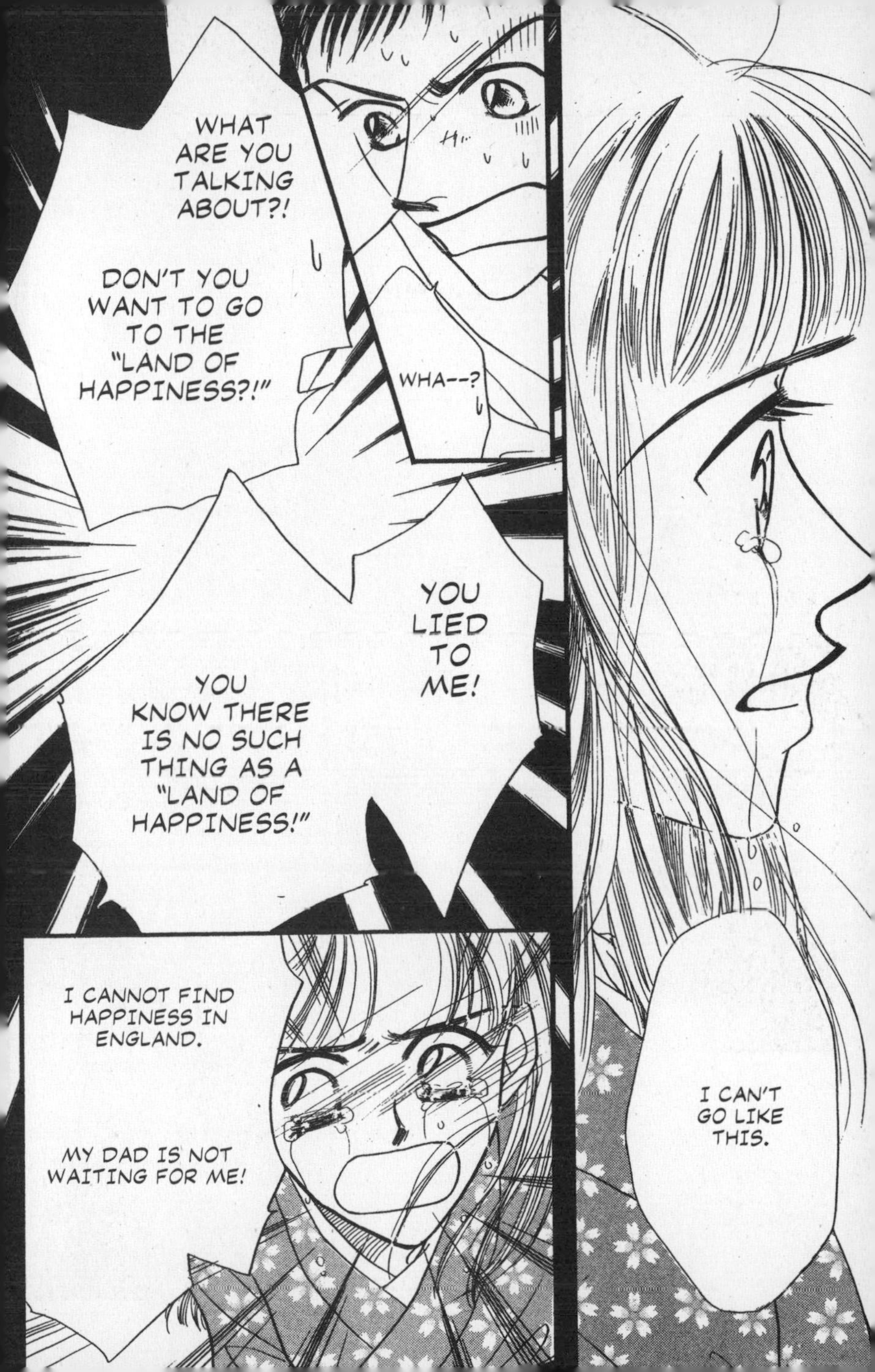
I CAN'T GO LIKE THIS.
WHAT ARE YOU TALKING ABOUT?!
DON'T YOU WANT TO GO TO THE "LAND OF HAPPINESS?!"
WHA--?
YOU LIED TO ME!
YOU KNOW THERE IS NO SUCH THING AS A "LAND OF HAPPINESS!"
I CANNOT FIND HAPPINESS IN ENGLAND.
MY DAD IS NOT WAITING FOR ME!

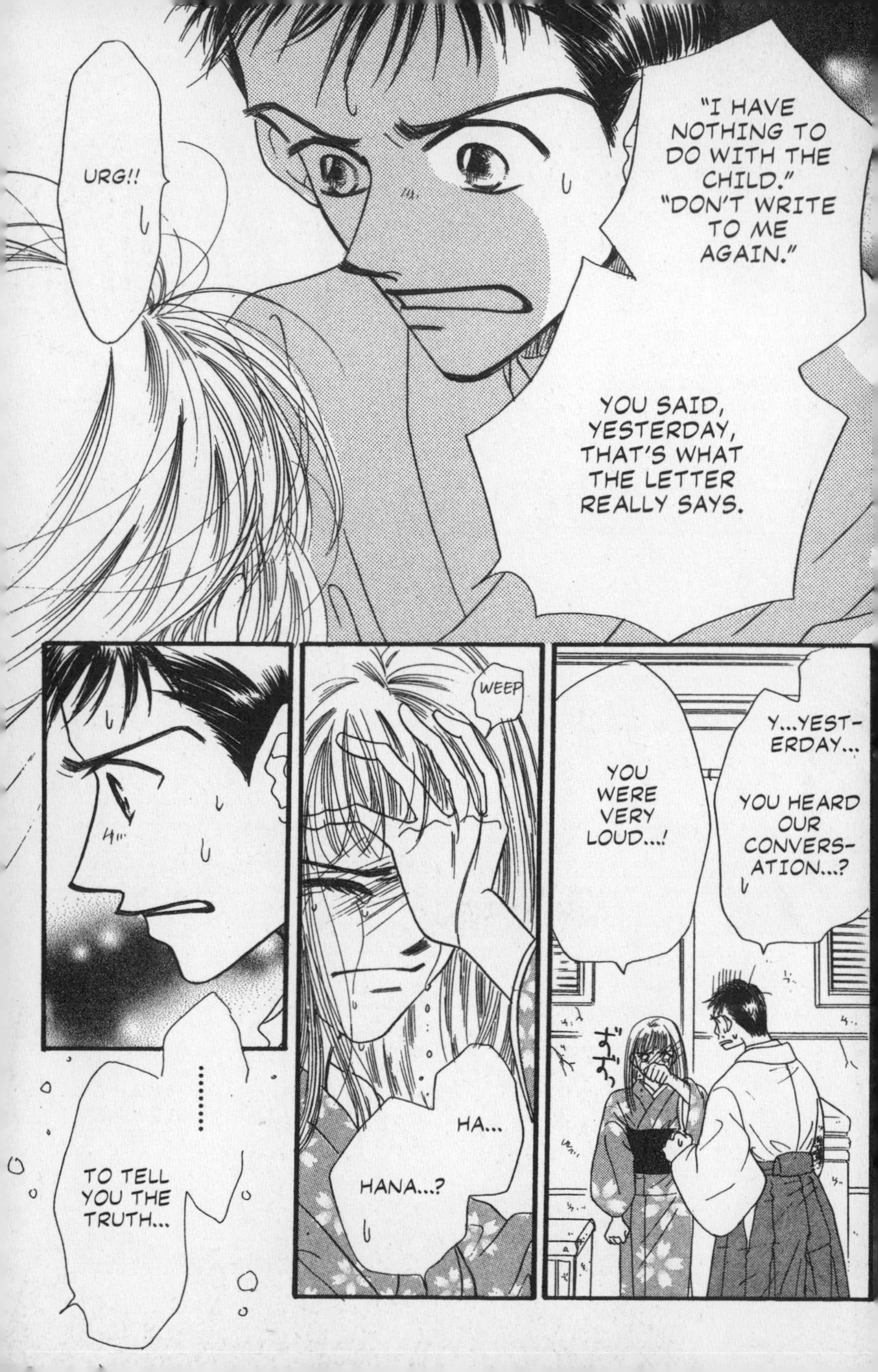
"I HAVE NOTHING TO DO WITH THE CHILD." "DON'T WRITE TO ME AGAIN."
YOU SAID, YESTERDAY, THAT'S WHAT THE LETTER REALLY SAYS.
URG!!
Y...YEST-ERDAY...
YOU HEARD OUR CONVERS-ATION...?
YOU WERE VERY LOUD...!
WEEP
HA...
HANA...?
......
TO TELL YOU THE TRUTH...

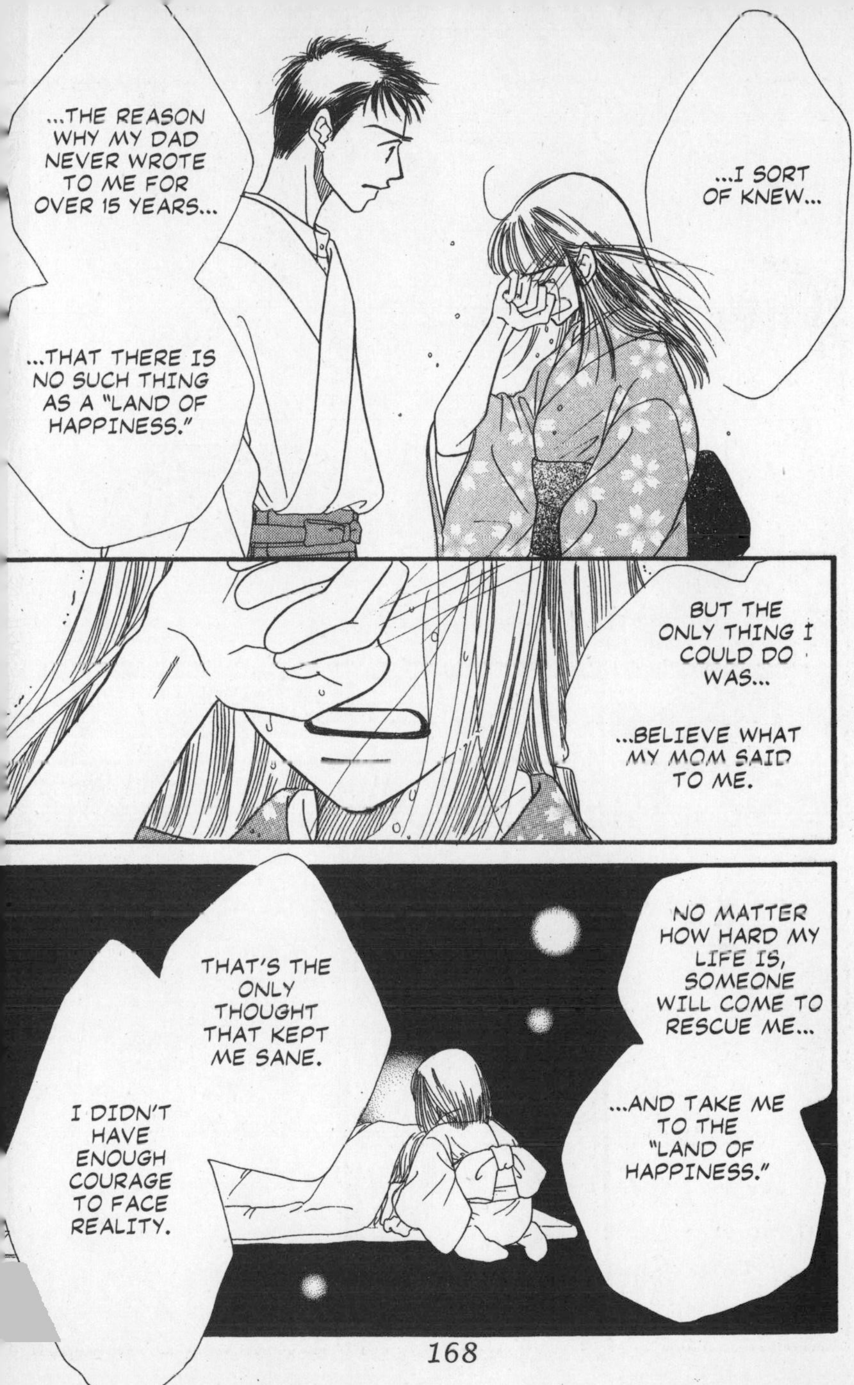
...I SORT OF KNEW...
...THE REASON WHY MY DAD NEVER WROTE TO ME FOR OVER 15 YEARS...
...THAT THERE IS NO SUCH THING AS A "LAND OF HAPPINESS."
BUT THE ONLY THING I COULD DO WAS...
...BELIEVE WHAT MY MOM SAID TO ME.
NO MATTER HOW HARD MY LIFE IS, SOMEONE WILL COME TO RESCUE ME...
...AND TAKE ME TO THE "LAND OF HAPPINESS."
THAT'S THE ONLY THOUGHT THAT KEPT ME SANE.
I DIDN'T HAVE ENOUGH COURAGE TO FACE REALITY.

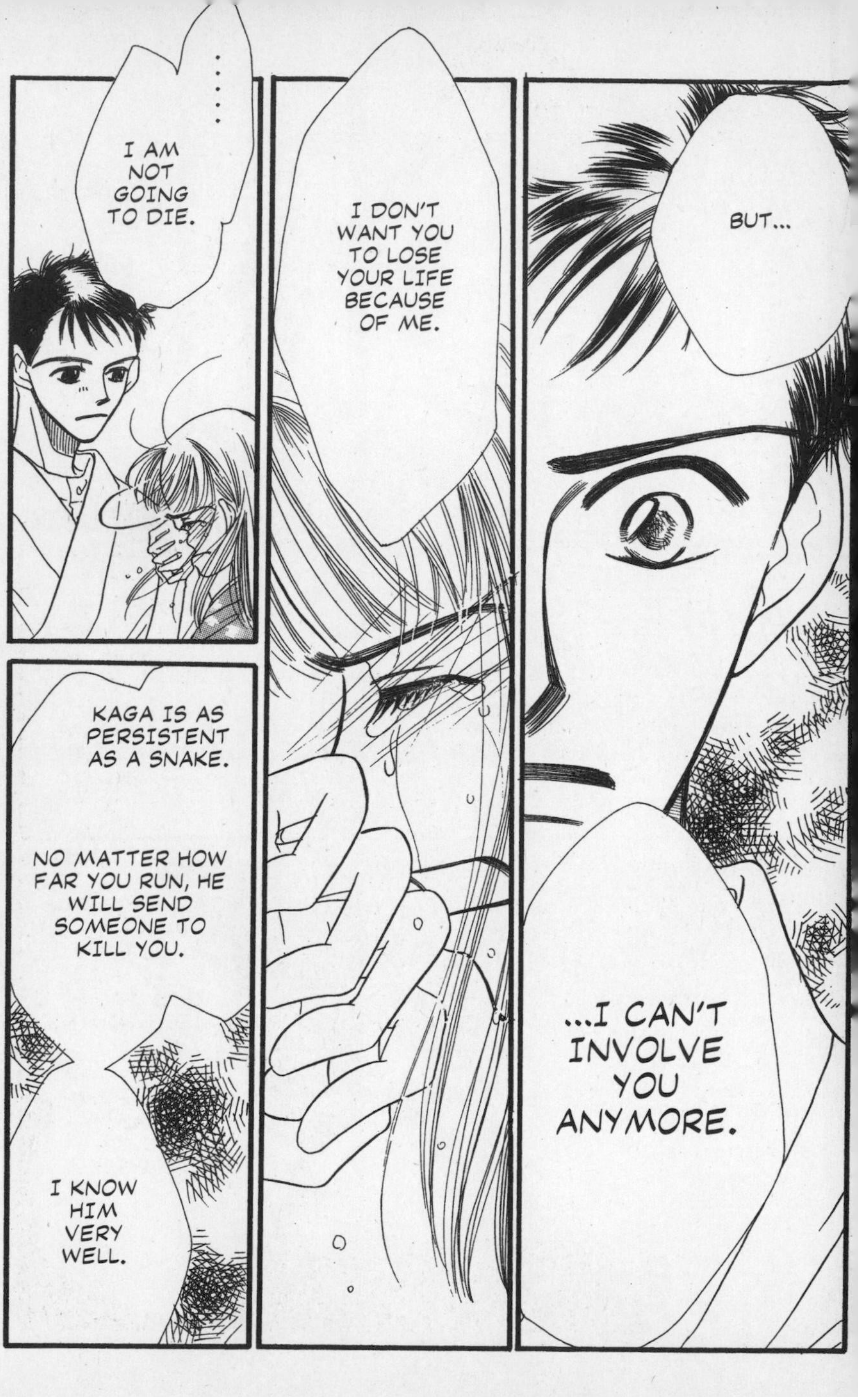
BUT...
...I CAN'T INVOLVE YOU ANYMORE.
I DON'T WANT YOU TO LOSE YOUR LIFE BECAUSE OF ME.
......
I AM NOT GOING TO DIE.
KAGA IS AS PERSISTENT AS A SNAKE.
NO MATTER HOW FAR YOU RUN, HE WILL SEND SOMEONE TO KILL YOU.
I KNOW HIM VERY WELL.

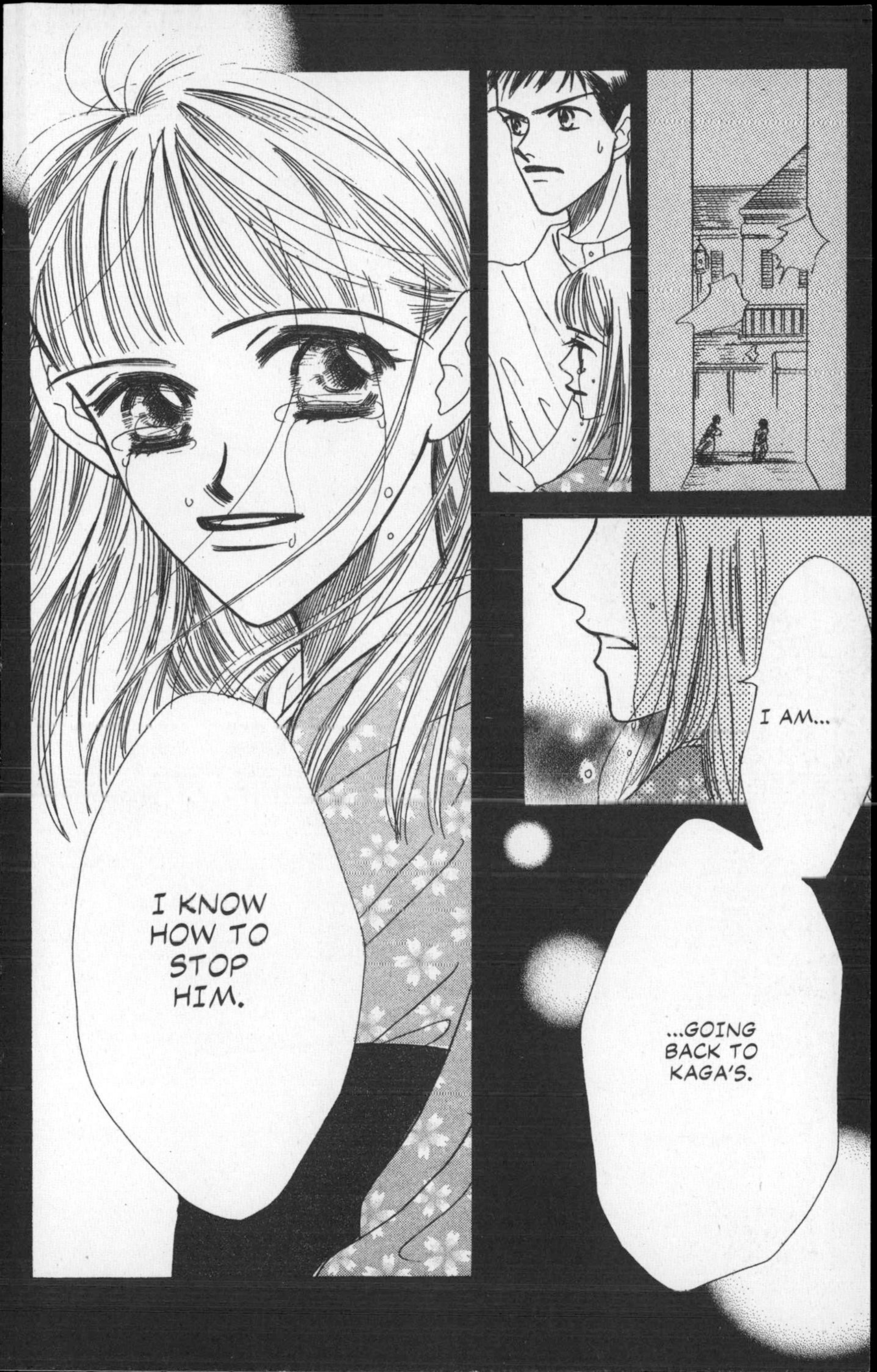
I AM...
...GOING BACK TO KAGA'S.
I KNOW HOW TO STOP HIM.

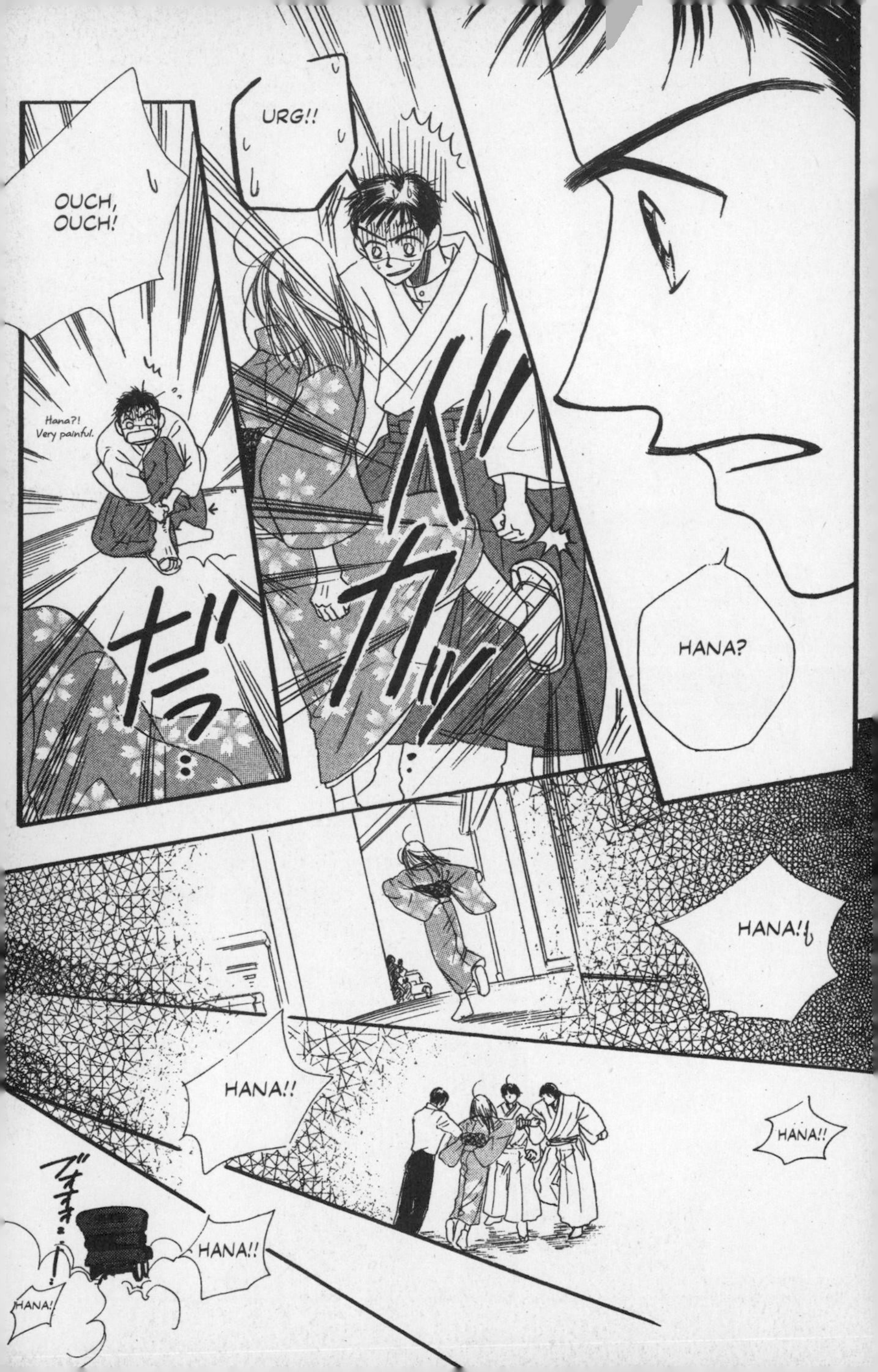
HANA?
URG!!
OUCH, OUCH!
Hana?! Very painful.
HANA!!
HANA!!
HANA!!
HANA!!
HANA!

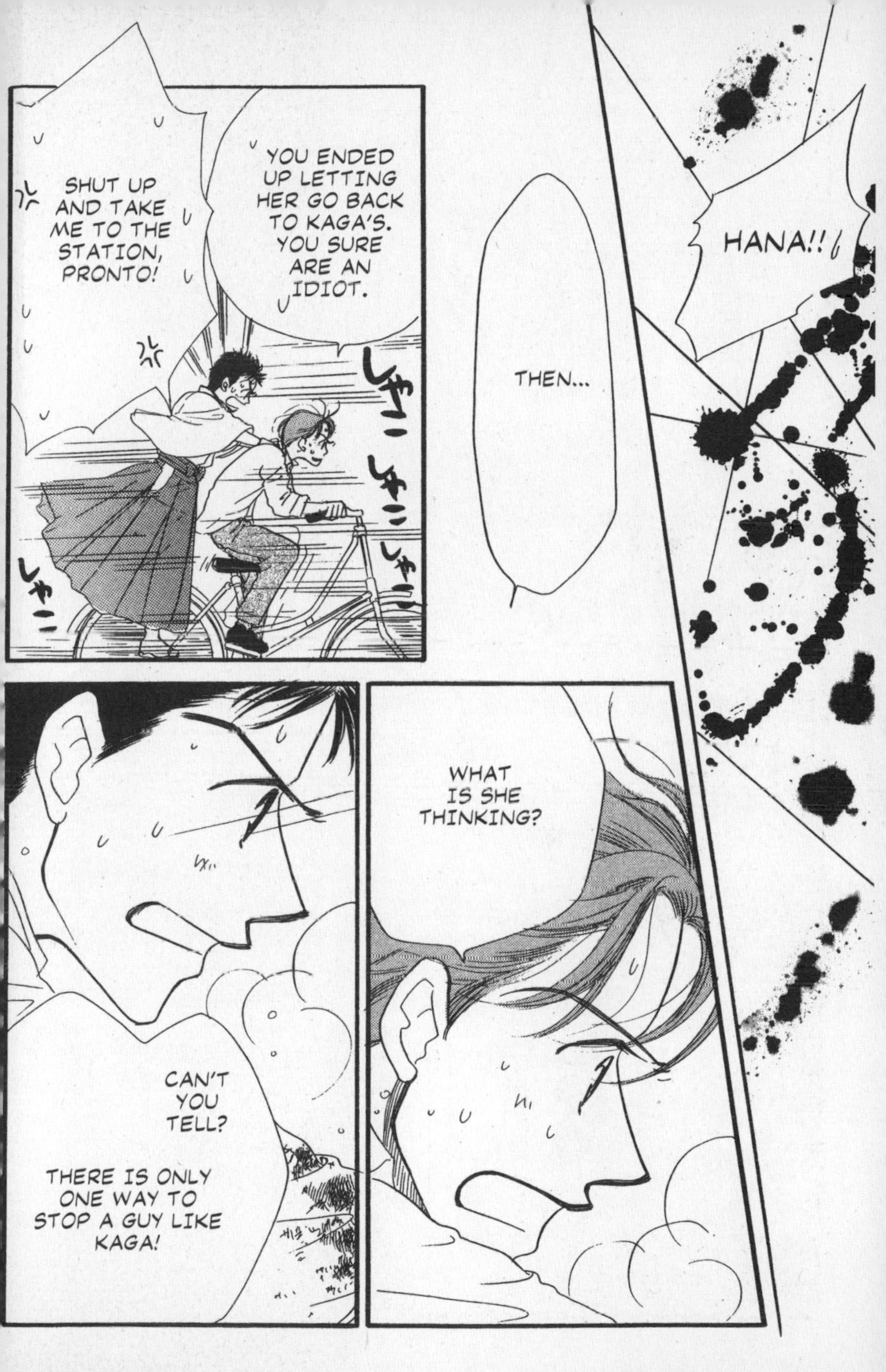
HANA!!
THEN...
YOU ENDED UP LETTING HER GO BACK TO KAGA'S. YOU SURE ARE AN IDIOT.
SHUT UP AND TAKE ME TO THE STATION, PRONTO!
WHAT IS SHE THINKING?
CAN'T YOU TELL?
THERE IS ONLY ONE WAY TO STOP A GUY LIKE KAGA!

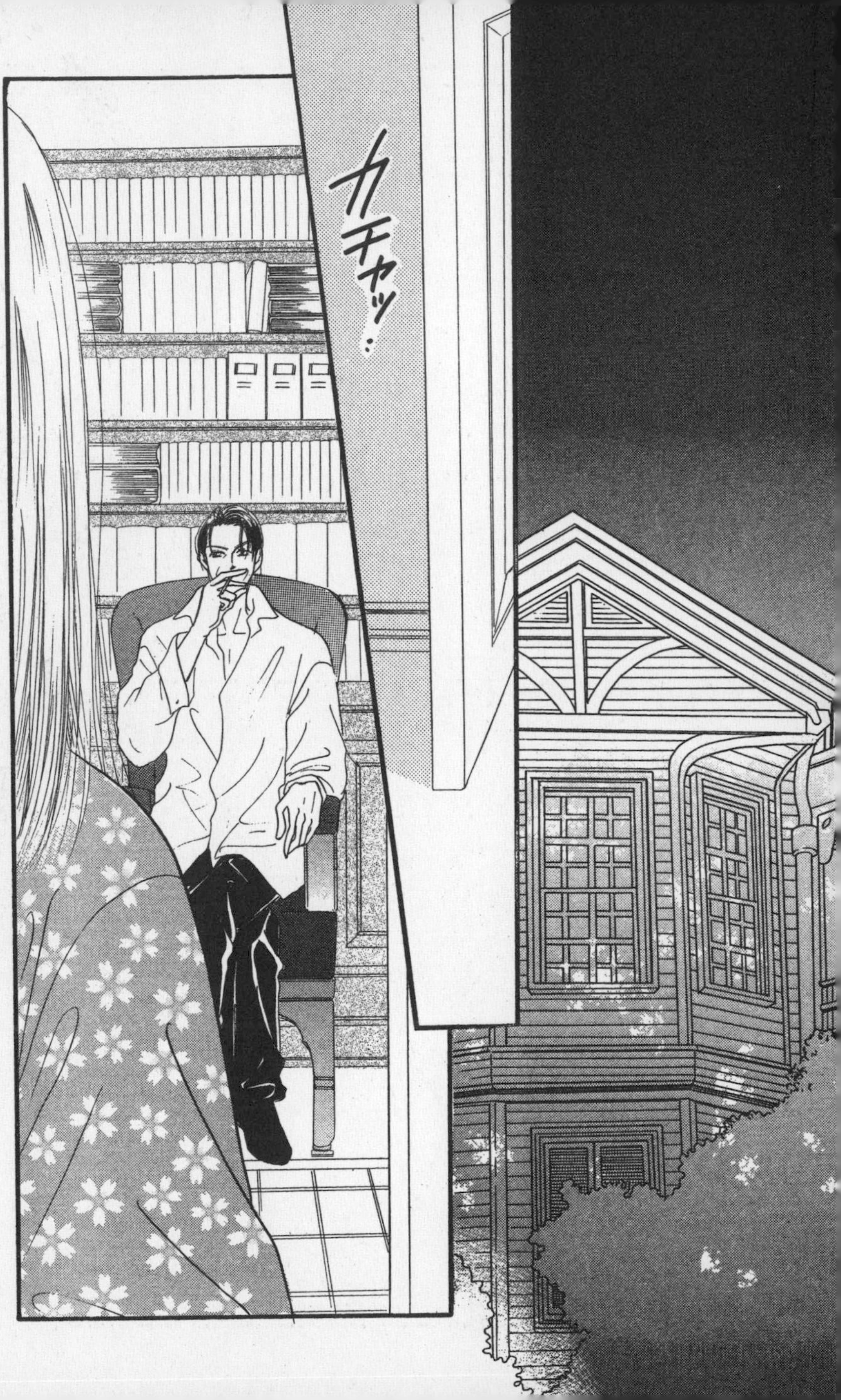
カチャッ…

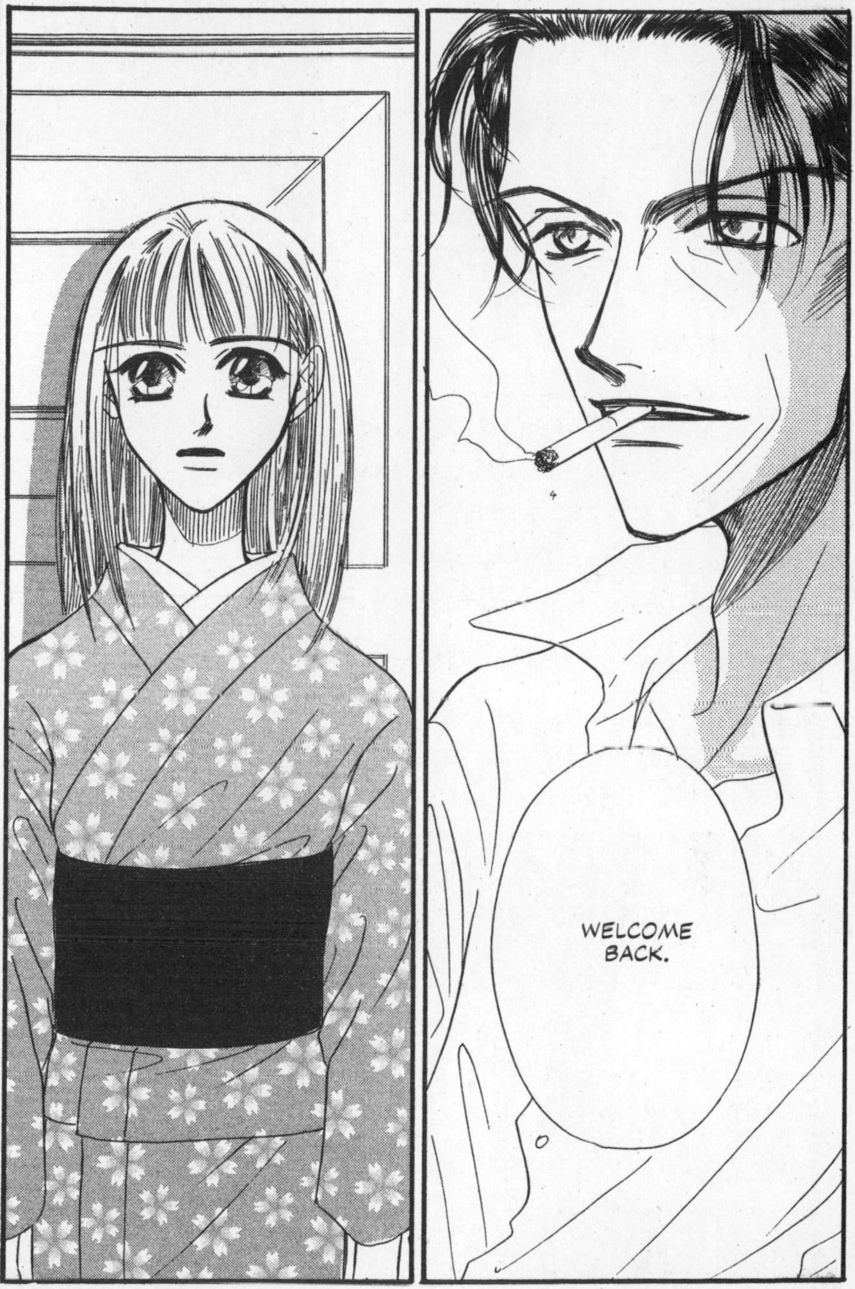
WELCOME BACK.

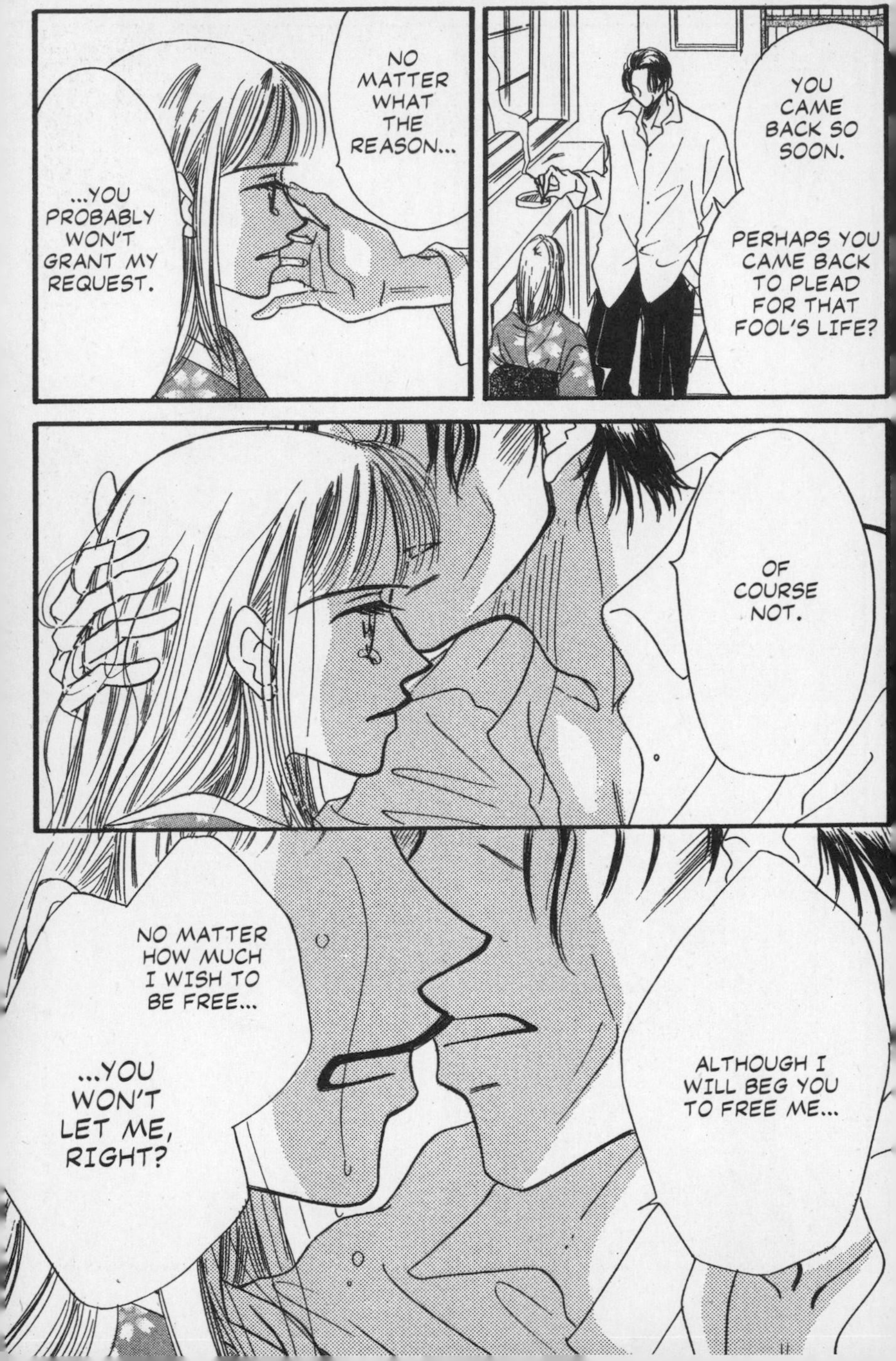
YOU CAME BACK SO SOON.
PERHAPS YOU CAME BACK TO PLEAD FOR THAT FOOL'S LIFE?
NO MATTER WHAT THE REASON...
...YOU PROBABLY WON'T GRANT MY REQUEST.
OF COURSE NOT.
ALTHOUGH I WILL BEG YOU TO FREE ME...
NO MATTER HOW MUCH I WISH TO BE FREE...
...YOU WON'T LET ME, RIGHT?

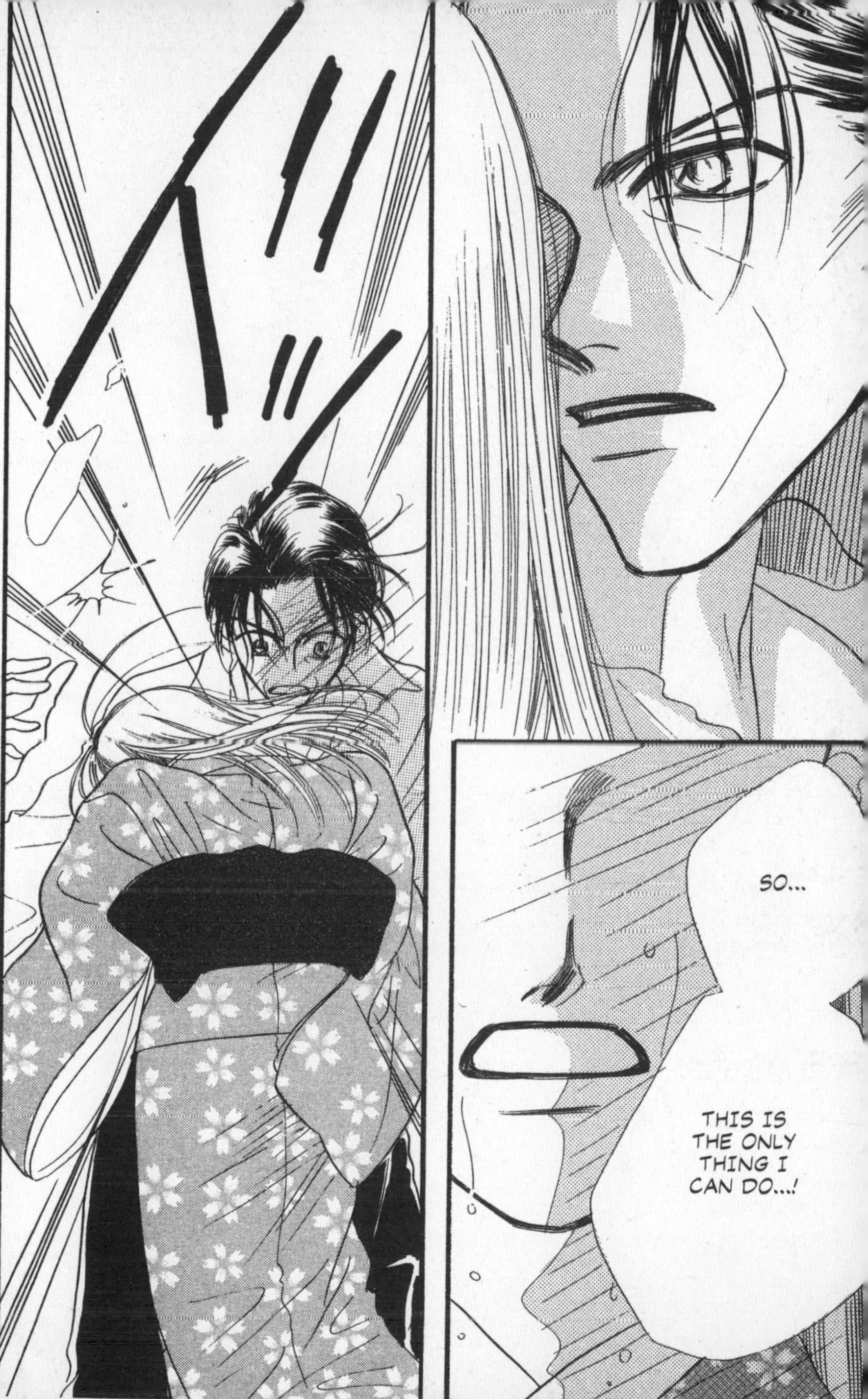
SO...
THIS IS THE ONLY THING I CAN DO...!

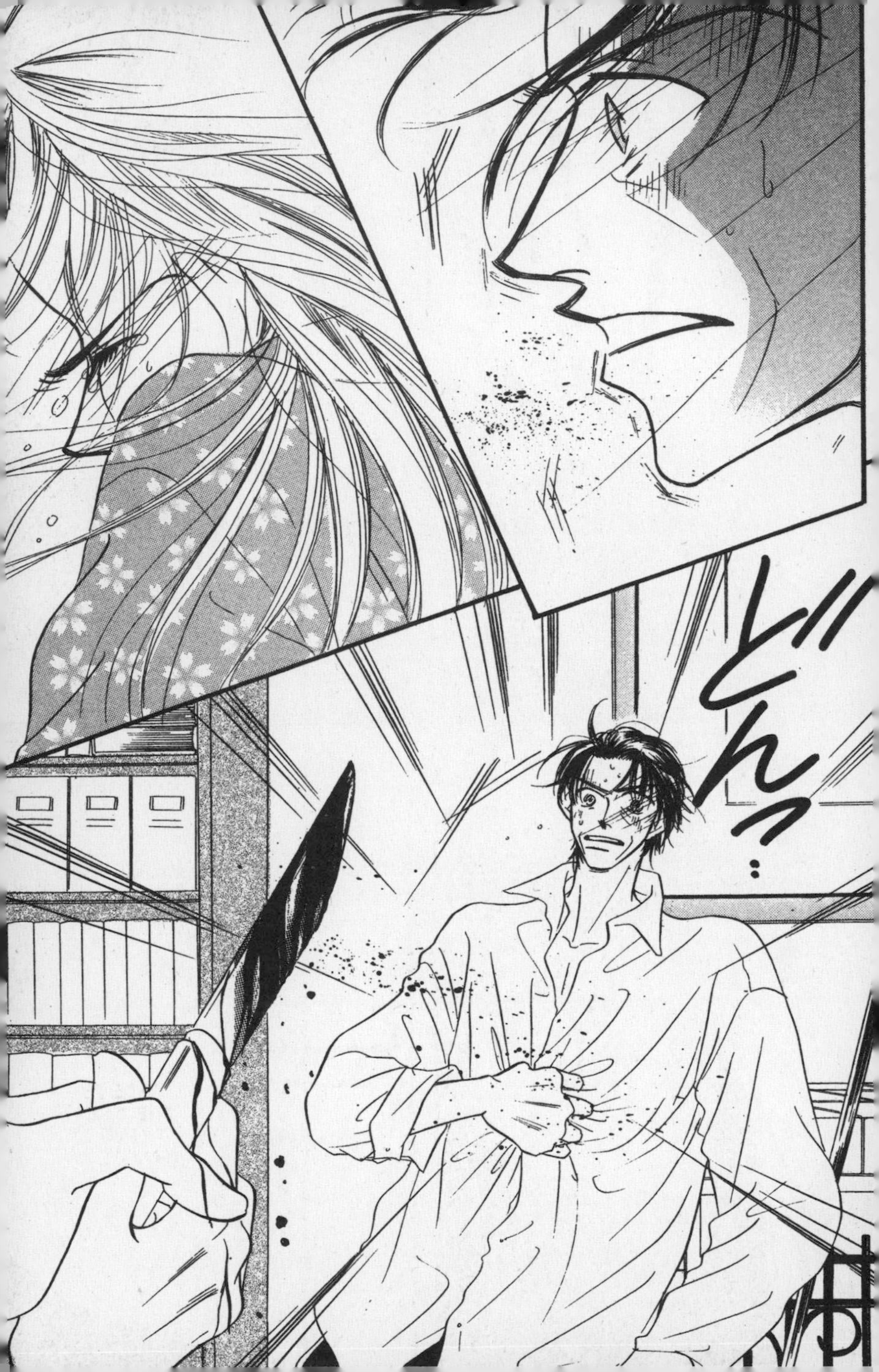
どんっ

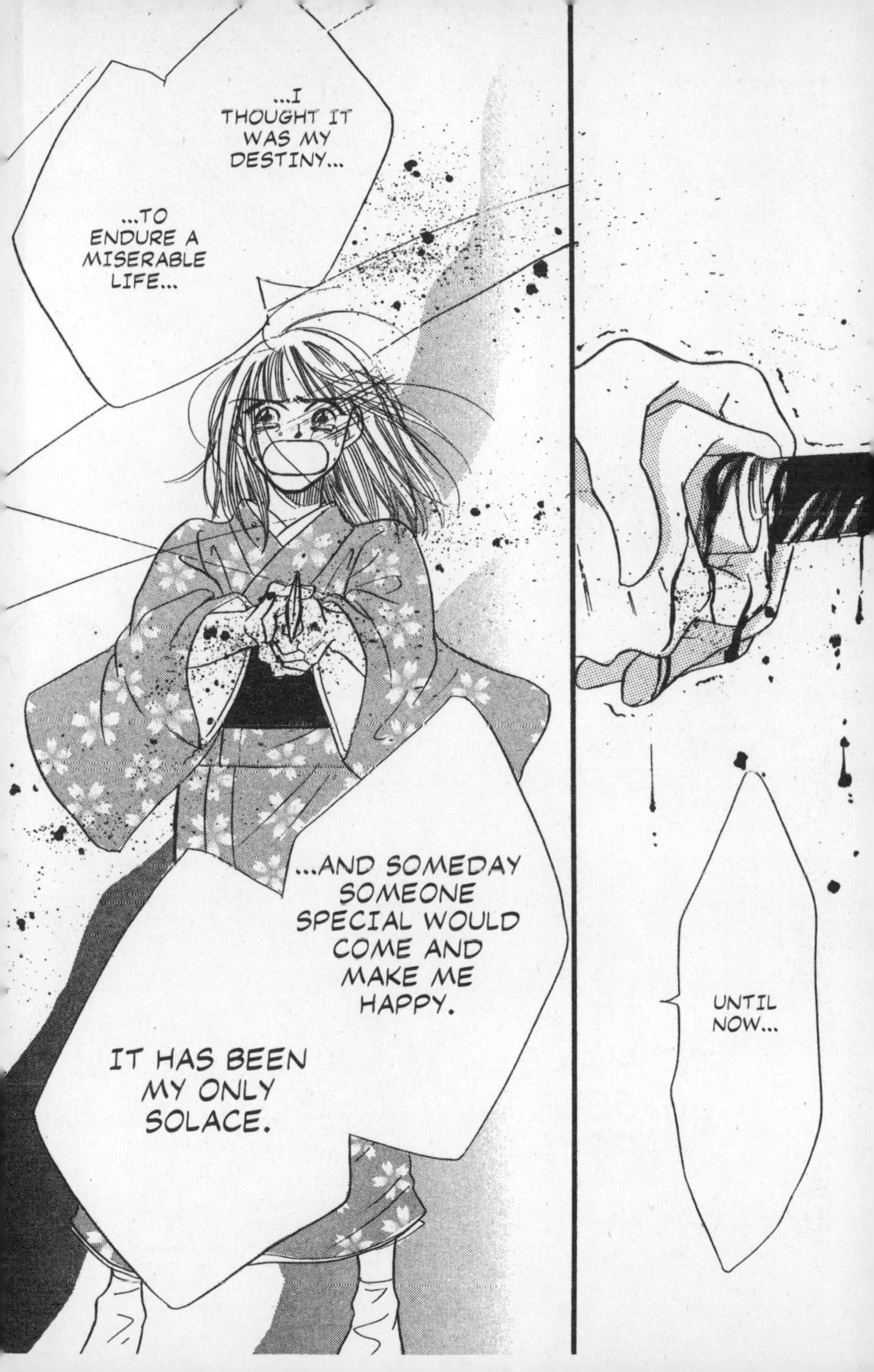
UNTIL NOW...
...I THOUGHT IT WAS MY DESTINY...
...TO ENDURE A MISERABLE LIFE...
...AND SOMEDAY SOMEONE SPECIAL WOULD COME AND MAKE ME HAPPY.
IT HAS BEEN MY ONLY SOLACE.

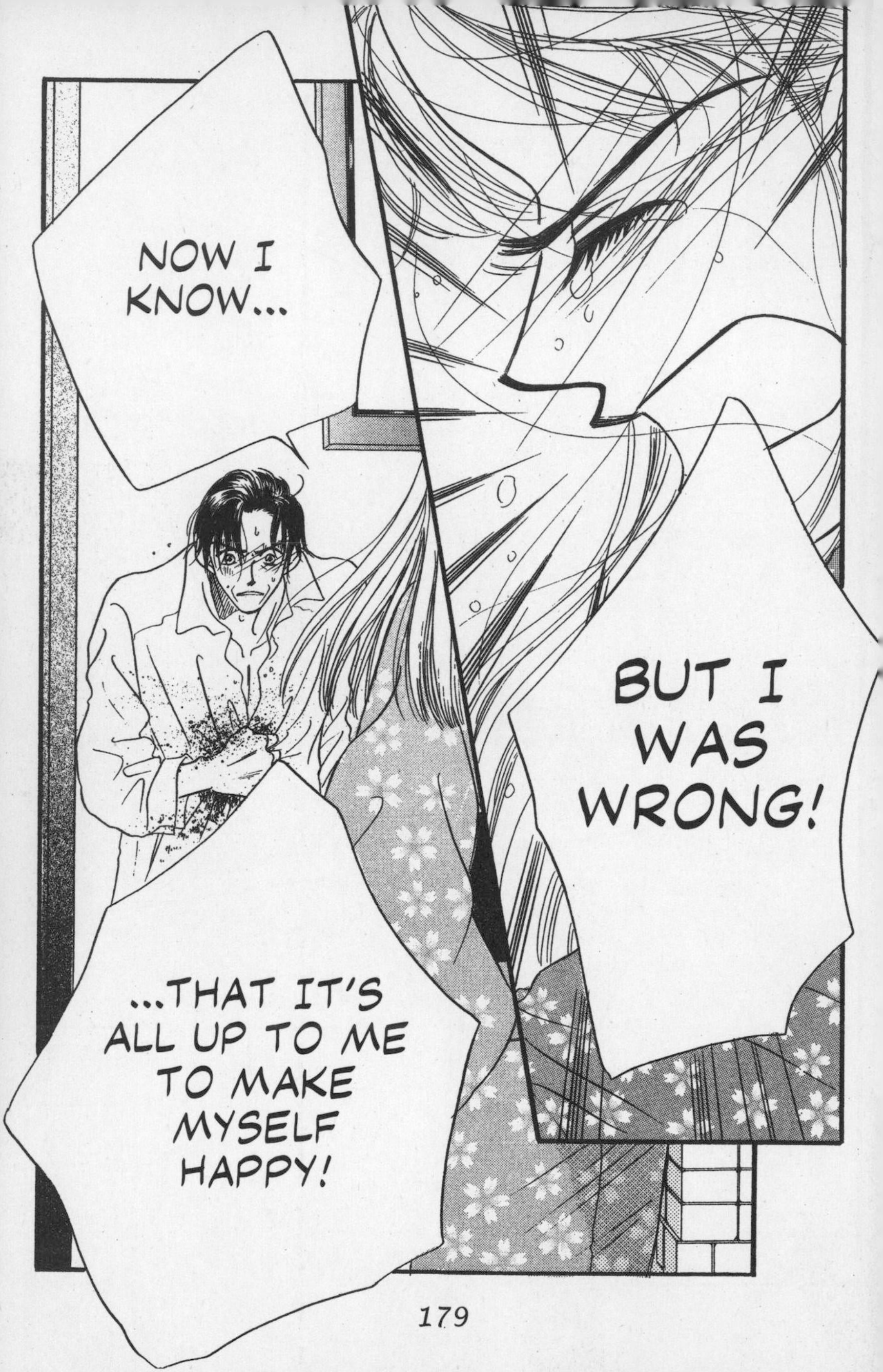
BUT I WAS WRONG!
NOW I KNOW...
...THAT IT'S ALL UP TO ME TO MAKE MYSELF HAPPY!

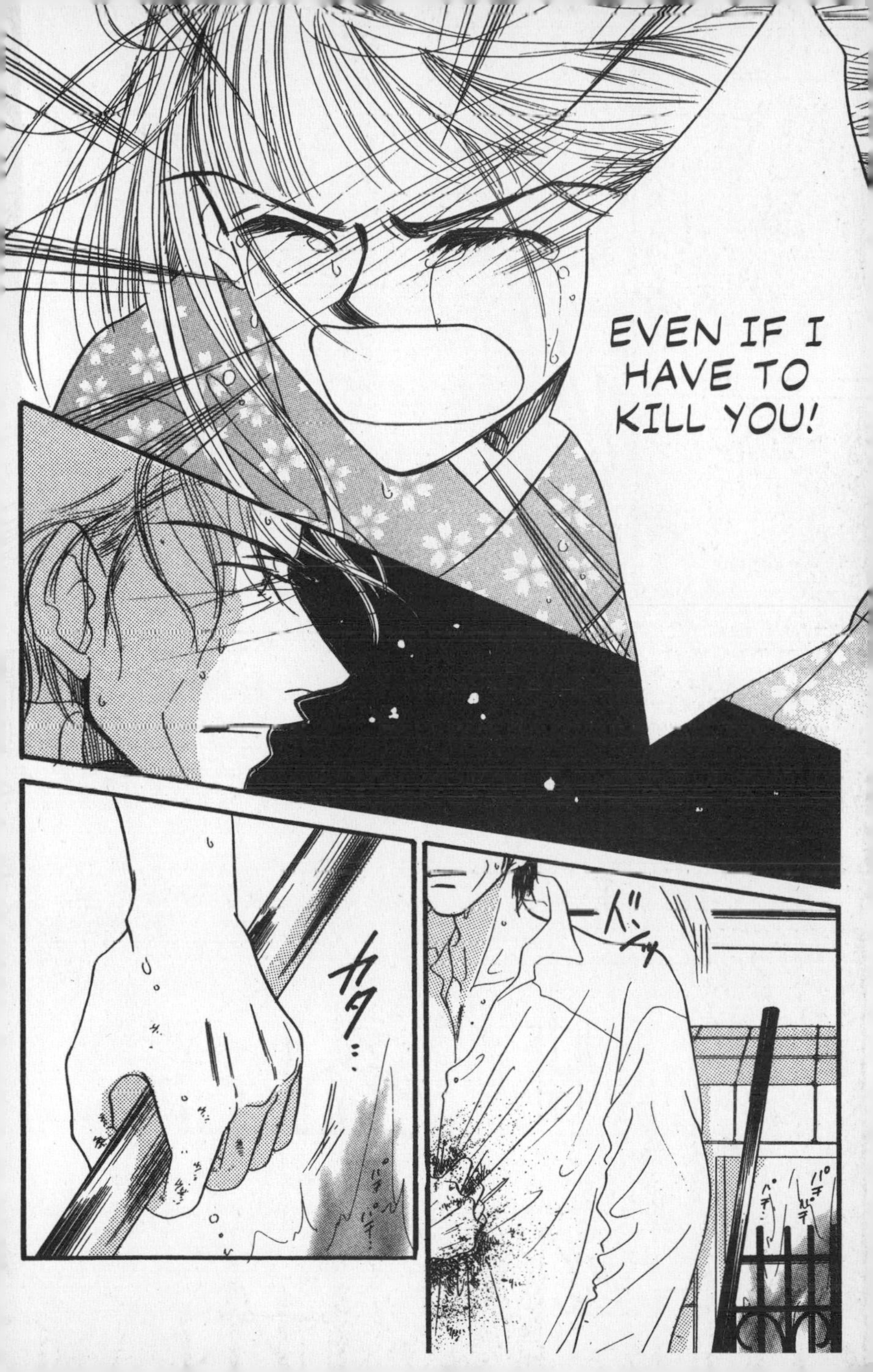
EVEN IF I HAVE TO KILL YOU!
カタ…

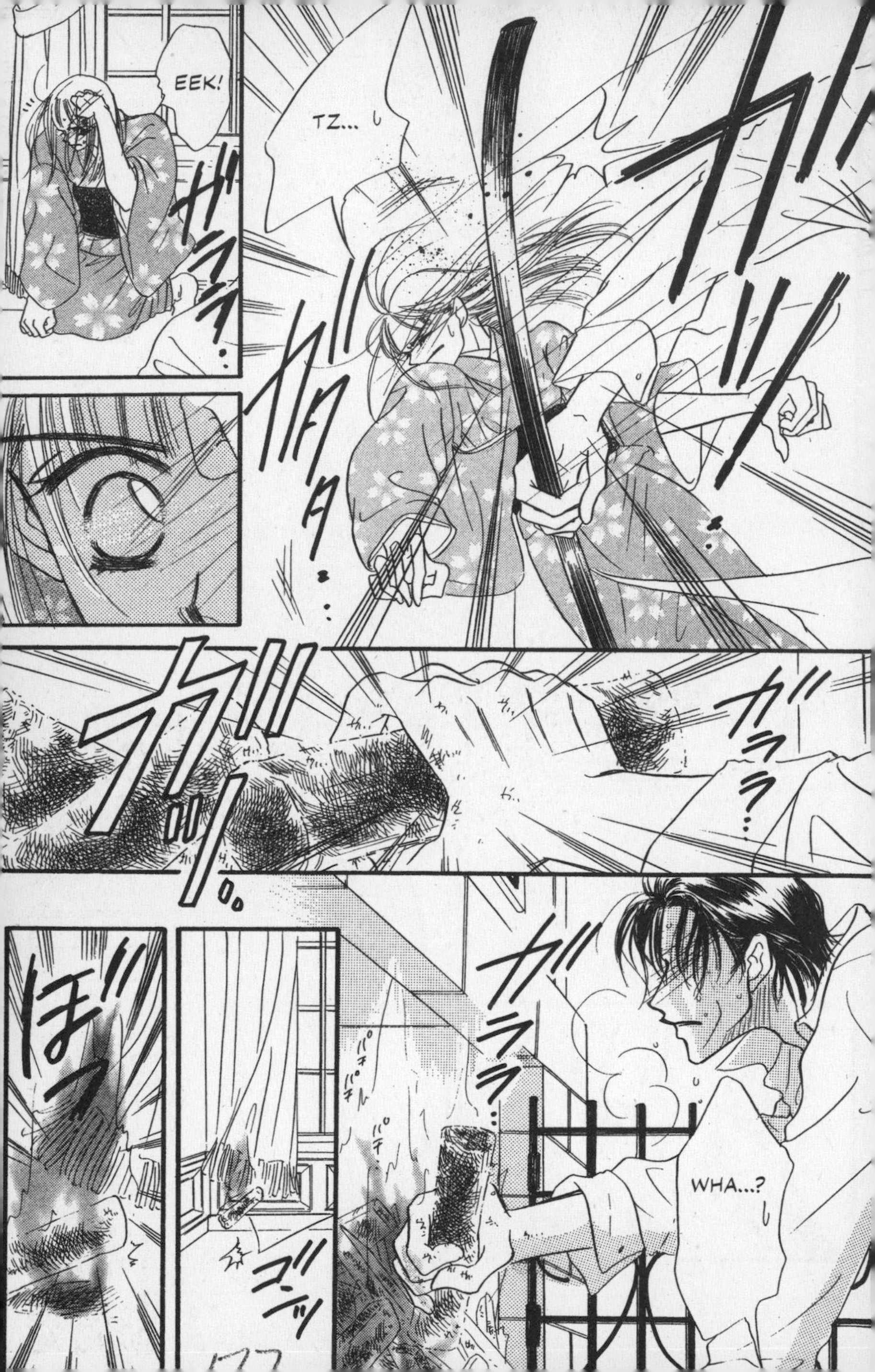

TZ...
EEK!
WHA...?

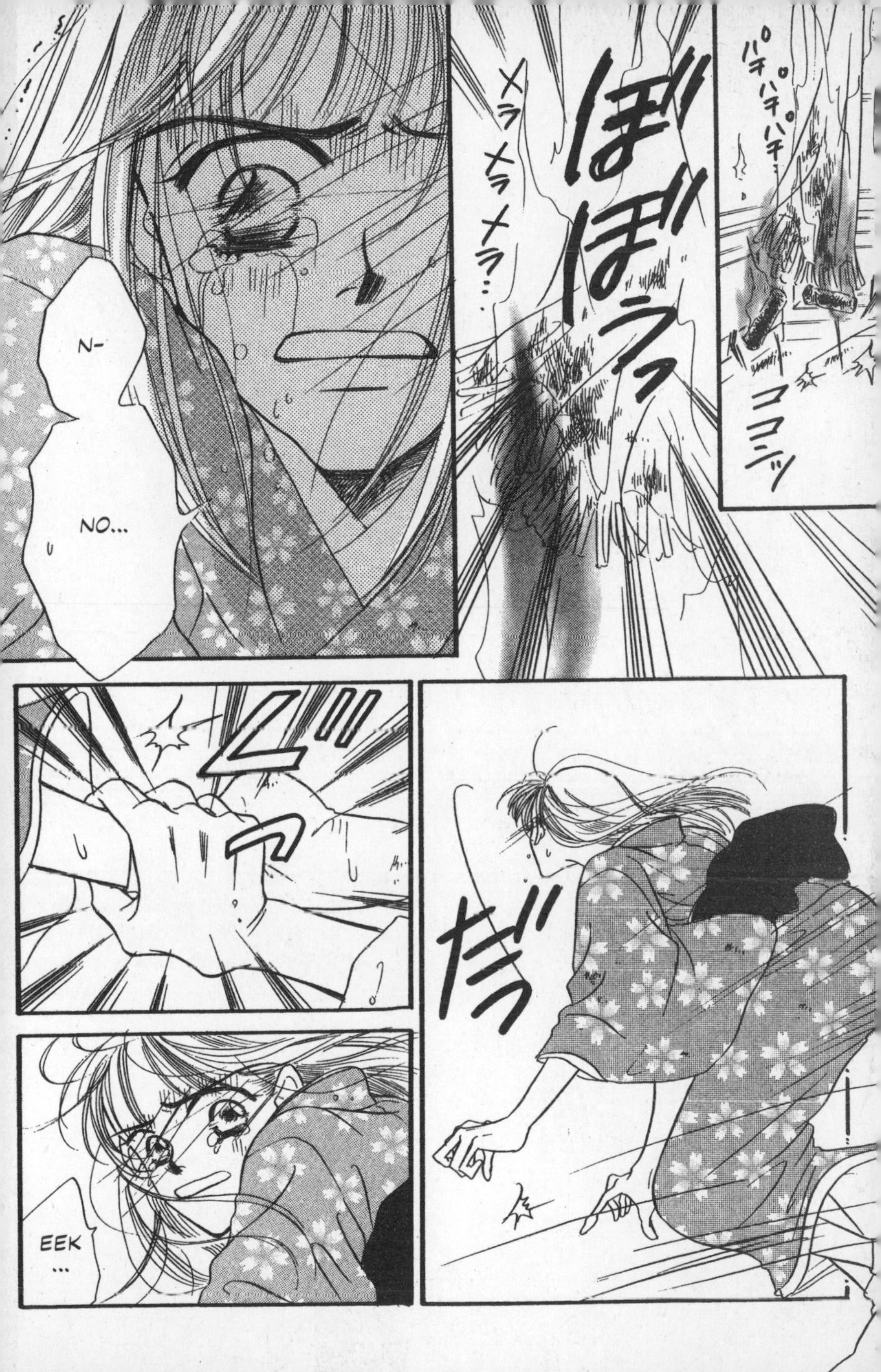
パチパチパチ…
ココンッ
ぼぼうっ
メラメラメラ…
N-
NO...
だっ
EEK
...

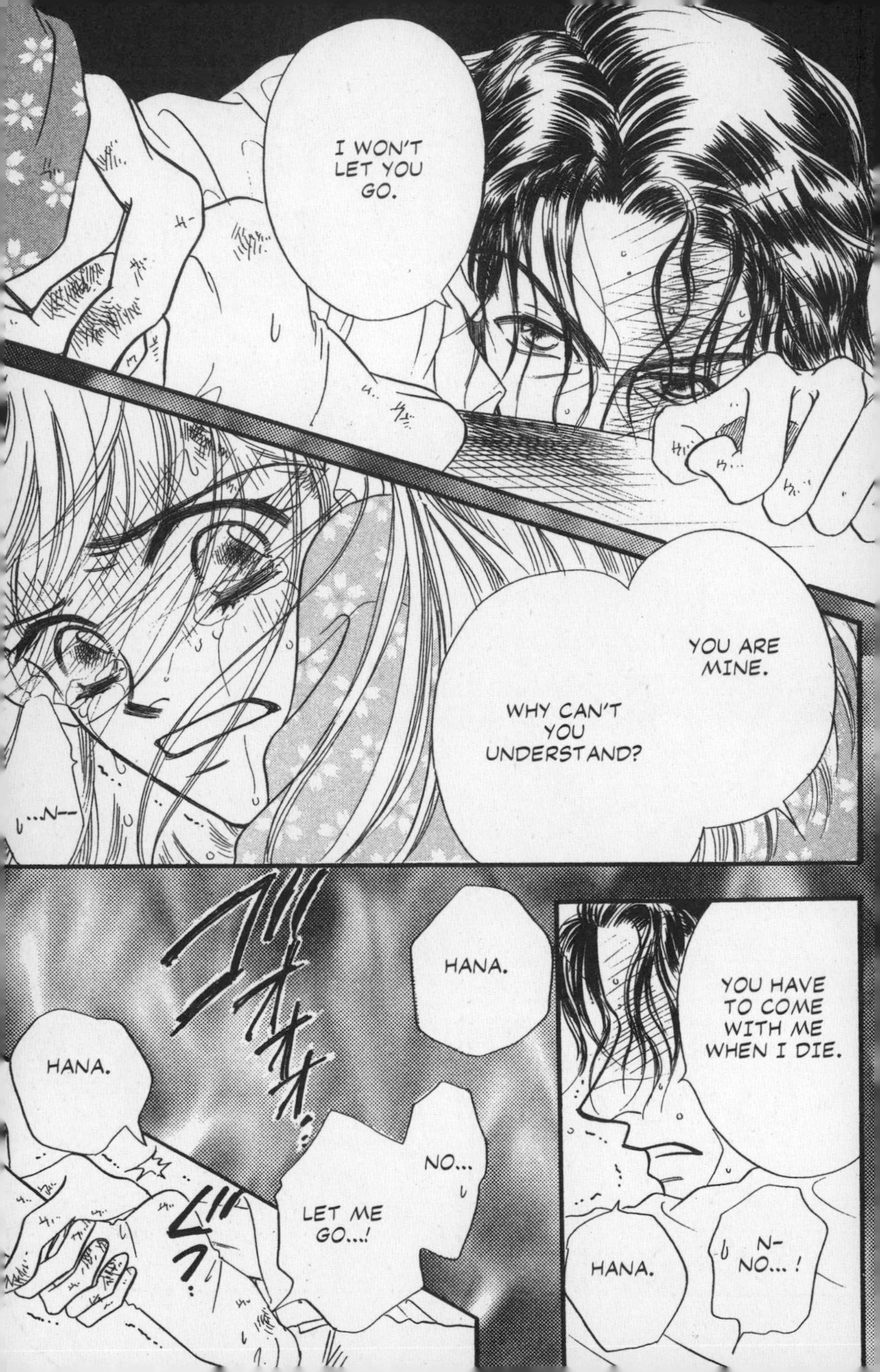
I WON'T LET YOU GO.
YOU ARE MINE.
WHY CAN'T YOU UNDERSTAND?
...N--
YOU HAVE TO COME WITH ME WHEN I DIE.
N- NO... !
HANA.
HANA.
NO...
LET ME GO...!
HANA.

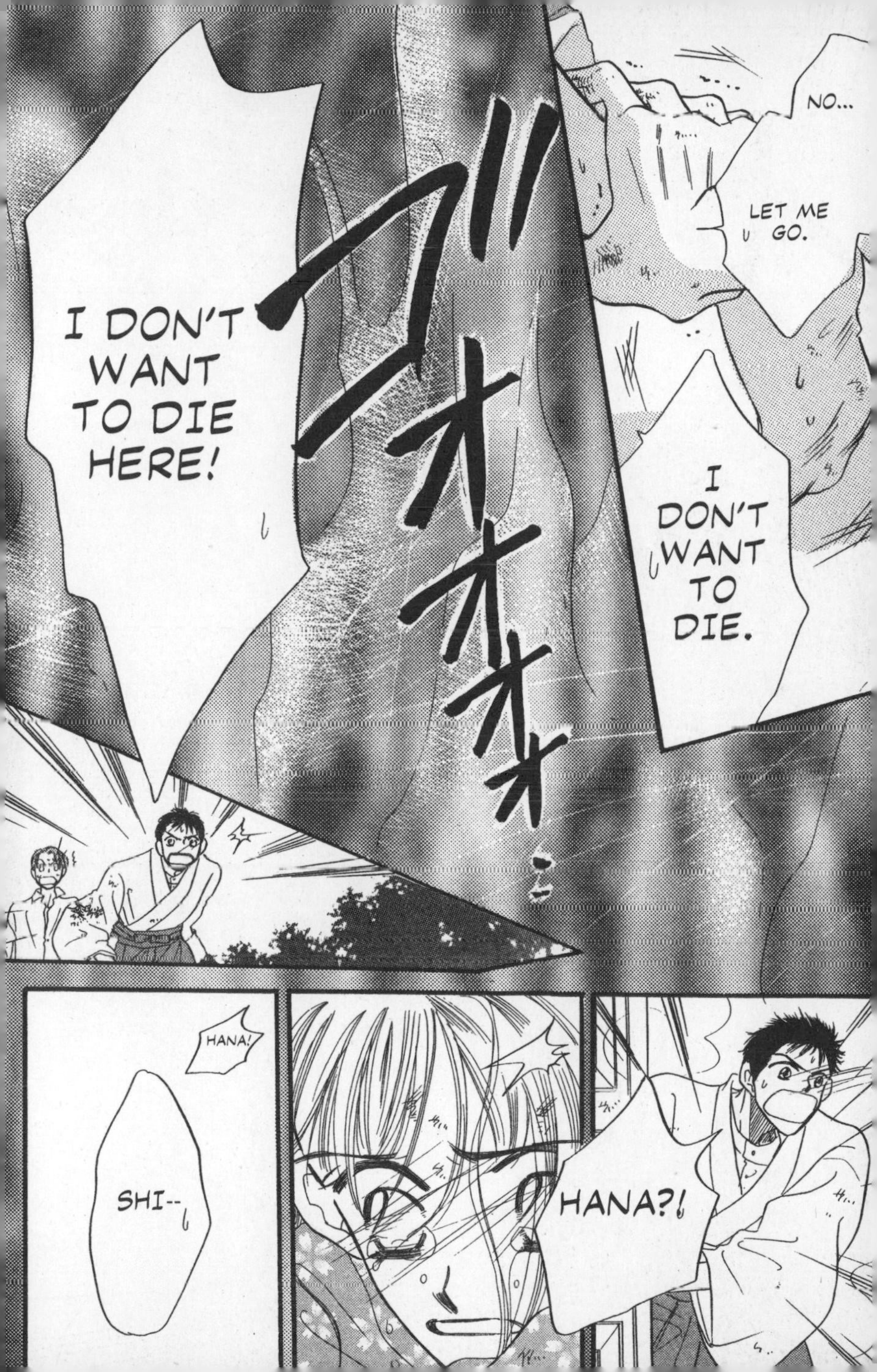
NO...
LET ME GO.
I DON'T WANT TO DIE.
I DON'T WANT TO DIE HERE!
ブオオオ
HANA?!
HANA!
SHI--

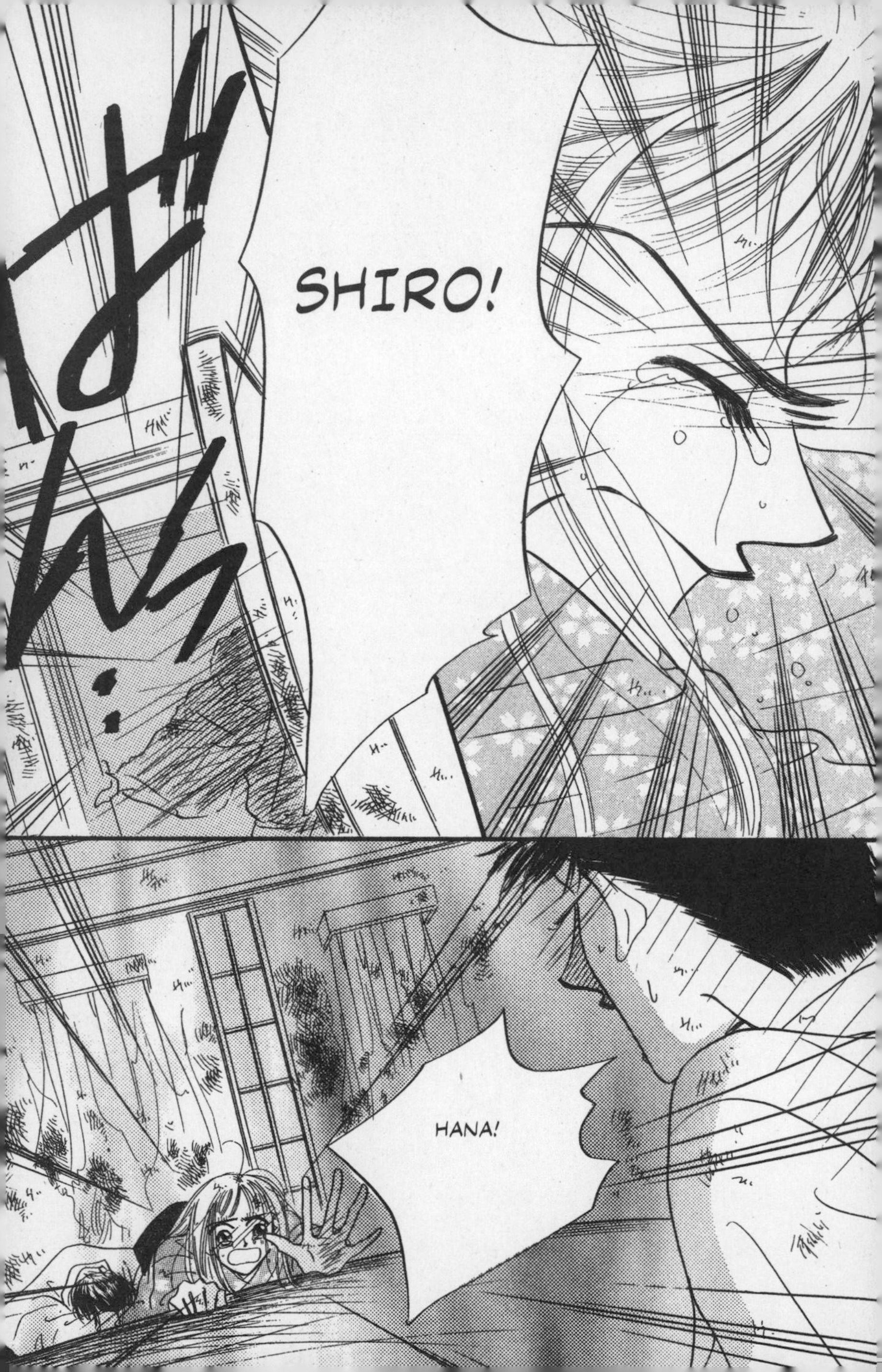

SHIRO!
はっ…
HANA!

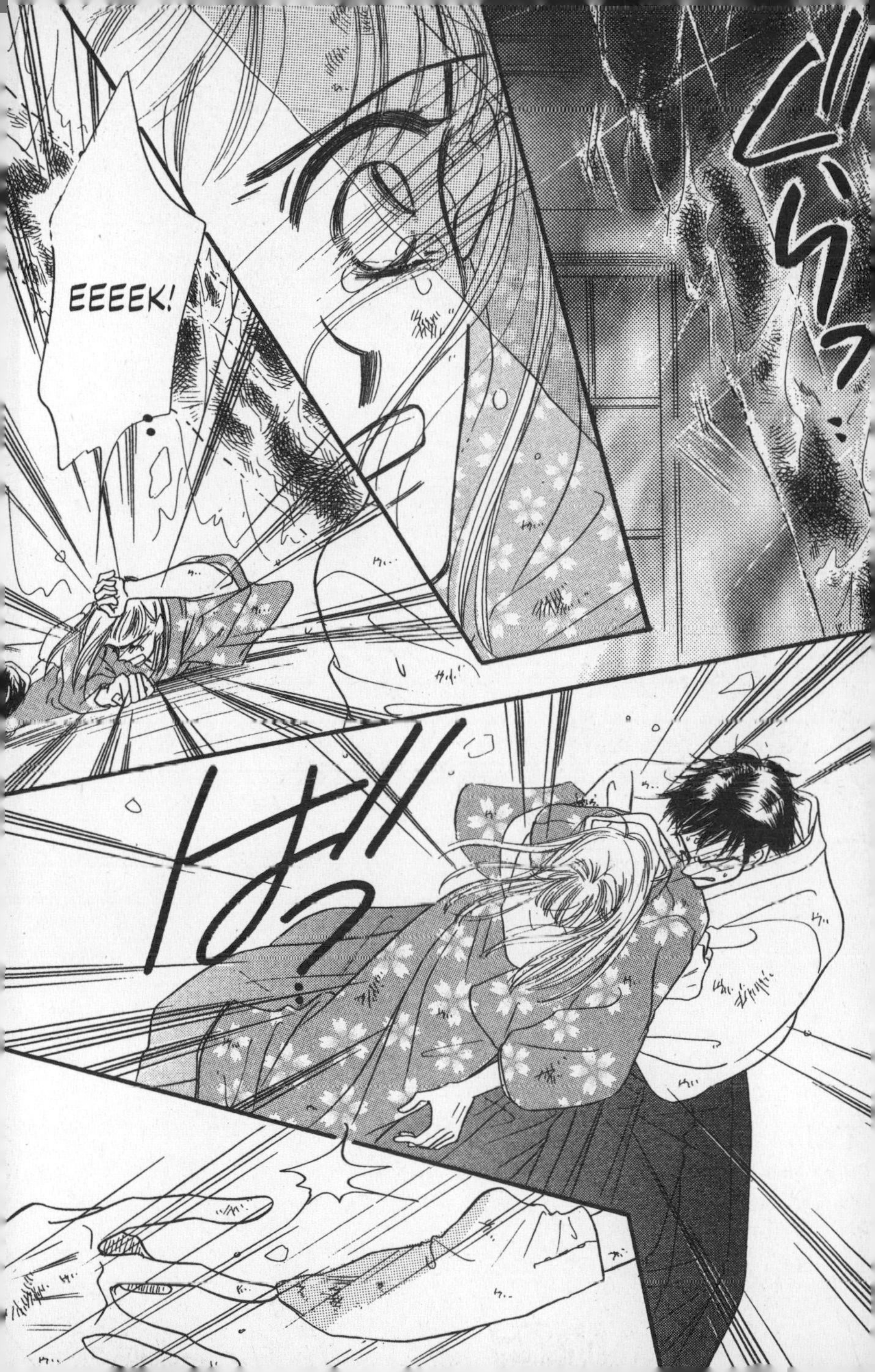
ぐらっ
EEEEK!
ばっ

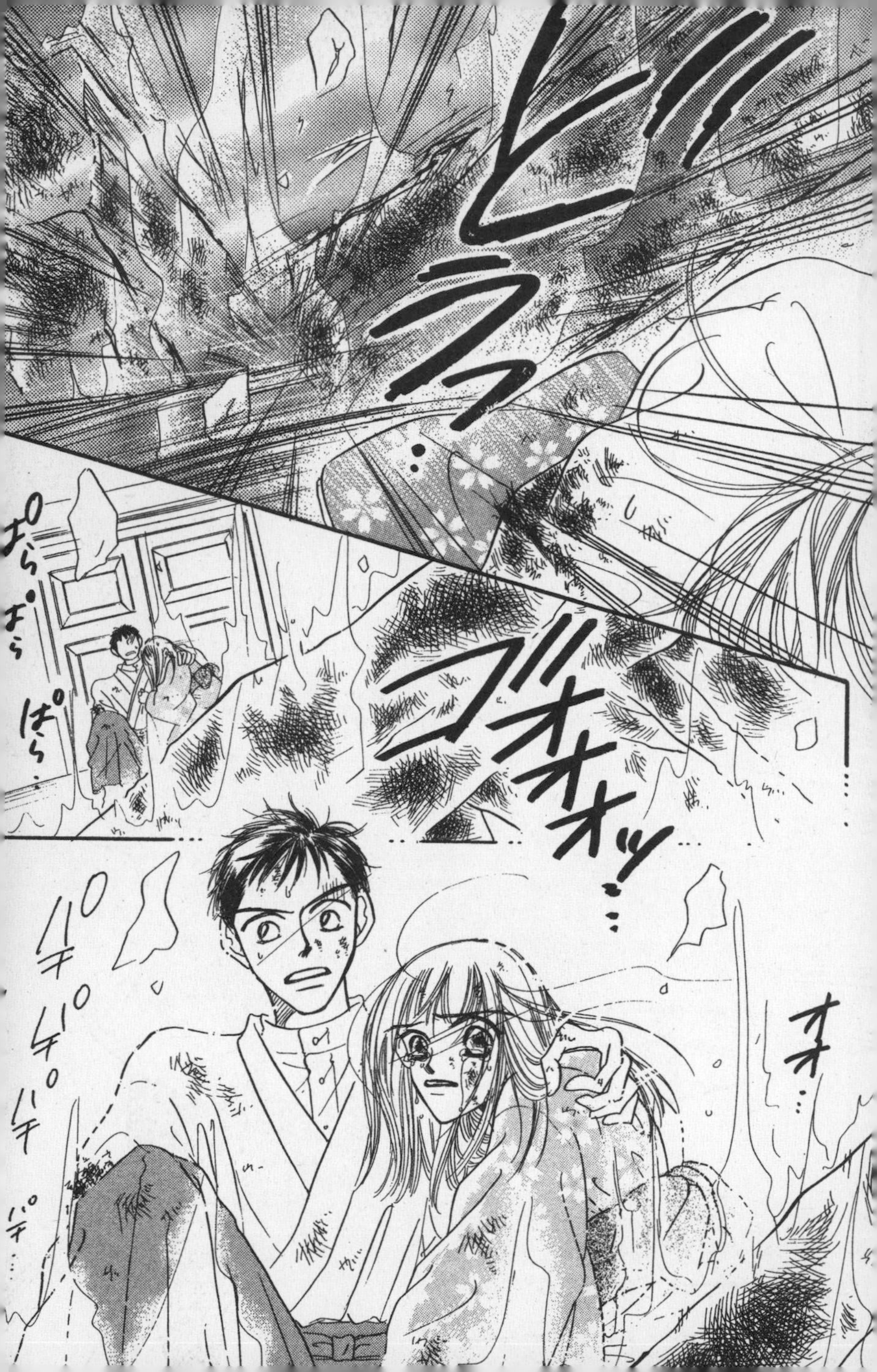
ドドドドドドン
ゴゴゴゴオオオッ...
ぱらぱら ぱら...
パチパチパチ パチ...
オオ...

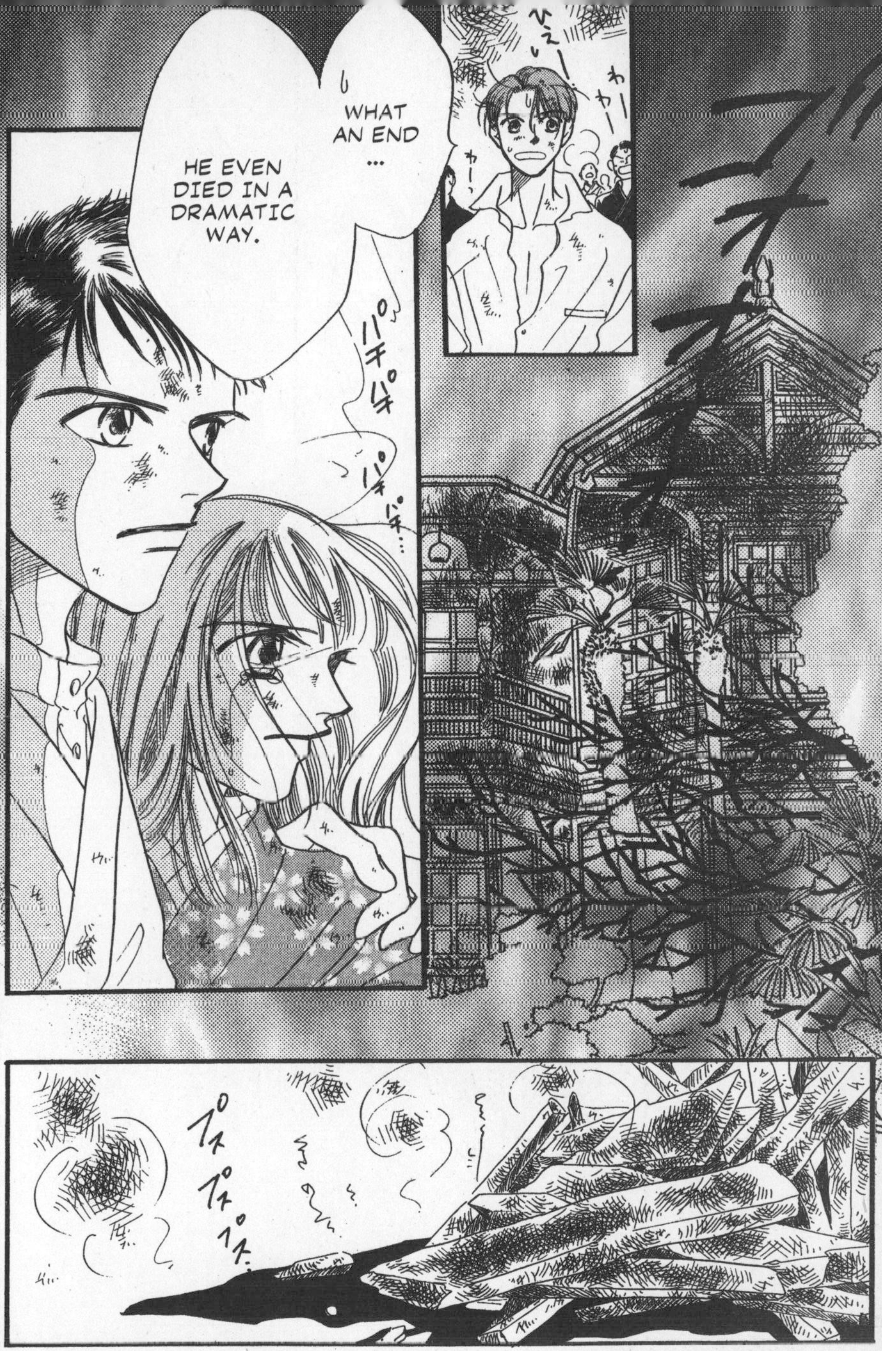
WHAT AN END ...
HE EVEN DIED IN A DRAMATIC WAY.
パチパチ
プスプスプス...

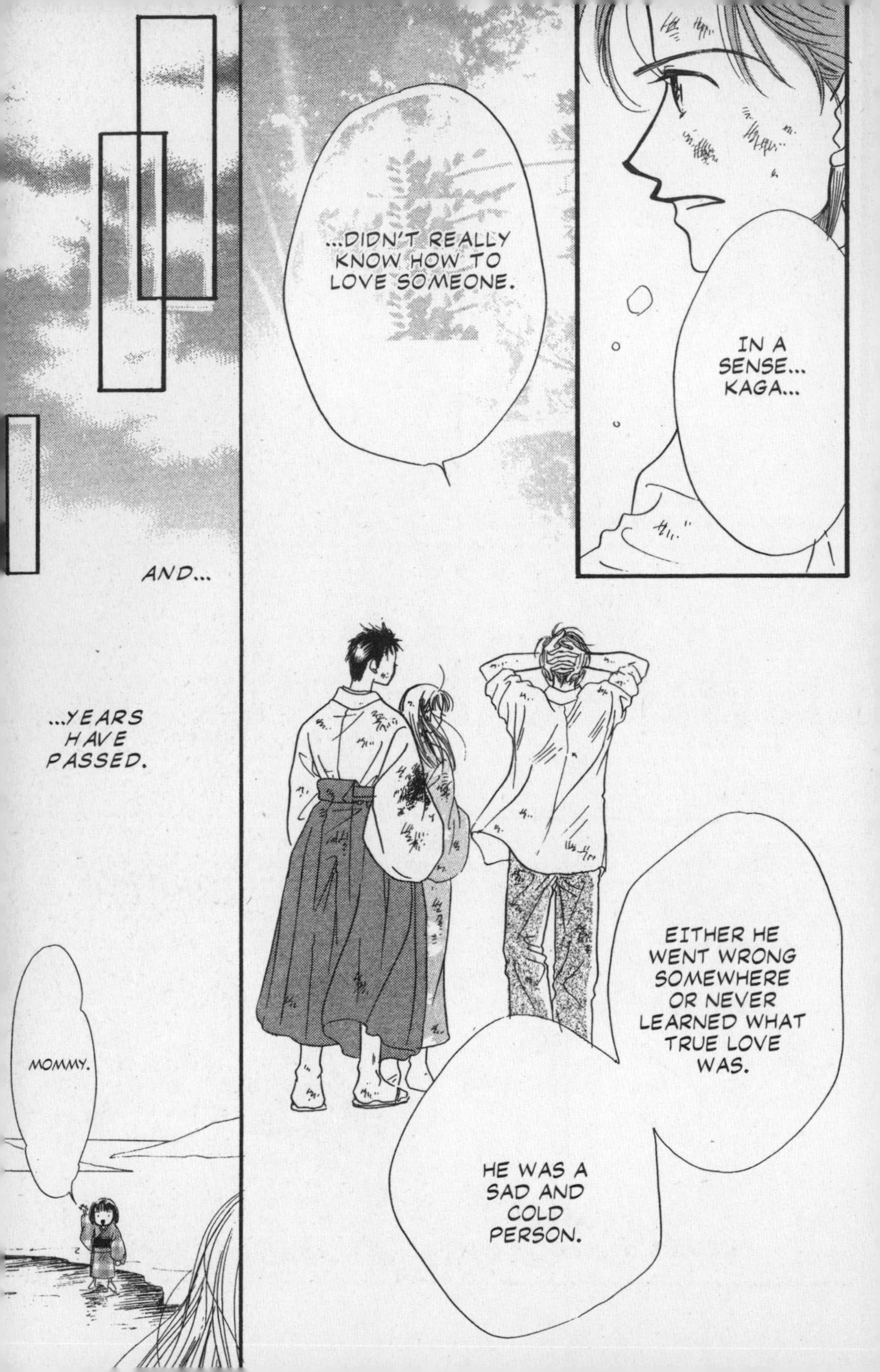
IN A SENSE... KAGA...
...DIDN'T REALLY KNOW HOW TO LOVE SOMEONE.
EITHER HE WENT WRONG SOMEWHERE OR NEVER LEARNED WHAT TRUE LOVE WAS.
HE WAS A SAD AND COLD PERSON.
AND...
...YEARS HAVE PASSED.
MOMMY.

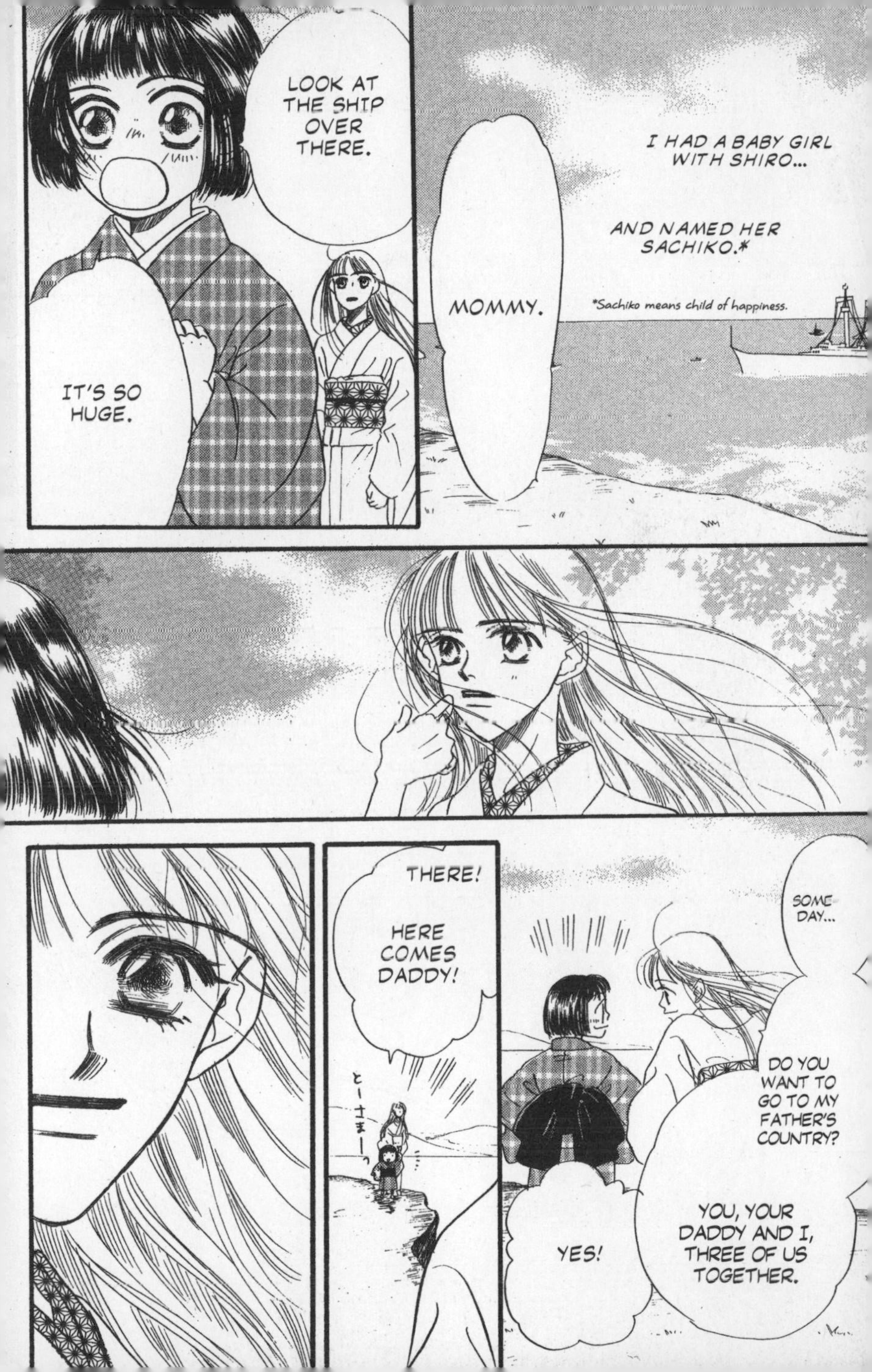
I HAD A BABY GIRL WITH SHIRO...
AND NAMED HER SACHIKO.*
*Sachiko means child of happiness.
MOMMY.
LOOK AT THE SHIP OVER THERE.
IT'S SO HUGE.
SOME DAY...
DO YOU WANT TO GO TO MY FATHER'S COUNTRY?
YOU, YOUR DADDY AND I, THREE OF US TOGETHER.
YES!
THERE!
HERE COMES DADDY!
とーさまー

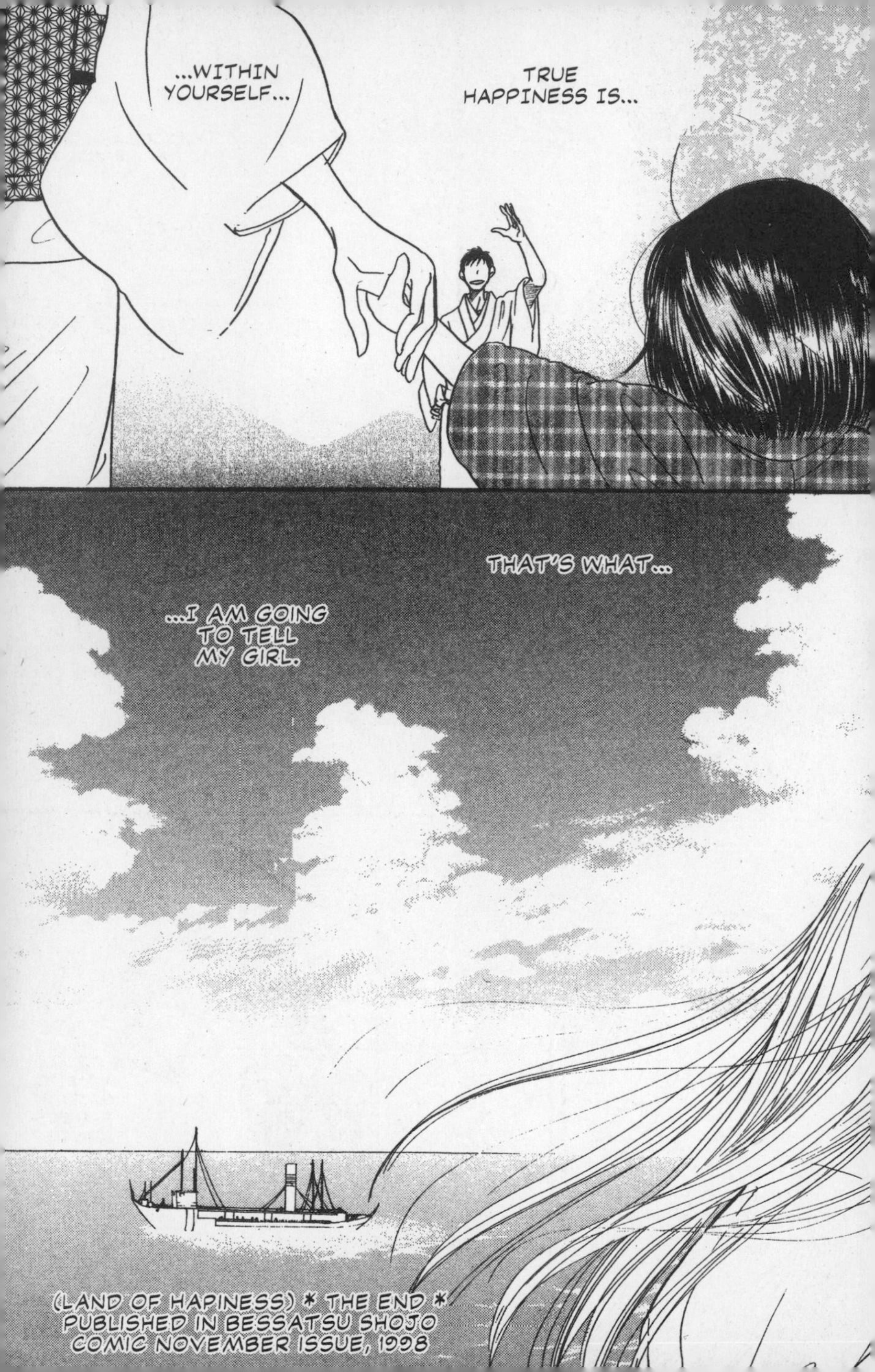
TRUE HAPPINESS IS...
...WITHIN YOURSELF...
THAT'S WHAT...
...I AM GOING TO TELL MY GIRL.
(LAND OF HAPINESS) * THE END *
PUBLISHED IN BESSATSU SHOJO COMIC NOVEMBER ISSUE, 1998

THANKS ♥ THANKS

Special thanks to
Members of Homura
Tomoi Ballet
Members of Shimoda Keiko
Ballet School
Hariyama Family
Ms. Minorikawa of Japan Arts
Ms. Mochizuki
My former editor,
my new editor.

SUZUNAMI. N
SUMIKO. N
SHOKO. K
SHIKI. K
KUMIKO. F
KUMIKO. S

And many more people who
helped me through the series.

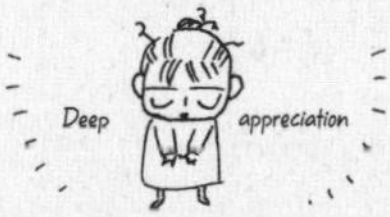
Deep
appreciation

I appreciate all the fans who
write me encouraging letters.
Sorry I am always behind
writing back to you all!! I
always enjoy reading letters
from fans. Please let me know
if you have any comments
regarding my works.

October 1998 Hinako Ashihara

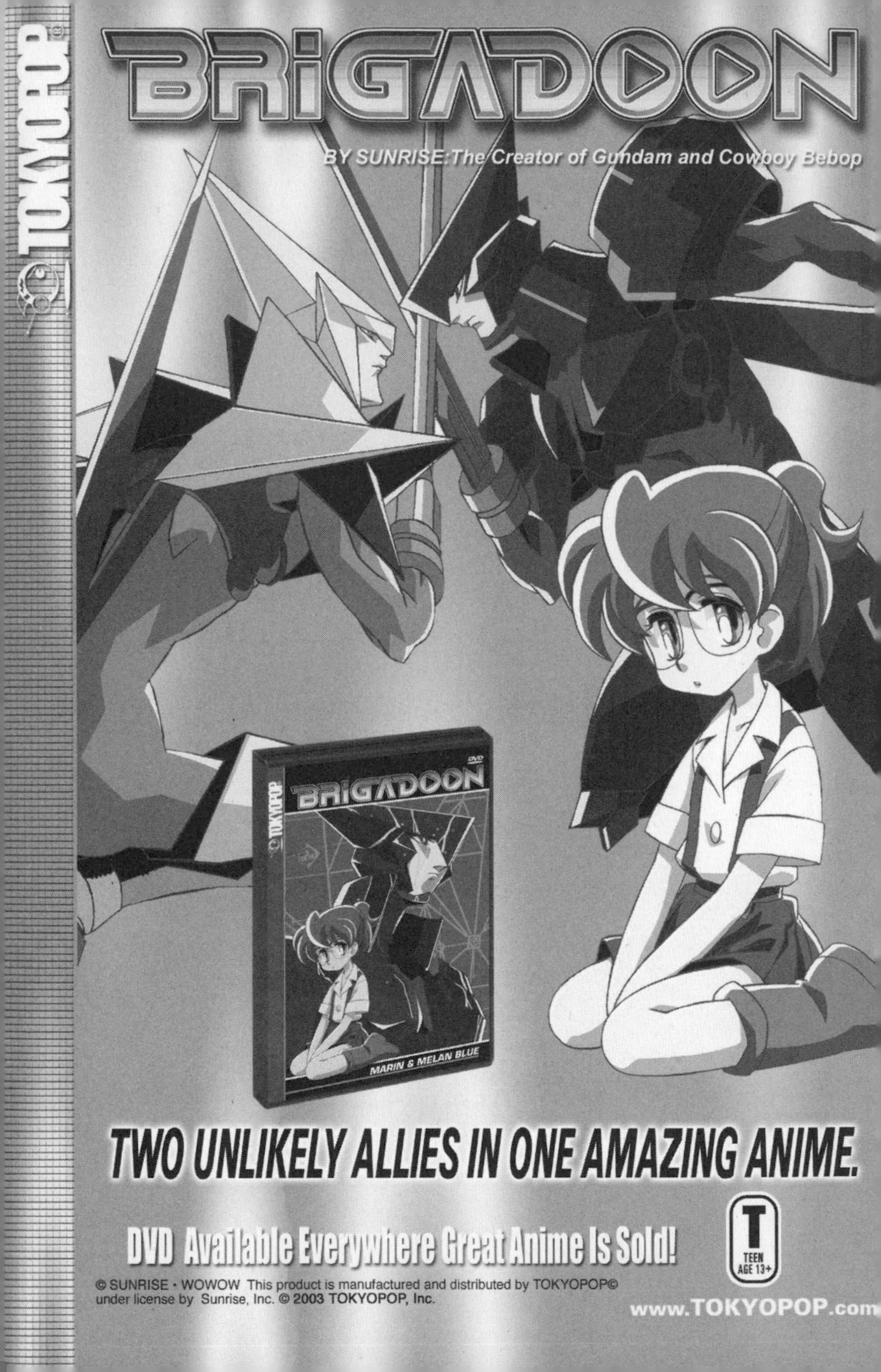
TOKYOPOP
BRIGADOON
BY SUNRISE:The Creator of Gundam and Cowboy Bebop
DVD
TOKYOPOP
BRIGADOON
MARIN & MELAN BLUE
TWO UNLIKELY ALLIES IN ONE AMAZING ANIME.
DVD Available Everywhere Great Anime Is Sold!
T
TEEN
AGE 13+
© SUNRISE · WOWOW This product is manufactured and distributed by TOKYOPOP©
under license by Sunrise, Inc. © 2003 TOKYOPOP, Inc.
www.TOKYOPOP.com

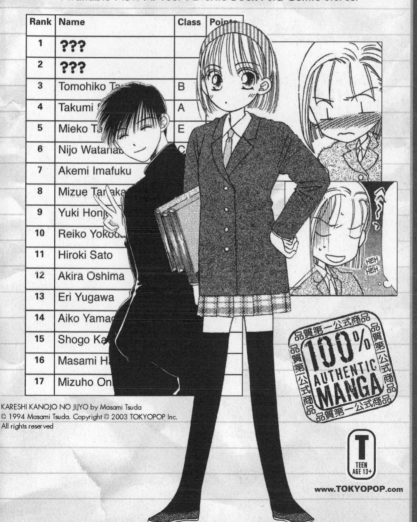

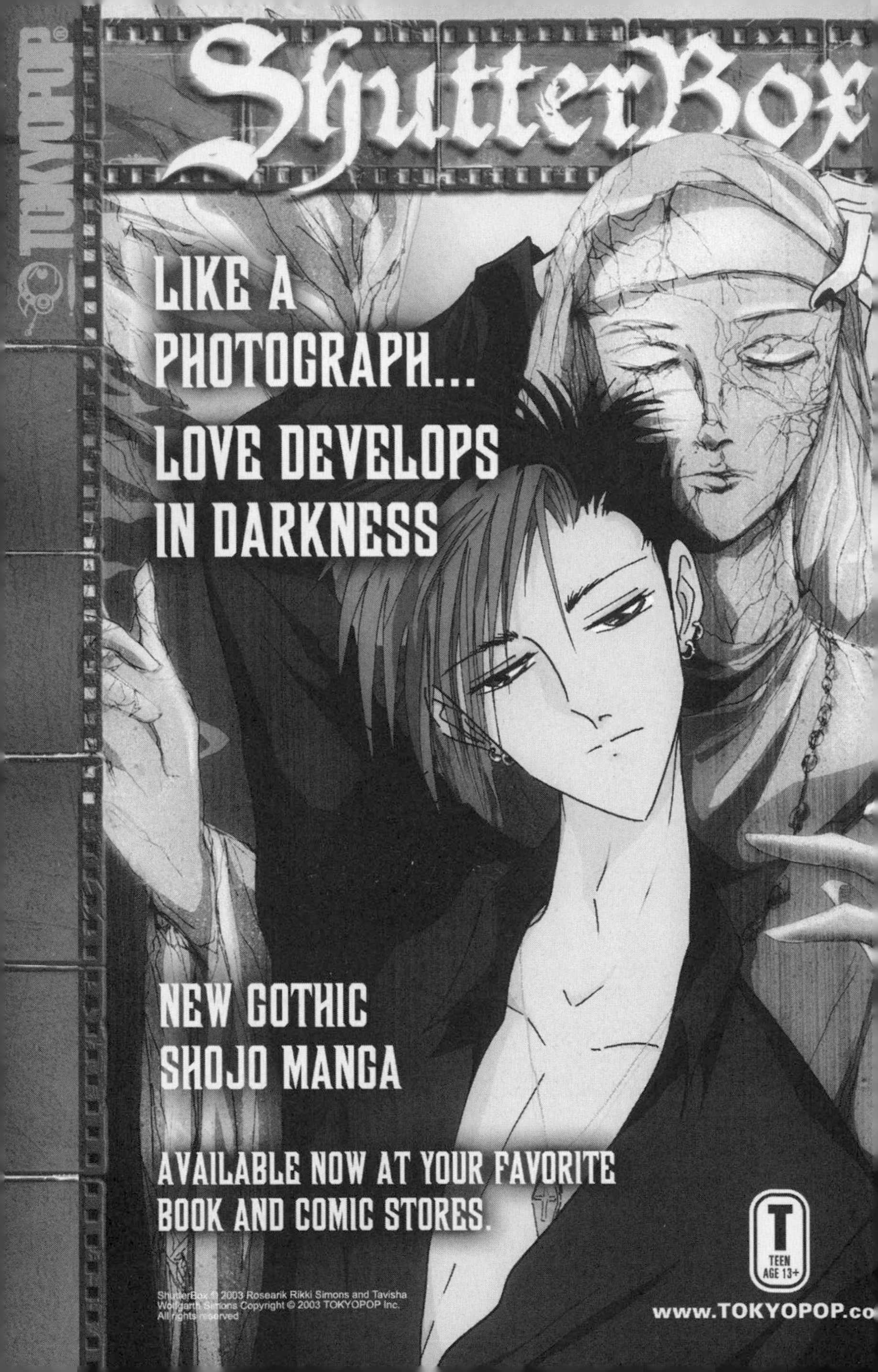

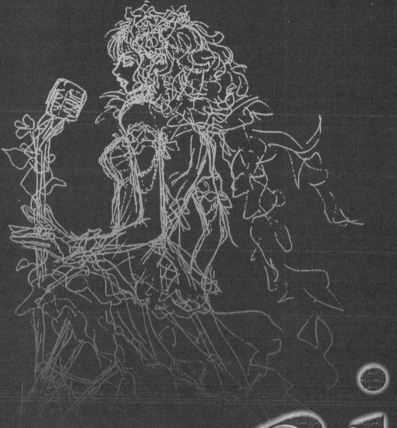

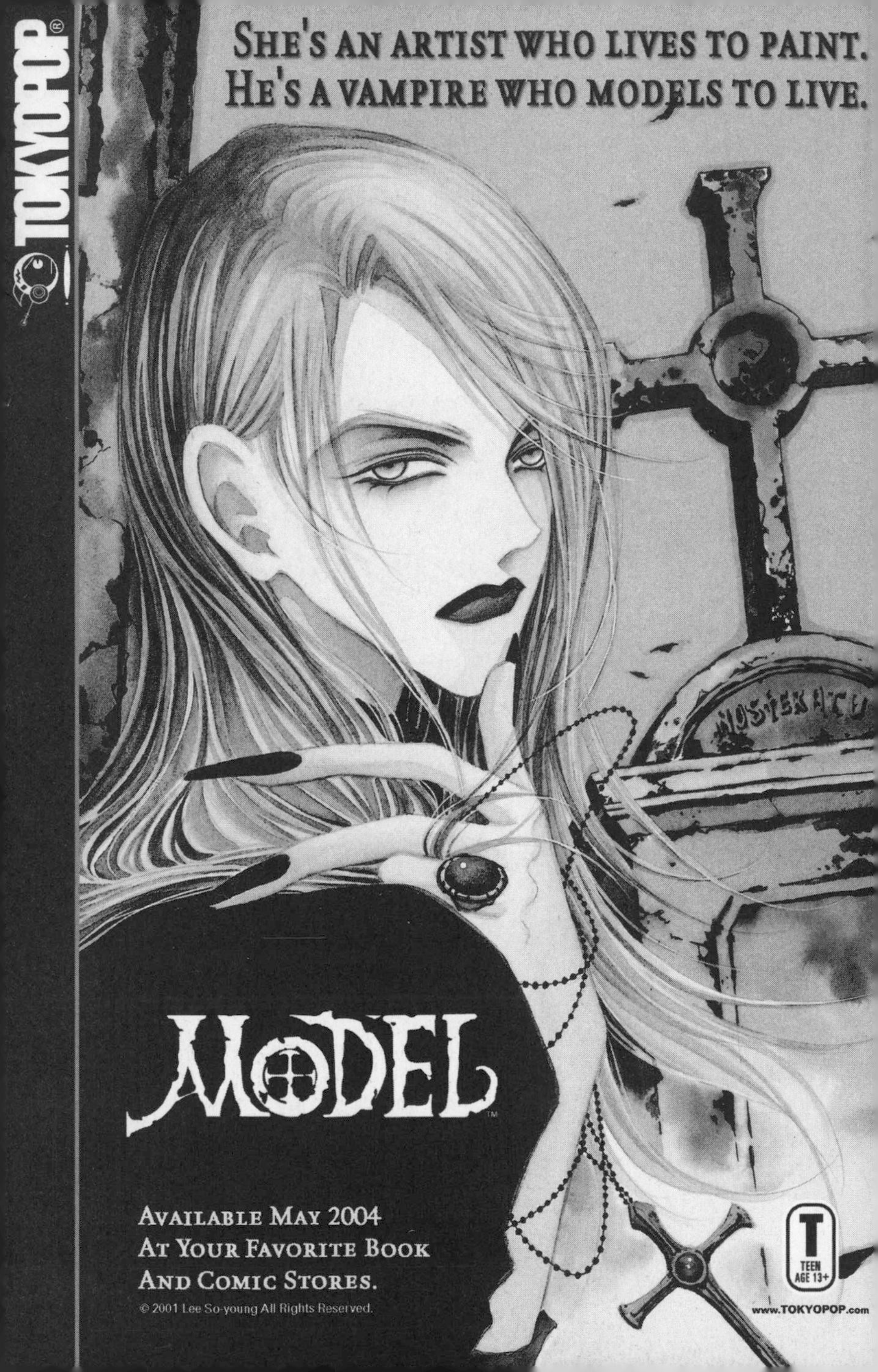

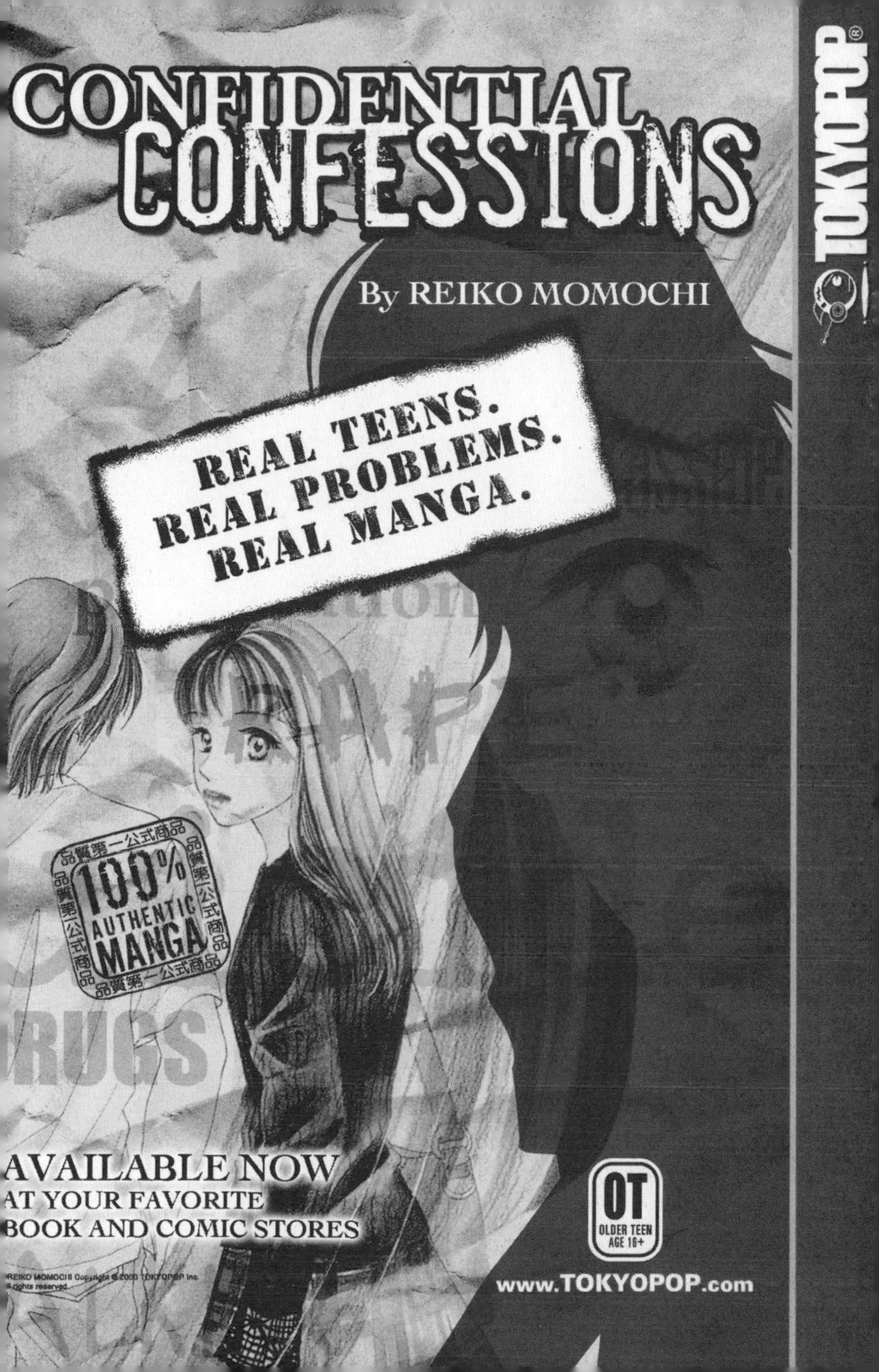

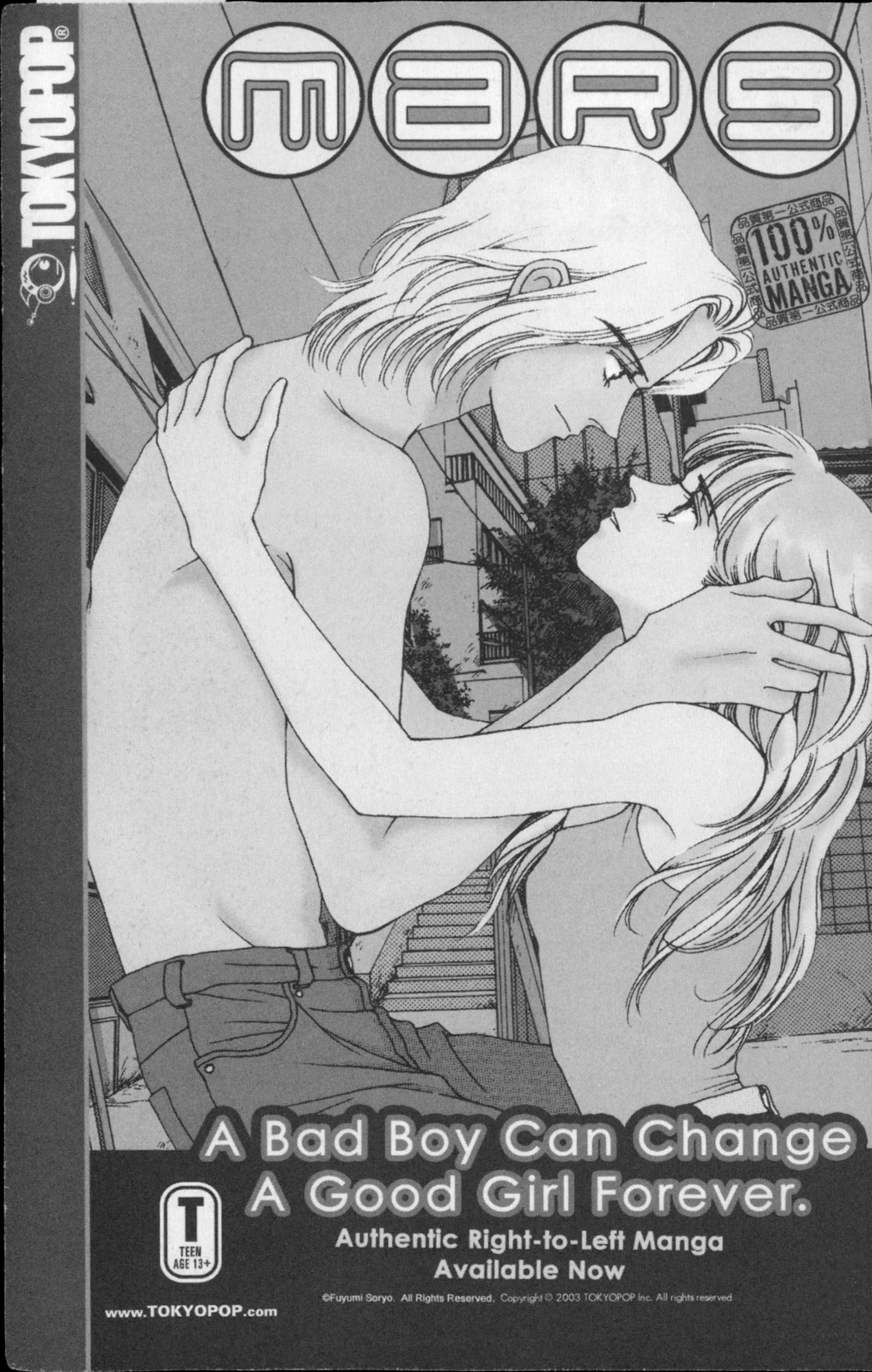

STOP!

This is the back of the book.
You wouldn't want to spoil a great ending!

This book is printed "manga-style," in the authentic Japanese right-to-left format. Since none of the artwork has been flipped or altered, readers get to experience the story just as the creator intended. You've been asking for it, so TOKYOPOP® delivered: authentic, hot-off-the-press, and far more fun!

DIRECTIONS

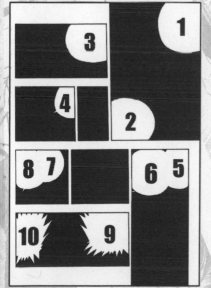

If this is your first time reading manga-style, here's a quick guide to help you understand how it works.

It's easy... just start in the top right panel and follow the numbers. Have fun, and look for more 100% authentic manga from TOKYOPOP®!

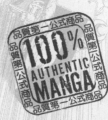